W9-CFC-423

PRAGUE
& THE BEST OF
THE CZECH REPUBLIC

1st Edition

Fodor's Travel Publications   New York, Toronto, London, Sydney, Auckland
www.fodors.com

Be a Fodor's Correspondent

Your opinion matters. It matters to us. It matters to your fellow Fodor's travelers, too. And we'd like to hear it. In fact, we *need* to hear it.

When you share your experiences and opinions, you become an active member of the Fodor's community. That means we'll not only use your feedback to make our books better, but we'll publish your names and comments whenever possible. Throughout our guides, look for "Word of Mouth," excerpts of your unvarnished feedback.

Here's how you can help improve Fodor's for all of us.

Tell us when we're right. We rely on local writers to give you an insider's perspective. But our writers and staff editors—who are the best in the business—depend on you. Your positive feedback is a vote to renew our recommendations for the next edition.

Tell us when we're wrong. We're proud that we update most of our guides every year. But we're not perfect. Things change. Hotels cut services. Museums change hours. Charming cafés lose charm. If our writer didn't quite capture the essence of a place, tell us how you'd do it differently. If any of our descriptions are inaccurate or inadequate, we'll incorporate your changes in the next edition and correct factual errors at fodors.com *immediately*.

Tell us what to include. You probably have had fantastic travel experiences that aren't yet in Fodor's. Why not share them with a community of like-minded travelers? Maybe you chanced upon a beach or bistro or B&B that you don't want to keep to yourself. Tell us why we should include it. And share your discoveries and experiences with everyone directly at fodors.com. Your input may lead us to add a new listing or highlight a place we cover with a "Highly Recommended" star or with our highest rating, "Fodor's Choice."

Give us your opinion instantly at our feedback center at www.fodors.com/feedback. You may also e-mail editors@fodors.com with the subject line "Prague Editor." Or send your nominations, comments, and complaints by mail to Prague Editor, Fodor's, 1745 Broadway, New York, NY 10019.

You and travelers like you are the heart of the Fodor's community. Make our community richer by sharing your experiences. Be a Fodor's correspondent.

Happy traveling!

Tim Jarrell, Publisher

FODOR'S PRAGUE & THE BEST OF THE CZECH REPUBLIC

Editor: Maria Teresa Hart

Writers: Sarah Amandolare, Alexander Basek, Mindy Kay Bricker, Raymond Johnston, Gary Lippman, Susan MacCallum-Whitcomb, Jacy Meyer

Production Editor: Carrie Parker

Maps & Illustrations: David Lindroth, *cartographer;* Bob Blake, Rebecca Baer, *map editors;* William Wu, *information graphics*

Design: Fabrizio La Rocca, *creative director;* Guido Caroti, Siobhan O'Hare, *art directors;* Tina Malaney, Nora Rosansky, Chie Ushio, Jessica Walsh, Ann McBride, *designers;* Melanie Marin, *senior picture editor*

Cover Photo: (View of Old Town Square from Old Town Hall Tower, Prague): Walter Bibikow/age fotostock

Production Manager: Angela L. McLean

1st Edition

ISBN 978-1-4000-0522-2

SPECIAL SALES

This book is available at special discounts for bulk purchases for sales promotions or premiums. Special editions, including personalized covers, excerpts of existing books, and corporate imprints, can be created in large quantities for special needs. For more information, write to Special Markets/Premium Sales, 1745 Broadway, MD 6-2, New York, New York 10019, or e-mail specialmarkets@randomhouse.com.

AN IMPORTANT TIP & AN INVITATION

Although all prices, opening times, and other details in this book are based on information supplied to us at press time, changes occur all the time in the travel world, and Fodor's cannot accept responsibility for facts that become outdated or for inadvertent errors or omissions. So **always confirm information when it matters,** especially if you're making a detour to visit a specific place. Your experiences—positive and negative—matter to us. If we have missed or misstated something, **please write to us.** We follow up on all suggestions. Contact the Prague & the Best of the Czech Republic editor at editors@fodors.com or c/o Fodor's at 1745 Broadway, New York, NY 10019.

PRINTED IN CHINA

10 9 8 7 6 5 4 3 2 1

CONTENTS

CONTENTS

MAPS

ABOUT THIS BOOK

Our Ratings

Sometimes you find terrific travel experiences and sometimes they just find you. But usually the burden is on you to select the right combination of experiences. That's where our ratings come in.

As travelers we've all discovered a place so wonderful that its worthiness is obvious. And sometimes that place is so unique that superlatives don't do it justice: you just have to be there to know. These sights, properties, and experiences get our highest rating, **Fodor's Choice**, indicated by orange stars throughout this book.

Black stars highlight sights and properties we deem **Highly Recommended**, places that our writers, editors, and readers praise again and again for consistency and excellence.

By default, there's another category: any place we include in this book is by definition worth your time, unless we say otherwise. And we will.

Disagree with any of our choices? Care to nominate a place or suggest that we rate one more highly? Visit our feedback center at www.fodors.com/feedback.

Budget Well

Hotel and restaurant price categories from ¢ to $$$$ are defined in the opening pages of each chapter. For attractions, we always give standard adult admission fees; reductions are usually available for children, students, and senior citizens. Want to pay with plastic? **AE, D, DC, MC, V** following restaurant and hotel listings indicate whether American Express, Discover, Diners Club, MasterCard, and Visa are accepted.

Restaurants

Unless we state otherwise, restaurants are open for lunch and dinner daily. We mention dress only when there's a specific requirement and reservations only when they're essential or not accepted—it's always best to book ahead.

Hotels

Hotels have private bath, phone, TV, and air-conditioning and operate on the European Plan (aka EP, meaning without meals), unless we specify that they use the Continental Plan (CP, with a continental breakfast), Breakfast Plan (BP, with a full breakfast), or Modified American Plan (MAP, with breakfast and dinner) or are all-inclusive (including all meals

and most activities). We always list facilities but not whether you'll be charged an extra fee to use them, so when pricing accommodations, find out what's included.

Listings

★	Fodor's Choice
★	Highly recommended
⊠	Physical address
⊹	Directions or Map coordinates
⌂	Mailing address
☎	Telephone
🖶	Fax
⊕	On the Web
✍	E-mail
✇	Admission fee
◷	Open/closed times
Ⓜ	Metro stations
▭	Credit cards

Hotels & Restaurants

▦	Hotel
⇥	Number of rooms
♿	Facilities
⏐❍⏐	Meal plans
✗	Restaurant
⌒	Reservations
🏛	Dress code
⌇	Smoking
🍷	BYOB

Outdoors

🏌	Golf
⛺	Camping

Other

☾	Family-friendly
⇨	See also
⊠	Branch address
☞	Take note

Experience
Prague

1

PRAGUE TODAY

"Golden Prague," "The City of a Hundred Spires," "The Heart of Europe": Prague goes by many names. But for its 1.2 million residents, the Czech capital is simply "home."

When the Iron Curtain parted in 1989, ending more than four decades of totalitarian rule, Prague moved to center stage and locals immediately started reveling in their new role. Then, late in 2008—just as Czechs were gearing up to commemorate the Velvet Revolution's 20th anniversary—the economic downturn hit. The republic as a whole has fared significantly better than some countries. Nevertheless, the global crisis has affected exports (which represent 80% of the GDP) as well as imports (namely free-spending foreign tourists).

Aside from worrying about the economy like the rest of us, here's a snapshot of what Pražaci (aka Praguers in Czech) are doing today.

. . . They're sprucing up local landmarks. Whether it's a case of civic pride or simply understanding what side their bread is buttered on (whatever side the tourists want), Praguers have embarked on an ambitious series of projects aimed at overhauling top historic sites: that's no

small feat during tough economic times. Work on the daunting stairway leading to the eastern gate of Pražský Hrad was recently completed; and restoration of Golden Lane, within the castle grounds, is next on the to-do list. Gaslights are also being installed to add a nostalgic glow to select parts of the city center. The big-ticket item, though, is a multiphase reconstruction of Karluv most (Charles Bridge) necessitated by the damaging flood of 2002. Controversial from the get-go, the project's bad press has been compounded by delays, and work isn't slated to be finished for several more years. The good news is that the bridge does remain open to pedestrians in the interim.

. . . They're building for the future. This emphasis on the past doesn't mean that locals live in an architectural time warp. Having emerged from World War II relatively unscathed, the city is admittedly blessed with buildings representing almost every prewar period, from romanesque to cubist. Yet contemporary constructions are equally impressive. Stanice Střížkov (a metro station in Střížkov that resembles a giant glass fish) is a case in point. It is only one of several new stations built in the past few years, the rationale behind

HOT TOPICS

Considering that they're traditionalists in many respects, Czechs are surprisingly tolerant of gays and lesbians. For instance, the republic legalized same-sex unions in 2006, and Vinohrady continues to be a welcoming—and vibrant—gay mecca.

Many eateries today do have smoking and no-smoking areas. But they're largely ineffective, and visitors concerned about *kouření* shouldn't hold their breath that rules will be enforced. Scratch that, holding your breath may be the best defense.

To see how thoroughly capitalism has trounced communism, just witness the number of upscale hotels that keep opening despite the recession. In 2009 alone, a quartet of five-star hotels—like Sheraton and Rocco Forte—began welcoming guests.

all of them being that the subway system must grow to keep pace with suburban sprawl. Given the cost, you see that only a small fraction of Greater Prague's residents can afford to live anywhere near the city center. That number will continue to dwindle as the poorer inner suburbs (think Holešovice and Žižkov) undergo commercial redevelopment, sending more renters fleeing to the fringes.

. . . They're craving caffeine. Maybe it's the long commute that has left locals needing a serious java jolt. Or maybe it's a reaction to the arrival of Starbucks, which debuted here in 2008. In any case, the world's most committed beer drinkers are suddenly reclaiming their coffee klatsch. The café tradition flourished in Prague from the heyday of the Austro-Hungarian Empire until the dawn of the Soviet Era. Needless to say, Communist officials weren't fond of coffeehouses that doubled as dissident hangouts, so before you could say "red scare," café culture started declining. Happily, it is at last making a comeback. *Grandes dames* like the Café Imperial (an art nouveau gem in Nové Město) have received a much-needed facelift, and new ones have opened their doors: perhaps the most notable being the

so-called charity cafés. These are not your average Joe, as the proceeds from them help fund social programs.

. . . And they're paying for everything with korunas. The Czech Republic was among the first of the former Soviet nations to be admitted into the European Union, in 2004. Then it was rightly seen as shining star of the Eastern Bloc (in yearbook terms, the country would have been voted "prettiest," "most popular," and "most likely to succeed"). However, it has yet to adopt the EU's common currency—the euro—despite innumerable promises and passed deadlines. Politicos now argue that 2012 (the latest target date) is untenable, so the euro may not be introduced until 2015. Conventional wisdom says that non-euro countries are a better value for vacationers. But before penny pinchers start high fiving each other, know this: Prague, because of its must-see status, defies the convention. In fact, this city hasn't been a certifiable bargain since the late 1990s, and today it is on a par pricewise with its Western European counterparts.

Although it doesn't register on many tourists' radars yet, locals are abuzz about the ongoing construction of the Blanka Tunnel: one component of a ring road that will eventually relieve traffic in the inner city. It's Prague's answer to Boston's "Big Dig."

Rail riders rejoice! Eurail, the venerable train-ticket packager, celebrated its 50th birthday in 2009 by giving purchasers a present: It added the Czech Republic to its extensive Global Pass and Select Pass network, bringing the number of participating countries to 21.

Czech foodies are embracing their roots—and their root vegetables. The national Association of Hotels & Restaurants and the Association of Master Chefs & Confectioners have created a program focusing on fine regional fare. For info, visit ⊕ *www.czechspecials.com.*

PRAGUE PLANNER

Prague Weather

Winters here can be bone-chillingly cold, with days that are overcast and dark (the sun tends to set by 5 PM). The maximum average temperature in December and January is 32°F, and the mercury frequently drops to the low 20sF. Things improve substantially in spring and summer. By July you can expect around 10 hours of sunshine per day. Showers, moreover, are infrequent and usually light and short, and temperatures hover in the high 70sF. Fall brings slightly cooler temperatures in the 60sF, as well as a riotous display of autumn foliage in parts of the city and countryside.

The words we use to designate different months are derived from Latin names and numbers. Czechs, on the other hand, use native words for climate-related events to reflect the importance of the four seasons. For instance, *únor* (our February) means "melting ice," and *listopad* (our November) means "falling leaves."

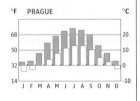

When to Go

Beautiful year-round, Prague is busiest over the Christmas and Easter holidays and during the summer months. Spring generally offers good weather, with a more relaxed level of tourism: flowers are blossoming, historic sites are open for business, and the Prague Spring Music Festival is in full swing. Once fall arrives, the trees are decked out with gold and scarlet leaves, and Czechs head to the woods in search of mushrooms (picking fungi is a time-honored pursuit here). In winter, crowd sizes and hotel costs drop along with the temperatures. You'll get a chance to see the photogenic capital blanketed in snow—the drawback is that some castles and museums (especially those outside of town) do close for the season. January and February usually bring the best skiing to Bohemian slopes, and finding a room at area ski resorts can be difficult. If you're not a skier, try visiting the mountains in late spring (April or May) or in fall, when the countryside is ablaze with brilliant colors and you have hotels and restaurants pretty much to yourself.

Hours

May through September, most of the city attractions open each day save Monday. Notable exceptions are the Jewish Museum (which shuts Saturday instead) and Prague Castle (which opens daily). Hours vary off-season, and many outlying sites close completely November through March.

Czech stores traditionally open weekdays from 9 AM to 6 PM and Saturday from 9 AM to 1 PM. Yet a growing number (including Prague's larger department stores, malls, and supermarkets) now boast extended evening and weekend hours. Ditto for shops in key tourist zones.

Restaurants typically welcome diners from 11 AM to 11 PM and start dishing out dinner around 6. Pubs have a similar schedule, but clubs are another matter altogether. Though they open a few hours earlier, clubs rev up around midnight, and don't close until 4 or 5 AM.

As for other services, most banks open weekdays from 8 AM to 5 PM. Most pharmacies open weekdays from 9 AM to 6 PM, though some maintain 24/7 hours for emergencies.

Getting Around

Central Prague is ideal for walking—provided you have enough leg muscle to handle the hills. If not, there's reliable **public transit** (⊕ www.dpp.cz). Basic, transferable tickets (good for 75 minutes) on city subways, buses, and trams are 26 Kč. Single-ride tickets, costing 18 Kč, allow one 20-minute ride on a tram or bus without transfer, *or* one 30-minute subway trip covering up to five metro stations.

The network is easy to negotiate: The caveat is that after buying your ticket you must time-stamp it at one of the machines found in stations or aboard trams. Miss this step and you potentially face a 950 Kč fine. Repeat riders should consider an unlimited-use transit pass. Prices start at 100 Kč a day. Like regular tickets, they're available from main stations, dispensing machines, and select newsstands.

Prefer taxis? Be warned. Local cabbies are notorious for overcharging, especially if hailed on the street or from a stand in touristy areas. Scams include doctoring the meter or "forgetting" to turn it on; then demanding an exorbitant sum. (FYI most rides should cost no more than 150 Kč to 250 Kč.) To avoid rip-offs, confirm an approximate fare up front. Better yet, call an honest radio-operated firm like **AAA Radiotaxi**(☎ 222–333–222 ⊕ www.aaa-taxi.cz).

If you're interested in exploring beyond the city, check our "Top Tours" or review the train and bus schedules at ⊕ www.idos.cz.

Prague by the Numbers

Prague neighborhoods are sometimes referred to by numbers corresponding to their postal district. There are 10 postal districts, but typically, visitors explore the following areas:

Prague 1: Staré Město (Old Town), Josefov (the Jewish Quarter), Hradčany (the Castle Area), Malá Strana (the Lesser Quarter), Northern Nové Město (New Town)

Prague 2: Southern Nové Město (New Town), Vyšehrad, western Vinohrady

Prague 3: Eastern Vinohrady, Žižkov

Prague 5: Smíchov

Prague 7: Letná, Holešovice

Safety

Although crime rates in Prague are relatively low, this is a major city, and travelers should exercise the usual precautions. For starters, that means being careful at night—even when visiting spots that seem safe by day. Prostitutes and drug dealers can make parts of Wenceslas Square feel sketchy after dark, and stag parties comprised of rowdy beer-addled lads can appear anywhere.

Regardless of the hour, be wary of pickpockets at crowded sites (like the Charles Bridge) and on public transit (the Number 22 tram, being popular with tourists, is a favorite among the sticky fingered). To be on the safe side, always keep your hands on purses, backpacks, cameras, and such rather than leaving them placed beside you.

Distribute cash, credit cards, ID, and other valuables between a deep front pocket, an inside jacket or vest pocket, and a discreet money pouch—please, no in-your-face fanny packs. Don't rifle in that pouch or flash wads of cash once you're in public. If you need an ATM top-up, choose a machine inside a bank building. One further tip: Ignore those ubiquitous guys offering to exchange currency at great rates on the street unless you want to end up with worthless bills.

WHAT'S WHERE

1 Old Town. Prague's historic heart is "tourist central," so it's often jam-packed with people. Most gather in Old Town Square to marvel at the architecture and watch the astronomical clock strike; then wander the narrow streets that radiate outward.

2 Josefov. The original Jewish Ghetto was largely razed in the 19th century, and art nouveau structures replaced many of its buildings. Yet the past is still apparent in the restored sites that comprise the Jewish Museum (including the Old Jewish Cemetery) and the active synagogues.

3 Malá Strana. The "Lesser Quarter" is filled with hilly cobblestone streets edged with baroque buildings. The stunning Church of St. Nicholas dominates the district.

4 Hradčany. The highlight here is Pražský Hrad. Said to be the world's largest ancient castle, it shelters a romanesque basilica, a Gothic cathedral, a renaissance garden, and a baroque palace within its walls.

5 Nové Město. Proving "new" is relative, Prague's New Town was laid out in the 14th century. Its focal point is Wenceslas Square: a grand boulevard lined with shops, restaurants, and hotels. Nové Město is also home to

BUBENEČ

DEJVICE
Evropská   Dejvická Ⓜ

Hradčanská Ⓜ

8
LETNÁ

4
HRADČANY
Pražský hrad ◆
(Prague Castle)

Patočkova

Malostranská Ⓜ

2
JOSEFOV
Náměstí
Republiky Ⓜ
Staroměstská Ⓜ

Charles ◆ STARE MĚSTO
Bridge   (OLD TOWN)

3
MALÁ STRANA
(LESSER QUARTER)

1 Ⓜ
Můstek Ⓜ

Národní
třída Ⓜ

Karlovo náměstí
Ⓜ   Muzeum Ⓜ

10
Plzeňská   SMÍCHOV

NOVÉ
MĚSTO Ⓜ
I.P.
Anděl Ⓜ
5   Pavlova Ⓜ

Smíchovské
nádraží Ⓜ
Radlická
Ⓜ

Vyšehrad Ⓜ

VYŠEHRAD
6

Pražského
povstání Ⓜ

RADLICE

Vltava

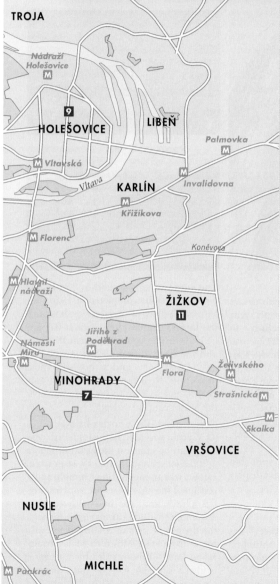

the National Museum, the State Opera House, and the National Theater.

6 Vyšehrad. Upriver from the Charles Bridge, compact Vyšehrad contains the remains of Prague's "other castle." A cemetery for the famed Czech artists is on the grounds, and river views are incomparable.

7 Vinohrady. As its name implies, this began as a wine-producing region, and it still has enough wine bars to attract *vino* lovers.

8 Letná. Known for its park, Letná is where some of the largest Velvet Revolution marches took place. Now protesters have been replaced by locals who rollerblade, bike, and walk on park paths.

9 Holešovice. Major redevelopment is in the works for this workaday neighborhood. For now its chief attraction is the National Gallery.

10 Smíchov. Today a busy commercial district, Smíchov is home to malls, multiplex theaters, and office complexes. New bars and eateries are also moving in.

11 Žižkov. Žižkov retains its counterculture reputation despite increasing gentrification. It reputedly has more drinking spots than anywhere else in Prague.

PRAGUE
TOP ATTRACTIONS

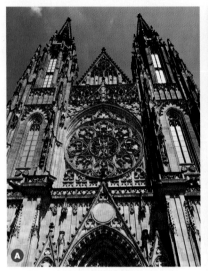

Pražský Hrad (Prague Castle)

(A) The nation's most-visited site draws more than 1.3 million people per year (even Barack Obama dropped by in 2010), and Czech history has been irrevocably intertwined with it from the 10th century onward. Attractions set inside the castle's imposing walls range from grand churches, manicured gardens, and regal residences—including the official presidential residence—to the higgledy-piggledy little cottages down Golden Lane. To set this all in context, it helps to make "The Story of Prague Castle" your first stop. It's an engaging multimedia display in the Old Royal Palace.

Chrám svatého Víta (St. Vitus's Cathedral)

(B) "The City of a Hundred Spires" has more than its fair share of churches. None, however, can top this glorious Gothic structure on the grounds of Prague Castle. Almost six centuries in the making

(the cornerstone was laid in 1344, and work was finally completed in 1929), St. Vitus's is a place of superlatives. It is both the largest church in the Czech Republic and—as the country's spiritual center and the final resting place for many of its beloved kings and saints—the most important. Replete with buttresses, gargoyles, and soaring spires, it is arguably the most beautiful as well.

Karluv most (The Charles Bridge)

(C) When it was built in the mid-14th century, Europe's longest medieval bridge (a 1,700-foot span supported by 16 graceful arches) was an engineering triumph, and it remained the only boat-free way to cross the Vltava until the mid-19th century. Assuming that you can navigate through the crowds, it is still a convenient way to get from Staré Město to Malá Strana. Being lined on both sides by statues, it is also a veritable gallery, and a magnet for romantics, history buffs, buskers, and

tourists. Photographers come in droves, too, because this icon is always ready for its close-up.

Staroměstské náměstí (Old Town Square)

(D) Dating back to the Middle Ages, this massive town square-cum-marketplace in the heart of Staré Město is rimmed with postcard-perfect sites. The most striking of these—quite literally—is the Astronomical Clock on the Old Town Hall tower, which marked its 600th birthday in 2010. Operating like a giant cuckoo clock, its meticulously carved wooden figures of the Twelve Apostles appear on the top of the hour from 9 AM to 9 PM. One spooky legend has it that local officials were so impressed by the mechanical marvel that they blinded the clockmaker to ensure that he could never duplicate it.

Židovské muzeum (The Jewish Museum)

(E) Rather than being a single bricks-and-mortar building, this museum is made up of six sites in the Josefov district. These include a Ceremonial Hall as well as four historic synagogues that house themed exhibits. The Pinkasova, with its Holocaust memorial, is most moving: The names of 77,297 Czech Jews murdered by the Nazis are inscribed on the main-floor walls, while impossibly poignant drawings made by children at the Terezín "transit" camp are displayed in an upper gallery. The museum also administers the Old Jewish Cemetery, which contains some 12,000 tilting headstones.

Chrám svatého Mikuláše (Church of St. Nicholas)

(F) Not to be confused with the 18th-century edifice in Staré Město that is dedicated to the same saint, this domed beauty

dominates the Malá Strana. A primo example of "high baroque," its extravagant interior features a gilded statue of St. Nick plus frescos depicting his life in addition to the usual paintings and putti. The church also hosts evening concerts from late March through early November, and again in the Christmas season (most showcase the music of Mozart, who himself played the organ here). Those who prefer the sound of pealing bells are welcome to climb the adjacent bell tower.

Obecní dům (Municipal House)

(G) Prague is compendium of architectural styles, and the remarkable range inevitably draws stares. For fans of art nouveau, though, this building takes the cake. Municipal House was built with nationalist zeal when the Austro-Hungarian Empire was waning. So it is no coincidence that the era's preeminent Czech artists were hired to decorate it, or that the main concert venue (Smetana Hall,

home to the Prague Symphony Orchestra) was named for the "The Father of Czech Music." Fittingly, the Republic of Czechoslovakia declared its independence from the balcony of Obecní dům in 1918.

Chrám svaté Barbory (St. Barbara's Cathedral)

(H) "Hi-Ho-Hi-Ho, it's off to church we go" could have been the theme song for the silver miners of Kutná Hora who financed the building of this grand cathedral to honor their patron saint. Like St. Vitus's Cathedral (aesthetically, its only rival), St. Barbara's was for centuries a work in progress: construction went on intermittently from 1388 to 1905. What makes this church so unusual, though, is the way metallurgy and liturgy intersect inside. Paying homage to both the blue collar and the clerical collar, it contains frescos portraying both religious scenes and scenes of mining and minting.

PRAGUE LIKE A LOCAL

With Prague so full of foreign visitors, it can be a little hard to uncover what life for residents is like. So put the sightseeing on hold for a while and try these activities, beloved by locals.

Pivo (Beer)

Every discussion about this republic begins and ends with beer That seems fair, given that Czechs aren't only the world's largest per capita consumers of beer, they also invented the modern pilsner, and their national brews set the gold standard globally. They are so good, in fact, that beer here commands the type of reverence usually reserved for fine wine. But if you want to drink it like a native, don't chug from a bottle or a can. Head to the nearest smoky pivnice, or pub, grab a seat at a table, and wait for the waiter to plunk down a mug in front of you. Turn to your neighbor, raise your glass, and say, Na zdraví, "To your health!" (any pronunciation suffices when you say it with feeling). Congratulations. You are now an honorary citizen.

Culture

Czechs survived three centuries of Austrian occupation (from 1620 to 1918) with nothing but a shared culture to unite them; and right across the class continuum they remain committed to the performing arts. Opera and orchestral music are the biggest draws, and you'll likely encounter touts advertising quick "greatest hits"–style concerts in churches all over town. However, these are targeted squarely at tourists, with nary a native in sight. So save your koruny for the real deal, like a performance by the Prague State Opera or the Czech Philharmonic. The weekly Prague Post carries a full listing of classical acts, plus concerts and club shows where you can rub elbow with local music enthusiasts. The quality of the performances is high, and the audience reaction is invariably heartfelt.

Parks

Like many city dwellers, residents of Prague are fond of their green spaces, which serve as a sort of communal backyard. Formal gardens—like Vrtba in Malá Strana—offer a grassy respite when leisure time is limited. Yet lounging in a park is preferable. Two of the most popular are Letenské Sady and Riegrovy Sady. Aside from walking shoes, follow the locals' lead by coming equipped with a book, blanket, and picnic. Since both parks have huge beer gardens, you should be prepared to stay awhile, too. Rather take a walk on the wild side? At Divoká Šárka (literally "Wild Sarka"), open fields, wooded paths, and a stream-fed pool lure nature lovers; conversely, Petřínské Sady, on Prague's highest hill, appeals to the upwardly mobile.

Spas

Prague locals love spa resorts, and there are plenty of Bohemian ones to pick from. The most famous of the bunch are concentrated in the so-called Spa Triangle made up of Karlovy Vary, Mariánské Lázně, and Františkovy Lázně, where mineral springs are abundant. Other prized resources also come into play. In addition to water, spas build their treatments around peat, natural gas, and even beer. Czech spas have a long tradition of welcoming visitors (past guests at Karlovy Vary, for example, include Peter the Great, Beethoven, Tolstoy, and Freud). However, one legacy of the communist era is that many still present treatments as medical procedures. In short, they focus on health more than hedonism. If you want full-on pampering, choose your locale carefully.

TOP EXPERIENCES

Rock Me Amadeus

Mozart is a civic obsession, so you can't leave Prague without hearing his music. The obvious choice is to attend an opera at the opulent Estates Theatre, where Don Giovanni (personally conducted by the maestro) premiered to an appreciative audience in 1787. Anyone who fears that opera may be a bit uppity can enjoy a more accessible performance—albeit with some strings attached—at the National Marionette Theatre. Tickets will cost anywhere from 250 Kč to 1,000 Kč at the former, about 590 Kč at the latter.

Word of Mouth: "We saw the puppet show at the National Marionette Theatre in/near Old Town Square. The show is Don Giovanni and we LOVED it. A highlight of our trip! Enjoy!"   —Kwoo

Raising the Bar

The king of beers in this part of the globe isn't Budweiser—though Czech Budvar runs a close second—but Plzeňský Prazdroj (aka Pilsner Urquell). The word "prazdroj" translates as "source," and you can discover that source by visiting the legendary brewery complex and adjacent brewery-themed museum in Plzeň, 55 mi southwest of Prague. The world-renowned pale lager was invented here in 1842. One taste and you'll understand why Czechs have an old proverb that says, "Where beer is brewed, life is good."

Wonder Water

A different kind of beverage is the drink du jour in Karlovy Vary. Accidentally discovered by Emperor Charles IV in the 1300s, the hot springs here provide water for sipping as well as spa-ing—which explains why most folks tote porcelain cups that they fill for free at thermal fountains. You can buy your own for a few bucks

(the unique little handle that doubles as a straw makes it a fun spa souvenir). Even without one, though, you will remember the experience. The curative water's sulfuric taste is unforgettably awful.

A Touch of Glass

The Czech Republic is synonymous with fine cut crystal, and purists contend that the very best is created by Moser, a glassmaker that has been operating in Karlovy Vary since 1857. Moser also has two Prague locations: the flagship store at Na Příkopě 12 (itself a work of art) and a second shop on Old Town Square. Looking for something more modern? Function coupled with contemporary form makes Artel in Staré Město a Fodor's Choice. Wherever you shop, be sure that pieces bear an official "Bohemia Crystal" sticker.

Novel Excursions

Paging all literature lovers! Czech-born author and existentialist poster boy Franz Kafka lived out his life in Prague, and retracing his footsteps offers a surprisingly comprehensive city tour. Former homes, for example, include buildings on Old Town Square and in Prague Castle (Dům U Minuty and 22 Golden Lane respectively). A suitably surreal bronze statue of him stands in the Jewish Quarter, where he worshipped; plus, there's a whole Kafka museum in Malá Strana. Organized Kafka walks are also broadly touted.

Cruise Control

The Vltava River (this country's longest) slices through Prague, offering ample on-the-water opportunities in the process. That's a good thing, because some people like standard-issue outings on big sightseeing vessels and some prefer a bit more quirkiness. Those who fall into the second category may sign on with Prague-Venice

Cruises and tool around in a little 19th-century canal boat. If you're eager to break free entirely and paddle your own rowboat, there are several waterfront rental companies that can set you up.

Hrad Choices

Bordering Germany and the former Austro-Hungarian Empire, Southern Bohemia long held a strategically important position that needed to be defended with a series of fortifications. Today that makes it a popular locale among castle connoisseurs. If you can only see one, make it Hrad Krumlov, which, in Czech terms, is second only in size to Pražský Hrad in Prague. Positioned high above the fairytale town of Český Krumlov, this fanciful castle comes complete with a tower, a dungeon, and a moat.

Market Research

Christmas markets, which start four Saturdays before Christmas Eve and run daily until New Year's, are hugely popular in Prague. A well-stocked one sets up on Wenceslas Square (named for the "good king" of carol fame). But Old Town Square's wins the "most festive" prize, because St. Nick appears there the afternoon of December 5 to separate the naughty children from the nice. After stocking up on crafts, carp, and cups of mulled wine, revelers return to the square December 24 for a candlelit midnight mass.

Word of Mouth: "European cities are always known for their beauty, but the charm of the cities reaches its peak during Christmas season specially Prague . . . Last year I was there to witness that and wouldn't want to miss the fun again."
—*rickwright3*

A Well-Orchestrated Event

Since 1946 the Prague Spring International Music Festival has been the most noteworthy event on the Czech cultural calendar. Opening with a tribute to native composer Bedřich Smetana on May 12 (the anniversary of his death), it features three weeks of A-list performances. Musicians gather in concert halls and churches to play from the entire classical repertoire; hence the demand for tickets is high. So, too, are some of the ticket prices. The upside is that others are affordable and, on occasion, available the day-of.

Make Way for Dumplings

Prague's Allegro restaurant sparked something of a food revolution when it earned outstanding international reviews for its Italian cuisine in 2008. Yet classic stick-to-your-ribs Czech cuisine remains both compelling and comforting. Try vepřo-knedlo-zelo, a fatty dish of roast pork and cabbage served with dumplings. Deep-fried potato pancakes and deep-fried cheese are other frequently ordered sides. If you're concerned about packing on pounds, just remind yourself that eating heavy food here is all part of the cultural experience.

GREAT ITINERARIES

Day 1: Arrival, Pražský Hrad (Prague Castle)

Even jet lag can't dampen the allure of Pražský Hrad, so it is a perfect place to hit on your first day in the city. The castle's ancient 18-acre property contains a slew of individual attractions conveniently linked by internal courtyards. The showstopper is St. Vitus's Cathedral (wherein lie the remains of fabled Czechs like Charles IV and St. Wenceslas). But don't forget to hit the Royal Palace and Lobkowicz Palace, too. Also worth a gander is Golden Lane: a row of crooked cottages, one of which was once occupied by Kafka. Diminutive to begin with, they look like dollhouses when compared with the supersize surrounding structures. Before calling it a day and descending from the castle, remember to take in the city view: aside from offering a photo op, it will also help you get your bearings!

Day 2: Josefov and Staré Město (Old Town)

Begin your day early in the Jewish Quarter. (Because it is best approached with a certain solemnity, and arriving ahead of the tour groups is a definite advantage.) Here you will find Europe's oldest active synagogue—the Staronová, erected in 1270—as well as the Jewish Museum. Once you've seen the latter's evocative exhibits and paid your respects at the topsy-turvy Old Jewish Cemetery, saunter over to Staré Město to explore its centuries-old—and certifiably touristy—tangle of streets. Prepare to linger around Old Town Square, ideally timing your arrival to coincide with the striking of the astronomical clock. Later you can retrace the "Royal Way" (so named for the kings who trod it) that links the square with the Powder Tower. The Municipal House, an eye-popping 20th-century addition to Staré Město's medieval streetscape, is right beside it.

Day 3: Malá Strana

You shouldn't be surprised if the neighborhood you visit today looks vaguely familiar: after all, it has been featured in a glut of period movies, ranging from *Amadeus* to *Van Helsing*. Filmmakers come because its cobbled streets, beautifully preserved baroque buildings, and gorgeous formal gardens conjure up a long-ago time. Since the area seems to have a surprise at every turn, aimless wandering is Malá Strana's main pleasure; however, there is one site that deserves thorough investigation: St. Nicholas Church—an 18th-century beauty dedicated to Ol' Saint Nick. If you choose to climb the 215 steep steps of the church bell tower, you can reward your aching feet afterward by resting in Vrtba Garden or taking an extended break in leafy Kampa Island Park before returning to Staré Město via the Charles Bridge.

Day 4: Day Trip to Kutná Hora

If you are ready for a break from the city. Kutná Hora—44 mi east of Prague—is a memorable destination for day-trippers. Rich deposits of silver put this town on the map in the 12th century, and the premiere local attractions are still tied to them. Chances are you will start your visit at St. Barbara's Cathedral, a divine Gothic sanctuary that was built with miners' donations. Afterward you can get the lowdown on mineralogy at the Czech Museum of Silver, then tour portions of an original silver mine and restored mint. (For a real heavy-metal experience, try coming in late June, when the town relives its glory days during the annual Royal Silvering Festival.) When in the area, it is also worth making a detour to suburban

Sedlec to see the somewhat spooky Kostnice Ossuary, a bizarre church decorated with human bones.

Day 5: Český Krumlov

For a vacation within your vacation, take an overnight trip to Český Krumlov in Southern Bohemia. *Timeless* is a word that is frequently used to describe this sublime spot—and little wonder. The architecturally coherent Old Town has a "long ago and far, far away" vibe due largely to a UNESCO World Heritage designation that protects hundreds of buildings in its historic center. When you factor in an enviable selection of hotels and restaurants, a river that embraces the town on three sides, plus that oh-so-atmospheric castle that overlooks it all, it is hard to imagine a more scenic town. The downside is that Český Krumlov can feel crowded, especially in high season. Nevertheless, you may escape the mob by exercising your options: try rafting on the Vltava River, mountain biking along marked trails, or hiking up to Hrad Krumlov.

Day 6: Karlovy Vary

Head back to České Budějovice and then westward in the direction of Plzeň—dropping in, perhaps to quaff a cold one in pilsner's birthplace—before stopping in Karlovy Vary. This spa town (Karlsbad in German) is scooped out of a forest and framed by mountains, so it has a stunning setting. It is also loaded with charm, thanks to streets laced with baroque buildings painted in pastel Baskin-Robbins colors. Yet it's the water (mineral-rich hot springs to be precise) that's the star attraction here. Since therapeutic spas began popping up around them in the 1500s, a historical Who's Who has come to "take the cure." Find out what all the fuss is about by taking a drink

and a dip; then towel off and retire to a Fodor's Choice hotel. One word to the wise: Book well ahead if you're arriving in July during Karlovy Vary's International Film Festival.

Day 7: Return to Prague

Depending on what time you get back to Prague, you might explore a new neighborhood or just rest up for a big night on the town. A tempting alternative is to indulge in some last-minute shopping, whether opting for upscale items on Pařížská Street or folksy mementos in Havelske Trziste. (Admit it. You're *dying* to have one of those omnipresent Mozart marionettes!) Before bedding down, revisit the Charles Bridge for a final floodlighted look at Golden Prague. Although you'll be hard pressed to take your eyes off the illuminated castle in the background, do take a moment to search among the many statues that decorate the span for the one depicting St. John Nepomuk. It's the eighth on the right, and—according to legend—travelers who rub it are bound to return.

■ TIP→ **When traveling outside of Prague, always compare prices and timing of buses versus trains. Often, bus travel is both cheaper and more direct.**

A WALK THROUGH OLD TOWN'S GREATEST HITS

There's a reason Old Town is congested with people practically every day of the week—it's stuffed with A-list attractions, surrounded with looping cobblestone streets, and bordered with eye-candy architecture from subtle *sgraffito* to bold baroque. This part of the city was made for walking and you can easily cover the neighborhood in half a day on foot.

The "Royal Way"

Start on the perimeter of Old Town by turning up onto **Na příkopě**. A short detour down the first street on your left, Havířská ulice, takes you to the 18th-century **Stavovské divadlo** (Estates Theater).

Return to Na příkopě, turn left, and continue to the street's end. Na příkopě ends abruptly at **náměstí Republiky** (Republic Square). Two stunning buildings, constructed hundreds of years apart, anchor the area. Centuries of grime have not diminished the majesty of the Gothic **Prašná brána**, with its stately spires looming above the square. Adjacent to this tower, the rapturous art nouveau **Obecní dům** concert hall and municipal center looks like a brightly decorated confection.

Walk through the archway of the massive **Prašná brána** and down the formal **Celetná ulice**, the first leg of the "Royal Way." The cubist building at Celetná No. 34 is **Dům U černé Matky boží**, the House of the Black Madonna, and now a museum of cubism. Look for the miniature Madonna placed on the corner of the building.

The Heart of Old Town

After a few blocks, Celetná opens onto the justly famous **Staroměstské náměstí**, the beating heart of Old Town with dazzling architecture on all sides. On the east side of the square, the double-spire church **Kostel Panny Marie před Týnem** rises from behind a row of patrician houses. To the immediate left of this, at No. 13, is **Dům U Kamenného zvonu** (House at the Stone Bell), a baroque town house that has been stripped down to its original Gothic elements. Next door, at No. 12, stands the gorgeous pink-and-ocher **Palác Kinských**, considered the most prominent example of late baroque–rococo in the area. At this end of the square, you can't help noticing the gigantic expressive **Jan Hus monument.**

Beyond the Jan Hus monument is the Gothic **Staroměstská radnice**, with its impressive 200-foot tower that gives the square its gravitas. As the hour approaches, join the people milling below the tower's 15th-century astronomical clock for a brief but spooky spectacle. The square's second church is the baroque **Kostel svatého Mikuláše.**

Toward the Clementinum

Turn left and continue along U Radnice proper a few yards until you come to **Malé náměstí**, a mini-square with arcades on one side. Look for tiny Karlova ulice, which begins in the southwest corner of the square, and take another quick right to stay on it (watch the signs—this medieval street often confounds visitors). The **České muzeum výtvarných umění** (Czech Museum of Fine Arts) attracts tried-and-true fans of 20th-century Czech art, but you may find yourself lured away by the exotic **Clam-Gallas palác**, at Husova 20.

A block north, the street opens onto Mariánské náměstí, where you'll find the entrance to the **Clementinum**, a grouping of historic buildings once used as a Jesuit stronghold.

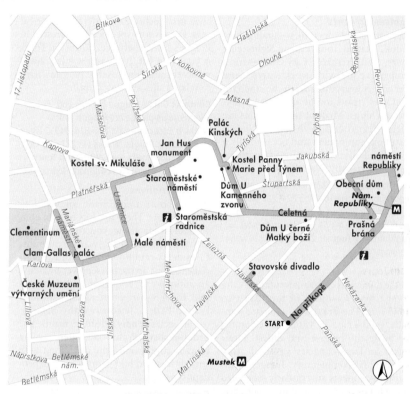

Where to Start:	The northern end of Wenceslas Square.
Time/Length:	Three to four hours.
Where to Stop:	The Clementinum complex.
Best Time to Go:	For fewer crowds, time your visit early morning on the weekends. Hit the Astronomical Clock 10 minutes before the hour.
Worst Time to Go:	Saturday afternoon when crowds are at their peak. Evenings are also surprisingly busy.
Highlights:	Obecní dům, Staroměstské náměstí, Staroměstská radnice, Dům U černé Matky boží, Clementinum.
Where to Refuel:	Café au Gourmand, just outside Old Town Square on Dlouhá street offers a tranquil garden where you can enjoy pastries or a sandwich. Around the corner from Obecní dům you'll also find the Hotel Paříž that serves up hearty omelets.

TOP TOURS

Sightseeing Tours

The most reliable operators—among them Čedok, Martin Tour, Prague Sightseeing Tours, and Premiant City Tour—are a competitive lot, with an extensive menu that covers everything from the standard "top sites" tours to pub crawls and folkloric evenings. Most of these options are offered year-round, with some including a walking component and occasionally a boat trip. Full-day excursions to outlying areas are typically available, too.

Contacts Čedok (☎ 221–447–242 ⊕ www.cedok.com). **Martin Tour** (☎ 224–212–473 ⊕ www.martintour.cz). **Prague Sightseeing Tours** (☎ 222–314–661 ⊕ www.pstours.cz). **Premiant City Tour** (☎ 224–946–922 ⊕ www.premiant.cz).

Boat Tours

Of the numerous companies running Valta River trips 12 months of the year, two stand out. The Prague Steamboat Company, established in 1865, scores points for being the biggest and oldest. Hour cuises on large-capacity vessels feature multilingual commentary. Longer meal-and-music junkets are regularly scheduled as well. For a more intimate experience, try a Prague–Venice cruise aboard a 19th century canal boat that holds fewer than three dozen passengers.

Contacts Prague Steamboat Company (☎ 224–931–013 ⊕ www.paroplavba.cz). **Prague-Venice Cruises** (☎ 775–311–717 ⊕ www.prague-venice.cz).

Specialized Walking Tours

Themed strolls are hugely popular, especially during the peak tourist season, and several providers (Guide-Prague, Prague Walks, and Prague Tours, Walks & Excursions being only three examples) lead tours focusing on, say, local authors, civic architecture, or different historical eras. For visitors specifically interested in Prague's Jewish heritage, Wittmann Tours is your best bet. It organizes informative walks through the Josefov plus day trips to related sites such as Terezín.

Contacts Guide-Prague (☎ 776–868–770 ⊕ www.guide-prague.cz). **Prague Tours, Walks & Excursions** (☎ 777–816–849 ⊕ www.praguer.com). **Prague Walks** (☎ 222–322–309 ⊕ www.praguewalks.com). **Wittmann Tours** (☎ 222–252–472 ⊕ www.wittmann-tours.com).

Fun Alternatives

If your boots aren't made for walking, don't despair. There are lots of cool conveyances that allow you to see Prague in style, at least in the warmer months. Consider a traditional horse-drawn carriage tour, or up the horsepower by riding an antique car (bookable on location in Old Town Square or in advance through Prague PG), a Jetsons-worthy Segway, or an eco-friendly electric train. For pedal pushers, Praha Bike offers cycling tours in and around the city along with straightforward bike rentals for independent types.

Contacts Ekoexpres (☎ 602–317–784 ⊕ www.ekoexpres.cz). **Pony Travel** (☎ 224–930–516 ⊕ www.ponytravelsro.cz). **Prague on Segway** (☎ 775–588–588 ⊕ www.pragueonsegway.com). **Prague PG** (☎ 222–518–259 ⊕ www.guidingprague.com). **Praha Bike** (☎ no phone ⊕ www.prahabike.cz).

Private Guides

Eager to take a private tour with a tailor-made itinerary? Lots of locals advertise themselves as guides. So it's wise to choose one registered by Prague Information Service **PIS Guide Office** (☎ 236–002–569 ⊕ www.pis.cz).

Exploring Prague

WORD OF MOUTH

"We enjoyed the Mucha Museum and a twilight walk along the river, over the Charles Bridge, and around Kampa Island. It was autumn, so the air was crisp and the leaves had turned many colors. Of course, the Prague Castle complex is amazing."

—Paul1950

By Gary
Lippman
and Sarah
Amandolare

Full of fairy-tale vistas, Prague is beautiful in a way that makes even the most jaded traveler stop and snap pictures. The city is physically divided in two by the Vltava River (also sometimes known by its German name, the Moldau), which runs from south to north with a single sharp turn to the east.

Originally, Prague was composed of five independent towns: Hradčany (the Castle Area), Malá Strana (Lesser Quarter), Staré Město (Old Town), Nové Město (New Town), and Josefov (Jewish Quarter), and these areas still make up the heart of Prague—what you think of when picturing its famed winding cobblestone streets and squares.

Hradčany, the seat of Czech royalty for hundreds of years, centers on the Pražský hrad (Prague Castle)—itself the site of the president's office. A cluster of white buildings yoked around the pointed steeples of a chapel, Prague Castle overlooks the city from a hilltop west of the Vltava River. Steps lead down from Hradčany to the Lesser Quarter, an area dense with ornate mansions built for the 17th- and 18th-century nobility.

The looming Karlův most (Charles Bridge) connects the Lesser Quarter with the Old Town. Old Town is hemmed in by the curving Vltava and three large commercial avenues: Revoluční to the east, Na příkopě to the southeast, and Národní třída to the south. A few blocks east of the bridge is the district's focal point: Staroměstské náměstí (Old Town Square), a former medieval marketplace laced with pastel-color baroque houses—easily one of the most beautiful central squares in Europe. To the north of Old Town Square the diminutive Jewish Quarter fans out around a tony avenue called Pařížská.

Beyond the former walls of the Old Town, the New Town fills in the south and east. The name "new" is a misnomer—New Town was laid out in the 14th century. (It's new only when compared with the neighboring Old Town.) Today this mostly commercial district includes the city's largest squares, Karlovo náměstí (Charles Square) and Václavské náměstí (Wenceslas Square).

PHOTO OP

As you walk uphill from Malá Strana to the Castle District, you'll get glorious views over the Prague rooftops. Many of the restaurants and hotels in this area have terraces where you can snap a photo, but you can also climb up the "Royal Way" or head to Petřín sady for more accessible vistas.

DID YOU KNOW?

Most of the statues that line the Charles Bridge aren't the originals. They're modern copies. But several of the originals can be viewed at the Lapidarium museum.

STARÉ MĚSTO (OLD TOWN)

Old Town is usually the first stop for any visitor. Old Town Square, its gorgeous houses, and the astronomical clock are blockbuster attractions. On the other hand, the north end of Wenceslas Square—its base, the opposite end from the statue and the museum—is also a good place to begin a tour of Old Town. This "T" intersection marks the border between the old and new worlds in Prague. A quick glance around shows the often jarring juxtaposition: centuries-old buildings sit side by side with modern retail names like Benetton and Starbucks.

GETTING HERE AND AROUND

There's little public transit in the Old Town, so walking is really the most practical way to get around; you could take a cab, but it's not worth the trouble. It takes about 15 minutes to walk from Náměstí Republiky to Staroměstská. If you're coming to the Old Town from another part of Prague, three metro stops circumscribe the area: Staroměstská on the west, náměstí Republiky on the east, and Můstek on the south, at the point where Old Town and Wenceslas Square meet.

TIMING

Wenceslas Square and Old Town Square teem with activity around the clock almost year-round. If you're in search of a little peace and quiet, you can find the streets at their most subdued on early weekend mornings or when it's cold. Remember to be in Old Town Square just before the hour if you want to see the astronomical clock in action.

TOP ATTRACTIONS

Clementinum. The origins of this massive complex—now part of the university—date back to the 12th and 13th centuries, but it's best known as the stronghold of the Jesuits, who occupied it for more than 200

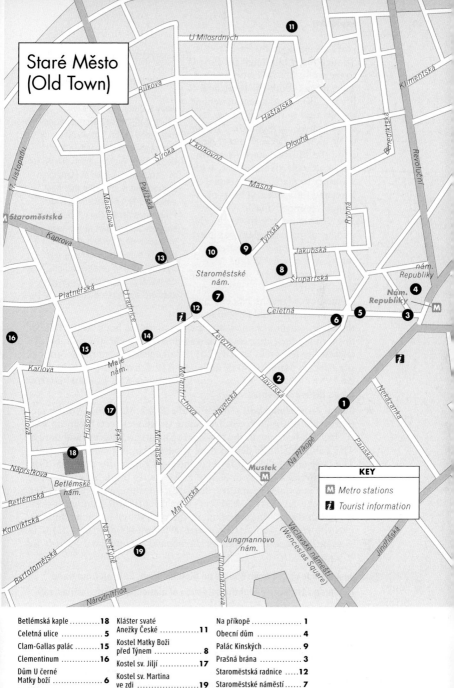

Staré Město (Old Town)

KEY

🅼 Metro stations

🅸 Tourist information

years beginning in the early 1600s. Though many buildings are closed to the public, it's well worth a visit. The Jesuits built a resplendent library, displaying fabulous ceiling murals that portray the three levels of knowledge, with the "Dome of Wisdom" as a centerpiece. Next door, the Mirror Chapel is a symphony of reflective surfaces, with acoustics to match. Mozart played here, and the space still hosts occasional chamber music concerts. The Astronomical Tower in the middle of the complex was used by Johannes Kepler, and afterward functioned as the "Prague Meridian," where the time was set each day. At high noon a timekeeper would appear on the balcony and wave a flag that could be seen from the castle, where a cannon was fired to mark the hour. At the time of this writing, the entire complex was closed for reconstruction, but it's expected to reopen in January 2011. Call ahead to confirm. ⊠ *Mariánské nám. 5, Staré Město* ☎ *222–220–879* ⊕ *www.klementinum.com* 🖃 *220 Kč entrance fee and tour* ☉ *Daily 10–8 in summer (shorter hours different months).*

SAVING FACE

In the Church of Our Lady Before Týn, find the grave marker (tucked away to the right of the main altar) of the great Danish astronomer Tycho Brahe. Tycho had a firm place in history: Johannes Kepler used Tycho's observations to formulate his laws of planetary motion. But it is legend that has endeared Tycho to the hearts of Prague residents. The robust Dane supposedly lost part of his nose in a duel. He quickly had a wax nose fashioned for everyday use but preferred to parade around on holidays and festive occasions sporting a bright metal one.

★ **Dům U černé Matky boží** *(House of the Black Madonna).* In the second decade of the 20th century, young Czech architects boldly applied cubism's radical reworking of visual space to architecture and design. This cubist building, designed by Josef Gočár, is a shining example. The museum inside, refurbished and now run by the National Gallery, showcases fine examples of every genre. Inside there are three floors of paintings, sculptures, drawings, furniture, and other "applied arts" in the cubist style. And don't miss the gift shop. Although pricey, it's worth discovering for some of the oddest-looking home furnishings you've ever seen. ⊠ *Ovocný trh 19, Staré Město* ☎ *224–211–732* ⊕ *www.ngprague.cz/en (under Permanent Exhibitions)* 🖃 *100 Kč* ☉ *Tues.–Sun. 10–6.*

QUICK BITES

Just outside of Old Town Square on Dlouhá Street, **Café au Gourmand** (⊠ *Dlouhá 10*) has a delightful selection of authentic French pastries, salads, and sandwiches. There's also a small garden in the back where you can sit with your snacks.

★ **Jan Hus monument.** Few memorials in Prague elicited as much controversy as this one, dedicated in July 1915, exactly 500 years after Hus was burned at the stake in Constance, Germany. Some maintain that the monument's Secessionist style (the inscription seems to come right from turn-of-the-20th-century Vienna) clashes with the Gothic and baroque style of the square. Others dispute the romantic depiction of

Hus, who appears here as tall and bearded in flowing garb, whereas the real Hus, as historians maintain, was short and had a baby face. Either way, the fiery preacher's influence is not in dispute. His ability to transform doctrinal disagreements, both literally and metaphorically, into the language of the common man made him into a religious and national symbol for the Czechs. ⊠ *Staroměstské nám., Staré Město.*

★ **Kostel Matky Boží před Týnem** (*Church of Our Lady Before Týn*). One of the best examples of Prague Gothic, this church's exterior is in part the work of Peter Parler, an architect responsible for many of Prague's iconic sights (including the Charles Bridge and Chrám svatého Víta, aka St. Vitus's Cathedral). Construction of its twin black-spire towers began later, by King Jiří of Poděbrad in 1461, during the heyday of the Hussites. Jiří had a gilded chalice, the symbol of the Hussites, proudly displayed on the front gable between the two towers. Following the defeat of the Czech Protestants by the Catholic Hapsburgs, the chalice was removed and eventually replaced by a Madonna. As a final blow, the chalice was melted down and made into the Madonna's glimmering halo (you can still see it by walking into the center of the square and looking up between the spires). The entrance to the church is through the arcades on Old Town Square, under the house at No. 14.

Much of the interior, including the tall nave, was rebuilt in the baroque style in the 17th century. Some Gothic pieces remain, however: look to the left of the main altar for a beautifully preserved set of early Gothic carvings. The main altar itself was painted by Karel Škréta, a luminary of the Czech baroque. ⊠ *Staroměstské nám., between Celetná and Týnská, Staré Město* ☎ *222–318–186* ⊕ *tynska.farnost.cz* ☉ *Weekdays 10–1, 3–5.*

QUICK BITES

In the Platýz courtyard immediately east of the church (also accessible from Národní), **Káva Káva Káva** (⊠ *Národní třída 37*) offers one of the best selections of coffee in town, along with a small assortment of pastries and desserts. You can pay extra to access the Internet on the computers downstairs, or use Wi-Fi for free if you spend 60 Kč or more.

Na příkopě. The name means "At the Moat" and harks back to the time when the street was indeed a moat separating the Old Town from the New Town. Today the pedestrian-only Na příkopě is prime shopping territory. Sleek modern buildings have been sandwiched between baroque palaces, the latter cut up inside to accommodate casinos, boutiques, and fast-food restaurants. The new structures are fairly identical inside, but at the end of the block, Slovanský dům (No. 22) is worth a look. This late-18th-century structure has been tastefully refurbished and now houses fashionable boutiques, stylish restaurants, and one of the city's first Western-style multiplex cinemas.

★ **Obecní dům** (*Municipal House*). The city's art nouveau showpiece still fills the role it had when it was completed in 1911 as a center for concerts, rotating art exhibits, and café society. The mature art nouveau style echoes the lengths the Czech middle class went to at the turn of the 20th century to imitate Paris. Much of the interior bears the work of Alfons Mucha, Max Švabinský, and other leading Czech artists. Mucha decorated the Hall of the Lord Mayor upstairs with impressive, magical frescoes depicting Czech history; unfortunately it's visible only as part of a guided tour. The beautiful **Smetanova síň** (Smetana Hall), which hosts concerts by the Prague Symphony Orchestra as well as international players, is on the second floor. The ground-floor restaurants are overcrowded with tourists but still impressive, with glimmering chandeliers and exquisite woodwork. There's also a beer hall in the cellar, with decent food and ceramic murals on the walls. ⊠ *Nám. Republiky 5, Staré Město* ☎ *222–002–100* ⊕ *www.obecnidum.cz* ☉ *Information center and box office daily 10–7.*

QUICK BITES

Head around the corner from Obecní dům to the café at the **Hotel Paříž** (⊠ *U Obecního domu 1, Staré Město* ☎ *224–222–151*) for the café analog of the Municipal House. It's a Jugendstil jewel tucked away on a quiet side street. The lauded, haute-cuisine Restaurant Sarah Bernhardt is next door. At the café, the "old Bohemian" omelet with potatoes and bacon is enough fuel for a full day of sightseeing.

Palác Kinských *(Kinský Palace).* This exuberant building, built in 1765 from Kilian Ignaz Dientzenhofer's design, is considered one of Prague's finest rococo, late-baroque structures. With its exaggerated pink overlay and numerous statues, it looks extravagant when contrasted with the somber baroque elements of other nearby buildings. (The interior, alas, was "modernized" under communism.) The palace once contained a German school—where Franz Kafka studied for nine misery-laden years—and holds the Collection of Prints and Drawings of the National Gallery, which includes pieces from the graphics collection. Communist leader Klement Gottwald, flanked by comrade Vladimír Clementis, first addressed the crowds from this building after seizing power in February 1948—an event recounted in the first chapter of Milan Kundera's novel *The Book of Laughter and Forgetting.* ⊠ *Staroměstské nám. 12, Staré Město* ☎ *224–810–758* ⊕ *www.ngprague.cz* 🎫 *100 Kč* ☉ *Tues.– Sun. 10–6.*

★ **Prašná brána** *(Powder Tower).* Once used as storage space for gunpowder, this dark, imposing tower—covered in a web of carvings—offers a striking view of the Old Town and Prague Castle from the top. King Vladislav II of Jagiello started construction of the tower—which replaced one of the city's 13 original gates—in 1475. At the time, kings of Bohemia maintained their royal residence next door, on the site now occupied by the Obecní dům. The tower was intended to be the grandest gate of all. Vladislav, however, was Polish, and heartily disliked by the rebellious Czech citizens of Prague. Nine years after he assumed power, and fearing for his life, he moved the royal court across the river to Prague Castle. Work on the tower was abandoned, and the half-finished structure remained a depository for gunpowder until the end of the 17th century. The golden spires were not added until the end of the 19th century. The ticket office is on the first floor, after you go up the dizzyingly narrow stairwell. ⊠ *Nám. Republiky, 5/1090, Staré Město* 🎫 *70 Kč* ☉ *Apr.–Sept., daily 10–10; Oct.–Mar., daily 10–8; Nov.–Feb., Daily 10–6.*

QUICK BITES

With an entrance diagonally opposite the astronomical clock, **Hotel U Prince** (✉ *Staroměstká nám. 29*) boasts an impressive rooftop view. Go through the arched entryway to the right and walk all the way to the back, where a golden angel with a trumpet stands watch over a glass-door elevator. Take the elevator to the rooftop bar, which has covered seating and portable heaters running in cold weather. Be forewarned though: The view doesn't come cheap.

PRAGUE PLAYS WITH PLASTER

Sgraffiti, plural for *sgraffito*, is a process where two contrasting shades of plaster are used on the façade of a building. Often the *sgraffiti* serve to highlight the original architecture; other times they can produce an optical illusion, painting brickwork and balconies from thin air. Walls can also be covered with lively classical pictures, which make houses resemble enormous Grecian vases. One of the best examples of *sgraffiti* is on Kafka's former residence, U Minuty, just next to the clock tower on Old Town Square.

Fodor's Choice
★

Staroměstské náměstí *(Old Town Square)*. The hype about Old Town Square is completely justified. Picture a perimeter of colorful baroque houses contrasting with the sweeping old-Gothic style of the Týn church in the background. The unexpectedly large size gives it a majestic presence as it opens up from feeder alleyways. As the heart of Old Town, the square grew to its present proportions when Prague's original marketplace moved away from the river in the 12th century. Its shape and appearance have changed little since that time. During the day the square pulses with activity, as musicians vie for the attention of visitors milling about. In summer the square's south end is dominated by sprawling outdoor restaurants. During the Easter and Christmas seasons it fills with wooden booths of vendors selling everything from simple wooden toys to fine glassware and mulled wine. At night the brightly lighted towers of the Týn church rise gloriously over the glowing baroque façades.

But the square's history is not all wine and music: During the 15th century the square was the focal point of conflict between Czech Hussites and German Catholics. In 1422 the radical Hussite preacher Jan Želivský was executed here for his part in storming the New Town's town hall three years earlier. In the 1419 uprising three Catholic consuls and seven German citizens were thrown out the window—the first of Prague's many famous defenestrations. Within a few years the Hussites had taken over the town, expelled the Germans, and set up their own administration.

Twenty-seven white crosses embedded in the square's paving stones, at the base of Old Town Hall, mark the spot where 27 Bohemian noblemen were killed by the Austrian Hapsburgs in 1621 during the dark days following the defeat of the Czechs at the Battle of White Mountain. The grotesque spectacle, designed to quash any further national or religious opposition, took about five hours to complete, as the men were put to the sword or hanged one by one.

One of the most interesting houses on Old Town Square juts out into the small extension leading into Malé náměstí. Trimmed with elegant cream-color 16th-century Renaissance *sgraffiti* of biblical and classical motifs, the house, called **U Minuty** (⊠ *2 Staroměstské nám., Staré Město*), was the young Franz Kafka's home in the 1890s.

Fodor's Choice ★ **Staroměstská radnice** *(Old Town Hall)*. This is a center of Prague life for tourists and locals alike. Hundreds of visitors gravitate here throughout the day to see the hour struck by the mechanical figures of the **astronomical clock**. Before the hour, look to the upper part of the clock, where a skeleton begins by tolling a death knell and turning an hourglass upside down. The 12 apostles promenade by, and then a cockerel flaps its wings and screeches as the hour finally strikes. To the right of the skeleton, the dreaded Turk nods his head, almost hinting at another invasion like those of the 16th and 17th centuries. This theatrical spectacle doesn't reveal the way this 15th-century marvel indicates the time—by the season, the zodiac sign, and the positions of the sun and moon. The calendar under the clock dates from the mid-19th century. While you're taking in the show, do note that thanks to the constant cycle of tourists moving through, the area is also popular with pickpockets.

Old Town Hall served as the center of administration for Old Town beginning in 1338, when King John of Luxembourg first granted the city council the right to a permanent location. The impressive 200-foot **Town Hall Tower,** where the clock is mounted, was first built in the 14th century. For a rare view of the Old Town and its maze of crooked streets and alleyways, climb the ramp or ride the elevator to the top of the tower.

Walking around the hall to the left, you can see it's actually a series of houses jutting into the square; they were purchased over the years and successively added to the complex. On the other side, jagged stonework reveals where a large, neo-Gothic wing once adjoined the tower until it was destroyed by fleeing Nazi troops in May 1945.

Guided tours of Old Town Hall depart from the main desk inside (most guides speak English, and English texts are on hand). Previously unseen parts of the tower were opened to the public in 2002, and you can now see the inside of the famous clock. ⊠ *Staroměstské nám., Staré Město* ⊙ *Mon. 11–6, Tues.–Sun. 9–6* ⊡ *Tower 100 Kč.*

WORTH NOTING

Betlémská kaple *(Bethlehem Chapel)*. The original church was built at the end of the 14th century, and the Czech religious reformer Jan Hus was a regular preacher here from 1402 until his exile in 1412. Here he gave the mass in "vulgar" Czech—not in Latin as the church in Rome demanded. After the Thirty Years' War in the 17th century, the chapel fell into the hands of the Jesuits and was demolished in 1786. Excavations carried out after World War I uncovered the original portal and three windows; the entire church was reconstructed during the 1950s. Although little remains of the first church, some remnants of Hus's teachings can still be read on the inside walls. A word of warning: Even though regular hours are posted, the church is not always open at those times, so it is suggested that you call ahead of your visit. ☒ *Betlémské nám. 5, Staré Město* ☏ *224–248–595* ☉ *50 Kč* ☉ *Tues.–Sun. 10–6:30.*

Celetná ulice. Most of this street's façades are styled in classic 17th- or 18th-century manner, but appearances are deceiving: Many of the houses in fact have parts that date back to the 12th century. Be sure to look above the street-level storefronts to see the fine examples of baroque detail.

Clam-Gallas palác *(Clam-Gallas Palace).* The work of Johann Bernhard Fischer von Erlach, the famed Viennese architectural virtuoso of the day, is showcased in this earth-tone palace. Construction began in 1713 and finished in 1729. Enter the building to glimpse the Italian frescoes depicting Apollo and the battered but intricately carved staircase, done by the master himself. Clam-Gallas palác is now used for art exhibitions and concerts. If you don't see anyone offering tickets at a table on the street, go inside and up to the desk on the second floor. ☒ *Husova 20, Staré Město* ☏ *236–002–019* ☉ *Free* ☉ *Tues.–Sun. 10–7 usually, depending on exhibits.*

Klášter svaté Anežky České *(St. Agnes's Convent).* Near the river between Pařížská and Revoluční streets, this peaceful complex has Prague's first buildings in the Gothic style. Built between the 1230s and the 1280s, the convent now provides a fitting home for the National Gallery's marvelous collection of Czech Gothic art, including altarpieces, portraits, and statues. ☒ *U Milosrdných 17, Staré Město* ☏ *224–810–628* ☉ *150 Kč–80 Kč; 80 Kč–40 Kč after 4 PM* ☉ *Tues.–Sun. 10–6.*

Kostel svatého Jiljí *(Church of St. Giles).* Replete with buttresses and a characteristic portal, this church's exterior is a powerful example of Gothic architecture. An important outpost of Czech Protestantism in the 16th century, the church reflects baroque style inside, with a design by Johann Bernhard Fischer von Erlach and sweeping frescoes by Václav Reiner. The interior can be viewed during the day from the vestibule or at the evening concerts held several times a week. ☒ *Husova 8, Staré Město* ☏ *224–220–235* ⊕ *www.kostel-praha.cz* ☉ *Free* ☉ *Mon. and Thurs. 4–6.*

Kostel svatého Martina ve zdi *(Church of St. Martin-in-the-Wall).* It was here in 1414 that Holy Communion was first given to the Bohemian laity in the form of both bread and wine. (The Catholic custom of the time dictated only bread would be offered to the masses, with wine reserved for priests and clergy.) From then on, the chalice came to symbolize the Hussite movement. The church is open for evening concerts, held several times each week, but that's the only way to see the rather plain interior. ☒ *Martinská 8, Staré Město* ⊕ *www.martinvezdi.cz* ☉*Open during concerts (see Web site for times) and during mass (Sun., 10:30 AM in German, 7:30 PM in Czech).*

Kostel svatého Mikuláše *(Church of St. Nicholas).* Designed in the 18th century by Prague's own master of late baroque, Kilian Ignaz Dientzenhofer, this church is probably less successful in capturing the style's lyric exuberance than its namesake across town, the Chrám svatého Mikuláše. But Dientzenhofer utilized the limited space to create a well-balanced structure. The interior is compact, with a beautiful, small

chandelier and an enormous black organ that overwhelms the rear of the church. Afternoon and evening concerts for visitors are held almost continuously—walk past and you're sure to get leafleted for one. ⊠ *Staroměstské nám., Staré Město* ⊕ *www.svmikulas.cz* ⊡ *Free* ☉ *Daily 10–4, except during mass on Sun. and holidays at 10* AM.

Malé náměstí *(Small Square).* Note the iron fountain dating from around 1560 in the center of the square. The colorfully painted house at No. 3 was originally a hardware store (and now, confusingly, is the site of a Hard Rock Cafe). It's not as old as it looks, but you can find authentic Gothic portals and Renaissance *sgraffiti* that reflect the square's true age in certain spots.

OFF THE BEATEN PATH

Muzeum hlavního města Prahy *(Museum of the City of Prague).* The high point of this museum is a paper model of Prague that shows what the city looked like before the Jewish ghetto was destroyed in a massive fire in 1689. Display boards—not all are in English—trace the history of the city from its origins through the 17th century. Though technically situated in Nové Město, this out-of-the-way museum is easy to reach from Old Town, because it's near the Florenc metro and bus station. ⊠ *Na Poříčí 52, Nové Město* ☎ *224–816–773* ⊕ *www.muzeumprahy.cz* ⊡ *120 Kč* ☉ *Tues.–Fri. and Sun. 9–6, Sat. 9–9* Ⓜ *Lines B and C: Florenc.*

Stavovské divadlo *(Estates Theater).* Built in the 1780s in the classical style, this opulent, green *palais* was a beacon of Czech-language culture in a city long dominated by German. It's best known for hosting the world premiere of Mozart's opera *Don Giovanni* in October 1787, with the composer himself conducting. Prague audiences were quick to acknowledge Mozart's genius: The opera was an instant hit here, though it flopped nearly everywhere else in Europe. Mozart wrote some of the opera's second act in Prague at the Villa Bertramka, where he was a frequent guest. You must attend a performance to see inside. But the statue of Mozart's "Commendatore" character just outside the theater, a haunting sight, especially after dark, is free to gaze at. ⊠ *Ovocný trh 1, Staré Město* ☎ *224–902–322 box office* ⊕ *www.narodni-divadlo.cz.*

2

JOSEFOV (JEWISH QUARTER)

For centuries Prague had an active, vital Jewish community that was an exuberant part of the city's culture. Much of that activity was concentrated in Josefov, the former Jewish ghetto, just a short walk north of Old Town Square. This area first became a Jewish settlement around the 12th century, but it didn't actually take on the physical aspects of a ghetto—walled off from the rest of the city—until much later.

The history of Prague's Jews, like those of much of Europe, is mostly a sad one. There were horrible pogroms in the late Middle Ages, followed by a period of relative prosperity under Rudolf II in the late 16th century, though the freedoms of Jews were still tightly restricted. It was Austrian Emperor Josef II—the ghetto's namesake—who did the most to improve the conditions of the city's Jews. His "Edict of Tolerance" in 1781 removed dress codes for Jews and opened the gates to the rest of the city.

The prosperity of the 19th century lifted the Jews out of poverty, and many of them chose to leave the ghetto. By the end of the century the number of poor gentiles, drunks, and prostitutes in the ghetto was growing, and the number of actual Jews was declining. At this time, city officials decided to clear the slum and raze the buildings. In their place they built many of the gorgeous turn-of-the-20th-century and art nouveau town houses you see today. Only a handful of the synagogues, the town hall, and the cemetery were preserved.

World War II and the Nazi occupation brought profound tragedy to the city's Jews. A staggering percentage were deported—many to Terezín, north of Prague, and then later to Polish death camps. Of the 40,000 Jews living in Prague before World War II, only about 1,200 returned after the war, and merely a handful live in the ghetto today.

The Nazi occupation contains a historic irony. Many of the treasures stored away in Prague's Jewish Museum were brought here from across

Central Europe on Hitler's orders. His idea was to form a museum dedicated to the soon-to-be extinct Jewish race.

Today, even with the crowds, the ghetto is a must-see. The Old Jewish Cemetery alone, with its incredibly forlorn overlay of headstone upon headstone going back centuries, merits the steep admission price the Jewish Museum charges to see its treasures. Don't feel compelled to linger long on the ghetto's streets after visiting, though—much of it is tourist-trap territory, filled with overpriced T-shirt, trinket, and toy shops—the same lousy souvenirs found everywhere in Prague.

A ticket to the Židovské muzeum v Praze (Prague Jewish Museum) includes admission to the Old Jewish Cemetery and collections installed in four surviving synagogues and the Ceremony Hall. The Staronová synagóga, or Old-New Synagogue, a functioning house of worship, does not technically belong to the museum, and requires a separate admission ticket.

GETTING HERE AND AROUND

The Jewish Quarter is one of the most heavily visited areas in Prague, especially in peak tourist seasons, when its tiny streets are jammed to bursting. The best way to visit is on foot—it's a short hop over from Old Town Square.

TIMING

The best time for a visit (read: quiet and less crowded) is early morning, when the museums and cemetery first open. The area itself is very compact, and a fairly thorough tour should take only half a day. Don't go on the Sabbath (Saturday), when all the museums are closed.

TOP ATTRACTIONS

Klausová synagóga (*Klausen Synagogue*). This baroque synagogue displays objects from Czech Jewish traditions, with an emphasis on celebrations and daily life. In the neo-Romanesque **Obřadní síň** (Ceremony Hall) that adjoins the Klausen Synagogue, the focus is more staid. You'll find a variety of Jewish funeral paraphernalia, including old gravestones, and medical instruments. Special attention is paid to the activities of the Jewish Burial Society through many fine objects and paintings. The building was built at the end of the 17th century in place of three small buildings (a synagogue, a school, and a ritual bath) that were destroyed in a fire that devastated the ghetto in 1689. ⊠ *U starého hřbitova 3A, Josefov* ☎ *221–711–511* ⊕ *www.jewishmuseum. cz* ⌲ *Combined ticket to museums and Old-New Synagogue 480 Kč; museums only, 300 Kč* ☉ *Apr.–Oct., Sun.–Fri. 9–6; Nov.–Mar., Sun.–Fri. 9–4:30.*

★ **Maiselova synagóga** (*Maisel Synagogue*). The history of Czech Jews from the 10th to the 18th century is illustrated, accompanied by some of the Prague Jewish Museum's most precious objects. The collection includes silver Torah shields and pointers, spice boxes, and candelabra; historic tombstones; and fine ceremonial textiles—some donated by Mordechai Maisel to the very synagogue he founded. The glitziest items come from the late 16th and early 17th centuries, a prosperous era for Prague's Jews. ⊠ *Maiselova 10, Josefov* ☎ *221–711–511* ⊕ *www.jewishmuseum. cz* ⌲ *Combined ticket to museums and Old-New Synagogue 480 Kč;*

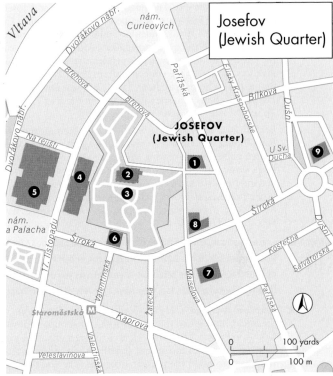

museums only, 300 Kč ☉ *Apr.–Oct., Sun.–Fri. 9–6; Nov.–Mar., Sun.–Fri. 9–4:30.*

Pinkasova synagóga *(Pinkas Synagogue).* Here you'll find two moving testimonies to the appalling crimes perpetrated against the Jews during World War II. One astounds by sheer numbers: The walls are covered with nearly 80,000 names of Bohemian and Moravian Jews murdered by the Nazis. Among them are the names of the paternal grandparents of former U.S. Secretary of State Madeleine Albright. The second is an exhibition of drawings made by children at the Nazi concentration camp Terezín. The Nazis used the camp for propaganda purposes to demonstrate their "humanity" toward the Jews, and for a time the prisoners were given relative freedom to lead "normal" lives. However, transports to death camps in Poland began in earnest in 1944, and many thousands of Terezín prisoners, including most of these children, later perished. The entrance to the Old Jewish Cemetery is through this synagogue. ⊠ *Široká 3, Josefov* ☎ *221–711–511* ⊕ *www.jewishmuseum. cz* ☒ *Combined ticket to museums and Old-New Synagogue 480 Kč; museums only, 300 Kč* ☉ *Apr.–Oct., Sun.–Fri. 9–6; Nov.–Mar., Sun.–Fri. 9–4:30.*

★ **Rudolfinum.** Thanks to a thorough makeover and exterior sandblasting, this neo-Renaissance monument now has some of the cleanest, brightest stonework in the city. Designed by Josef Zítek and Josef Schulz and completed in 1884—it was named for then Hapsburg Crown Prince Rudolf—the low-slung sandstone building was meant to be a combination concert hall and exhibition gallery. After 1918 it was converted into the parliament of the newly independent Czechoslovakia until German invaders reinstated the concert hall in 1939. Now the Czech Philharmonic has its home base here. The 1,200-seat **Dvořákova síň** (Dvořák Hall) has superb acoustics (the box office faces 17 Listopadu Street). To see the hall, you must attend a concert.

Behind Dvořák Hall sits a set of large exhibition rooms, the **Galerie Rudolfinum** (⊕ *www.galerierudolfinum.cz*), an innovative, state-supported gallery with rotating shows of contemporary art. Four or five large shows are mounted here annually, showcasing excellent Czech and international artists. ⊠ *Alšovo nábřeží 12, Josefov* ☎ *227–059–111 box office, 227–059–309 gallery* ⊕ *www.rudolfinum.org* ⊠ *Gallery 70 Kč–150 Kč, depending on exhibition* ☉ *Gallery Tues., Wed., and Fri.–Sun. 10–6, Thurs. 10–8.*

QUICK
BITES

Crave a culinary change from constant meat and potatoes? Try Les Moules (⊠ *Pařížská 19/203* ☎ 222–315–022), at the end of Maiselova. There's a nice open terrace and a fine selection of mussels, as you'd expect from the name. If you're tired of pilsner, too, they have a variety of Belgian Trappist beers.

★ **Staronová synagóga** *(Old-New Synagogue, or Altneuschul).* Dating from the mid-13th century, this is one of the most important works of early Gothic in Prague. The name refers to the legend that the synagogue was built on the site of an ancient Jewish temple, and the temple's stones were used to build the present structure. The entrance, with its vault supported by two pillars, is the oldest part of the synagogue. Amazingly, the synagogue has survived fires, the razing of the ghetto, and the Nazi occupation intact; it's still in active use. As the oldest functioning synagogue in Europe, it's a living storehouse of Bohemian Jewish life. Note that men are required to cover their heads inside, and during services men and women sit apart. ⊠ *Červená 2, Josefov* ☎ *221–711–511* ⊕ *www.jewishmuseum.cz* ⊠ *Combined ticket to Old-New Synagogue and museums 480 Kč; Old-New Synagogue only, 200 Kč* ☉ *Apr.–Oct., Sun.–Fri. 9–6; Nov.–Mar., Sun.–Fri. 9–4:30.*

Fodor's Choice
★ **Starý židovský hřbitov** *(Old Jewish Cemetery).* An unforgettable sight, this cemetery is where all Jews living in Prague from the 15th century to 1787 were laid to rest. The lack of any space in the tiny ghetto forced graves to be piled on top of one another. Tilted at crazy angles, the 12,000 visible tombstones are but a fraction of countless thousands more buried below. Walk the path amid the gravestones; the relief symbols you see represent the names and professions of the deceased. The oldest marked grave belongs to the poet Avigdor Kara, who died in 1439; the grave is not accessible from the pathway, but the original tombstone can be seen in the Maisel Synagogue. The best-known marker belongs to Jehuda ben Bezalel, the famed Rabbi Loew (died 1609), a chief rabbi of Prague and a profound scholar, credited with creating the mythical Golem. Even today, small scraps of paper bearing

wishes are stuffed into the cracks of the rabbi's tomb with the hope that he will grant them. Loew's grave lies near the exit. ⊠ *Široká 3, enter through Pinkasova synagóga, Josefov* ☎ *221–711–511* ⊕ *www. jewishmuseum.cz* ⊠ *Combined ticket to museums and Old-New Synagogue 480 Kč; museums only, 300 Kč* ⊙ *Apr.–Oct., Sun.–Fri. 9–6; Nov.–Mar., Sun.–Fri. 9–4:30.*

U(P)M *(Museum of Decorative Arts)*. In a custom-built art nouveau building from 1897, this wonderfully laid-out museum of exquisite local prints, books, ceramics, textiles, clocks, and furniture will please anyone from the biggest decorative arts expert to those that just appreciate a little *Antiques Roadshow* on the weekend. Superb rotating exhibits, too. ⊠ *Ulice 17, Listopadu 2, Josefov* ☎ *225–093–111* ⊕ *www.upm.cz* ⊠ *120 Kč, free Tues. 5–7* ⊙ *Tues. 10–7, Wed.–Sun. 10–6.*

TOURIST TRAPS

Walking through Old Town Square and on Celetná it's almost impossible not to be accosted by boys in Mozart costumes or guides selling hour-long bus tours. Just know: Most of the concerts are dismissed as "tourist music" by locals. There are better performers in the city's much more authentic classical music venues. As for the tours, remember that Prague is blessed with a fantastic and efficient public transportation system—why shell out to take a bus when you can ride a tram with the same view?

WORTH NOTING

Španělská synagóga *(Spanish Synagogue)*. This domed, Moorish-style synagogue was built in 1868 on the site of the city's oldest synagogue, the Altschul. Here the historical exposition that begins in the Maisel Synagogue continues to the post–World War II period. The displays are not very compelling, but the building's painstakingly restored interior definitely is. ⊠ *Vězeňská 1, Josefov* ☎ *221–711–511* ⊕ *www. jewishmuseum.cz* ⊠ *Combined ticket to museums and Old-New Synagogue 480 Kč; museums only, 300 Kč* ⊙ *Apr.–Oct., Sun.–Fri. 9–6; Nov.–Mar., Sun.–Fri. 9–4:30.*

Židovská radnice *(Jewish Town Hall)*. The hall was the creation of Mordechai Maisel, an influential Jewish leader at the end of the 16th century. Restored in the 18th century, it was given a clock and bell tower at that time. A second clock, with Hebrew numbers, keeps time counterclockwise. Now a Jewish Community Center, the building also houses Shalom, a kosher restaurant. Neither the hall nor the restaurant is open to the public, but the beautiful building is worth seeing from the outside. ⊠ *Maiselova 18, Josefov* ☎ *222–319–002.*

MALÁ STRANA (LESSER QUARTER)

Established in 1257, this is Prague's most perfectly formed—yet totally asymmetrical—neighborhood. Also known as "Little Town," it was home to the merchants and craftsmen who served the royal court. Though not nearly as confusing as the labyrinth that is Old Town, the streets in the Lesser Quarter can baffle, but they also bewitch, and today the area holds embassies, Czech government offices, historical attractions, and galleries mixed in with the usual glut of pubs, restaurants, and souvenir shops.

GETTING HERE AND AROUND

The Metro's A line will lead you to Malá Strana, the Malostranká station being the most central stop. But there's no better way to arrive at Malá Strana than via a scenic downhill walk from the Castle or a lovely stroll from Old Town across the Charles Bridge.

TIMING

Note that the heat builds up during the day in this area—as do the crowds—so it's best visited before noon or in early evening. On literally every block there are plenty of cafés in which to stop, sip coffee or tea, and people-watch, and a wealth of gardens and parks ideal for resting in cool shade. As with the other most popular neighborhoods of Prague—Old Town, New Town, and the Castle Area—there are fewer crowds in the early morning, or the bitter cold. (The former is preferable over the latter.)

TOP ATTRACTIONS

Chrám svatého Mikuláše *(Church of St. Nicholas)*. With dynamic curves, this church is one of the purest and most ambitious examples of high baroque. The celebrated architect Christoph Dientzenhofer began the Jesuit church in 1704 on the site of one of the more active Hussite

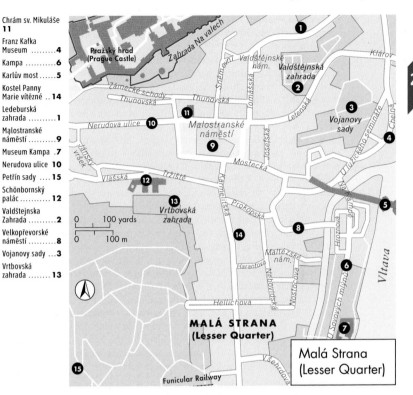

churches of 15th-century Prague. Work on the building was taken over by his son Kilian Ignaz Dientzenhofer, who built the dome and presbytery. Anselmo Lurago completed the whole thing in 1755 by adding the bell tower. The juxtaposition of the broad, full-bodied dome with the slender bell tower is one of the many striking architectural contrasts that mark the Prague skyline. Inside, the vast pink-and-green space is impossible to take in with a single glance. Every corner bristles with life, guiding the eye first to the dramatic statues, then to the hectic frescoes, and on to the shining faux-marble pillars. Many of the statues are the work of Ignaz Platzer and constitute his last blaze of success. Platzer's workshop was forced to declare bankruptcy when the centralizing and secularizing reforms of Joseph II toward the end of the 18th century brought an end to the flamboyant baroque era. The tower, with an entrance on the side of the church, is open in summer. The church also hosts chamber music concerts in summer, which complement this eye-popping setting but do not reflect the true caliber of classical music in Prague. For that, check the schedule posted across the street at **Líchtenský palác,** where the faculty of HAMU, the city's premier music academy, often gives performances. ⊠ *Malostranské nám., Malá Strana* ⊕ *www.psalterium.cz* ⊠ *60 Kč* ⊗ *Daily 9–4:30 for sightseeing, 8:30–9* AM *for prayer; no admission charge for prayer.*

★ **Franz Kafka Museum.** The great early-20th-century Jewish author Kafka wasn't Czech, and he wrote in German, but he lived in Prague nearly his entire short, anguished life, so it's fitting that he's finally gotten the shrine he deserves here. Because the museum's designers believed in channeling Kafka's darkly paranoid and paradoxical work, they created exhibits true to this spirit. And even if the results are often goofy, they get an "A-plus" for effort. Facsimiles of manuscripts, documents, first editions, photographs, and newspaper obits are displayed in glass vitrines, which in turn are situated in "Kafkaesque" settings: huge open filing cabinets, stone gardens, piles of coal. Also abounding are scary projections, pockets of shadow, and the author's quotes painted on stark planked walls ("The Messiah will only come when we no longer need him"), while each of the neurotic scribe's "failed fiancées" gets her own table hung from the ceiling by chains. The basement level of the museum gets even freakier, with expressionistic representations of Kafka's work itself, including a model of the horrible torture machine from the "Penal Colony" story. Not a place for young children, or even lovers on a first date, but fascinating to anyone interested in Prague's cultural history. Other Kafka sites in Prague include his home on Golden Lane, his Old Town birthplace at Náměstí Franze Kafky 3, and Jaroslav Rona's trippy bronze sculpture of the writer on nearby Desni Street. (Speaking of sculptures, take a gander at the animatronic "Piss" statue in the Kafka Museum's courtyard. This rendition of a couple urinating into a fountain shaped like the Czech Republic was made by local *enfant terrible* sculptor David Černy, who also did the babies crawling up the Žižkov TV Tower.) ✉ *Hergetova Cihelna, Cihelna 2b, Malá Strana* ☎ *257–535–507* 🌐 *www.kafkamuseum.cz* 🎫 *180 Kč* ⏲ *Daily 10–6.*

Kampa. Prague's largest "island" is cut off from the "mainland" by the narrow Čertovka streamlet. The name Čertovka, or Devil's Stream, reputedly refers to a cranky old lady who once lived on Maltese Square (given the river's present dirty state, the name remains appropriate). During the 2002 floods, the well-kept lawns of the **Kampa Gardens,** which occupy much of the island, were covered as was much of the lower portion of Malá Strana. Evidence of flood damage occasionally marks the landscape, along with a sign indicating where the waters crested.

NEED A BREAK?

The second location of this old favorite, Bohemia Bagel (✉ *Lázenská 19*) is steps from the Charles Bridge. A welcome addition for homesick expats, this was the first restaurant to offer homemade bagels in Prague, along with soups and salads.

Fodor's Choice ★ **Karlův most** *(Charles Bridge).* This is Prague's signature monument, and worth the denomination. The view from the foot of the bridge on the Old Town side, encompassing the towers and domes of the Lesser Quarter and the soaring spires of St. Vitus's Cathedral, is nothing short of breathtaking. This heavenly vista subtly changes in perspective as you walk across the bridge, attended by a host of baroque saints that decorate the bridge's peaceful Gothic stones. At night its drama is spellbinding: St. Vitus's Cathedral lit in a ghostly green, the Castle in monumental yellow, and the Church of St. Nicholas in a voluptuous pink,

The Kafka Museum pays tribute to the surreal spirit of Kafka's work.

all viewed through the menacing silhouettes of the bowed statues and the Gothic towers. Night is the best time to visit the bridge, which is choked with visitors, vendors, and beggars by day. The later the hour, the thinner the crowds—though the bridge is never truly empty, even at daybreak. Tourists with flash cameras are there all hours of the night, and as dawn is breaking, revelers from the dance clubs at the east end of the bridge weave their way homeward, singing loudly and debating where to go for breakfast.

When the Přemyslid princes set up residence in Prague during the 10th century, there was a ford across the Vltava here—a vital link along one of Europe's major trading routes. After several wooden bridges and the first stone bridge washed away in floods, Charles IV appointed the 27-year-old German Peter Parler, the architect of St. Vitus's Cathedral, to build a new structure in 1357. It became one of the wonders of the world in the Middle Ages.

After 1620, following the disastrous defeat of Czech Protestants by Catholic Hapsburgs at the Battle of White Mountain, the bridge became a symbol of the Counter-Reformation's vigorous re-Catholicization efforts. The many baroque statues that appeared in the late 17th century, commissioned by Catholics, came to symbolize the totality of the Austrian (hence Catholic) triumph. The Czech writer Milan Kundera sees the statues from this perspective: "The thousands of saints looking out from all sides, threatening you, following you, hypnotizing you, are the raging hordes of occupiers who invaded Bohemia 350 years ago to tear the people's faith and language from their hearts."

The religious conflict is less obvious nowadays, leaving behind an artistic tension between baroque and Gothic that gives the bridge its allure. Take a closer look at some of the statues while walking toward the Lesser Quarter. The third one on the right, a bronze crucifix from the mid-17th century, is the oldest of all. It's mounted on the location of a wooden cross destroyed in a battle with the Swedes (the golden Hebrew inscription was reputedly financed by a Jew accused of defiling the cross). The fifth on the left, which shows St. Frances Xavier carrying four pagan princes (an Indian, Moor, Chinese, and Tartar) ready for conversion, represents an outstanding piece of baroque sculpture. Eighth on the right is the statue of St. John of Nepomuk, who according to legend was wrapped in chains and thrown to his death from this bridge. Touching the statue is supposed to bring good luck or, according to some versions of the story, a return visit to Prague. On the left-hand side, sticking out from the bridge between the 9th and 10th statues (the latter has a wonderfully expressive vanquished Satan), stands a Roland (Bruncvík) statue. This knightly figure, bearing the coat of arms of the Old Town, was once a reminder that this part of the bridge belonged to the Old Town before Prague became a unified city in 1784.

For many art historians the most valuable statue is the 12th on the left, near the Lesser Quarter end. Mathias Braun's statue of St. Luitgarde depicts the blind saint kissing Christ's wounds. The most compelling grouping, however, is the second from the end on the left, a work of Ferdinand Maxmilian Brokoff (son of Johann) from 1714. Here the saints are incidental; the main attraction is the Turk, his face expressing extreme boredom at guarding the Christians imprisoned in the cage at his side. When the statue was erected, just 31 years after the second Turkish siege of Vienna, it scandalized the Prague public, who smeared it with mud. All but a couple of the bridge's surviving baroque statues, including St. Luitgarde and the Turk, have been replaced by modern copies. Several can be viewed in the Lapidarium museum at the Výstaviště exhibition grounds in Prague 7; a few more occupy a man-made cavern at Vyšehrad.

Staroměstská mostecká věž (Old Town Bridge Tower), at the bridge entrance on the Old Town side, is where Peter Parler, the architect of the Charles Bridge, began his bridge building. The carved façades he designed for the sides of the tower were destroyed by Swedish soldiers in 1648, at the end of the Thirty Years' War. The sculptures facing the Old Town, however, are still intact (although some are recent copies). They depict an old and gout-ridden Charles IV with his son, who became Wenceslas IV. Above them are two of Bohemia's patron saints, Adalbert of Prague and Sigismund. The top of the tower offers a spectacular view of the city for 70 Kč; it's open daily from 10 to 10, year-round.

Kostel Panny Marie vítězné (*Church of Our Lady Victorious*). This aging, well-appointed church on the Lesser Quarter's main street is the unlikely home of Prague's most famous religious artifact, the *Pražské Jezulátko* (Infant Jesus of Prague). Originally brought to Prague from Spain in the 16th century, the wax doll holds a reputation for bestowing miracles on many who have prayed for its help. A measure of its widespread attraction is reflected in the prayer books on the kneelers in front of the

statue, which have prayers of inter-
cession in 20 different languages.
The "Bambino," as he's known
locally, has an enormous and
incredibly ornate wardrobe, some
of which is on display in a museum
upstairs. Nuns from a nearby convent change the outfit on the statue
regularly. Don't miss the souvenir
shop (accessible via a doorway to
the right of the main altar), where
the Bambino's custodians flex their
marketing skills. ⊠ *Karmelitská
9A, Malá Strana* ⌷ *Free* ☉ *Mon.–
Sat. 9:30–5:30, Sun. 1–6 (museum and gift shop); Mon.–Sat. 8:30–7,
Sun. 8:30–8 (church).*

> **WORD OF MOUTH**

"One of the special treats for me
was to walk on the Charles bridge
after midnight when the bridge
lights were all turned off so it was
almost pitch black but there were
street musicians playing beautiful
music and we could really appreciate the beauty of the city lights
and the beaconing castle complex
on hilltop."   —DAX

2

Malostranské náměstí *(Lesser Quarter Square)*. Another one of the many
classic examples of Prague's charm, this square is flanked on the east
and south sides by arcaded houses dating from the 16th and 17th centuries. The Czech Parliament resides partly in the gaudy yellow-and-
green palace on the square's north side, partly in a building on Sněmovní
Street, behind the palace. The huge bulk of the Church of St. Nicholas
divides the lower, busier section—buzzing with restaurants, street vendors, clubs, and shops—from the slightly quieter upper part.

★ **Museum Kampa**. The spotlighted jewel on Kampa Island is a remodeled
flour mill that now displays a private collection of paintings by Czech
artist František Kupka and first-rate temporary exhibitions by both
Czech and other Central European visual wizards. The museum was
hit hard by the 2002 flood; waters rose up 19½ feet in the building and
courtyard. But the museum rebounded quickly and now includes an
elegant restaurant with an outdoor terrace that offers a splendid view
of the river and historic buildings on the opposite bank. ⊠ *U Sovových
mlýnů 2, Malá Strana* ☎ *257–286–147* ⊕ *www.museumkampa.cz*
⌷ *220 Kč* ☉ *Daily 10–6.*

Nerudova ulice. This steep street used to be the last leg of the "Royal
Way," the king's procession before his coronation. As king, he made
the ascent on horseback, not huffing and puffing on foot like today's
visitors. It was named for the 19th-century Czech journalist and poet
Jan Neruda, after whom Chilean poet Pablo Neruda renamed himself.
Until Joseph II's administrative reforms in the late 18th century, house
numbering was unknown in Prague. Each house bore a name, depicted
on the façade, and these are particularly prominent on Nerudova ulice.
No. 6, **U červeného orla** (At the Red Eagle), proudly displays a faded
painting of a crimson eagle. No. 12 is known as **U tří housliček** (At
the Three Fiddles); in the early 18th century three generations of the
Edlinger violin-making family lived here. Joseph II's scheme numbered
each house according to its position in the "town" (here the Lesser
Quarter) to which it belonged, rather than its sequence on the street.
The red plates record the original house numbers, but the blue ones

DID YOU KNOW?

According to popular superstition, touching the eighth statue on the right of the Charles Bridge, St. John of Nepomuk, is said to bring a return visit to Prague.

are the numbers used in addresses today. Many architectural guides refer to the old, red-number plates, much to the confusion of visitors.

Two large palaces break the unity of the houses on Nerudova ulice. Both were designed by the adventurous baroque architect Giovanni Santini, one of the popular Italian builders hired by wealthy nobles in the early 18th century. The **Morzin Palace,** on the left at No. 5, is now the Romanian Embassy. The fascinating façade, created in 1713 with an allegory of night and day, is the work of Ferdinand Brokoff, of Charles Bridge statue fame. Across the street at No. 20 is the **Thun-Hohenstein Palace,** now the Italian Embassy. The gateway with two enormous eagles (the emblem of the Kolovrat family, who owned the building at the time) is the work of the other great Charles Bridge statue sculptor, Mathias Braun. Santini himself lived at No. 14, the **Valkoun House.**

The archway at Nerudova No. 13 is a prime example of the many winding passageways that give the Lesser Quarter its captivatingly ghostly character at night. Higher up the street at No. 33 is the **Bretfeld Palace,** a rococo house on the corner of Jánský vršek. The relief of St. Nicholas on the façade was created by Ignaz Platzer, a sculptor known for his classical and rococo work. But it's the building's historical associations that give it intrigue: Mozart, his librettist partner Lorenzo da Ponte, and the aging but still infamous philanderer and music lover Casanova stayed here at the time of the world premiere of *Don Giovanni* in 1787.

☾ **Petřín sady.** For a superb view of the city—from a slightly more soli-
★ tary perch—the top of Petřín Hill includes a charming playground for children and adults alike, with a miniature Eiffel Tower. The park is laced with footpaths, with several buildings clustered together near the tower. Just keep going gradually upward until you reach the base, where you can also find a mirror maze (*bludiště*) in a small structure, and the seemingly abandoned svatý Vavřinec (St. Lawrence) church. The peaceful area is an ideal spot for an afternoon of wandering. You can walk up from Karmelitská ulice or Újezd down in the Lesser Quarter, or ride the funicular railway from U lanové dráhy ulice, off Újezd. You can also stroll over from Strahov klášter (Strahov Monastery). Regular public-transportation tickets are valid on the funicular. Lines for the funicular can be long on a clear day, and they move slowly. (If the line is far outside the terminal door, you're in for at least a 30-minute wait, if not longer.) To descend, take the funicular or meander on foot down past the Stations of the Cross on the pathways leading back to the Lesser Quarter. A number of paths meander down the face of the hillside through fruit orchards, and finally back to Karmelitská; a wide path goes to Strahov Monastery. The funicular, an attraction in itself, is run as an extension of the tram system. The station at the top opens onto a rose garden, a lovely destination in the summer months.

As you exit the funicular at the top of Petřín Hill, the rounded dome to your left is **Štefánik Observatory** (☎ *257–320–540* ⊕ *www.observatory. cz*), a working astronomical facility with some fine displays (though not many in English). Both day and night telescope viewings are available.

A large children's play area in Petřín sady is dominated by the nearly 200-foot **Petřínská rozheldna** (*Petřín Tower*), a smaller replica of the

Eiffel Tower with a marvelous view of the city from the top. This is not an attraction for the timid; the only way to the viewing platforms is via a circular stairway that wraps around the outside of the tower, a safe but dizzying ascent. The hardy who make the climb will be rewarded with a dazzlingly view.

A stone's throw from the Petřín Tower, the **Bludiste na Petřína** (*Mirror Maze* ☎ *257–315–212*) is an amusement-park attraction with, as the name suggests, a variety of amusingly distorted mirrors. It's great fun for the kids. ⊠ *Petřín Hill* 🎫 *Observatory 55 Kč, Tower 100 Kč, Maze 70 Kč* ☙ *Observatory: Jan. and Feb., Tues.–Fri. 6–8 PM, weekends 11–8; Mar., Tues.–Fri. 7–9 PM, weekends 11–6, and 7–9; Apr.–Aug., Tues.–Fri. 2–7 and 9–11, weekends 11–7, and 9–11; Sept., Tues.–Fri. 2–6 and 8–10, weekends 11–6, and 8–10; Oct., Tues.–Fri. 7–9, weekends 11–6, and 7–9; Nov. and Dec., Tues.–Fri. 6–8, weekends 11–8. Tower and Maze: Daily 10–10.*

Valdštejnska Zahrada *(Wallenstein Palace Gardens).* With its idiosyncratic high-walled gardens and superb, vaulted Renaissance *sala terrena* (room opening onto a garden), this palace displays superbly elegant grounds. Walking around the formal paths, you come across numerous fountains and statues depicting figures from classical mythology or warriors dispatching a variety of beasts. (See if you can spot the live white peacock that has made this garden its home.) However, nothing beats the trippy "Grotto," a huge dripstone wall packed with imaginative rock formations, like little faces and animals hidden in the charcoal-colored landscape, and what's billed as "illusory hints of secret corridors." Here, truly, staring at the wall is a form of entertainment. Next to the wall sits an aviary with some large owls (look up; they're usually perched in the upper reaches). Albrecht von Wallenstein, onetime owner of the house and gardens, began a meteoric military career in 1622, when the Austrian emperor Ferdinand II retained him to save the empire from the Swedes and Protestants during the Thirty Years' War. Wallenstein, wealthy by marriage, offered to raise an army of 20,000 men at his own cost and lead them personally. Ferdinand II accepted and showered Wallenstein with confiscated land and titles. Wallenstein's first acquisition was this enormous area. After knocking down 23 houses, a brick factory, and three gardens, in 1623 he began to build his magnificent palace. Most of the palace itself now serves the Czech Senate as meeting chamber and offices. The palace's cavernous former *Jízdárna*, or riding school, now hosts occasional art exhibitions. ⊠ *Letenská 10, Malá Strana* 🎫 *Free* ☙ *Apr.–May and Oct., weekdays 7:30–6, weekends 10–6; June–Sept., weekdays 7:30–7, weekends 10–7.*

Vrtbovská zahrada *(Vrtba Garden).* An unobtrusive door on noisy Karmelitská hides the entranceway to a fascinating sanctuary with one of the best views of the Lesser Quarter. The street door opens onto the intimate courtyard of the Vrtbovský palác (Vrtba Palace), which is now private housing. Two Renaissance wings flank the courtyard; the left one was built in 1575, the right one in 1591. The original owner of the latter house was one of the 27 Bohemian nobles executed by the Hapsburgs in 1621. The house was given as confiscated property to Count Sezima of Vrtba, who bought the neighboring property and turned the buildings into a late-Renaissance palace. The Vrtba Garden was created a century later. Built in five levels rising behind the courtyard in a wave of statuary-bedecked staircases and formal terraces reaching toward a seashell-decorated pavilion at the top, it's a popular spot for weddings, receptions, and occasional concerts. (The fenced-off garden immediately behind and above belongs to the U.S. Embassy—hence the U.S. flag that often flies there.) The powerful stone figure of Atlas that caps the entranceway in the courtyard and most of the other statues of mythological figures are from the workshop of Mathias Braun, per-

haps the best of the Czech baroque sculptors. ⊠ *Karmelitská 25, Malá Strana* ☎ *257–531–480*⊕ *www.vrtbovska.cz* ⊡ *55 Kč* ۞ *Apr.–Oct., daily 10–6.*

WORTH NOTING

Ledeburská zahrada *(Ledeburg Garden)*. Rows of steeply banked baroque gardens rise behind the palaces of Valdštejnská ulice here. It's a climb if you enter from the street side, but the many shady arbors and niches are worth the exertion. The garden, with frescoes and statuary, was restored with support from a fund headed by Czech president Václav Havel and Britain's Prince Charles. Renovation seems to be never-ending at the lower entrance, but don't be deterred by the barriers and construction equipment—press on through the courtyard and up the stairs. You can also enter directly from the upper, south gardens of Prague Castle in summer. ⊠ *Valdštejnské nám. 3, Malá Strana* ⊡ *79 Kč* ۞ *Apr. and Oct., daily 9–6; May and Sept., daily 9–7; June and July, daily 9–9; Aug., daily 9–8.*

Schönbornský palác *(Schönborn Palace)*. Franz Kafka had an apartment in this massive baroque building at the top of Tržiště ulice in mid-1917, after moving from Zlatá ulička, or Golden Lane. The U.S. Embassy and consular office now occupy this prime location. Though security is stepped down compared with earlier in the decade, the many police, guards, and jersey barriers don't offer much of an invitation to linger. ⊠ *Tržiště 365/15 at Vlašská, Malá Strana.*

Velkopřevorské náměstí *(Grand Priory Square)*. This square is south and slightly west of the Charles Bridge, next to the Čertovka. The Grand Prior's Palace fronting the square is considered one of the finest baroque buildings in the Lesser Quarter, though it's now part of the Embassy of the Sovereign Military Order of Malta—the contemporary (and very real) descendant of the Knights of Malta. Alas, it's closed to the public. Opposite is the flamboyant orange-and-white stucco façade of the

The John Lennon Peace Wall on Kampa Island continues to be marked with free spirited, anti-war graffiti years after his death.

Buquoy Palace, built in 1719 by Giovanni Santini and the present home of the French Embassy. The so-called **John Lennon Peace Wall,** leading to a bridge over the Čertovka, was once a kind of monument to youthful rebellion, emblazoned with a large painted head of the former Beatle. But Lennon's visage is nowhere to be seen these days; the wall is usually covered instead with political and music-related graffiti.

Vojanovy sady *(Vojan Park).* Once the gardens of the Monastery of the Discalced Carmelites, later taken over by the Order of the English Virgins, this walled garden is now part of the Ministry of Finance. With its weeping willows, fruit trees, and benches, it provides another peaceful haven in summer. Exhibitions of modern sculpture are occasionally held here, contrasting sharply with the two baroque chapels and the graceful Ignaz Platzer statue of John of Nepomuk standing on a fish at the entrance. At the other end of the park you can find a terrace with a formal rose garden and a pair of peacocks that like to aggressively preen for visitors under the trellises. The park is surrounded by the high walls of the old monastery and new Ministry of Finance buildings, with only an occasional glimpse of a tower or spire to remind you of the world beyond. ⊠ *U lužického semináře 43/17, between Letenská ulice and Míšeňská ulice, Malá Strana* ☎ *257–531–839* ⊕ *www.vojanovysady.cz* ⊙ *Nov.–Mar., daily 8–5; Apr.–Oct., daily 8–7.*

HRADČANY (CASTLE AREA)

To the west of Prague Castle is the residential Hradčany (Castle Area), a town that during the early 14th century emerged from a collection of monasteries and churches. The concentration of history packed into Prague Castle and Hradčany challenges those not versed in the ups and downs of Bohemian kings, religious uprisings, wars, and oppression—but there's no shame in taking it all in on a purely aesthetic level.

GETTING HERE AND AROUND

There's a rise from river level of nearly 1,300 vertical feet to get to the Castle Area, so if you're on foot, be prepared for a climb. Pace yourself, not only to catch your breath but also to get views of the colorful jumble of terra-cotta-tile rooftops and the spires of the city center. The best subway approach is via line A, while bus enthusiasts should climb onto a 22 or 23.

TIMING

To do justice to the subtle charms of Hradčany once you arrive, allow at least two hours just for ambling and admiring the passing buildings and views of the city. The Strahovský klášter halls need about a half hour to take in, more if you tour the small picture gallery there, and the Loreta and its treasures need an equal length of time at least. The Národní galerie in the Šternberský palác deserves a minimum of a couple of hours. Keep in mind that several places are not open on Monday, and that early morning is the least crowded time to visit.

TOP ATTRACTIONS

★ **Hradčanské náměstí** *(Hradčany Square)*. With its fabulous mixture of baroque and Renaissance houses, topped by the Castle itself, this square had a prominent role in the film *Amadeus* (as a substitute for Vienna). Czech director Miloš Forman used the house at No. 7 for Mozart's residence, where the composer was haunted by the masked figure he thought was his father. The flamboyant rococo Arcibiskupský palác (Archbishop's Palace), on the left as you face the Castle, was the Viennese archbishop's palace. Sadly, the plush interior shown off in the film is rarely open to the public. For a brief time after World War II, No. 11 was home to a little girl named Marie Jana Korbelová, better known as Madeleine Albright.

★ **Národní galerie** *(National Gallery).* Housed in the 18th-century **Šternberský palác** (Sternberg Palace), this collection, though impressive, feels fairly limited when compared with nearby museums in Germany and Austria. During the time when Berlin, Dresden, and Vienna were building up superlative old-master galleries, Prague languished, neglected by her Viennese rulers. Works by Rubens and Rembrandt are on display; some other key pieces in the collection wait in the wings. Other branches of the National Gallery are scattered around town. ⊠ *Hradčanské nám. 15, Hradčany* ☎ *233–090–570* ⊕ *www.ngprague. cz* ☜ *150 Kč (reduced to 80Kč, Tues.–Sun. 4–6)* ☉ *Tues.–Sun. 10–6.*

Schwarzenberský palác *(Schwarzenberg Palace).* A boxy palace with an extravagant façade, this space is now home to a permanent exhibition of baroque sculpture and paintings created in lands that made up the Bohemian realm. Among the Czech masters featured are Peter Brandl, Maximilian Brokof, and the sculptor Mathias Braun (whose work you've seen on the Charles Bridge). ⊠ *Hradčanské nám. 185/2, Hradčany* ☎ *222–321–459* ⊕ *www.ngprague.cz* ☜ *150 Kč (reduced to 80 Kč, Tues.–Sun. 4–6)* ☉ *Tues.–Sun. 10–6.*

WORTH NOTING

Loreta *(Loreto Church).* The seductive lines of this church were a conscious move on the part of Counter-Reformation Jesuits in the 17th century, who wanted to build up the cult of Mary and attract Protestant Bohemians back to the fold. According to legend, angels had carried Mary's house from Nazareth and dropped it in a patch of laurel trees in Ancona, Italy. Known as *Loreto* (from the Latin for laurel), it immediately became a destination of pilgrimage. The Prague Loreto was one of many symbolic reenactments of this scene across Europe, and it worked: Pilgrims came in droves. The graceful façade, with its voluptuous tower, was built in 1720 by the ubiquitous Kilian Ignaz Dientzenhofer, the architect of the two St. Nicholas churches in Prague. A small exhibition upstairs displays the religious treasures presented to Mary in thanks for various services, including a monstrance (a vessel for the consecrated Eucharist) spectacularly studded with 6,500 diamonds. ⊠ *Loretánské nám. 7, Hradčany* ⊕ *www.loreta.cz* ☜ *110 Kč, 100 Kč photography fee* ☉ *Tues.–Sun. 9–12:15 and 1–4:30.*

Nový Svět. This picturesque, winding little alley, with façades from the 17th and 18th centuries, once housed Prague's poorest residents, but now many of the homes are used as artists' studios. The last house on the street, No. 1, was the home of the Danish-born astronomer Tycho Brahe. Supposedly Tycho was constantly disturbed during his nightly stargazing by the neighboring Loreto's church bells. He ended up com-

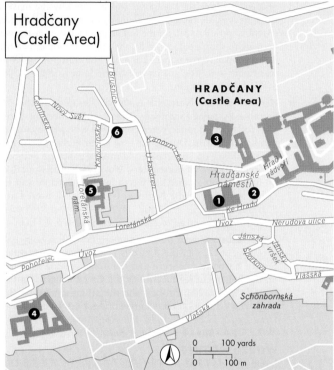

Hradčany
(Castle Area)

HRADČANY
(Castle Area)

plaining to his patron, Emperor Rudolf II, who instructed the Capuchin monks to finish their services before the first star appeared in the sky.

Strahovský klášter *(Strahov Monastery).* Founded by the Premonstratensian order in 1140, the monastery remained theirs until 1952, when the communists suppressed all religious orders and turned the entire complex into the **Památník národního písemnictví** (Museum of National Literature). The major building of interest is the **Strahov Library**, with its collection of early Czech manuscripts, the 10th-century Strahov New Testament, and the collected works of famed Danish astronomer Tycho Brahe. (Note that the library is closed at this writing and scheduled to reopen in 2011.) Also of note is the late-18th-century **Philosophical Hall.** Its ceilings are engulfed in a startling sky-blue fresco that depicts an unusual cast of characters, including Socrates' nagging wife Xanthippe; Greek astronomer Thales, with his trusty telescope; and a collection of Greek philosophers mingling with Descartes, Diderot, and Voltaire. On the premises is the order's small art gallery, highlighted by late-Gothic altars and paintings from Rudolf II's time, and a pub where you can sample the beer that the monks brew. ⊠ *Strahovské nádvoří 1/132, Hradčany* ☎ *233–107–716 library, 233–107–730 gallery* ⊕ *www.strahovskyklaster.cz* 💲 *60 Kč gallery, 80 Kč library* ☉ *Gallery 9–noon and 12:30–5 daily; library 9–noon and 1–5 daily.*

DID YOU KNOW?

The Loreto Church was built to symbolically reenact the legend of the Virgin Mary's house being carried by angels to Ancona, Italy.

PRAŽSKÝ HRAD (PRAGUE CASTLE)

Despite its monolithic presence, Prague Castle is not a single structure but a collection of structures dating from the 10th to the 20th century, all linked by internal courtyards. The most important are the cathedral, the Chrám svatého Víta, clearly visible soaring above the castle walls, and the Královský palác, the official residence of kings and presidents and still the center of political power in the Czech Republic.

Informační středisko *(Castle Information Office).* This is the place to come for entrance tickets, guided tours, audio-tour players, and tickets to cultural events held at the castle. You can wander around a great deal of the castle for free, especially as admission to St. Vitus's is now gratis once again. There are two tour options, with tickets valid for two days. The shorter tour (at a cheaper price) allows entrance to the Royal Palace, Golden Lane, the Daliborka Tower, St. George's Basilica, and the permanent exhibition on the history of the castle, "The Story of Prague Castle." This will provide more than enough castle quality time for most people. A more expensive, longer tour also includes the powder tower, the convent of St. George, and the Picture Gallery, in addition to sites included in the cheaper tour. If you just want to walk through the castle grounds, note that the gates close at midnight from April through October and at 11 PM the rest of the year, and the gardens are open from April through October only. ⊠ *Třetí nádvoří, across from entrance to St. Vitus's Cathedral, Pražský Hrad* ☎ *224–372–423* ⊕ *www.hrad.cz* ✉ Long Tour 350 Kč, Short Tour 250 Kč, ¿Story of Prague Castle" exhibit 140 Kč, Picture Gallery 150 Kč (free Mon. 4–6), Powder Tower 70 Kč, Photo fee 50 Kč ☉ Castle grounds open daily Apr.–Oct., 5 AM–midnight; Jan.–Mar., Nov. and Dec., 6 AM–11 PM; Premises requiring tickets (Old Royal Palace, "The Story of Prague Castleî exhibit, St. George's Basilica, Convent of St. George, Golden Lane and Daliborka Tower, Picture Gallery, Powder Tower), open daily

Apr.–Oct. 9–6; Jan.–Mar., Nov. and Dec. 9–4. Castle Gardens and Stag Moat open daily, Apr. and Oct. 10–6, May and Sept. 10–7, June and July 10–9, Aug. 10–8.

GETTING HERE AND AROUND

As with the neighboring environs, the best public transportation here is via the metro's Line A or by buses 22 or 23. Taxis work, too, of course, but they can be expensive. The Castle is compact and easily navigated. But be forewarned: The Castle, especially Chrám svatého Víta, teems with huge crowds practically year-round. **Zlatá ulička** (the Golden Lane) became so packed that in 2002 an admission fee was imposed for it.

TIMING

The Castle is at its best in early morning and late evening, when it holds an air of mystery. (It's incomparably beautiful when it snows.) The cathedral deserves an hour—but budget more time, as the number of visitors allowed in is limited, and the lines can be long. Another hour should be spent in the Královský palác, and you can easily spend an entire day taking in the museums, the views of the city, and the hidden nooks of the Castle. Remember that some sights, such as the Lobkovický palác and the National Gallery branch at Klášter svatého Jiří, are not open on Monday.

TOP ATTRACTIONS

★ **Bazilika svatého Jiří** *(St. George's Basilica)*. Inside, this church looks more or less as it did in the 12th century; it's the best-preserved Romanesque relic in the country. The effect is at once barnlike and peaceful, as the warm golden yellow of the stone walls and the small arched windows exude a sense of enduring harmony. Prince Vratislav I originally built it in the 10th century, though only the foundations remain from that time. The father of Prince Wenceslas (of Christmas carol fame) dedicated it to St. George (of dragon fame), a figure supposedly more agreeable to the still largely pagan people. The outside was remodeled during early baroque times, although the striking rusty-red color is in keeping with the look of the Romanesque edifice. The painted, house-shape tomb at the front of the church holds Vratislav's remains. Up the steps, in a chapel to the right, is the tomb Peter Parler designed for St. Ludmila, grandmother of St. Wenceslas. ⊠ *Nám. U sv. Jiří, Pražský Hrad* ☎ 224–373–208 ⊕ *www.hrad.cz* 🎟 *Included in 2-day castle ticket (250 Kč–350 Kč)* ⊙ *Apr.–Oct. 9–6; Jan.–Mar., Nov. andDec. 9–4.*

Fodor's Choice **Chrám svatého Víta** *(St. Vitus's Cathedral)*. With its graceful, soaring
★ towers, this Gothic cathedral—among the most beautiful in Europe—is the spiritual heart of Prague Castle and of the Czech Republic itself. The cathedral has a long and complicated history, beginning in the 10th century and continuing to its completion in 1929. To hear its history in depth, English-speaking guided tours of the cathedral and the Královský palác can be arranged at the information office across from the cathedral entrance.

Once you enter the cathedral, pause to take in the vast but delicate beauty of the Gothic and neo-Gothic interior. Colorful light filters through the brilliant stained-glass windows. This western third of the structure, including the façade and the two towers you can see from outside, was not completed until 1929, following the initiative of the Union for the Completion of the Cathedral. Don't let the neo-Gothic illusion keep you from examining this new section. The six stained-glass windows to your left and right and the large rose window behind are modern masterpieces. Take a good look at the third window up on the left. The familiar art nouveau flamboyance, depicting the blessing of Sts. Cyril and Methodius (9th-century missionaries to the Slavs), is the work of Alfons Mucha, the Czech founder of the style. He achieved the subtle coloring by painting rather than staining the glass.

Walking halfway up the right-hand aisle, you will find the **Svatová-clavská kaple** (Chapel of St. Wenceslas). With a tomb holding the saint's remains, walls covered in semi-precious stones, and paintings depicting the life of Wenceslas, this square chapel is the ancient core of the cathedral. Stylistically, it represents a high point of the dense, richly decorated—though rather gloomy—Gothic favored by Charles IV and his successors. Wenceslas (the "good king" of the Christmas carol) was a determined Christian in an era of widespread paganism. Around 925, as prince of Bohemia, he founded a rotunda church dedicated to St. Vitus on this site. But the prince's brother, Boleslav, was impatient to take power, and he ambushed and killed Wenceslas in 935 near a church at Stará Boleslav, northeast of Prague. Wenceslas was originally buried in that church, but so many miracles happened at his grave that he rapidly became a symbol of piety for the common people, something that greatly irritated the new Prince Boleslav. Boleslav was finally forced to honor his brother by reburying the body in the St. Vitus Rotunda. Shortly afterward, Wenceslas was canonized.

The rotunda was replaced by a Romanesque basilica in the late 11th century. Work began on the existing building in 1344. For the first few years the chief architect was the Frenchman Mathias d'Arras, but after his death in 1352 the work continued under the direction of 22-year-old German architect Peter Parler, who went on to build the Charles Bridge and many other Prague treasures.

The small door in the back of the chapel leads to the **Korunní komora** (Crown Chamber), the Bohemian crown jewels' repository. It remains locked with seven keys held by seven important people (including the president) and rarely opens to the public.

A little beyond the Chapel of St. Wenceslas on the same side, stairs lead down to the underground **royal crypt,** interesting primarily for the information it provides about the cathedral's history. As you descend the stairs, you can see parts of the old Romanesque basilica and portions of the foundations of the rotunda. Moving into the second room, you find a rather eclectic group of royal remains ensconced in sarcophagi dating from the 1930s. In the center is Charles IV, who died in 1378. Rudolf II, patron of Renaissance Prague, is entombed at the rear in his original tin coffin. To his right is Maria Amalia, the only child of Empress Maria Theresa to reside in Prague. Ascending the wooden steps back into the cathedral brings you to the white-marble **Kralovské mausoleum** (Royal Mausoleum), atop which lie stone statues of the first two Hapsburg kings to rule in Bohemia, Ferdinand I and Maximilian II, and another of Ferdinand's consort, Anne Jagiello.

Pražský hrad
(Prague Castle)

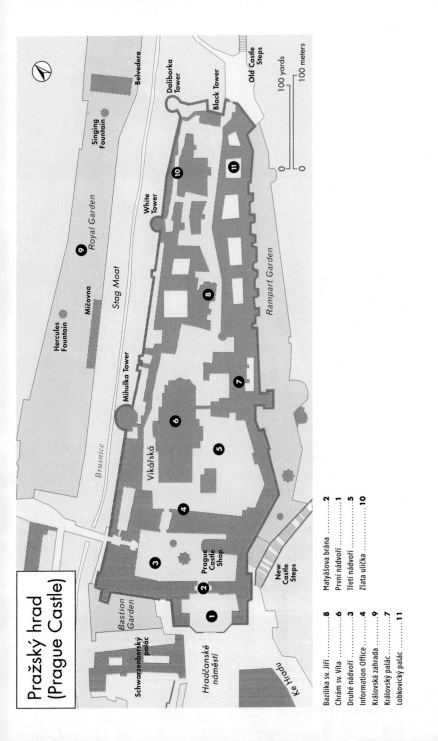

Schwarzenberský
palác

Bastion
Garden

Hradčanské
náměstí

K Hradu

Prague
Castle
Shop

New
Castle
Steps

Vikářská

Mihulka Tower

Brusnice

Hercules
Fountain

Míčovna

Stag Moat

Royal Garden

Singing
Fountain

Belvedere

White
Tower

Daliborka
Tower

Black Tower

Rampart Garden

Old Castle
Steps

100 yards

100 meters

Bazilika sv. Jiří **8**
Chrám sv. Víta **6**
Druhé nádvoří **3**
Information Office **4**
Královská zahrada **9**
Královský palác **7**
Lobkovický palác **11**

Matyášova brána **2**
První nádvoří **1**
Třetí nádvoří **5**
Zlatá ulička **10**

The cathedral's **Kralovské oratorium** (Royal Oratory) was used by the kings and their families when attending mass. Built in 1493, the work represents a perfect example of late Gothic. It's laced on the outside with a stone network of gnarled branches, similar in pattern to the ceiling vaulting in the Královský palác. The oratory connects to the palace by an elevated covered walkway, which you can see from outside.

A few more steps toward the east end, you can't fail to catch sight of the ornate silver **sarcophagus of St. John of Nepomuk**. According to legend, when Nepomuk's body was exhumed in 1721 to be reinterred, the tongue was found to be still intact and pumping with blood. This strange tale served a highly political purpose: The Catholic Church and the Hapsburgs were seeking a new folk hero to replace the Protestant forerunner Jan Hus, whom they despised. The 14th-century priest Nepomuk, killed during a power struggle with King Václav IV, was sainted and reburied a few years later with great ceremony in a 3,700-pound silver tomb, replete with angels and cherubim; the tongue was enshrined in its own reliquary.

The eight chapels around the back of the cathedral are the work of the original architect, Mathias d'Arras. A number of old tombstones, including some badly worn grave markers of medieval royalty, can be seen within, amid furnishings from later periods. Opposite the wooden relief, depicting the Protestants' looting of the cathedral in 1619, is the **Valdštejnská kaple** (Wallenstein Chapel). Since the 19th century the chapel has housed the Gothic tombstones of its two architects, d'Arras and Peter Parler, who died in 1352 and 1399, respectively. If you look up to the balcony, you can just make out the busts of these two men, designed by Parler's workshop. The other busts around the triforium depict royalty and other VIPs of the time.

The Hussite wars in the 15th century put an end to the first phase of the cathedral's construction. During the short era of illusory peace before the Thirty Years' War, the massive south tower was completed, but lack of money quashed any idea of finishing the building, and the cathedral was closed in by a wall built across from the Chapel of St. Wenceslas. Not until the 20th century was the western side of the cathedral, with its two towers, completed in the spirit of Parler's conception.

A key element of the cathedral's teeming, rich exterior decoration is the **Last Judgment mosaic** above the ceremonial entrance, called the Golden Portal, on the south side. The use of mosaic is quite rare in countries north of the Alps; this work, constructed from 1 million glass and stone tesserae, dates from the 1370s. The once-clouded glass now sparkles again, thanks to many years of restoration funded by the Getty Conservation Institute. The central field shows Christ in glory, adored by Charles IV and his consort, Elizabeth of Pomerania, as well as several saints; the risen dead and attendant angels are on the left; and on the right the flames of Hell lick around the figure of Satan. ⊠ *St. Vitus's Cathedral, Pražský Hrad* ☎ *257–531–622* ⊕ *www.hrad. cz* ⊡ *Free* ☉ *Apr.–Oct., daily 5–midnight; Jan.–Mar., Nov. and Dec., daily 6–11* PM.

Druhé nádvoří *(Second Courtyard)*. Except for the view of the spires of St. Vitus's Cathedral, the exterior courtyard offers little for the eye to feast on. Empress Maria Theresa's court architect, Nicolò Pacassi, received imperial approval to remake the castle in the 1760s, as it was badly damaged by Prussian shelling during the Seven Years' War in 1757. The Second Courtyard was the main victim of Pacassi's attempts at imparting classical grandeur to what had been a picturesque collection of Gothic and Renaissance styles. This courtyard also houses the rather gaudy **Kaple svatého Kříže** (Chapel of the Holy Cross), with decorations from the 18th and 19th centuries, which now serves as a souvenir and ticket stand.

Built in the late 16th and early 17th century, the Second Courtyard was originally part of a reconstruction program commissioned by Rudolf II. He amassed a large and famed collection of fine and decorative art, scientific instruments, philosophical and alchemical books, natural wonders, coins, and a hodgepodge of other treasures. The bulk of the collection was looted by the Swedes during the Thirty Years' War, removed to Vienna when the imperial capital returned there after Rudolf's death, or auctioned off during the 18th century. Artworks that survived the turmoil, for the most part acquired after Rudolf's time, are displayed in the **Obrazárna** (Picture Gallery) on the courtyard's left side as you face St. Vitus's. In rooms redecorated by the current official castle architect, Bořek Šípek, there are good Renaissance, mannerist, and baroque paintings that demonstrate the luxurious tastes of Rudolf's court. Across the passageway by the gallery entrance is the **Císařská konírna** (Imperial Stable), where temporary exhibitions are held. The passageway at the northern end of the courtyard forms the northern entrance to the castle, and leads out over a luxurious ravine known as the **Jelení příkop** (Stag Moat), which can be entered either here or at the lower end via the metal catwalk off Chotkova ulice, when it isn't closed for sporadic renovations. ⊠ *Obrazárna: 2nd Courtyard, Pražský Hrad* ☎ *224–373–208* ⊕ *www.hrad.cz* ⊠ *Courtyard free, Picture Gallery 150 Kč or 250 Kč–350 Kč as part of a 2-day ticket, free Mon. 4–6* ☉ *Picture Gallery daily Apr.–Oct. 9–6; Jan.–Mar., Nov. and Dec. 9–4.*

Královská zahrada *(Royal Garden)*. This peaceful swath of greenery affords lovely views of St. Vitus's Cathedral and the Castle's walls and bastions. Originally laid out in the 16th century, it endured devastation in war, neglect in times of peace, and many redesigns, reaching its present parklike form early in the 20th century. Luckily, its Renaissance treasures survived. One of these is the long, narrow **Míčovna** (Ball Game Hall), built by Bonifaz Wohlmut in 1568, its garden front completely covered by a dense tangle of allegorical *sgraffiti*.

The **Královský letohrádek** (Royal Summer Palace, also known as the Belvedere), at the garden's eastern end, deserves its unusual reputation as one of the most beautiful Renaissance structures north of the Alps. Italian architects began it; Wohlmut finished it off in the 1560s with a copper roof like an upturned boat's keel riding above the graceful arcades of the ground floor. During the 18th and 19th centuries military engineers tested artillery in the interior, which had already lost its rich furnishings to Swedish soldiers during their siege of the city in

1648. The Renaissance-style *giardinetto* (little garden) adjoining the summer palace centers on another masterwork, the Italian-designed, Czech-produced Singing Fountain, which resonates from the sound of falling water. ☒ *U Prašného mostu ulice and Mariánské hradby ulice near Chotkovy Park, Pražský Hrad* ☎ *224–373–238* ⊕ *www.hrad.cz* ⊙ *Apr. and Oct., daily 10–6; May and Sept., daily 10–7; June and July, daily 10–9; Aug., daily 10–8.*

★ **Královský palác** *(Royal Palace).* A jumble of styles and add-ons from different eras are gathered in this palace. The best way to grasp its size is from within the **Vladislavský sál** (Vladislav Hall), the largest secular Gothic interior space in Central Europe. Benedikt Ried completed the hall in 1493. (He was to late Bohemian Gothic what Peter Parler was to the earlier version.) The room imparts a sense of space and light, softened by the sensuous lines of the vaulted ceilings and brought to a dignified close by the simple oblong form of the early Renaissance windows. In its heyday, the hall held jousting tournaments, festive markets, banquets, and coronations. In more recent times, it has been used to inaugurate presidents, from the communist leader Klement Gottwald in 1948 to Václav Havel in 1989, 1993, and 1998, and Václav Klaus in 2003 and 2008.

From the front of the hall, turn right into the rooms of the **Česká kancelář** (Bohemian Chancellery). This wing was built by Benedikt Ried only 10 years after the hall was completed, but it shows a much stronger Renaissance influence. Pass through the portal into the last chamber of the chancellery. In 1618 this room was the site of the second defenestration of Prague, an event that marked the beginning of the Bohemian rebellion and, ultimately, the Thirty Years' War throughout Europe. The square window used in this protest is on the left as you enter the room.

At the back of Vladislav Hall a staircase leads up to a gallery of the **Kaple všech svatých** (All Saints' Chapel). Little remains of Peter Parler's original work, but the church contains some fine works of art. The large room to the left of the staircase is the **Stará sněmovna** (council chamber), where the Bohemian nobles met with the king in a prototype parliament of sorts. The descent from Vladislav Hall toward what remains of the **Romanský palác** (Romanesque Palace) is by way of a wide, shallow set of steps. This **Jezdecké schody** (Riders' Staircase) was the entranceway for knights who came for the jousting tournaments. ☒ *Royal Palace, Třetí nádvoří, Pražský Hrad* ☎ *224–373–208* ☒ *Requires 2-day castle ticket, 250 Kč–350 Kč* ⊙ *Apr.–Oct., daily 9–6; Jan.–Mar., Nov. and Dec., daily 9–4.*

QUICK BITES

Break for a coffee, pastry, or even lunch and enjoy one of the loveliest views of the city from the outdoor terrace of the **Lobkowicz Palace Café** (☒ *Lobkovický palác, Jirska 3, Pražský Hrad* ☎ *233–356–978* ⊕ *www. lobkowiczevents.cz*). The menu is a touch expensive, but full of delicious sandwiches, including ham and cheese, tuna, and smoked salmon, beverages, and desserts. It's an enchanting place to while away an hour.

Lobkovický palác *(Lobkowicz Palace).* Greatly benefiting from a recent renovation, this palace is a showcase for baroque and rococo styling.

Part of the Prague Castle complex, the Royal Palace has a splendid vaulted ceiling.

Exhibits trace the ancestry of the Lobkowicz family, who were great patrons of the arts in their heyday. (Beethoven was one of the artists who received their funding.) The audio tour adds a personal touch: it's narrated by William Lobwicz, the family scion who spearheaded the property's restitution and rehabilitation, and includes quite a few anecdotes about the family through the years. Although inside Prague Castle, this museum has a separate admission. ✉ *Jiřská 3, Pražský Hrad* ⊕ *www.lobkowiczevents.cz* ✉ *275 Kč* ☉ *Daily 10–6.*

★ **Zlatá ulička** *(Golden Lane).* A jumbled collection of tiny, ancient, brightly colored houses crouched under the fortification wall look remarkably like a set for *Snow White and the Seven Dwarfs.* Purportedly, these were the lodgings for an international group of alchemists whom Rudolf II brought to the court to produce gold. But the truth is a little less romantic: The houses were built during the 16th century for the castle guards. By the early 20th century Golden Lane had become the home of poor artists and writers. Franz Kafka, who lived at No. 22 in 1916 and 1917, described the house on first sight as "so small, so dirty, impossible to live in, and lacking everything necessary." But he soon came to love the place. As he wrote to his fiancée: "Life here is something special, to close out the world not just by shutting the door to a room or apartment but to the whole house, to step out into the snow of the silent lane." The lane now holds tiny stores selling books, music, and crafts, and has become so popular that an admission fee is charged. The houses are cute, but crowds can be uncomfortable, and the fact remains that you are paying money for the privilege of shopping in jammed little stores. Within the walls above Golden Lane, a timber-roof **corridor** (enter between No. 23 and No. 24) is lined with replica suits of armor and weapons (some of them for sale), mock torture chambers, and the like. A shooting range allows you to fire five bolts from a crossbow for 50 Kč. Note that at the time of this writing the Golden Lane was closed, with plans to reopen in May 2011. ⊠ *Pražský Hrad* ☎ *257–531–622* ⊕ *www.hrad.cz* 📧 *Included in combination 2-day castle ticket for 250 Kč–350 Kč* ☉ *Golden Lane and Corridor, Apr.–Oct., daily 9–6; Jan.– Mar., Nov. and Dec., daily 9–4.*

WORTH NOTING

Matyášova brána *(Matthias Gate).* Built in 1614, this stone gate once stood alone in front of the moats and bridges that surrounded the castle. Under the Hapsburgs, the gate survived by being grafted as a relief onto the palace building. As you go through it, notice the ceremonial white-marble entrance halls on either side that lead up to the Czech president's reception rooms (which are only rarely open to the public).

První nádvoří *(First Courtyard).* During a formal renovation the main entrance to Prague Castle from Hradčanské náměstí was stripped of some grand touches. But any first-time visitor will still be suitably impressed. Going through the wrought-iron gate, guarded at ground level by Czech soldiers and from above by the ferocious *Battling Titans* (a copy of Ignaz Platzer's original 18th-century work), you enter this courtyard, built on the site of old moats and gates that once separated the Castle from the surrounding buildings and thus protected the vulnerable western flank. The courtyard is one of the more recent additions to the Castle, designed by Maria Theresa's court architect, Nicolò Pacassi, in the 1760s. Today it forms part of the presidential office complex. Pacassi's reconstruction was intended to unify the eclectic collection of buildings that made up the Castle, but the effect of his work is somewhat flat. ■TIP➔ **Try to come by on the hour to witness the changing of the guards at noon; it features a flag ceremony in the First Courtyard, which is greeted with fanfare.**

Třetí nádvoří *(Third Courtyard).* The contrast between the cool, dark interior of St. Vitus's Cathedral and the brightly colored Pacassi façades of the Third Courtyard just outside is startling. Noted Slovenian architect Josip Plečnik created the courtyard's clean lines in the 1930s, but the modern look is a deception. Plečnik's paving was intended to cover an underground world of house foundations, streets, and walls dating from the 9th through 12th centuries and rediscovered when the cathedral was completed. (You can see a few archways through a grating in a wall of the cathedral.) Plečnik added a few features to catch the eye: a granite obelisk to commemorate the fallen of World War I, a black-marble pedestal for the Gothic statue of St. George (a copy of the National Gallery's original statue), an inconspicuous entrance to his Bull Staircase leading down to the south garden, and a peculiar golden ball topping the eagle fountain near the eastern end of the courtyard.

DID YOU KNOW?

It used to be believed that the Golden Lane housed alchemists, but in actuality they were homes for the castle guards and later artists like Franz Kafka, who lived at No. 22.

NOVÉ MĚSTO (NEW TOWN) AND VYŠEHRAD

To this day, Charles IV's building projects are tightly woven into the daily lives of Prague citizens. His most extensive scheme, Nové Město, or the New Town, is still such a lively, vibrant area you may hardly realize that its streets and squares were planned as far back as 1348. In other words, the area is about as "new" as the Charles Bridge.

As Prague outgrew its Old Town parameters, Charles IV extended the city's fortifications. A high wall surrounded the newly developed 2½-square-km (1½-square-mi) area south and east of the Old Town, tripling the walled territory on the Vltava's right bank. The wall extended south to link with the fortifications of the citadel called Vyšehrad. In the mid-19th century, construction boomed in Romantic and neo-Renaissance styles. Wenceslas Square and avenues such as Vodičkova, Na Poříčí, and Spálená saw a welter of development. One of the most important structures was the Národní divadlo (National Theater), meant to symbolize in stone the revival of the Czechs' history, language, and sense of national pride. This national feeling was compounded in 1918 with the creation of an independent Czechoslovak state, and with it a new era of modernist architecture, particularly on the outer fringes of the Old Town and in the New Town. One of modernism's most unexpected products was cubist architecture, a form unique to Prague, which produced four notable examples at the foot of ancient Vyšehrad.

Václavské náměstí is a long, gently sloping boulevard rather than an actual square. More than Old Town Square, it's the commercial heart of Prague today as much as it was a hundred years ago. At the end of November 1989, hundreds of thousands of Czechs gathered here to demand an end to the communist government. The image beamed to television sets around the world showed thousands of Czechs jangling their keys as a signal of protest—"Time to leave."

GETTING HERE AND AROUND

The best metro stops for this area are those at Karlovo náměstí, Muzeum, and Můstek, with all three lines, A, B and C, running close to it. The C line will get you closest to Vyšehrad (the High Castle).

TIMING

New Town is best done as a two-part affair: Start with Václavské náměstí and Karlovo náměstí, and then hit the castle Vyšehrad and its cubist houses as a separate trip, on a different day—or at least after a fortifying lunch. It's an arduous uphill walk from the houses to the

bluff. The castle grounds can easily absorb several hours. Vyšehrad is open every day, year-round, and the views are stunning on a day with clear skies.

TOP ATTRACTIONS

Cubist houses. Bordered to the north by Nové Město and to the south by Nusle, Vyšehrad is mostly visited for its citadel high above the river on a rocky outcropping. However, fans of 20th-century architecture—you know who you are—will find cubist gems between the area's riverfront street and the homes that dot the hills on the other side. Prague's cubist architecture followed a great Czech tradition: embracing new ideas, while adapting them to existing artistic and social contexts to create something sui generis. Between 1912 and 1914 Josef Chochol (1880–1956) designed several of the city's dozen or so cubist projects. His apartment house **Neklanova No. 30,** on the corner of Neklanova and Přemyslova, is a masterpiece in concrete. The pyramidal, kaleidoscopic window moldings and roof cornices make an expressive link to the baroque yet are wholly novel; the faceted corner balcony column, meanwhile, alludes to Gothic forerunners. On the same street, at **Neklanova No. 2,** is another apartment house attributed to Chochol. Like the building at Neklanova No. 30, it uses pyramidal shapes and a suggestion of Gothic columns. Nearby, Chochol's **villa,** on the embankment at Libušina 3, has an undulating effect, created by smoothly articulated forms. The wall and gate around the back of the house use triangular moldings and metal grating to create an effect of controlled energy. The **three-family house,** about 100 yards away from the villa at Rašínovo nábřeží 6–10, was completed slightly earlier, when Chochol's cubist style was still developing. Here the design is touched with baroque and neoclassical influence, with a mansard roof and end gables.

Karlovo náměstí (*Charles Square*). This square began life as a cattle market, a function chosen by Charles IV when he established the New Town in 1348. The horse market (now Wenceslas Square) quickly overtook it as a livestock-trading center, and an untidy collection of shacks

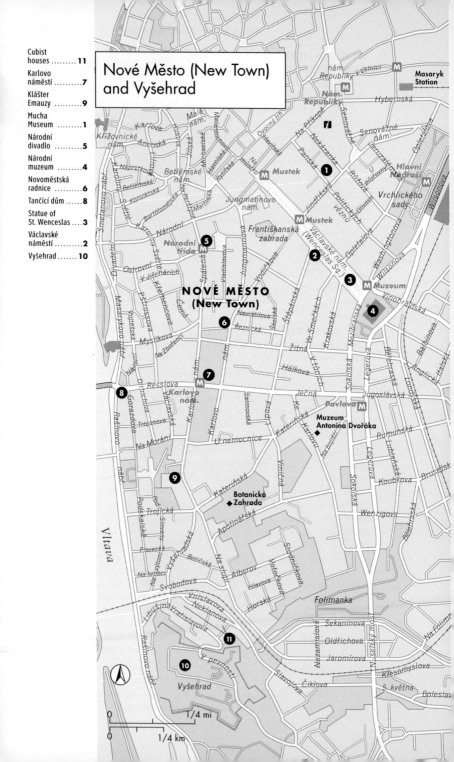

Nové Město (New Town) and Vyšehrad

accumulated here until the mid-1800s, when it became a green park named for its patron. The glassy, modern Ernst and Young building clashes with surrounding older architecture, but it's quite representative of Prague's past and present united in one spot. ⊠ *Bounded by Řeznická on the north, U Nemocnice on the south, Karlovo nám. on the west, and Vodičkova on the east, Nové Město.*

2

QUICK BITES

Parched from your circuit of the square? Walk up Ječná Street from Karlovo Náměstí to Lipová 15, where you'll find **Pivovarksy Dům** (☎ *296–216–666* ▭ *AE, DC, MC, V*). They brew their own beers on the premises, including limited-edition flavors with coffee and banana, and pair them with Czech culinary staples.

★ **Mucha Museum.** For decades it was almost impossible to find an Alfons Mucha original in his homeland, but in 1998 this private museum opened with nearly 100 works from this justly famous Czech artist's long career. Everything you expect to see from the man famed for his art nové (or art nouveau) style is here—the theater posters of actress Sarah Bernhardt, the eye-popping advertising posters, and the sinuous, intricate designs. Also exhibited are paintings, photographs taken in Mucha's studio (one shows Paul Gauguin playing the piano in his underwear), and even Czechoslovak banknotes designed by Mucha. ⊠ *Panská 7, 1 block off Wenceslas Sq., across from Palace Hotel, Nové Město* ☎ *224–216–415* ⊕ *www.mucha.cz* ▭ *180 Kč* ☯ *Daily 10–6.*

★ **Národní divadlo** *(National Theater).* Statues representing Drama and Opera rise above the riverfront side entrances to this theater, and two gigantic chariots flank figures of Apollo and the nine Muses above the main façade. The performance space lacks restraint as well—it's filled with gilding, voluptuous plaster figures, and plush upholstery. The idea for a Czech national theater began during the revolutionary decade of the 1840s. In a telling display of national pride, donations to fund the plan poured in from all over the country, from people of every socioeconomic stratum. The cornerstone was laid in 1868, and the "National Theater generation" who built the neo-Renaissance structure became the architectural and artistic establishment for decades to come. Its designer, Josef Zítek, was the leading neo-Renaissance architect in Bohemia. The nearly finished interior was gutted by a fire in 1881, and Zítek's onetime student Josef Schulz saw the reconstruction through to completion two years later. Today it's still the country's leading dramatic stage. ⊠ *Národní třída 2, Nové Město* ☎ *224–901–448 box office* ⊕ *www.narodni-divadlo.cz.*

Fodor'sChoice ★ **Tančící dům** *(Dancing House).* This whimsical building, one of Prague's most popular, came to life in 1996 as a team effort from architect Frank Gehry (of Guggenheim Bilbao fame) and his Croatian-Czech collaborator Vlado Milunic. A wasp-waisted glass-and-steel tower sways into the main columned structure as though they were a couple on the dance floor—the "Fred and Ginger" effect gave the building its nickname. It's notable for a Gehry piece as it's more grounded in the surrounding area than his larger projects. ⊠ *Rašínovo nábř. 80, Nové Město.*

The Dancing House earned the nickname "Fred and Ginger" for pairing a curving, feminine tower with a solid, straight one.

★ **Václavské náměstí** *(Wenceslas Square)*. Some 500,000 students and citizens gathered here in the heady days of November 1989 to protest the policies of the former communist regime. After a week of demonstrations, the government capitulated without a shot fired or the loss of a single life. After that the first democratic government in 40 years (under playwright-president Václav Havel) was swept into office. This peaceful transfer of power is referred to as the "Velvet Revolution" (the subsequent "Velvet Divorce" from Slovakia took effect in 1993). It's fitting that the 1989 revolution took place on Wenceslas Square: Throughout much of Czech history, the square has served as the focal point for popular discontent. The long "square" was first laid out by Charles IV in 1348, and began its existence as a horse market at the center of the New Town.

At No. 25, the **Hotel Europa** (✉ *Vaclavske nám. 25* ☎ *224–215–387* ⊕ *www.evropahotel.cz*) is an art nouveau gem, with elegant stained glass and mosaics in the café and an unfortunately named "Titanic" restaurant. Note in particular the ornate sculpture work of two figures supporting a glass egg on top of the building and the exterior mural. In 1906, when the hotel opened, this was a place for the elite; now the dilapidated rooms reflect more a sense of sadly faded grandeur that, thankfully, hasn't extended to the public spaces.

☾ **Vyšehrad**. Bedřich Smetana's symphonic poem *Vyšehrad* opens with four
★ bardic harp chords that echo the legends surrounding this ancient fortress. Today the flat-top bluff stands over the right bank of the Vltava as a green, tree-dotted expanse showing few signs that splendid medieval monuments once made it a landmark to rival Prague Castle.

The Vyšehrad, or the "High Castle," was constructed by Vratislav II (ruled 1061–92), a Přemyslid duke who became the first king of Bohemia. He made the fortified hilltop his capital. Under subsequent rulers it fell into disuse until the 14th century, when Charles IV transformed the site into an ensemble of palaces, the main church, battlements, and a massive gatehouse called *Špička*, whose scant remains are on V Pevnosti ulice. By the 17th century royalty had long since departed, and most of the structures they built were crumbling. Vyšehrad was turned into a fortress.

Vyšehrad's place in the modern Czech imagination is largely thanks to the National Revivalists of the 19th century, particularly writer Alois Jirásek. Jirásek mined medieval chronicles for legends and facts to glorify the early Czechs, and that era of Czech history is very much in the popular consciousness today.

Traces of the citadel's distant past can be found at every turn, and are reflected even in the structure chosen for the visitor center, the remains of a Gothic stone fortification wall known as **Špička**, or Peak Gate, at the corner of V Pevnosti and U Podolského Sanatoria. Farther ahead is the sculpture-covered **Leopold Gate**, which stands next to brick walls enlarged during the 1742 occupation by the French. Out of the gate, a heavily restored **Romanesque rotunda**, built by Vratislav II in the 11th century, stands on the corner of K Rotundě and Soběslavova. It's considered the oldest fully intact Romanesque building in the city. Down Soběslavova are the excavated foundations and a few embossed floor tiles from the late-10th-century **Basilika svatého Vavřince** (St. Lawrence Basilica, closed to the public). The foundations, discovered in 1884 while workers were creating a cesspool, are in a baroque structure at Soběslavova 14. The remains are from one of the few early medieval buildings to have survived in the area and are worth a look. On the western side of Vyšehrad, part of the fortifications stand next to the surprisingly confined foundation mounds of a medieval palace overlooking a ruined watchtower called **Libuše's Bath,** which precariously juts out of a rocky outcropping over the river. A nearby plot of grass hosts a statue of Libuše and her consort Přemysl, one of four large, sculpted images of couples from Czech legend by J. V. Myslbek (1848–1922), the sculptor of the St. Wenceslas monument.

The military history of the fortress and the city is covered in a small exhibit inside the Cihelná brána (Brick Gate), but the real attraction is the **casemates**, a long, dark passageway within the walls that ends at a dank hall used to store several original, pollution-scarred Charles Bridge sculptures. A guided tour into the casemates and the statue storage room starts at the military history exhibit; it has a separate admission fee.

Fodor's Choice
★ With its neo-Gothic spires, **Kapitulní kostel svatých Petra a Pavla** (*Chapter Church of Sts. Peter and Paul* ✉ K rotundě 10, Vyšehrad ☎ 224–911–353) dominates the plateau as it has since the 11th century. Next to the church lies the burial ground of the nation's revered cultural figures. Most of the buildings still standing are from the 19th century, but scattered among them are a few older structures and some

foundation stones of the medieval palaces. Surrounding the ruins are gargantuan, excellently preserved brick fortifications built from the 17th to the mid-19th century; their broad tops allow you to take in sweeping vistas along the riverbank. The church is open daily from 9 to noon and 1 to 5, with an admission charge of 30 Kč.

A concrete result of the national revival was the establishment of the **Hřbitov** (cemetery) in the 1860s, adjacent to the Church of Sts. Peter and Paul. It filled the fortress with the remains of luminaries from the arts and sciences. The grave of Smetana faces the Slavín, a mausoleum for more than 50 honored men and women, including Alfons Mucha, sculptor Jan Štursa, inventor František Křižík, and the opera diva Ema Destinnová. All are guarded by a winged genius who hovers above the inscription AČ ZEMŘELI, JEŠTĚ MLUVÍ ("Although they have died, they yet speak"). Antonín Dvořák (1841–1904) rests in the arcade along the north wall of the cemetery. Among the many writers buried here are Jan Neruda, Božena Němcová, Karel Čapek, and the Romantic poet Karel Hynek Mácha, whose grave was visited by students on their momentous November 17, 1989, protest march. ⊠ V Pevnosti 159/5b, Vyšehrad ☎ 241–410–348 ⊕ www.praha-vysehrad. cz ⊠ Grounds and cemetery free, casemates tour 50 Kč, military history exhibit (Fortress Vyšehrad) 20 Kč ☉ Grounds daily. Casemates and military history exhibit, Apr.–Oct., daily 9:30–6; Nov.–Mar., daily 9:30–5. Cemetery, daily 8–5 Ⓜ Line C: Vyšehrad.

> **TAKING YOU FOR A RIDE**
>
> Sadly, Prague has a reputation for dishonest taxi drivers. In an honest cab, the meter starts at about 300 Kč and increases by 25 Kč per km (½ mi) or 4 Kč per minute at rest. These days the best way to avoid getting ripped off is to ask your hotel or restaurant to call a cab for you. (AAA Taxi is the best-known and most trustworthy company.) But the chance of hailing an honest cab has improved. The city launched "Fair Place" taxi points throughout 121 locations (most of them tourist-central) in town. The signs at these locations include prices for popular destinations and prices in English, German, and Czech.

QUICK BITES

If you're worn out after the long uphill climb to the bluff, **Café Fresco** (⊠ Lumírova 1715/33) serves up Italian salads and panini, plus a revivifying set of espresso drinks. It's on the way to or from the Vyšehrad metro stop. And if your legs are really killing you, there's also a Thai massage studio next door.

WORTH NOTING

Klášter Emauzy (Emmaus Monastery). Another of Charles IV's gifts to the city, the Benedictine monastery sits south of Karlovo náměstí. It's often called Na Slovanech, literally "At the Slavs," which refers to its purpose when it was established in 1347. The emperor invited Croatian monks here to celebrate mass in Old Slavonic, and thus cultivate religion among the Slavs in a city largely controlled by Germans. A faded but substantially complete cycle of biblical scenes by Charles's

Next to the Church of Sts. Peter and Paul lies the burial ground for several of Prague's most famous citizens.

court artists lines the four cloister walls. The frescoes, and especially the abbey church, suffered heavy damage from a raid by Allied bombers on February 14, 1945; it's believed they may have mistaken Prague for Dresden, 121 km (75 mi) away. The church lost its spires, and the interior remained a blackened shell until a renovation was begun in 1998; the church reopened to the public in 2003. ⊠ *Vyšehradská 49, cloister entrance on left at rear of church, Vyšehrad* ⊕ *www.emauzy.cz* ⌷ *30 Kč* ☉ *Weekdays 11–5.*

Národní muzeum (*National Museum*). Built between 1885 and 1890, this grandiose edifice seems an incongruous venue for a rather tired collection of stones, bones, minerals, and coins by day. But bathed in nighttime lighting, the building comes into its own, displaying an imposing structure designed by Prague architect Josef Schulz. And many of the exhibits have gone "interactive," with helpful (though pricey) audio guides also available. ⊠ *Václavské nám. 68, Nové Město* ☎ *224–497–111* ⊕ *www.nm.cz* ⌷ *150 Kč; free 1st Thurs. of month, 2–6 PM* ☉ *Mon., Tues., and Thurs.–Sun. 10–6, Wed. 9–6, 1st Wed. of month, 10–8. Closed 1st Tues. of month.*

Novoměstská radnice (*New Town Hall*). At the northern edge of Karlovo náměstí, the New Town Hall has a late-Gothic tower similar to that of the Old Town Hall, plus three tall Renaissance gables that add a Dutch flair. The first defenestration in Prague occurred here on July 30, 1419, when a mob of townspeople, followers of the martyred religious reformer Jan Hus, hurled Catholic town councilors out the windows. Historical exhibitions and contemporary art shows are held regularly in the gallery, and you can climb the tower for a view of the New Town.

Prague's Plaques

The famous, the forgotten, and the victims.

Throughout the center of town a large number of plaques and even busts are attached to the sides of buildings marking the famous and sometimes not-so-famous people who lived or worked there. Composer Frederick Chopin can be found across from Obecní dům (the Municipal House) on the side of the Czech National Bank. Scientists like Albert Einstein—who was friends with author Franz Kafka, according to a marker on Old Town Square—also turn up. Some Czech figures like composer Bedřich Smetana or painter Josef Manés might be recognizable, while many plaques commemorate totally obscure teachers, civic organizers, or members of the 19th-century national awakening.

One set of plaques stands out from the rest—those marking the victims of the Prague Uprising that took place May 5–8, 1945. These mark where Prague citizens who tried to battle the German army at the end of World War II were killed. Many plaques depict a hand with two upraised fingers and the phrase "věrni zůstaneme," meaning "remain faithful." Foil-covered wreaths are still regularly hung underneath them. A marker like that can be seen at náměstí Franze Kafky, below and a few feet to the right of a bust of Kafka.

The area around Wenceslas Square has several, including one on the side of the main Post Office on Jindřišská Street. Two plaques can even be found on the back of the plinth of the Jan Hus statue on Old Town Square.

Some of the more touching ones have black-and-white photographs of the victims, such a marker for 23-year-old Viktorie Krupková, who was killed on Újezd near Říční Street, just across from Petřín.

The area around Czech Radio headquarters on Vinohradská Street in Vinohrady has many, as well as some plaques for victims of the 1968 Soviet invasion. Fighting for control of the radio station was fierce both times.

—Raymond Johnston

As in Old Town, this town hall is a popular venue for weddings. ✉ 23 *Karlovo nám., at Vodičkova, Nové Město* ⊕ *www.novomestskaradnice. cz* 🗼 *Tower and admission to exhibits on tower premises, 50 Kč; gallery shows have varying prices; not included in Tower admission fee* ☉ *Tower and gallery Tues.–Sun. 10–6.*

Statue of St. Wenceslas. Josef Václav Myslbek's huge equestrian representation of St. Wenceslas with other Czech patron saints around him has been a traditional meeting place for locals: in 1939 (when Czechs gathered to oppose Hitler's annexation of Bohemia and Moravia), in 1969 (when the student Jan Palach set himself on fire, protesting the Soviet Union's bloody invasion), and in 1989 (when many thousands successfully gathered here and all along the square to demand the end of the communist government). ✉ *Václavské nám., Nové Město.*

DID YOU KNOW?

The gorgeous architecture for the National Museum was created by Prague architect Josef Schulz. (And it's even more stunning at night.)

VINOHRADY AND ŽIŽKOV

From Riegrovy Park the eclectic apartment buildings and villas of the elegant residential neighborhood called Vinohrady extend eastward and southward. The pastel-tint formation of turn-of-the-20th-century houses—which not long ago were still crumbling after years of neglect—are now chockablock with upscale flats, slick offices, eternally packed restaurants, and all manner of shops.

Much of the development lies on or near Vinohradská, the main street, which extends from the top of Wenceslas Square to a belt of enormous cemeteries about 3 km (2 mi) eastward. Yet the flavor of daily life persists: smoky old pubs still ply their trade on the quiet side streets; the stately theater, Divadlo na Vinohradech, keeps putting on excellent shows as it has for decades; and on the squares and in the parks nearly everyone still practices Prague's favorite form of outdoor exercise—walking the dog.

For Prague residents, Žižkov is synonymous with pubs. There are more places to knock back a Pilsner Urquell or a shot of Fernet Stock per square inch here than anywhere else in the city, giving it a kind of seedy reputation that it doesn't deserve. Nowadays the district is starting to recoup. Some of the city's coolest cafés, clubs, and trendy apartments have opened up here. There are still some—in fact, lots of—crumbling, run-down areas, but it's also one of the most interesting districts in the city for its nightlight and dining.

GETTING HERE AND AROUND
Any subway line—A, B or C—will bring you here.

TIMING
Here, unlike central Prague, you won't need to worry about timing your visit to avoid bands of roving tourists. Happily, this area is mostly occupied by locals. But if you'd like to hit the Antonín Dvořák Museum

or the Church of the Most Sacred Heart, you'll still need to arrive in the afternoon at the latest.

TOP ATTRACTIONS

Kostel Nejsvětějšího Srdce Páně *(Church of the Most Sacred Heart).* If you've had your fill of Romanesque, Gothic, and baroque, this church will give you a look at a startling modernist art deco edifice. Designed in 1927 by Slovenian architect Josip Plečnik (the same architect commissioned to update Prague Castle), the church resembles a luxury ocean liner more than a place of worship. The effect was purposeful, as during the 1920s and 1930s the avant-garde imitated mammoth objects of modern technology. Plečnik used many modern elements on the inside. You may be able to find someone at the back entrance of the church who will let you walk up the long ramp into the fascinating glass clock tower. It's hard to miss the structure, which looms as you exit the metro. ⊠ *Nám. Jiřího z Poděbrad, Vinohrady* ☎ *Free (entrance only allowed 40 mins before and after mass)* ⊘ *Mass, Mon.–Sat., 8 AM and 6 PM; Sun., 9 AM, 11 AM, 6 PM* Ⓜ *Line A: Jiřího z Poděbrad.*

Muzeum Antonína Dvořáka *(Antonín Dvořák Museum).* The stately baroque red-and-yellow villa housing this museum displays the 19th-century Czech composer's scores, photographs, viola, piano, and other memorabilia. The statues in the garden date from about 1735; the house is from 1720. Check the schedule for classical performances, as recitals are often held in the first floor of the two-story villa. ⊠ *Ke Karlovu 20, Vinohrady* ☎ *224–918–013* 🎫 *50 Kč; free 1st Thurs. of month 2–closing* ⊘ *Apr.–Sept., Tues., Wed., Fri.–Sun. 10–1:30 and 2–5, Thurs. 11–3:30 and 4–7, 1st Thurs. of month 10–7; Oct.–Mar., Tues.–Sun. 10–1:30 and 2–5, 1st Thurs. of month 10–5* Ⓜ *Line C: I.P. Pavlova.*

National Memorial. On Vítkov Hill, one of the high points in the city, this stone building contains one outstanding feature: the largest equestrian statue in the world—a 16.5-ton metal sculpture of one-eyed Hussite leader Jan Žižka on horseback. In the past the 20th-century memorial was a final resting place for postwar presidents; now the eerily quiet mausoleum is a popular spot for movie shoots, especially since its late 2009 reopening. ⊠ *U Památníku, Žižkov* ☎ *222–781–676* ⊕ *www. nm.cz* 🎫 *110 Kč; free 1st Thurs. of month 2–6* ⊘ *Tues. and Thurs.–Sun. 10–6, Wed. 9–6* Ⓜ *Lines B and C: Florenc.*

WORTH NOTING

Nový židovský hřbitov *(New Jewish Cemetery).* Tens of thousands of Czechs were placed in Vinohrady's cemeteries. In this, the newest of the city's half-dozen Jewish burial grounds, you can find the modest **tombstone of Franz Kafka,** which seems grossly inadequate to Kafka's fame but oddly in proportion to his own modest sense of self. The cemetery is usually open, although guards sometimes inexplicably seal off the grounds. Men may be required to wear a yarmulke (you can buy one here if you need to). Turn right at the main cemetery gate and follow the wall for about 100 yards. Kafka's thin white tombstone lies at the front of section 21. City maps may label the cemetery *Židovské hřbitovy.* ⊠ *Vinohradská at Jana Želivského, Vinohrady* ☎ *226–235–*

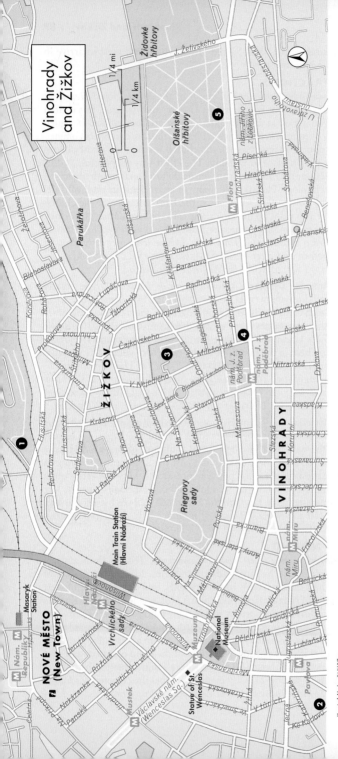

Vinohrady and Žižkov

Kostel Nejsvětějšího
Srdce Páně **4**

Muzeum Antonína
Dvořáka **2**

National Memorial **1**

Nový židovský
hřbitov **5**

Žižkov TV Tower **3**

CLOSE UP

Václav Havel

One of the great men to emerge from the anti-communist revolutions was the Czech playwright and dissident Václav Havel. The author of several anti-communist, absurdist plays and a series of moving essays on the moral corruption of communism, Havel captured the support of the students leading the Velvet Revolution and went on to head the country. He quickly assumed the leadership of the anti-communist opposition, and was a crucial force in negotiating the agreement that eventually led the communists to peacefully relinquish power after 40 years of authoritarian rule.

Havel's rapid ascent from a lowly dissident to the Czech chief executive—in a matter of weeks—proves the weight of his writings. In essays like "The Power of the Powerless" Havel spoke of the power of ordinary citizens to internally and peacefully resist the communist authorities. His voice, it's safe to say, became the country's conscience.

Before 1989 he was jailed several times for his writings, and when the 1989 events came around, he was one of the few public personalities who were not compromised by the previous regime.

Havel's time as president—from 1990 until 2003, with some breaks—was a mixed affair. But if there was a success, it was in his image abroad. It's no stretch to say that much of the adoration and attention the Czechs received after 1989 was because of their universally respected president.

---

248 ⊗ *Apr.–Sept., Sun.–Thurs. 9–5, Fri. 9–2; Oct.–Mar., Sun.–Thurs. 9–4, Fri. 9–2* Ⓜ *Line A: Želivského.*

Žižkov TV Tower. Looking like a rocket ready to blast off (or a "ptak," as the Czechs would say), the Žižkov TV Tower came under fire from area residents, who claimed it gave their children cancer soon after it began operating in 1990. The eighth-floor platform, reached by a high-speed elevator, gives a bird's-eye view of the numerous courtyards and apartment blocks that make up the city, but in truth it's almost too tall to provide a good view. Once back down on the ground, look up its 709-foot gray steel legs at the bronze statues of babies crawling on the structure, which were created by local provocateur artist David Černy. ⊠ *Mahlerovy sady, Žižkov* ⊕ *www.tower.cz* ✆ *120 Kč* ⊗ *Daily 10* AM*–11:30* PM Ⓜ *Line A: Jiřího z Poděbrad.*

LETNÁ, HOLEŠOVICE, AND TROJA

These are three inessential but delightful places to visit if your itinerary will allow. From above the Vltava's left bank, the large, grassy plateau called Letná gives you one of the classic views of the Old Town and the many bridges crossing the river. Beer gardens, tennis, and Frisbee attract people of all ages, while amateur soccer players emulate the professionals of Prague's top team, Sparta, which plays in the stadium just across the road.

The rapidly gentrifying neighborhood of Holešovice features many urban riches of its own, while north of Holešovice on the bank of the Vltava, the City Gallery Prague has a branch at Troja Château. Nearby are the Prague Botanical Gardens and the zoo.

GETTING HERE AND AROUND

The C line—or a taxi—will bring you to these environs fastest. On foot, get to Letná from the Old Town by walking north on Pařížská Street north. Then cross the Čechův Bridge and climb the stairs. From Letná, 10 minutes of strolling will bring you down into the rapidly gentrifying neighborhood of Holešovice. Just north along Dukelských hrdinů Street is Stromovka—a royal hunting preserve turned gracious park.

TOP ATTRACTIONS

Botanická zahrada *(Botanical Gardens).* The garden's newest addition is Fata Morgana, a snaking 429-foot greenhouse that simulates three different environments and has been drawing large crowds ever since it opened to visitors in summer 2004. Its path first takes you through a semi-desert environment, then through a tunnel beneath a tropical lake and into a rain forest; you end up cooling off in a room devoted to plants found in tropical mountains. Sliding doors and computer-controlled climate systems help keep it all together. ⊠ *Nadvorni 134, Troja* ☎ *234–148–111* ⊕ *www.botgarden.cz* ✉ *120 Kč, Fata Morgana*

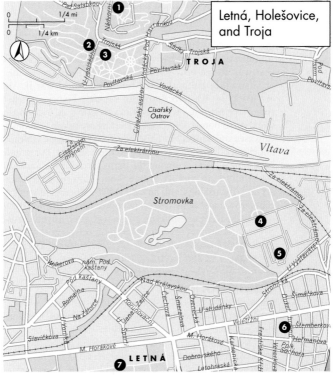

Letná, Holešovice, and Troja

and Open Air Exhibitions; 50 Kč, Open Air Exhibitions only ☉ Open-Air Expositions, Nov.–Feb., daily 9–4; Mar., daily 9–5; Apr. and Oct., daily 9–6; May–Sept., daily 9–7. Fata Morgana, same hours but closed Mon. Ⓜ *Line C: Nádraží Holešovice, then Bus 112.*

Křižikova fontána *(Kříž Fountain).* This pressurized-water and colored-light show was originally built for the Jubilee Industrial Exhibition of 1891. Occasionally, live music accompanies the spectacle of lights, but more often recorded programs of film music, classics, or rock play over the illuminated dancing waters. František Křížík, who built the fountain, was a famous inventor of his day and a friend of Thomas Edison. ⊠ *Výstaviště, exhibition grounds, Holešovice* ☎ *723–665–694* ⊕ *www.krizikovafontana.cz* ⊠ *200 Kč* Ⓜ *Line C: Nádraží Holešovice.*

Letenské sady *(Letná Park).* Come to this large, shady park for an unforgettable view of Prague's bridges. From the enormous concrete pedestal at the center of the park, the largest statue of Stalin in Eastern Europe once beckoned to citizens on the Old Town Square far below. The statue was ripped down in 1962, just seven years after it was completed. On sunny Sundays expatriates often meet up here to play ultimate Frisbee. Head east on Milady Horáové Street after exiting the metro. ⊠ *Letná* Ⓜ *Line A: Hradčanská.*

★ **Veletržní palác** *(Trade Fair Palace)* The National Gallery's **Sbírka moderního a soucasného umění** (Collection of Modern and Contemporary

Art) has been renamed, in English, "Collection of 19th, 20th, and 21st Century Art," but it remains the keystone of the city's visual-arts scene that it has been since its opening in 1995. Touring the vast spaces of this 1920s constructivist exposition hall filled to the brim with quirky, stimulating, comprehensive modern and contemporary local art is the best way to see how Czechs surfed the forefront of the avant-garde wave until the cultural freeze following World War II. Also on display are works by Western European—mostly French—artists from Delacroix to the present—with paintings by Gauguin, Picasso, and Braque an unexpected bonus. Especially haunting are Jakub Schikanaeder's moody canvases and Arnost Hofbauer's hushed pilgrimage tableau (which eerily anticipates Christina's World by Andrew Wyeth). But painting is only the beginning—also occupying the many levels of the museum are collage, cubist sculpture, vintage gramophones, futuristic architectural models, art deco furnishings, and an exhaustive gathering of work from this new century, some of which is just as engrossing as the older stuff. A portrait of Ronald Reagan emblazoned on a toaster, anyone? Also, watch the papers and posters for information on traveling shows and temporary exhibits. ⊠ *Dukelských hrdinů 47, Holešovice* ☎ *224–301–111* ⊕ *www. ngprague.cz* 🖃 *200 Kč 10–4; 100 Kč 4–6; free 3–8 1st Wed. of month* ☉ *Tues.–Sun. 10–6, Thurs. 10–9* Ⓜ *Line C: Vltavská.*

WORTH NOTING

Lapidárium. A fascinating display of 11th- to 19th-century sculptures rescued from torn-down buildings (or the vicissitudes of Prague's weather) is sheltered here. Original Charles Bridge statues can be found here, along with a towering bronze monument to Field Marshall Radetsky, a leader of the 19th-century Austrian army. Pieces of a marble fountain that once stood in Old Town Square now occupy most of one room. For horse lovers, there are several fine equestrian statues inside. ⊠ *Výstaviště 422, Holešovice* ☎ *233–375–636* ⊕ *www.nm.cz* 🖃 *50 Kč; free 1st Thurs. of month, 2–6* ☉ *Tues., Thurs., Fri., noon–6, Wed. 10–4* Ⓜ *Line C: Vltavská.*

Trojský zámek *(Troja Château).* Built in the late 17th century for the Czech nobleman Count Šternberg, this sprawling summer residence, modeled on a classical Italian villa, had the first French-style gardens in Bohemia. Inside, rich frescoes that took more than 20 years to complete depict the stories of emperors. Outside, a sweeping staircase is adorned with statues of the sons of Mother Earth. The City Gallery Prague manages this chateau and provides information. ⊠ *U trojského zámku 1, Troja* ☎ *283–851–614* ⊕ *www.citygalleryprague.cz* 🖃 *120 Kč* ☉ *Tues.–Sun. 10–6, except Fri. 1–7* Ⓜ *Line C: Nádraží Holešovice, then Bus 112.*

Zoologická zahrada v Praze *(Prague Zoo).* Flora, fauna, and fresh air are the main things you can find in Prague's zoo. Hit hard by the floods in 2002—134 animals perished—the zoo has been cleaned up and offers a break from the bustle of the city. Covering 160 acres on a slope overlooking the Vltava River, the zoo has thousands of animals representing 500 species. Take the chairlift for an outstanding view of the area. ⊠ *U trojského zámku 3, Troja* ☎ *296–112–111* ⊕ *www.zoopraha.cz* 🖃 *150 Kč* ☉ *Nov.–Feb., daily 9–4; Mar., daily 9–5; Apr., May, Sept., and Oct., daily 9–6; June–Aug., daily 9–7* Ⓜ *Line C: Nádraží Holešovice, then Bus 112.*

Where to Eat

WORD OF MOUTH

"I would try a restaurant in Mala Strana (Lesser Town)—it is the area under the Prague Castle. It is less noisy compared to Old Town and Wenceslas Square. The surroundings are beautiful and there are nice restaurants, particularly if you are not on very tight budget."

—city_mountain_beach

By Alexander Basek

Foodies and vegetarians, rejoice! Prague is no longer a culinary backwater, with endless pork knuckles and bread dumplings. Now it's a bustling culinary hub of Central Europe. The city boasts award-winning restaurants, blossoming celebrity chefs, and an annual food festival.

A legion of venues are transforming heavy Czech food into delicate dishes, and even quality Asian fare can be found where once there was little beyond microwaved spring rolls. Prague's chefs and diners alike are both salivating at what lies ahead for them.

The development of Prague as a whole has much to do with its culinary upgrades. Once upon a time in the 1990s, Prague's best restaurants were full of Americans and Russians on vacation. Thanks to an uptick in local entrepreneurship and a resurgence of interest in cooking, Czechs are filling these exclusive dining rooms in increasing numbers. As locals, they clamored for fresher, more vibrant fare, and Prague's chefs have responded in force. No longer does haute cuisine here equate with heavy doses of foie or game—though there's no shortage of them. These days seafood, Eastern flavors, and seasonal ingredients are coming to the fore at long last.

Alas, what still needs an upgrade is the service. English is widely spoken, but tourist traps in the center are perfectly content to be brusque, or worse, to try to tack phony cover charges onto the bill. For the most part, these places are near the Castle or in Old Town; if a man is needling you to come in, keep walking.

Classic Czech fare is best sampled in a *hospoda*, or pub. These local joints have menus that usually include dishes for which Czech cuisine is justly (in)famous: pork and sauerkraut with bread dumplings, roast duck, beef stew, and, for the vegetarian, fried cheese. In recent years Czech brewers like Staropramen and Budvar have opened branded pubs (Potrefená Husa and Budvarka, respectively). These restaurants are to the Czech pub what a Swiss timepiece is to a plastic watch—light-years ahead in terms of the quality of ingredients and service. If you're looking to dip a toe into the waters of Czech cuisine, these pubs are an excellent place to begin.

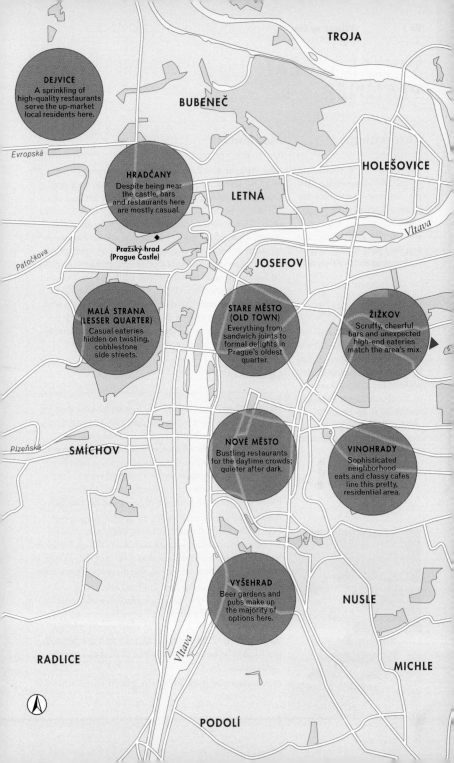

DEJVICE
A sprinkling of high-quality restaurants serve the up-market local residents here.

TROJA

BUBENEČ

HOLEŠOVICE

Evropská

HRADČANY
Despite being near the castle, bars and restaurants here are mostly casual.

LETNÁ

Vltava

Patočkova

◆
**Pražský hrad
(Prague Castle)**

JOSEFOV

**MALÁ STRANA
(LESSER QUARTER)**
Casual eateries hidden on twisting, cobblestone side streets.

**STARE MĚSTO
(OLD TOWN)**
Everything from sandwich joints to formal delights in Prague's oldest quarter.

ŽIŽKOV
Scruffy, cheerful bars and unexpected high-end eateries match the area's mix.

Plzeňská

SMÍCHOV

NOVÉ MĚSTO
Bustling restaurants for the daytime crowds; quieter after dark.

VINOHRADY
Sophisticated neighborhood eats and classy cafes line this pretty, residential area.

VYŠEHRAD
Beer gardens and pubs make up the majority of options here.

NUSLE

RADLICE

Vltava

MICHLE

PODOLÍ

WHERE TO EAT PLANNER

Reservations

The need for a reservation varies with the season and the weather—warm summer weather presents the biggest challenge. If you have your heart set on a particular spot and it's a busy time of day, it's best to drop in or call ahead.

Smoking

Restaurants and pubs can decide whether to allow smoking; smaller ones tend to ban it, larger ones have dedicated sections or just allow it outside. In traditional Czech establishments such as hospody and *pivnice* (beer halls), you may be overwhelmed by the amount of cigarette smoke.

Mealtimes

Most restaurants in Prague are open from about 11 AM to 11 PM. This closing time is very regular with traditional Czech restaurants and *hospody* (pubs); their kitchens usually shut down by 10 PM, and sometimes earlier if it's a slow night. A small number of restaurants serve the late-night crowd, especially in the city center, but don't put off dinner too long, or you may have trouble finding an open kitchen. Some restaurants in neighborhoods outside the center close on Sunday or open only for dinner, but in the heavily touristed areas hours remain the same every day. Mealtimes hold to the European standard. Lunch runs from noon until 2 PM; dinner starts at 6 PM and runs until about 8 or 9 PM. Czechs don't generally linger over meals, but you'll rarely feel any pressure from the staff to vacate your table.

Wine

Sure, the Czech Republic is more famous for beer than for wine, but wines are coming into their own now, especially the whites, which are suited to this relatively northern climate. You can almost always order wines by the glass, though more expensive vintages are usually available by the bottle only. So-called *archiví* (vintage) wines, despite being expensive, are not necessarily better. Moravian wines, such as those from Valtice, are often the best bets.

The most popular Czech whites are Müller-Thurgau and Ryzlink (Riesling); of these, domestic Rieslings tend to be the better choice. Czech sauvignon blanc, though harder to find, can be of exceptional quality. After that, four or five varietals can appear on menus, and these are hit and miss.

Two of the most popular reds are frankovka and svatovavřinecké. If you're in an inexpensive restaurant, you may find that the frankovkas are inferior, so try to avoid them. After these, cabernet sauvignon is popular, but regardless of the variety, the Czech reds are generally much lighter in body than the wines of Australia, France, or California.

Most restaurants, aside from pubs, offer a selection of international wines.

Paying

In a more traditional dining venue, such as a Czech *restaurace* or hospoda, it's possible that the person you ordered from will not be the person who tallies your bill. In that case, you may hear your waiter say *kolega,* meaning a colleague will bring the bill. This situation is less likely in more modern establishments. In the bulk of low- and mid-price restaurants the waiter or bill person will tally your bill in front of you and stand by while you pull together the money to pay. If you want to do it the Czech way, quickly add on a suitable amount for a tip in your head, and say this new total when you hand over your money. If you need a bit of time, it's best to politely smile and say *moment, prosím* (one moment, please). Don't panic if you miss the moment; many people don't make the calculation quickly enough and just leave the money on the table. In the places frequented by tourists, particularly in the city center, the waiter (or a colleague) may expect this already and just leave the bill on the table for you.

Tipping in the Czech Republic has been based traditionally on rounding up the tab to a convenient number rather than calculating a percentage and adding it on, and in the hospody around the city (especially out of the tourist area) this is still how it's done. For example, paying 150 Kč on a bill of 137 Kč would be perfectly acceptable (though locals might stop at 140 Kč). At the better places, a 10% tip is common to recognize good food and service.

PRICES

In better restaurants, prices are slightly lower but generally comparable to what you would find in North America or Western Europe. In traditional Czech restaurants and hospody, especially outside the city center, price levels are much lower, and can drop to a rock-bottom 90 Kč on the denní lístek (daily menu).

Watch for a couvert (cover charge), which may appear in smaller print on a menu. Though a bit annoying, it's legitimate and is meant to cover bread, a caddy of condiments, and/or service. Remember that side orders usually have to be ordered separately, and will be tabulated accordingly. Taxes are included with all meal prices listed in the menu.

Menus

Most restaurants post menus outside. Prix-fixe menus are not popular in the evening, but many restaurants offer a *denní lístek* (daily menu) of three or four items that usually include a soup starter and a simple main course. If you want to try a traditional Czech meal, such as *svíčková* (beef in cream sauce) or *guláš* (a bit thicker and less oily than the Hungarian version), you may find that it's offered only at lunchtime in most restaurants outside of central Prague.

Using the Map

Throughout the chapter, you'll see mapping symbols and coordinates (⊕ *D2)* after property names or reviews. To locate the property on a map, turn to the Where to Eat map. The letter and number following the ⊕ symbol are the restaurant's coordinates on the map grid.

WHAT IT COSTS IN CZECH KORUNA

	¢	$	$$	$$$	$$$$
Restaurants	under 100 Kč	100 Kč–150 Kč	150 Kč–300 Kč	300 Kč–500 Kč	over 500 Kč

Prices are per person for a main course at dinner and include 19% V.A.T.

STARÉ MĚSTO

Staré Město hosts a microcosm of Czech dining, from basement pubs to four-star eats and everything in between. With the right game plan, diners can find anything that tickles their fancy.

There is no shortage of restaurants in Prague's historic center; on the contrary, there are more places and types of cuisine to try here than anywhere else in the city. It's an embarrassment of riches, as long as you know where to look. Many restaurants, especially those on *Pařížská*, Prague's version of Fifth Avenue, go the expensive, international cuisine route that was so popular in the 1990s (and is slightly out of step with today's scene). In recent years several new restaurants have opened just outside the square toward *Náměstí Republiky*; you'll be able to find everything from Asian to vegetarian in these winding streets.

As for the tourist traps, they're easy to spot: if there is someone hustling for patrons outside the restaurant and displaying overexposed pictures of some meat and potatoes posted outside, you'll do well to eat elsewhere.

DINING AROUND OLD TOWN SQUARE

Knowing what areas to avoid in this neighborhood is quite simple. Rule number one: Don't eat on Old Town Square proper, as the restaurants are almost uniformly tourist traps. Moreover, far superior options are close at hand; walk past the Týn church to find restaurants like Apostila and Maitrea. If you're looking for a fancier meal, it's also worth exploring the area around Dlouhá to the northeast of the square, which boasts fine dining, wine bars, and high-end Czech eateries in a fairly compact space.

HUNTING FOR DUMPLINGS

Czech food gets a bad rap. Sure, when it's bad, it's very, very bad. But these days many traditional restaurants are offering classic Czech cuisine done right.

Throughout the city, restaurants from the Kolkovna group uphold the standards for traditional Czech cuisine in a sleek environment with good service. One favorite is the intimate Olympia location (⊠ *Vítězná 7* ☎ *251-511-080*).

Many Czech brewers have created restaurant "concepts" in recent years, and they're great for trying Czech food in a casual, friendly locale. Any of the Potrefena Husa restaurants are a fine choice; the one on Platnéřská (⊠ *Platnéřská 9* ☎ *224-813-892*) is one of the best.

Finally, the most recent—and best—entrant into the Czech food game is Lokal (⊠ *Dlouhá 33* ☎ *222-316-265*). The dishes here, all variations on the meals Czechs know and love, use high-quality ingredients and are second to none.

GOOD FOOD ON THE GO

There are plenty of bakeries and sandwich shops that offer nibbles to take away when goulash fatigue sets in.

Among the best is Bakeshop Praha (⊠ *Kozi 1* ☎ *222-315-874*), which sells everything from avocado BLTs to entire pies. Though it gets crowded during peak lunch hours, there is indoor seating if you want to stay in.

Even closer to Old Town Square is Au Gourmand (⊠ *Dlouhá 10* ☎ *222-329-060*), which has a certain Gallic flair. It too has a few seats and a in the back of the space where you can enjoy a salade niçoise or a tomato and mozzarella sandwich.

Finally, Paneria (⊠ *Kaprova 3* ☎ *224-827-912*) and Culinaria (⊠ *Skořepka 9* ☎ *224-231-017*) offers reliable sandwich and salad options, respectively.

AND TO DRINK . . .

3

Pivovarsky Klub
(⊠ *Křižíkova 17* ☎ *222-315-777*)
Here's a pub with the beer aficionado in mind. Typically, a local pub only offers three or so different beers on draft, from a single producer. Here there are six beers on tap, all of which are from artisanal beermakers like Regent. The drafts constantly rotate, so it's a situation of beer today, gone tomorrow, replaced by a new keg once the old one is finished. The Klub also offers traditional Czech eats, including pork knee and goulash, both of which are employed to absorb the massive amounts of beers the Klub's clientele imbibes.

WORD OF MOUTH

"We happily dove into our first real hot lunches of pork, kraut, and dumplings . . . This was our initiation into Czech organization, with the little slips of paper tallying our beers and food and our waiter calculating the bill longhand. (I'd like to see the teens at the local brass 'n fern try this!)"
—AHaugeto

MALÁ STRANA

Malá Strana has come into its own as dining scene of late. Gone are the expat hangouts, for the most part, replaced by more ambitious eateries and friendly Czech pubs.

Overall, restaurants in Malá Strana tend to be less formal than in Old Town, though there are pockets of high-end dining near Charles Bridge and the embassies. For the most part, establishments here serve tourists and locals alike, which makes for some more consistent dining.

Because it does get a bit quiet on this side of the river after dark, many of the hotels in Malá Strana have excellent restaurants, from the rooftop at the Aria to combination Asian and Czech menu at the Mandarin to the classic continental fare of the Augustine's Monastery restaurant.

If you want to eat near the Charles Bridge, hang a left or right—there are plenty of good options on either side, just avoid the spots directly uphill.

CAFÉS

Cafés in Malá Strana tend to be less grand than their counterparts in Old Town, which are sustained by tourist traffic and locals working in the area. So instead of fin-de-siècle decoration and hustling waiters in vests, you'll find workday venues with wooden chairs and cushy couches on which to relax, have a pastry, and regroup. It's not that one is more authentic than the other, since the Czechs have lived with their grand cafés for a century or more, but rather they serve different purposes. Either way, you'll likely get some quality coffee (from an Italian source, most likely) and a comfortable chair in which to relax.

HAUTE CZECH

Czech cuisine isn't limited to the more rustic dishes you'll find at pubs; it can also go upscale and experimental.

The "top" spot—literally—for haute Czech is Céleste (✉ *Rašínovo nábř. 80* ☎ *221–984–160*), on the roof of Dancing House. A substantial portion of the menu is devoted to Czech dishes. If you want to try a suckling pig with black pudding while gazing at Prague Castle, this is your spot.

Diners who want to go all out with haute Czech fare should head to La Degustation (✉ *Haštalská 18* ☎ *222–311–234*), which serves a seven-course tasting menu of reinterpreted Czech standards.

For traditional Czech cuisine with an upscale twist, try Perpetuum (✉ *Na hutích 9* ☎ *233–323–429*). By focusing on duck, an ingredient Czech chefs revere, Perpetuum uses the fowl as the base for nearly all of the menu.

Don't be limited to restaurants that focus on Czech food, either; many high-end "continental" restaurants will feature a local dish, too. Among the best is the duck liver with wild mushrooms at the Monastery (✉ *Letenská 18* ☎ *266–112–233*); it's one of the city's richest courses.

SCENIC SPOTS

Prague's best views belong to Céleste, on top of Frank Gehry's Dancing House (✉ *Rašínovo nábř. 80* ☎ *221–984–160*). If you're visiting in the summer months, sit on the terrace. Across the river, the Aria hotel's Coda Restaurant (✉ *Tržiště 9* ☎ *225–334–111*) boasts a superb view of the Castle; it feels so close, you could click a wine glass against its walls. And, if the Charles Bridge is your ideal vista, try the terrace at Hergetova Cihelna (✉ *Cihelná 2b* ☎ *296–826–103*). They keep blankets and heat lamps for when the nights get nippy.

AND TO DRINK . . .

U Bílého Lva
(✉ *Na Bělidle 30*
☎ *257–310–356*)
This unassuming pub in Smíchov, just down the street from the Novy Smíchov shopping center, is a fine example of a friendly Czech pub. With wooden tables and chairs, a projection screen showing whatever is the sports match du jour, and an owner who oversees the operation from a perch behind the bar, U Bílého Lva hits just the right notes. It's nothing fancy—unless you order the excellent duck breast with cheesy potatoes—but what it does, it does well. It's well worth the trip.

WORD OF MOUTH

"My fondest memory is of the very first bar we found on arrival. [My husband was] desperate to have a Czech beer. On the recommendation of our cab driver, we went into a typical Czech bar . . . As we drank we took in the décor—Václav Havel's portrait in one corner, Dubček in the middle, and a nice bust of Stalin in the window. We never could find that bar again!" —annhig

BEST BETS FOR PRAGUE DINING

With thousands of restaurants to choose from, how will you decide where to eat? Fodor's writers and editors have selected their favorite restaurants by price, cuisine, and experience. Fodor's Choice properties represent the "best of the best" in every price category. You can also search by neighborhood for excellent eats. Or find specific details about a restaurant in the full reviews, listed alphabetically later in the chapter.

RESTAURANT REVIEWS

Listed alphabetically within neighborhoods.

STARÉ MĚSTO

$$$$ ✗**Allegro**. Compared to other celebrity chefs, Andrea Accordi keeps
ITALIAN out of the spotlight, yet he's the most celebrated and well-known chef
Fodor's Choice in the city. And his reputation is well deserved; Accordi's cooking at
★ the Four Seasons is some of the best—the most thoughtful and delicate—of any in Prague. Even fish, the bane of many a Czech restaurant
kitchen, arrives here as sea bass with lemon, sea snails, and calamari
salad—all intricate flavors. It pairs nicely with the Four Seasons own
vibe, that of unquestioning luxury. Servers move seamlessly, the courses
are expertly timed, and the sommelier eagerly suggests his recommendations. Despite the high prices and reverent treatment of the ingredients, the light, airy dining room is quite welcoming. And in a nod to
the economy, concessions have been made: there's a kids' menu, and
Accordi has also rolled out a lower-priced set of dishes, more rustically
prepared, that were inspired by a recent visit from his grandmother.
⊠ *Four Seasons Prague, Veleslavinova 21, Staré Město* ☏ *221–427–000*
⊕ *www.fourseasons.com* ⌲ *Reservations essential* ▭ *AE, DC, MC, V*
Ⓜ *Line A: Staroměstská* ✛ *A2.*

$$$ ✗**Apostila**. Most Italian restaurants in Prague go the classic route, which
ITALIAN makes the food at Apostilla high concept in comparison. And that's
exciting for diners who are are looking for a fresh take; here you'll find
asparagus soup with both green and white asparagus placed side by
side in the same bowl like a springtime yin and yang. Another strength
is seafood: Try the scallops atop a beet puree and shrimp with cherry
tomatoes among them. All this culinary verve—and the prime location
behind the Týn cathedral—comes at a price; so come during lunch,
when specials keep the prices down to some extent. ⊠ *Týnská ulička
2, Staré Město* ☏ *224–828–888* ⊕ *www.apostila-prague.cz* ▭ *AE, V*
Ⓜ *Line B: Náměstí Republiky* ✛ *D2.*

$ ✗**Beas**. Right behind the soaring spires of Old Town's Týn cathedral,
VEGETARIAN this simple eatery serves classic North Indian fare on shiny metal trays
at a main counter. Don't expect upscale service: you're going to bus
your own table, but these dishes are worth the extra work. Flavors of
great curries, *dhals* (stewed lentils), grilled flatbreads, fragrant basmati
rice, rich grilled eggplant, and other vegetarian delights make you forget
that nothing you're eating contains eggs, meat, or fish. Though meal
prices are already exceptionally low, plenty of that local rarity, free tap
water, makes it even easier on the wallet. ⊠ *Týnská 19, Staré Město*
☏ *608–035–727* ⊕ *www.beas-dhaba.cz* ▭ *No credit cards* Ⓜ *Line B:
Nám. Republiky* ✛ *D2.*

$ ✗**Bohemia Bagel**. A lifeline to American breakfast when it opened in
DELICATESSEN the '90s, today Bohemia Bagel remains popular with visitors and expats
today looking for a taste of home. Offerings include the classic BLT, lox
with cream cheese and capers, as well as eggs, pancakes, and a surpris-
ingly good hamburger. ⊠ *Masná 2, Staré Město* ☏ *224–812–560* ⊕ *www.
bohemiabagel.cz* ▭ *No credit cards* Ⓜ *Line A: Staroměstská* ✛ *D1.*

$$$–$$$$
MEDITERRANEAN
Fodor's Choice
★

✗ **Céleste.** Prague's most scenic meal, Céleste occupies the top floor of Frank Gehry's iconic Dancing House along the Vltava River. Run by the team behind the late, great Angel restaurant, the food and service at Céleste live up to the quality of the Castle views, the best in the city. The room is decorated conservatively, but with modern flourishes, including an eye-popping chandelier. The food operates on much the same principle: A pork terrine or an asparagus soup will appear basic, but it'll be brought to life by a dash of drama (in the case of the soup, white nettles and foie gras). The kitchen handles seafood as well as meat, and the monkfish served with artichokes is exquisite. Of course, diners pay a premium for the view, and the wine list, though extensive, suffers from extreme mark-up. Still, for a special occasion, it's an ideal meal. ☒ *Rašínovo nábřeží 80, Staré Město* ☎ *221–984–160* ⊕ *www. celesterestaurant.cz* ⚖ *Reservations essential* ▭ *AE, MC, V* ⊙ *Closed Sun.* Ⓜ *Line B: Karlovo Nám* ✛ *A6.*

$$$
ITALIAN

✗ **Divinis.** The austere decor—white fabric chairs, untreated wood tables and floors—at this wine-centric Italian restaurant on a quiet street near the Týn cathedral belies the quality and complexity of its food. Whether you sample a platter with warm lardo and salumi atop crostini, or try something more complex like a marinated octopus salad that's spicily piquant, the dishes are skillfully prepared and attractively presented. Beef cheeks braised with Marsala and spinach or pork belly and lentils make excellent entrées, but if you're not up for a huge meal, opt for the more ethereal pastas, which incorporate seasonal ingredients and high-end fillips like foie gras and duck. The all-Italian wine list is one of the city's best. ☒ *Týnská 21, Staré Město* ☎ *222–325–440* ⊕ *www. divinis.cz* ⚖ *Reservations essential* ▭ *AE, V* ⊙ *Closed Sun.* Ⓜ *Line A: Staroměstská* ✛ *D1.*

¢
CAFÉ

✗ **Káva Káva Káva.** Still one of the city's best purveyors of Arabica beans, this American-style café serves a mean cuppa joe. You can also surf the Net for a few more crowns downstairs or for free on your own laptop via Wi-Fi. ☒ *Národní 37, Staré Město* ☎ *224–228–862* ⊕ *www.kava-coffee.cz* ▭ *No credit cards* Ⓜ *Line A: Můstek* ✛ *B5.*

$$
CAFÉ

✗ **Kavárna Obecní dům.** This is multitasking made easy: you can relax with a beverage while also drinking in the opulent art nouveau surroundings in this famous building's magnificent café. ☒ *Nám. Republiky 5, Staré Město* ☎ *222–002–763* ▭ *AE, DC, MC, V* Ⓜ *Line B: Náměstí Republiky* ✛ *F2.*

$–$$
EASTERN
EUROPEAN
Fodor's Choice
★

✗ **Kavárna Slavia.** Easily the city's best-known café, Slavia serves good coffee, drinks, and light snacks, as well as the greatest hits of Czech cuisine: roast duck with potato dumplings and sauerkraut, beef goulash, and roast smoked pork with white cabbage and potato pancakes. Sandwiches and quotidian pasta plates offer lighter, less-expensive options, though aesthetes can make a full meal out of the rich views of the National Theater, the Vltava, and Prague Castle. This spectacular location has a historic air that winds from the days of Viktor Oliva's painting *The Absinthe Drinker* (which hangs in the main room), through the era of the playwright and regular patron Václav Havel, and continues into the modern day. ☒ *Smetanovo nábř. 1012/2, Staré Město* ☎ *224–218–493* ⊕ *www.cafeslavia.cz* ▭ *AE, MC, V* Ⓜ *Line B: Národní Třida* ✛ *A5.*

In mild weather Allegro offers terrace dining.

$$–$$$
ITALIAN

✕ **Kogo.** Long a favorite of American expats, this Italian mainstay in the Slovanský Dům shopping mall is of a far higher quality than the immediate surroundings suggest. The cavernous interior is frenzied with businessmen at lunch, who negotiate while wolfing down the well-done Italian standards. Fresh pastas (fettuccine with bacon and mushrooms, tagliatelle with a dollop of lamb ragout) are so firm they taste as if they've been in the water for only seconds. The seafood case near the host's stand is a tip that fresh fish is another specialty here, including a salt-roasted dorado and skewers of shrimp and cuttlefish. Kogo's outdoor seating—yes, it's a mall restaurant with a courtyard—is covered and open year-round. ⊠ *Na Příkopě 22, Staré Město* ☎ *221–451–259* ⊕ *www.kogo.cz* ▭ *AE, V* Ⓜ *Line B: Náměstí Republiky* ✥ *E3.*

$$
EASTERN EUROPEAN

✕ **Kolkovna.** For Czechs, this chainlet remains one of the most popular spots to take visitors for a taste of local cuisine without the stress of tourist rip-offs. And it's a solid choice. The wood-and-copper decor gives off an appropriate air of a brewery taproom, and you can wash down traditional meals—such as *svíčková* (beef tenderloin in cream sauce), roast duck, and fried pork cutlets, or upgrades of traditional food, such as turkey steak with Roquefort sauce and walnuts—with a mug of unpasteurized Pilsner Urquell. ⊠ *V Kolkovně, Staré Město* ☎ *224–818–701* ⊕ *www.kolkovna.cz* ▭ *AE, MC, V* Ⓜ *Line A: Staroměstská* ✥ *C1.*

$$$
ITALIAN
Fodor's Choice
★

✕ **La Finestra.** Prague's hottest table, La Finestra is the meaty counterpart to its sister restaurant Aromi, right down to the wooden tables and brick walls. Catering to local gourmands and boldface names, this restaurant lives up to the hype. As at Aromi, waiters display an array of freshly caught fish that comprise the day's specials, but here they also do the same with meat, including dry-aged cuts flown in from

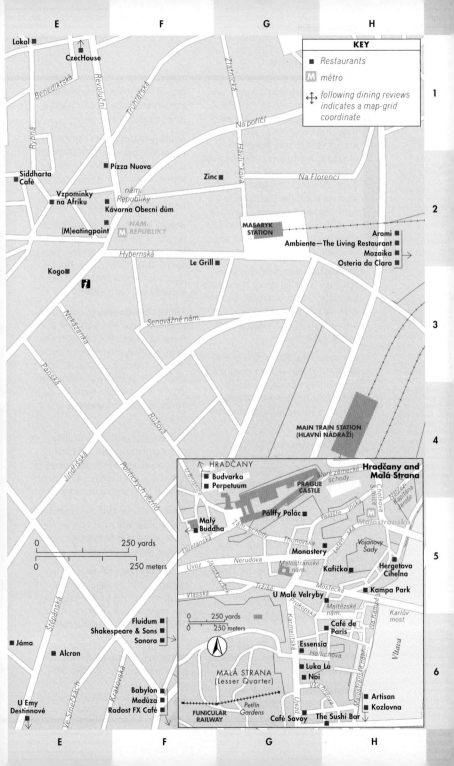

CLOSE UP

On the Menu

Traditional Czech food is hearty, with big portions of meat and something starchy on the side, such as dumplings or potatoes. Herbs and spices are not used heavily, though dill, marjoram, and caraway make frequent appearances, and garlic is a mainstay. Aside from these, the flavor comes from the meat. The Czechs know what they're doing when it comes to smoking meat—the natural way—and smoked *uzený* (pork) makes its way into many meals.

Bramborák (*bram*-bohr-ahk). Available from fast-food stands throughout the city as well as in restaurants, this large (6- to 8-inch) potato pancake is flavored with marjoram and deep-fried.

Bezmasá jídla. This section of the menu lists dishes without meat. Listings often include *čočka* (stewed lentils), *smažený sýr* (fried cheese), and *rizoto se zeleninou* (risotto with vegetables).

Česnečka (*ches*-netch-kah). A Czech standby, this garlic soup is a thin—usually meatless—garlic-laced broth containing small pieces of potato, served with fried bread cubes.

Cibulačka (*tsi*-boo-latch-kah). A close relative of česnečka—though a little less potent—this onion soup is typically served with bread, and cheese is sprinkled on top. Unlike the French version, it's not made from meat broth, so it's usually quite light.

Čočky (*choch*-kee). In this traditional dish green lentils are stewed with or without smoked meat. An egg and pickle are usually served with the meatless version.

Ďábelské toasty (*dya*-bel-skeh). Devil's toasts are a mixture of cooked ground beef, tomatoes, onions, and peppers served on fried or toasted white bread.

Guláš (*goo*-laush). Less oily than its Hungarian counterpart, Czech goulash is cubes of beef or pork stewed and served in thin gravy. It's often served with *houskové knedlíky* (bread dumplings) and chopped onions on top.

Hotová jídla (*ho*-to-vah *yee*'dla). This section of the menu contains dishes that are premade and ready to be served. Listed here you can find the most traditional favorites *svíčková* (stewed beef) and goulash.

Jídla na objednávku (*yee*'dla na *ob*-yeh'd-nahv-koo). This section of the menu lists dishes that are cooked to order, including a selection of chicken and pork cutlets, as well as beefsteak, prepared in various ways. Often, they differ in their use of ingredients, such as onions, garlic, mushrooms, or cheese.

Klobása (kloh-*bah*-sa). A mainstay of the *občerstveni* (fast-food stand), this smoked sausage is also served in restaurants as an addition to certain types of guláš and soups or by itself.

Kulajda (koo-*lie*-dah). This traditional creamy soup with fresh or dried forest mushrooms is flavored with wine vinegar, caraway, and dill.

Moučníky (*moe*-ooch-*nik*kee). The dessert section on any traditional Czech menu is not terribly long, but you might see *palačinky* (sweet pancakes), *zmrzlina* (ice cream), *compot* (fruit compote), or *dort* (cake).

Nakládaný Hermelín (*nah*-kla-den-ee). A favorite snack of cafés and pubs that consists of a small round of *hermelín* (a soft cheese closely resembling Camembert) pickled in oil, onions, and herbs and served with dark rye bread.

Palačinky (pala-*ching*-kee). Typically served with jam or ice cream inside and whipped cream on top, these pancakes resemble crepes, but are made with a thicker batter.

Přílohy (*pr'zhee*-lo-hee). In traditional Czech restaurants side orders aren't included with main courses, so look for them in this menu section. Regular dishes include *hranolky* (french fries), *Americké brambory* (literally, American potatoes; actually, fried potato wedges), and *ryže* (rice).

Smažený sýr (*sma*-zhe-nee *see*'r). A postwar addition to the traditional Czech diet, this staple is literally translated as "fried cheese." A thick slab of an Edamlike cheese is breaded and deep fried, ideally giving it a crusty shell and a warm gooey interior. It's commonly served with tartar sauce—for liberally spreading on top—and fries.

Studené předkrmy (*stoo*-den-eh *pr'zhed*-krmy). The section of cold appetizers on a Czech menu is typically a short one, and usually includes *utopenec* (pickled pork sandwich), *tlačenka* (head cheese), and *šunkova rolka* (ham roll with horseradish cream).

Svíčková (*svitch*-koh-vah). Though technically this means a tenderloin cut of beef, on menus it's actually a dish consisting of two to four slabs of stewed beef, usually rump roast; in better restaurants you can get real tenderloin covered with a creamy sauce of pureed root vegetables, garnished with a dollop of whipping cream, cranberry sauce, and a slice of lemon. It's served with *houskové knedlíky* (bread dumplings).

Teplé předkrmy (*teh*-pleh *pr'*zhed-kr-mee). Warm appetizers on a Czech menu ordinarily include *topinka* (toasted or fried dark bread, rubbed with garlic cloves) and *ďabělské toasty* (devil's toasts).

Utopenec (*oo*-toe-pen-etts). Literally translated as "drowned man," utopenec is uncooked pork sausage that has been pickled in vinegar. It's not only a common appetizer in Czech restaurants, but a ubiquitous beer-snack staple in Czech pubs.

Vepřo-knedlo-zelo (*veh*-pr'zho-kne'dlo-zhe-lo). An affectionately shortened name for the three foods that appear on one plate, this popular family dish consists of roast pork, dumplings, and cabbage stewed with a bit of caraway.

Zelňačka (zell-*n'yatch*-kah). Cabbage is the main ingredient in this hearty soup whose flavor is accentuated by caraway and smoked pork or sausage. It can be a filling meal by itself when served in a small round loaf of bread.

The modern vibe at Céleste matches the architecture of its home, the Dancing House.

Italy. Complimenting this array of protein are fried chickpeas and fresh foccacia to nibble on and expertly crafted, al dente pastas like oxtail agnolotti and spaghetti with sea urchin. Obviously the steaks, which often feed at least two if not three, are a hot-ticket item—don't miss the veal or aged rib eye, if it's available. ⊠ *Platnéřská 13, Staré Město* ☎ *222–325–325* ⊕ *www.lafinestra.cz* ⌂ *Reservations essential* ▤ *AE, MC, V* Ⓜ *Line A: Staroměstská* ✛ *B2.*

$$$–$$$$ ✕ **La Veranda.** Aphrodisiac menus and seasonal specials are but two of
ECLECTIC the reasons to consider this elegant dining room and lounge near the Jewish Quarter. A third is Radek David, a culinary juggernaut with an eye for unusual flavor combinations, sending out dishes like baked quail with pea pods, octopus carpaccio, duck foie gras with pickled rhubarb, and mozzarella baked with eggplant and confited cherry tomatoes. Despite the achievements and the acclaim, La Veranda remains somewhat overlooked, making a visit to this stylish, softly lighted room feel like you've been let in on a wonderful secret. ⊠ *Elišky Krásnohorské 2, Staré Město* ☎ *224–814–733* ⊕ *www.laveranda.cz* ▤ *AE, DC, MC, V* Ⓜ *Line A: Staroměstská* ✛ *C1.*

$$$ ✕ **Le Grill.** The expressive decor at Le Grill, Kempinski Hybernská's
CONTINENTAL hotel restaurant, is as wild as the service is formal. It makes for a fun combination, as guests are treated with efficient, Austro-Hungarian imperiousness under purple glass chandeliers while seated in chairs that resemble chess pawns. Contrast that with the more traditional European menu here, which rotates with seasonal ingredients. The downside is that you might get three courses of asparagus in the springtime. But otherwise dishes are made with finesse, like a silky venison tartare topped with a quail egg, or tender rack of lamb atop a ratatouille. Skip

the more classic Czech dishes, which come out a bit too heavy, but be sure to sample something from the expansive local wine list. ⊠ *Hybernská 12, Staré Město* ☎ *226–226–111* ⊕ *www.kempinski.com* ▭ *AE, MC, V* Ⓜ *Line B: Náměstí Republiky* ✛ *G2.*

$$$$ ✕ **Le Terroir.** The finest wines available to humanity can be found here,
FRENCH along with cuisine of the extremely rich variety: beef neck with honey and crème fraiche, scallops atop green-pea puree, red mullet with peppers, and grilled duck with marinated pears. Don't forget the cheese course, as this restaurant has its own cheese room stocking rarities from France and Italy. But wine provides the real lure; bottles here start around $20 and head into the upper stratosphere, with the list separated into minute geographic distinctions. (The listing for "Bordeaux" has nine subcategories.) The clublike cellar is romantic and chic, but open-air dining on the patio is a must in spring and summer. ⊠ *Vejvodova 1, Staré Město* ☎ *222–220–260* ⊕ *www.leterroir.cz* ▭ *AE, MC, V* Ⓜ *Line A or B: Můstek* ✛ *C4.*

$–$$ ✕ **Lokal.** Who would have guessed that the most exciting new restaurant
CZECH of the past year wouldn't even have an English menu on hand? That's
Fodor's Choice precisely the case at Lokal, which takes the Czech pub concept to the
★ next level with fresh, local ingredients, all manner of interesting beers, and friendly, efficient service. (Your waiter will happily translate that menu for you). It makes for an idealized version of a corner restaurant out of another era, right down to the stark white walls, waiters in vests, and bathrooms wallpapered with old pinups and airplane posters. Many of the dishes have a modern twist: schnitzel is made from pork neck and served atop buttery whipped potatoes, while the Czech classic of svíčková is tangy and fresh, not often the case at most pubs. If you're skeptical about Czech food, Lokal is just the place to change your mind. ⊠ *Dlouhá 33, Staré Město* ☎ *222–316–265* ⊕ *www.ambi.cz* ✍ *Reservations essential* ▭ *No credit cards* Ⓜ *Line B: Náměstí Republiky* ✛ *E1.*

$–$$ ✕ **Maitrea.** From the owners of the ever-popular—but ever-crowded and
VEGETARIAN tiny—Leka Hlava comes this larger vegetarian restaurant. If you're tired of meat and potatoes, Maitrea is a good bet. In fact, it's a good bet even if you're not tired of Czech cuisine, as they make a vegetarian version of classics like svíčková and goulash. The interior design is a bit space age, with swoopy fabric light fixtures reminiscent of giant white mushrooms. Actually, they're reminiscent of the mushrooms in a lot of the dishes, including a few pastas like a rich three-mushroom fettuccine medley. It isn't fancy, but for a dose of culinary chlorophyll it's one of the best options in the city. ⊠ *Týnská ulička 6, Staré Město* ☎ *221–711–631* ⊕ *www.restaurace-maitrea.cz* ▭ *AE, MC, V* Ⓜ *Line A: Staroměstská* ✛ *D1.*

$$–$$$ ✕ **(M)eatingpoint.** Ignore the silly, Jersey Shore–type name and you'll
ECLECTIC find a restaurant that's a cut above your typical hotel dining experience. Inside the King's Court hotel and looking out on Náměstí Republiky, (M)eatingpoint caters to international tastes. (The menu, which is written in English and Russian, should be a hint.) The decor suffers from too much flashiness: purple velvet chairs, disco chandelier, and a busy patterned carpet feel distracting. Nonetheless, the food hits the right notes, from crisp, tender calamari with a spicy tomato coulis to

tuna and salmon tartare appetizers (not as common in Prague as in the States). The pastas here are also excellent, including a fresh tagliatelle with mushrooms and bacon. And if you want to stick to the Czech standards, there are some clever spins on these as well, like a duck with white cabbage. ⊠ *U Obecního domu 3, Staré Město* 🖀 *224–222– 888* ⊕ *www.hotelkingscourt.cz* ▭ *AE, DC, MC, V* Ⓜ *Line B: Náměstí Republiky* ✛ *F2.*

$$–$$$ ✕ **Pepe Nero Pizzeria.** Whether Pepe Nero serves some of the best pizza
ITALIAN in Prague is the source of constant debate among locals, but one thing is for sure: they have the city's best mozzarella. Tangy and creamy, the cheese is as authentic as can be. It tops the panoply of pizzas here, including pepperoni, mushroom, and red-pepper pies. For the carb-phobic, the mozzarella also appears in the caprese and Vesuviana salads, both large enough for two, and several of the pasta dishes. The modern, angular, white interior bustles with Italians bantering with the staff during crucial Serie A soccer matches. ⊠ *Bílkova 4, Staré Město* 🖀 *222–315–543* ▭ *AE, DC, MC, V* Ⓜ *Line A: Staroměstská* ✛ *C1.*

$$ ✕ **Pizza Nuova.** Turning out pies in the true Neapolitan style, Pizza
ITALIAN Nuova serves chewy pizzas that tend to get a bit soggy in the cen-ter—100% authentic, if not the easiest to eat. The huge bi-level space, decked out in light and dark wood, also boasts a small outdoor eat-ing area on Náměstí Republiky. During the day it fills with business-men taking lunches and families with tots; at night the ambience turns downright swanky. All the pies come with authentic ingredients: San Marzano tomatoes, buffalo mozzarella, Grana Padano cheese. Skip the pastas and salads, which are secondary to what comes out of the wood-fired ovens. ⊠ *Revoluční 1, Staré Město* 🖀 *221–803–308* ⊕ *www.ambi. cz* ▭ *AE, MC, V* Ⓜ *Line B: Náměstí Republiky* ✛ *F2.*

$$ ✕ **Siddharta Café.** The decor offers a hint of how this casual restaurant
ASIAN in the Buddha Bar Hotel operates, combining Eastern and Western influences. The bright red and yellow gilded ceiling and chinoiserie throughout should tip you off that this isn't exactly authentic Asian fare. But the trick is to ignore the dishes' names and just enjoy the food, because the food is well made, just not what you'd expect. "Tuna sushi" actually involves warm cooked tuna drizzled with balsamic vin-egar; lovely, but definitely not sushi. Another tasty option is to get your beef with peppers and udon noodles or with a béarnaise sauce, a wel-come chance to try a little bit of everything. ⊠ *Jakubská 8, Staré Město* 🖀 *221–776–404* ⊕ *www.buddha-bar-hotel.cz* ▭ *AE, MC, V* Ⓜ *Line B: Náměstí Republiky* ✛ *E2.*

$$–$$$ ✕ **U Závoje.** This gastronomic beachhead contains a wine bar and wine
CONTINENTAL store, a day café, a cheese shop, a brandy retailer, and this exclusive cellar restaurant—which raids all the best supplies upstairs. Fine wines from around the world are given a place of pride in the restaurant, sup-ported by elaborate cuisine: grilled foie gras with sour-cherry coulis, venison ragout, or roasted chicken with favas and risotto. Be sure to save room—the pear tartar and wine-battered French toast represent a sweet pinnacle for desserts in Central Europe. ⊠ *Havelská 25, Staré Město* 🖀 *226–006–111* ⊕ *www.uzavoje.cz* ▭ *MC, V* Ⓜ *Line A or B: Můstek* ✛ *D3.*

CAFE CULTURE

Prague has a rapidly evolving café culture, and finding a good cup of coffee here is now as easy as in any large city in Europe. Coffee standards took a beating under communism, but a clutch of new Italian- and American-inspired cafés have opened up. These are meshing with the older, traditional coffeehouses from the 19th and 20th centuries, and today's cafés run the gamut from the historic to the literary to the trendy. Most cafés are licensed to sell alcohol, and are open until at least 11 PM, some transforming into virtual bars by night. In all the following you can sit down with a small snack and a hit of java. As a general rule, the old-fashioned-looking cafés serve traditional Czech snacks, such as marinated cheese, whereas those with splashy new façades carry a selection of more Western-style desserts, such as carrot cake and tiramisu.

¢ ✕ **Vzpomínky na Afriku**. This tiny shop behind the Kotva department
CAFÉ store sells the widest selection of premium coffees in town, served here or to go along with pastries and sandwiches. ✉ *Templová 7, Staré Město* ☎ *603–544–492* ▭ *No credit cards* Ⓜ *Line B: Náměstí Republiky* ✛ *E2.*

$$–$$$ ✕ **Yami**. Yami makes up for a lack of finesse with quantity. Take, for
JAPANESE example, the fusion roll: a mound of maki sushi filled with unusual ingredients like roast beef, cucumber, and sweet omelets. Traditional sushi recipes are good, as are the savory Korean dishes, making this casual eatery in Old Town's bar zone a favorite for those on their way out for the night. Draft Budvar and decent wines are on hand to get you started. ✉ *Masná 3, Staré Město* ☎ *222–312–756* ⊕ *www.iyami. cz* ▭ *AE, MC, V* Ⓜ *Line A: Staromětská* ✛ *D1.*

$$$$ ✕ **Zinc**. The story behind Zinc is a case of culinary musical chairs. Celeb-
CONTINENTAL chef Gordon Ramsay shuttered his restaurant, maze, in the local Hilton. Soon afterward, the hotel brought in Ari Munandar, who was cooking at the Mandarin Oriental across the river, to run the restaurant here. The result? A successful mix of European and Asian flavors that's bringing in the crowds (including President Obama during his most recent visit). Sink back into the dark banquettes under an open skylight and sample plates like miso-glazed sea bass and tuna-salmon sashimi with quince ponzu. There are plenty of straight-up classics too, like rack of lamb and chicken with foie-gras foam. It's not as ambitious as Ramsay was, but it's more consistent, and for a Hilton, that's the sweet spot. ✉ *V Celnici 7, Staré Město* ☎ *221–822–300* ⊕ *www.hiltonpragueoldtown. com* ▭ *AE, DC, MC, V* Ⓜ *Line B: Náměstí Republiky* ✛ *G2.*

JOSEFOV

$$$$ ✕ **Barock**. As a break from sightseeing, the location can't be beat:
ASIAN Barock's sidewalk tables overlook the Old-New Synagogue. Most of the buzz here is for the appearance: walls bathed in matte scarlet, deep-dish orange chairs, and recessed mood lighting make a chic statement suited to the stylish address on boutique-heavy Pařížská. Barock's clientele

is more fanny pack than jet set these days, but both camps seem to like the open-passport approach in the kitchen: crunchy Vietnamese spring rolls, spicy Thai soups and curries, fresh Mediterranean seafood, continental salads, and hearty Czech classics like roast duck all meet on the same menu. ⊠ *Pařížská 24, Josefov* ☎ *222–329–221* ⊕ *www. barockrestaurant.cz* ▤ *AE, DC, MC, V* Ⓜ *Line A: Staroměstská* ✛ *C1.*

$$$ ✕**Pravda.** Pravda offers a menu that bounces from country to coun-
ECLECTIC try like a backpacking student—and the menu lists the provenance of each dish. Grilled prawns with sambal, New Zealand lamb with Peruvian potatoes, Argentinean beef, traditional Czech duck, and bouillabaisse St. Tropez are just a few of the intercontinental specialties on the menu. It's no longer the hot spot it once was, but unlike scene-y Barock across the street, they've never lost their focus on the food, and that helps to lure in an engaging mix of tourists, businessmen, and, from time to time, models. ⊠ *Pařížská 17, Josefov* ☎ *222–326–203* ⊕ *www. pravdarestaurant.cz* ▤ *AE, DC, MC, V* Ⓜ *Line A: Staroměstská* ✛ *C1.*

MALÁ STRANA

$$ ✕**Café de Paris.** The twin stars of the show at this Swiss import are beef
FRENCH entrecote and French fries. Café de Paris even makes its own "secret sauce" (think béarnaise with a hint of mustard). If meat and frites are your fancy, waiters subsequently arrive bearing trays of them to serve to each diner's tableside. The look is classic French bistro, down to the old photographs and red banquettes lining the walls, which makes sense considering its location near the French Embassy. There are a few other things on the limited menu, like Caesar salad and a rotating option of soups, but there's little reason to stray from the specialties of the house. ⊠ *Maltézské nám. 4, Malá Strana* ☎ *603–160–718* ⊕ *www.cafedeparis. cz* ⌂ *Reservations essential* ▤ *AE, V* Ⓜ *Line A: Malostranská* ✛ *H6.*

$$$–$$$$ ✕**Essensia.** The refined look of Essensia, with arched whitewashed ceil-
ECLECTIC ings and gray high-backed chairs, is practically a given considering it's inside the Mandarin Oriental hotel. But it's food that has been more of a question mark, thanks to a new chef in the kitchen (Jiří Stift recently took the reins from Ari Munandar after he went to Hilton). Stift has altered the focus of the restaurant, moving it back toward European fare. Now the menu is truly split, with locally sourced Czech dishes on one half and authentic pan-Asian fare on the other both sharing the spotlight. For the most part, this works, though Stift's strength is clearly continental fare; dishes like pork cheeks sous vide with watercress risotto just have more heft than simpler items like king crab leg spring rolls. However, even with the changes, Essensia serves some of the best Asian dishes in the city. ⊠ *Nebovidska 1, Malá Strana* ☎ *233–088–888* ⊕ *www.mandarinoriental.com* ▤ *AE, DC, MC, V* Ⓜ *Line A: Malostranská* ✛ *G6.*

$$$ ✕**Hergetova Cihelna.** Between the attractive staff and sleek, minimal-
ECLECTIC ist interior, there's no shortage of glamour at Hergetova Cihelna. The most gorgeous thing, however, is the view of Charles Bridge from the expansive terrace. It makes Cihelna ideal for a leisurely lunch or a late-night cocktail—blankets are draped on the back of each chair if it gets chilly. The food runs the gamut from one of the city's better hamburgers

to flaky duck spring rolls, "sashimi pizza," and even black risotto. It's reliable fare; not exquisite, but then again, it's tough to compete with the vista. Surprisingly, Cihelna also serves one of the better margaritas in Prague. ⊠ *Cihelná 2b, Malá Strana* ☎ *296–826–103* ⊕ *www.kampagroup.com* ⊟ *AE, MC, V* Ⓜ *Line A: Malostranská* ✛ *H5.*

¢ ✗ **Kafíčko.** The "Little Coffee" grinds freshly roasted beans from Brazil, CAFÉ Kenya, Colombia, and other renowned growing regions. Superlative strudel and small snacks in a peaceful setting make this a pleasant stop for refueling near Charles Bridge. ⊠ *Míšeňská 10, Malá Strana* ☎ *724–151–795* ⊟ *No credit cards* Ⓜ *Line A: Malostranská* ✛ *H5.*

$$$–$$$$ ✗ **Kampa Park.** The zenith of riverside dining is offered at this legendary CONTINENTAL restaurant just off Charles Bridge, known almost as much for its chic decor and celebrity guests as it is for elegant continental cuisine and great wines—it's the kind of place where European royals and heads of state mingle with their head-of-studio counterparts from Hollywood. But the real star power arrives on the plate, courtesy of Kampa's executive chef Marek Raditsch, whose sophisticated cooking blends seasonal ingredients with worldly culinary technique: halibut with black truffles and crispy bacon, seared turbot with pumpkin puree, venison with veal tongue in cardamom sauce. Incredible foods and incredible views. ⊠ *Na Kampě 8/b, Malá Strana* ☎ *257–532–685* ⊕ *www.kampagroup.com* ⊟ *AE, DC, MC, V* Ⓜ *Line A: Malostranská* ✛ *H5.*

$$ ✗ **Luka Lu.** The decor is almost comically ominous—what's with the MEDITERRANEAN musical instruments and juxtaposed pictures of wolves and babies on the walls?—but the ambience is friendly at this pan-Balkan restaurant on a busy stretch of the Malá Strana. Their authentic kitchen cooks delicately spiced mincemeat sausages called *čevapčiči*, roasted lamb, and a "gourmet" *pljeskavice*, essentially an open-faced hamburger topped with bacon and cheese. Taking cues from Croatian cuisine, the menu branches out to more Mediterranean fare, including caprese salad, salmon carpaccio, and an excellent selection of no-nonsense grilled fish. The outdoor seating in summer is ideal for people-watching, and offers relief from the suspicious styling inside. ⊠ *Újezd 33, Malá Strana* ☎ *257–212–388* ⊕ *lukalu.cz* ⊟ *MC, V* Ⓜ *Line A: Malostranská* ✛ *G6.*

$$$ ✗ **Monastery.** The Augustine hotel's high-end restaurant, the Monastery CONTINENTAL can be as hushed as its namesake on some evenings, which is a shame— it deserves to be full. The 100-seat space is done up in neutral tones with whimsical light fixtures, cozy booths, and an expanse of outdoor seating in the hotel's courtyard. The kitchen turns out a mix of flawlessly executed continental dishes like fried duck livers on toast with mushrooms and a veal chop with spring vegetables. Pair that with an excellent wine list that includes some well-priced bottles of Moravian wine and courteous service, and the only drawback is that you might end up taking an inadvertent vow of poverty after paying your check. ⊠ *Letenska 12, Malá Strana* ☎ *266–112–233* ⊕ *www.theaugustine.com* ⊟ *AE, MC, V* Ⓜ *Line A: Malostranská* ✛ *H5.*

$$ ✗ **Noi.** A lounge-y spot on a well-trafficked stretch of Újezd, Noi delivers THAI on the promise of its Zen interior—it shares a building, and a sensibility, Fodor's Choice with a modern furniture store next door—by cooking excellent Thai ★ classics. The lithe staff is quick to accommodate its hip clientele at low

AL FRESCO SPRING TO AUTUMN?

Prague doesn't have the warmest climate, but diners cling to their al fresco options. Even into the late fall, you'll find outdoor cafés turning tables, although they'll also turn on the heating lamps and sometimes offer patrons a blanket.

tables surrounded by Buddha statues. And the kitchen excels at standards like a citrusy pad thai and addictive fried shrimp cakes. Curries, which run from tingly to tear-inducing hot, are cut by the creaminess of coconut milk and jasmine rice. One caveat for those who like to beat the heat with quality quaff: Noi has only Stella on tap. ⊠ *Újezd 19, Malá Strana* ☎ *257–311–411* ⊕ *www.noirestaurant.cz* ▭ *AE, V* Ⓜ *Line A: Malostranská* ✛ *G6.*

$$$–$$$$
CONTINENTAL
✕ **Pálffy Palác.** Tucked inside an establishment that's literally palatial, age-old elegance and artful continental cuisine combine on the second story of a baroque palazzo just below Prague Castle. A favorite for special occasions and affairs to remember, Pálffy is one of the few ancient locations in Prague to maintain a feel for the past without seeming stuffy, kitschy, or fake. Instead, it's all high ceilings, candlelight, and haute cuisine: baked yellowfin with fennel puree, young bull steak with veggie sauce, and ostrich carpaccio. The overall effect is elegant, yet lighthearted. ⊠ *Valdštejnská 14, Malá Strana* ☎ *257–530–522* ⊕ *www.palffy.cz* ▭ *AE, MC, V* Ⓜ *Line A: Malostranská* ✛ *G5.*

$$$–$$$$
JAPANESE
✕ **The Sushi Bar.** This narrow little room across the river from the National Theater is home to some of the city's best sushi, courtesy of the fish market next door. The selection is first-rate by Central European standards. Beyond sushi, the menu also includes a great seaweed salad and a rich vegetable stew. Though prices for individual pieces of sushi start relatively low, bills can rise quickly, depending on how many you order. ⊠ *Zborovská 49, Malá Strana* ☎ *603–244–882* ⊕ *www.sushi.cz* ▭ *DC, MC, V* Ⓜ *Line B: Národní Třida* ✛ *H6.*

$$–$$$
SEAFOOD
✕ **U Malé Velryby.** No restaurant in Prague embraces the doing-more-with-less aesthetic more fully than U Malí Velryby (Little Whale). Hidden away on Maltézské náměstí, the menu is the greatest hits of seafood dishes from across the continent, all prepared in a postage stamp–size open kitchen that's only slightly smaller than the cramped, unadorned dining room. You'll find Russian-style smoked salmon on blinis, a heaping helping of paella, a spicy calamari ceviche, and crab pappardelle. The tapas menu is an excellent way to sample little bites of dishes that will appear on the menu as appetizers or entrées in following weeks. Be warned: the opening hours here are erratic. ⊠ *Maltézské nám. 15, Malá Strana* ☎ *257–214–703* ⊕ *www.umalevelryby.cz* ▭ *MC, V* ☻ *Closed Sun.* Ⓜ *Line A: Malostranská* ✛ *H5.*

HRADČANY

$$
VIETNAMESE
✕ **Malý Buddha.** Bamboo, wood, paper, incense—and the random creepy mask on the wall—are all part of the decor at this earthy hilltop hideaway near Prague Castle. Spring rolls, vegetable and mixed stir-fries, fish, and shark steaks come in generous portions. The drink list is unusual, with ginseng wine, herbal drinks, and mystery shots of exotic alcoholic concoctions. This restaurant was one of the first in the city with a no-smoking policy—a rarity in Prague—so the aromas are pure. It's as much about the atmosphere as the food here, which isn't complex but is cooked with heart. ⊠ *Úvoz 46, Hradčany* ☎ *220–513–894* ⊕ *www.malybuddha.cz* ▭ *No credit cards* ☻ *Closed Mon.* Ⓜ *Line A: Hradčanská* ✛ *F5.*

NOVÉ MĚSTO (NEW TOWN)

$$$$

SEAFOOD

✗ **Alcron**. An intimate salon of just seven tables, Alcron remains the city's seafood mecca. Though dating from 1998, this semicircular room's Jazz Age murals give it a classic presence. Main courses feature creative interpretations of traditional fish recipes from around the world, including seasonal specials such as smoked eel with truffled scrambled eggs, scallops with caviar, lobster bisque, and langoustines with seared foie gras. The limited seating arrangements mean reservations are a must. ⊠ *Radisson Blu Alcron Hotel, Štěpánská 40, Nové Město* ☎ *222–820–038* ⊕ *www.radissonblu.com* ⌧ *Reservations essential* ☰ *AE, DC, MC, V* ☉ *Closed Sun.* Ⓜ *Line A: Můstek* ✛ *E6.*

$$$–$$$$

EASTERN
EUROPEAN

✗ **Černý Kohout**. Cozy, comfortable, and full of European charm, the "Black Rooster" serves classic Czech cuisine in a continental context, bringing a strong French touch to such traditional fare as Czech lamb from the Šumava National Forest and roasted Slovak peppers, as well as adding an Italian influence in the risotto with Czech forest mushrooms. Special menus often highlight the cuisine of distinct regions within the country. Graceful service with upscale surroundings gives the impression of something from a bygone era. Thrifty diners, take note: Midweek brings a three-course business lunch of the same high quality for a much lower price. ⊠ *Vojtěšská 9, Nové Město* ☎ *251–681–191* ☰ *AE, DC, MC, V* Ⓜ *Line B: Národní Třída* ✛ *A6.*

$$$–$$$$

EASTERN
EUROPEAN

✗ **CzecHouse**. This is a favorite spot of convention-goers staying at the Hilton, and the new chef Miroslav Hanzal is a great addition. Spying on his work through the window into the kitchen, diners can watch him add haute flair to Czech classics like svíčková (marinated beef with cream sauce) or experiment with dishes like white and green asparagus salad with egg yolk. Czech wines are similarly of a higher standard, though beer goes very well with most recipes. Hanzal is also a whiz with the restaurant's wide selection of U.S. beef. Although those in the city center will have to hop on the metro to Florenc, the food and the excellent service are worth the trip. ⊠ *Pobřezní 1, Karlín* ☎ *224–842–125* ⊕ *www.hiltonprague.cz* ☰ *AE, DC, MC, V* ✛ *E1.*

$

CAFÉ

✗ **The Globe Bookstore & Coffeehouse**. Prague's first English-language bookstore with a café draws both foreigners and Czechs for its books, brunch, and memories of the go-go '90s. The recently upgraded menu includes an excellent burger, passable salads, and more adventurous items like Thai curry. Use the Internet or hook up your own laptop. ⊠ *Pštrossova 6, Nové Město* ☎ *224–934–203* ⊕ *www.globebookstore.cz* ☰ *AE, MC, V* Ⓜ *Line A or B: Můstek* ✛ *A6.*

$$–$$$

ECLECTIC

✗ **Jáma**. American expatriates, Czech politicians, international consultants, and a constant crowd of students make this Czech-American hybrid pub feel like a place where everyone is welcome—especially when there's a big football game. Though just hanging out is of primary importance, the food is leagues ahead of most pubs of this type, with decent Tex-Mex dishes (hearty burritos, crisp nachos, and refreshing taco salads) mixing it up with Czech classics (roast beef with cream sauce, and hearty goulash) and international pub standards (big Caesar salads and juicy burgers). Lunchtime brings inexpensive three-course menus. The owner, a sommelier, also has a stash of high-quality

French and Italian wines at moderate prices. ⊠ *V Jámě 7, Nové Město* ☎ *224–222–383* ⊕ *www.jamapub.cz* ⊟ *AE, DC, MC, V* Ⓜ *Line A or B: Můstek* ⊕ *E6.*

¢ ✗ **Jazz Café č. 14.** Old-fashioned Parisian charm radiates from marble
CAFÉ floors, dim wall lamps, and old oak tables in this large but cozy café. It's frequented by students from nearby Charles University. Marinated hermelín cheese makes a good snack, or sometimes a complete meal. ⊠ *Opatovická 14, Nové Město* ☎ *224–934–674* ⊟ *No credit cards* Ⓜ *Line B: Národní Třída* ⊕ *B6.*

$$–$$$ ✗ **Karavanseraj.** A quirky Lebanese/Indian restaurant popular with the
MIDDLE EASTERN backpacker set, Karavanseraj serves specialties as diverse as Baghdad-style spiced lamb sausages in tomato sauce and as common as Czech lunchmeat. The chef views himself as a cultural ambassador, apparent both in the tomelike menu jammed with photos of foreign lands and the austere restaurant's few decorations, which include pictures and knickknacks from abroad. Dishes like sag paneer are described on the menu as best eaten only after diners "successfully levitate," though more grounded eaters will be happy with the assortment of Lebanese meze, kebabs, and mixed veggie platters. Be sure to try the Algerian-style *burek*, a meat pastry. ⊠ *Masarykovo nábř. 22, Nové Město* ☎ *224–930–390* ⊕ *www.klubcestovatelu.cz* ⊟ *No credit cards* Ⓜ *Line B: Národní Třída* ⊕ *A6.*

¢ ✗ **Kavárna Divadlo Komedie.** A smattering of foreigners mingle with
CAFÉ Czech performers and other locals at this "Comedy Theater" café while sipping small coffees or holding big, thick glasses of Hoegaarden beer. The restored functionalist interior features double marble staircases, which lead to the theater downstairs. ⊠ *Jungmannova 1, Nové Město* ☎ *603–148–162* ⊕ *www.divadlokomedie.cz* ⊟ *No credit cards* Ⓜ *Line A or B: Můstek* ⊕ *C6.*

$$ ✗ **Lemon Leaf.** Lemon Leaf serves a long list of Thai classics to an appre-
THAI ciative, dedicated clientele. Airy and luminous, with big pots of plants, tall windows, and funky lamps, this spot provides a solid alternative to European cuisine for lunch or dinner. Crunchy spring rolls and traditional Thai soups reeling with flavor are essential openers to one of the noodle dishes or spicy curries, but keep an eye on the little flame symbols in the menu that denote the hotness of dishes. ⊠ *Myslíkova 14, Nové Město* ☎ *224–919–056* ⊕ *www.lemon.cz* ⊟ *AE, MC, V* Ⓜ *Line B: Národní Třída* ⊕ *A6.*

$–$$ ✗ **Pastacaffé.** Great coffees by the Tonino Lamborghini brand and fresh
ITALIAN pastas turn this quiet New Town café into a small corner of Milan. Large salads, quick panini, *piadini,* and antipasti round out the menu. Plenty of light and fresh air from the large windows invite all-day loungers, but when the coffee kicks in, people get up and *go.* The cheap, simple dishes are expertly prepared. ⊠ *Vodičkova 8, Nové Město* ☎ *222–231–869* ⊕ *www.ambi.cz* ⊟ *AE, DC, MC, V* Ⓜ *Line A or B: Můstek* ⊕ *D6.*

$$–$$$ ✗ **Potrefená Husa.** Owned and operated by the Prague-based Staro-
EASTERN pramen brewery, Potrefená Husa (the "Wounded Goose") is a Czech
EUROPEAN "gastropub." The interior screams upscale sports bar—as do the fans, crowding the bar area to watch local hockey or soccer matches. Here

you'll find lighter and marginally healthier versions of Czech and Slovak classics. The choices vary slightly from location to location—it's a chainlet—but standards like grilled sirloin and *haluška* (dumplings) with farmer cheese and bacon are found at every one. At the New Town branch there's a fantastic "burger" that's not a burger at all: It's a pork loin sandwich with barbecue sauce and cheese. ⊠ *Resslova 1, Nové Město* ☎ *224–918–691* ⊕ *www.potrefenahusa.cz* ▭ *AE, MC, V* Ⓜ *Line B: Národní Třída* ⚓ *A6.*

$$–$$$
VEGETARIAN

✕ **Radost FX Café.** Rave on: This vegetarian restaurant and café sits right above the venerable Radost FX nightclub. Though it's no longer the only place in the city to get American breakfast of a passable burrito, it's still an excellent spot to pass the time. The menu includes extremely satisfying Tex-Mex, pasta dishes, and the ever-popular Popeye "burger." The service isn't fast, but really, what's the rush? ⊠ *Bělehradská 120, Nové Město* ☎ *224–254–776* ⊕ *www.radostfx.cz* ▭ *No credit cards* Ⓜ *Line C: I.P. Pavlova* ⚓ *F6.*

$$
CONTINENTAL

✕ **Universal.** Prices here have doggedly remained unchanged since it opened in the late 1990s, much to customers' delight. Universal is a continental cornucopia of excellent salads, classically European main courses, titanic side orders of scalloped potatoes, luscious lemon tarts, and sweet profiteroles. An affordable midday menu makes it even more alluring at lunchtime, and the cheap house wine draws out after-dinner conversations. Reservations are advisable. ⊠ *V Jirchářích 6, Nové Město* ☎ *224–934–416* ⊕ *www.universalrestaurant.cz* ▭ *MC, V* Ⓜ *Line B: Národní Třída* ⚓ *A6.*

VINOHRADY AND ŽIŽKOV

VINOHRADY

$$–$$$
MEXICAN

✕ **Ambiente—The Living Restaurant.** The first of what has become a small chain of successful restaurants helped champion the concept of attentive service, a foreign notion to Prague waitstaff when it opened in the 1990s. This branch still retains the original Mexican theme that made it famous, but pasta and steaks also figure strongly on the expanded menu. It's a suitable stop before or after a stroll through nearby Riegrovy sady, one of the city's grand hilltop parks. ⊠ *Mánesova 59, Vinohrady* ☎ *222–727–851* ⊕ *www.ambi.cz* ▭ *AE, DC, MC, V* Ⓜ *Line A: Jiřího z Poděbrad* ⚓ *H2.*

$$$
ITALIAN

✕ **Aromi.** Gracious, gregarious, and extremely confident, Aromi is arguably the city's second-best Italian restaurant and proud of it: It's considerably less stiff than Allegro in Staré Město, but with the same great service and a festive air, showcasing the overlooked fare of Le Marche. Classic pastas made in-house and fresh seafood shown off tableside are two of the crowd favorites, as are the superb salads and well-chosen Italian wines. Leave room for a post-dessert treat: Aromi stocks an exclusive list of rare grappas. ⊠ *Mánesova 78, Vinohrady* ☎ *222–713–222* ⊕ *www.aromi.cz* ▭ *MC, V* Ⓜ *Line A: Jiřího z Poděbrad* ⚓ *H2.*

$$
MIDDLE EASTERN

✕ **Babylon.** Babylon boasts dishes from places as diverse as Cyprus, Morocco, and Lebanon in a basement space filled with expansive murals of lions and mythical beasts. This culinary showcase draws adventurous diners and people looking for a taste of home. Lamb is a particular strength—in either the couscous with vegetables or a *tukka*, dipped in a mild chili sauce. The grilled *halloumi* (Greek cheese), tender octopus, and creamy *tzatiki* (yogurt and cucumber dip) are all winners as well. Weekend afternoons are a great time to visit, as Babylon fills with families eating leisurely lunches. ⊠ *Pod Karlovem 12, Vinohrady* ☎ *222–561–021* ⊟ *AE, V* Ⓜ *Line A: Náměstí Míru* ⟡ *F6.*

¢ ✕ **Medúza.** The old-fashioned, CAFÉ black-and-white photographs on the walls, burnished chairs, old lacquered tables, and a general "grandma's parlor" feel make this student-y place instantly inviting. The menu offers a selection of mostly vegetarian snacks and *palačinky* (filled pancakes) that go perfectly with a glass of wine. ⊠ *Belgická 17, Vinohrady* ☎ *222–515–107* ⊕ *www.meduza.cz* ⊟ *No credit cards* Ⓜ *Line A: Náměstí Míru* ⟡ *F6.*

> ### THE SWEET LIFE
>
> There are a few uniquely Czech treats around—great as a snack or a little gift.
>
> *Tatranka:* Delicious wafer candy bars, covered with chocolate and wrapped in paper.
>
> *Kofola:* This alternative to Coke from the pre-1989 era tastes like a spicier Dr Pepper.
>
> *Karlovarske oplatky:* Crunchy, sweet, flat wafer cookies filled with sugar or chocolate about as big as a dinner plate.
>
> *Fidorka:* Chocolate-coated wafers in coconut, peanut, and other flavors. Foil-wrapped, about one-fourth as thick as a hockey puck.

$$–$$$ ✕ **Mozaika.** Pushing the outer orbits of eclectic, this cellar restaurant ECLECTIC in a leafy residential neighborhood offers Thai-style curried mussels, hearty roast-beef salads, grilled veal chops, and what some consider to be the best (and weirdest) hamburger in Prague, served on a homemade spinach bun and topped with sugary caramelized onions, grilled mushrooms, and rich Swiss cheese. The result? Delicious meals, without the attitude and the concomitant kick in the wallet from your average pricey spot. That means it's popular, so reservations are especially recommended. Linger in the modern dining room to view a rotating exhibit of original art hanging on the walls. ⊠ *Nitranská 13, Vinohrady* ☎ *224–253–011* ⊕ *www.restaurantmozaika.cz* ⊟ *AE, DC, MC, V* Ⓜ *Line A: Jiřího z Poděbrad* ⟡ *H2.*

$$–$$$ ✕ **U Emy Destinnové.** An American cooking in the house where the cel-ITALIAN ebrated Czech opera singer Ema Destinnová was born? Somehow chef Steven Trumpfheller makes it work at this basement restaurant. The interior replicates a 1950s Czech living room, right down to the natty couches and chatty diners eating as though enjoying a Sunday supper at mom's house. But the modern food is beyond mom's stovetop. It's a hybrid of Italian and Czech influences: Pistachio-crusted venison arrives with a cranberry sage reduction; tagliatelle comes with shrimp and asparagus. U Emy Destinnové's seafood selections are also top-notch, particularly the calamari stuffed with shrimp or crab and mushrooms. ⊠ *Kateřinská 7, Vinohrady* ☎ *224–918–425* ⊕ *www.uemydestinove.cz* ⊟ *AE, MC, V* ⊘ *Closed Sun.* Ⓜ *Line A: Náměstí Míru* ⟡ *E6.*

ŽIŽKOV

$$–$$$
MEDITERRANEAN

✕ **Fluidum.** There's some ambitious fare at this earnest restaurant just steps from the Jiřího z Poděbrad metro. In a neighborhood better known for pubs, Fluidum courts business lunchers with a colorful interior and daily specials and foodies with its multicourse tasting menus. The dishes here are more ambitious than expected; duck breast has a coffee and dried plum sauce, while the tuna comes with a bitter chocolate sauce—they believe in dessert first, it would seem. The starters are set to win over skeptics, particularly the fish fillet with root veggies. ✉ *Lucemburská 6, Žižkov* ☎ *222–211–702* ⊕ *www.fluidumrestaurant. cz* ▭ *AE, DC, MC, V* Ⓜ *Line A: Jiřího z Poděbrad* ✛ *F6.*

$$–$$$
MEXICAN
Fodor's Choice
★

✕ **Sonora.** This local secret hidden on a sleepy Žižkov side street serves up quality—and spicy—Mexican standards paired with the single best selection of tequilas in Prague. Unlike a lot of Czech-Mex, the kitchen here is unafraid of the heat, from the moderately piquant fried jalapeños to thermonuclear chipotles with adobo sauce. Milder concoctions add balance, including a crispy chicken chimichanga that makes an encore appearance stuffed with bananas and vanilla ice cream (minus the chicken, of course). Quality *añejos* round out the drinks list, which features 220 different kinds of tequila and makes for some raucous evenings. Adding desert-outpost feel, the outdoor seating is penned in by a wood fence. ✉ *Radhošťská 5, Žižkov* ☎ *222–711–029* ⊕ *www. sonoras.cz* ▭ *MC, V* Ⓜ *Line A: Jiřího z Poděbrad* ✛ *F6.*

SMÍCHOV

$$$
ECLECTIC
Fodor's Choice
★

✕ **Artisan.** Hidden on a side street off Ujezd, Artisan is a secret spot worth the trouble it takes to find. (Look for signs pointing the way from the tram stop.) Decorated with muted earth tones and indirect lighting, it can feel a little dark, but the food brightens the experience. Aran Halvorsen, the owner of beloved Czech-Mex spot Banditos, expanded his repertoire here with more ambitious, globally inspired dishes. Case in point, the Thai chicken salad that's crunchy, spicy, and not too sweet. Solid bets are the open-faced ravioli with duck ragout and the hickory-smoked hamburger. Hit this venue at lunch, when the outdoor patio in a courtyard is a treat and there's a 135 Kč, three-course business menu. ✉ *Rošických 4, Smíchov* ☎ *257–218–277* ⊕ *www.artisanrestaurant.cz* ▭ *AE, V* Ⓜ *Line B: Anděl* ✛ *H6.*

$–$$
CONTINENTAL

✕ **Café Savoy.** Stellar service and elegant meals of high quality at moderate prices are de rigueur here. This restored café, a onetime favorite of the city's fin-de-siècle Jewish community, serves everything from meal-sized split-pea and cream of spinach soups to Wiener schnitzel, with huge salads complemented by fresh breads from the in-house bakery. The house cake, topped with marzipan, makes a properly sweet finish. If you're looking for eggs, Savoy's breakfasts are without question some of Prague's best. It's just south of Malá Strana, but easily walkable from Malostranske namesti. ✉ *Vitěznŝ 1, Smíchov* ☎ *257–311–562* ⊕ *www. ambi.cz* ▭ *AE, DC, MC, V* Ⓜ *Line A: Malostranská* ✛ *G6.*

$–$$
CZECH

✕ **Kozlovna.** The newest of the brewery-owned chains in Prague, Kozlovna is affiliated with the Velkopopovicky Kozel beer. But aside from the animal horns outside the front door and the company's brews

Guests at Artisan can choose between the outdoor patio or the dark, cozy interior.

on tap, the branding is unobtrusive and the environment is friend and bustling. They serve huge portions of expertly made Czech classics at low prices, and naturally everything goes great with beer: ribs, venison, and a sinus-clearing garlic soup are all superlative versions of the pub food you'll find elsewhere, without the intense premium you pay for a sleek environment and competent service. Just don't get too ambitious—sometimes the daily specials, especially anything that involves pasta, overreach. ⊠ *Lidická 20, Smíchov* ☎ *257–210–862* ⊕ *www.kozlovna. eu* ▭ *No credit cards* Ⓜ *Line B: Anděl* ✛ *H6.*

VRŠOVICE

$$ ╳ **Osteria da Clara.** Replacing the beloved—though infrequently vis-

ECLECTIC ited—Valletta, Osteria da Clara is an unassuming Italian spot that gets by on the hustle and charm of the staff. When the kitchen isn't over-whelmed—which happens when the austere white dining room gets beyond half-full—it pumps out lovely, unpretentious Italian cuisine, like crostini with chicken liver, polenta, and tomatoes. Pastas are supe-rior to the meatier entrées, like the spaghetti with anchovies and garlic, and the pasta with sausage and cream. The tiramisu isn't Prague's best, but it may be Prague's biggest. ⊠ *Mexická 7, Vršovice* ☎ *271/726–548* ⌖ *Reservations essential* ⊕ *www.daclara.com* ▭ *AE, MC, V* Ⓜ *Line A: Flora* ✛ *H2.*

¢ ╳ **Shakespeare & Sons.** Czechs and expats frequent this tranquil book-

CAFÉ store/café out of the city center, which offers Bernard beer, occasional readings, performances, and assorted happenings. The charming book room at the back has the strange power to make hours disappear while you browse. ⊠ *Krymská 12, Vršovice* ☎ *271–740–839* ⊕ *www.shakes. cz* ▭ *AE, MC, V* Ⓜ *Line A: Náměstí Míru* ✛ *F6.*

DEJVICE

$–$$
EASTERN
EUROPEAN

✕ **Budvarka**. Owned by Czech brewer Budvar, Budvarka is a pumped-up pub. From the selection of beers to the rough-hewn wood tables, everything here is larger than life. The samples of rare Budvar brews (Budvar Pale Ale or the famed "Bud Strong") are worth the trip to this neighborhood alone. The food is upscale Czech grub, including an entire section of the menu meant to pair with beer, which includes potatoes cooked in lard and pickled hermelín cheese. The Flinstonian ribs are so huge that they require special presentation on a raised metal tray. Bring an appetite, or at the very least, a hungry friend. ⊠ *Wuchterlova 22, Dejvice* ☎ *222–960–820* ⊕ *www.budvarkadejvice.cz* ▭ *MC, V* Ⓜ *Line A: Dejvická* ✛ *F4.*

$$
EASTERN
EUROPEAN

✕ **Perpetuum**. The country's greatest culinary resource—wild duck—gets a makeover here with culinary flourishes from the rest of the continent. Starters include an over-the-top pairing of duck livers and guanciale—two great tastes that taste great together—as well as hearty salads and soups with seasonal ingredients. That merely sets the stage for the main courses, with more duck like duck breast stuffed with mushrooms and even a duck confit with tomato risotto. As if they were competing for a medal in hedonism, Perpetuum also includes one of the city's best wine lists, featuring the country's best vintages, like the crisp whites from cult producer Dobrá vinice. The whole experience is sinfully, painfully rich. ⊠ *Na hutích 9, Dejvice* ☎ *222–522–784* ⊕ *www.restauraceperpetuum. cz* ▭ *MC, V* ☾ *Closed Mon.* Ⓜ *Line A: Dejvická* ✛ *F4.*

Where to Stay

By Alexander
Basek

Sometimes, too much of a good thing is really too much of a good thing. Prague's hotel market has grown by leaps and bounds in the past decade, adding luxury hoteliers with fusion restaurants, boffo room amenities, and properties with beer-theme spa treatments, astronomical thread counts, even on-site monks.

Alas, after all that building, the city is in something of a hotel hangover, with more hotel beds than Vienna and not enough people to fill them. But that can work in your favor; while prices remain high during peak season, essentially May through September or October, they plummet in the shoulder and low periods, with room rates at half or a third of their highs. Just remember that this time period is not for everyone; wintertime in Prague is beautiful, but it gets cold and daylight is at a premium. Moreover, prices are down compared to two years ago—the bubble has clearly burst.

The most desirable neighborhoods to stay in are the Old Town (Staré Město), the Lesser Quarter (Malá Strana), the Castle Area (Hradčany), and the New Town (Nové Město). Neighborhoods outside the center, like Smíchov and Vinohrady, are easily accessible by Prague's inexpensive, highly efficient metro and tram system.

If you'd prefer to try something a bit different from a chain or five-star hotel, the vast majority of hotels and pensions are privately owned and operated. Private hotels can certainly be quaint and atmospheric, but they can also be stripped down—lacking a/c, breakfast, or amenities—which is a fine line; one person's shabby chic can be another person's just plain shabby. If you want to really go local, try renting an apartment in the city. Several agencies now help book rooms in private apartments, and you can find some very nice places at more reasonable prices. On the flip side, remember that there's no shortage of three- and four-star "design hotels" that boast sleek rooms and free Wi-Fi for about the same price; you don't have to go without unless that's the vacation you want to have.

WHERE SHOULD I STAY?

	NEIGHBORHOOD VIBE	PROS	CONS
Staré Město	The city's ancient center; tourists, nightlife, museums, and monuments.	Everything at your fingertips, including fantastic restaurants and Old Town Square.	Everyone else at your doorstep, visiting those very same things.
Malá Strana	With evocative, cobblestone alleys and Embassy Row, the Lesser Quarter is as authentic as Old Town but with fewer crowds.	Easy access to Old Town (just across the river); churches galore.	Hilly layout can mean a schlep to your hotel; not as hopping as Old Town come nightfall.
Hradčany	The neighborhood surrounding Prague Castle, this is a mix of gardens and historic buildings from every era.	Beautiful greenery; St. Vitus's Cathedral and the Castle within walking distance.	Far from the action; fewer high-end eateries and far less street life.
Nové Město	The area near Wenceslas Square, "new" only means less than 800 years old.	Bustles with activity during the day; a short walk to Old Town; National Museum and lots of shopping.	Gets seedier after dark; the shopping is ample but cheap stores are in short supply.
Vinohrady	Leafy residential streets: think of it as Prague's Greenwich Village.	Quiet; filled with locals; charming restaurants and bars.	A tram ride or walk to the center; not as tourist-friendly as other locales.
Smíchov	Just south of Malá Strana, Smíchov boasts a similar look with cobblestone, streets along the Vltava.	Lots of shopping thanks to the Novy Smíchov Mall; near the Staropramen brewery.	Not easy walking distance to Old Town; lack of subway options.
Žižkov	Down the hill from Vinohrady, Žižkov is the edgy little brother to the more buttoned-up Vinohrady.	Great bars and music venues; a lively arts scene with the people to match.	A bit gritty and dirty; not walking distance to many other central locations.
Eastern and Western Suburbs	Ride the metro to the end and you'll find yourself among the locals—and the communist housing blocks.	Cheap; so locals-only; you'll feel really cool.	Far from anything; not much in the way of redeeming design or architecture of interest.

4

WHERE TO STAY PLANNER

Strategy

Where should we stay? With hundreds of Prague hotels, it may seem like a daunting question. But fret not—our expert writers and editors have done most of the legwork. The selections here represent the best this city has to offer—from the best budget hostels to the sleekest designer hotels. Scan "Best Bets" on the following pages for top recommendations by price and experience. Or find a review quickly in the listings. Search by neighborhood, then alphabetically. Happy hunting!

Word of Mouth

"Wenceslas Square wouldn't be my first choice of area for accommodation. I'd rather avoid it! [I'd pick] Malá Strana or Old Town areas where things are quieter and with a bit more old city-like atmosphere. (That's why I visit Prague.)"   —kappa

"I stay in Wenceslas Square all the time, and like it, so to each his own. I use public transportation a lot, so I love walking out the door & being at a tram or metro stop. With that said, if it's your first time there, maybe Old Town or Malá Strana will give you more of the ambience you want."   —amp322

Reservations

During the peak season (May through October, excluding July and August), or over major holidays, reservations are a must; reserve 90 days in advance to stay in the hotel and room of your choice. For the remainder of the year, reserve 30 days in advance. If possible, call or e-mail to double-check your reservation before you come to avoid any hassles on arrival. Note that many hotel rooms use two single beds pushed together; if you are counting on a proper double bed, ensure this with the reservations desk when booking your room.

Family Travel

Hotels in Prague are more family-friendly than ever before. The proliferation of high-end chains has helped mightily, as properties offer the same options they do on the other side of the Atlantic. Plus, there are plenty of options no matter where you stay. Suites at the Mamaison Suite Hotel Pachtuv Palace, for example, are an excellent value, and offer scads of space for little ones to run around in. (Don't worry, the chandeliers are quite high up). The Four Seasons, meanwhile, provides amenities like bathrobes and coloring books on request; it also boasts a highly acclaimed restaurant that also has a children's menu. Most hotels in Prague will have cribs or extra beds for an additional fee, and can arrange babysitting services given fair warning, but more complicated requests—say, a stroller—might be harder to accommodate. Best to bring what you can ahead of time; especially at the smaller, less expensive properties, options will be more limited. Also, bear in mind that standard rooms in Prague tend to be on the small side, and that if you're traveling with a child, a larger room might be a wise decision if it's within your budget.

Facilities

In most cases, cable TV, breakfast, and some kind of Internet connection are offered in hotels in all price ranges. Wi-Fi Internet access is breaking onto the scene, though Wi-Fi networks can be spotty, and usually function only in the lobby and other public areas. Hotels at $$ and $$$ ranges usually have restaurants, cafés, room service, private baths, and hair dryers. At $$$$ hotels you can expect luxury amenities like robes, a sauna, steam bath, pool, concierge, and babysitting—oh, yes, and air-conditioning, which is woefully absent at cheaper hotels. (Many of Prague's older buildings are legally prohibited from installing air-conditioning for architectural reasons, but most of the upscale hotels somehow circumvented the rules.)

Star Ratings

A word to star-rating aficionados: unlike many other countries, the Czech Republic doesn't have an official rating system, so hotels rate themselves. They invariably toss on a couple stars more than they actually merit.

Prices

Many hotels in Prague go by a three-season system: The lowest rates are charged from November through mid-March, excluding Christmas and New Year's, when high-season rates are charged; the middle season is July and August; the high season, from the end of March through June and again from mid-August through the end of October, brings the highest rates. Easter sees higher-than-high-season rates, and some hotels increase the prices for other holidays and trade fairs. Always ask first.

In This Chapter

4

Using the Map

Throughout the chapter, you'll see mapping symbols and coordinates (⊕ F2) after property names or reviews. To locate the property on a map, turn to the Where to Stay map. The letter and number following the ⊕ symbol are the property's coordinates on the map grid.

WHAT IT COSTS IN KORUNA AND EUROS

	¢	$	$$	$$$	$$$$
HOTELS in koruna	under 1,200 Kč	1,200 Kč–2,200 Kč	2,200 Kč–4,000 Kč	4,000 Kč–6,500 Kč	over 6,500 Kč
HOTELS in euros	under €50	€50–€92	€92–€168	€168–€273	over €273

Prices are for two people in a double room with a private bath and breakfast during peak season (March through October, excluding July and August).

BEST BETS FOR PRAGUE LODGING

Fodor's offers a selective listing of quality lodging experiences at every price range, from the city's best budget hostel to its most sophisticated luxury hotel. Here we've compiled our top recommendations by price and experience. The very best properties—in other words, those that provide a particularly remarkable experience in their price range—are designated in the listings with the Fodor's Choice logo.

Fodor's Choice ★

Alchymist Grand Hotel and Spa, p. 139
The Augustine, p. 142
Golden Well, p. 143
Hotel Le Palais, p. 150
Hotel Salvator, p. 148
Mamaison Suite Hotel Pachtuv Palace, p. 136
Mandarin Oriental Prague, p. 145
Sax Vintage Design Hotel, p. 145

By Price

$
Hotel Salvator, p. 148

$$
King's Court, p. 136
Sax Vintage Design Hotel, p. 145

$$$
Golden Well, p. 143
Icon Hotel & Lounge, p. 149

Leonardo, p. 136
Maximilian, p. 138

$$$$
Alcymist Grand Hotel and Spa, p. 139
The Augustine, p. 142
Hotel Le Palais, p. 150
Kempinski Hybernská, p. 135
Mamaison Suite Hotel Pachtuv Palace, p. 136
Mandarin Oriental Prague, p. 145

By Experience

BEST BEDS
Four Seasons Prague, p. 131
Icon Hotel & Lounge, p. 149
Kempinski Hybernská, p. 135

BEST BREAKFAST
Golden Well, p. 143
Josef, p. 135

Mamaison Suite Hotel Pachtuv Palace, p. 136
Maximilian, p. 138

BEST CONCIERGE
The Augustine, p. 142
Four Seasons, p. 131
Mandarin Oriental, p. 145

BEST FOR BUSINESS TRAVELERS
Andel's Hotel Prague, p. 152
Kempinski Hybernská, p. 135
Radisson Blu Alcron Hotel, p. 149

BEST DESIGN
Alchymist Grand Hotel and Spa, p. 139
The Augustine, p. 142
Sax Vintage Design Hotel, p. 145

BEST DINING
Four Seasons, p. 131
Golden Well, p. 143

Mandarin Oriental Prague, p. 145

BEST SPAS
Alchymist Grand Hotel and Spa, p. 139
The Augustine, p. 142
Icon Hotel & Lounge, p. 149
Mandarin Oriental Prague, p. 145

BEST VIEWS
Four Seasons Prague, p. 131
Mamaison Suite Hotel Pachtuv Palace, p. 136
Mamaison Hotel Riverside Prague, p. 153

MOST KID-FRIENDLY
Four Seasons, p. 131
Hotel Le Palais, p. 150
Mandarin Oriental Prague, p. 145

MOST ROMANTIC
The Augustine, p. 142
Alchymist, p. 139
Mamaison Suite Hotel Pachtuv Palace, p. 136

QUAINT AND COZY
Golden Well, p. 143
Mamaison Hotel Riverside Prague, p. 153
Romantik Hotel U Raka, p. 146

YOUNG AND HAPPENING
The Augustine, p. 142
Icon Hotel & Lounge, p. 149
King's Court, p. 136

HOTEL REVIEWS

Listed alphabetically by neighborhood.

STARÉ MĚSTO (OLD TOWN)

Staré Město, Prague's Old Town, is a highly desirable neighborhood to lodge in. The mix of baroque and Gothic buildings provides a storybook feeling. Hotels here are of the old-made-new variety. Don't be surprised to be standing in a hotel lobby that was originally built in the 17th century but looks and smells like a fresh coat of plaster and paint was added a month ago. Trendy restaurants, hip cafés, superior clubs, and the city's best clothing boutiques are all in this area.

$$$$ ☷ **Buddha Bar Hotel.** With so many luxurious Prague hotels incorporating Czech design and history, it's hard to see the appeal of the more conceptually muddled Buddha Bar Hotel—especially when it comes at a premium price. (The concept is Chinoiserie-meets-art nouveau, as best we can tell.) The excessive qualities of both are interwoven in a clever way, with the designs from the hotel's original 100-year-old structure meshed with Chinese script and Buddhas throughout. Traverse the dark hallways and you'll note the design announces itself even here—each room has a lighted white tile with its number on the floor, like a space-age welcome mat. In the rooms themselves you'll find more of the same: black-lacquer cabinetry, silky smooth linens, and freestanding bathtubs with a mosaic of a dragon on the exterior. This being a hotel linked with a nightclub/restaurant, you can even dial in the television to play the same tunes the DJ is spinning in the bi-level basement eatery. The spa is so small that in-room treatments are recommended (often with those famed "Buddha Bar" mixes playing in the background). At peak times the lobby hums with a motley collection of moneyed European characters chatting with the Czech staff wearing Chinese outfits. Guests get to use a separate entrance for the Buddha Bar, and breakfast is served in the more continental Siddhartha Café. **Pros:** stylish design; Mecca for clubgoing hipsters. **Cons:** overpriced; inattentive staff. ✉ *Jakubská 8, Staré Město* ☎ *221–776–300* ⊕ *www.buddha-bar-hotel.cz* ⟳ *36 rooms, 3 suites* ♨ *In-room: a/c, Internet. In-hotel: 2 restaurants, room service, bar, spa, laundry service, Wi-Fi hotspot* ▭ *AE, D, DC, MC, V* ⎟◎⎟ *EP* Ⓜ *Line C: Nám. Republiky* ⊕ *G3.*

$$$$ ☷ **Four Seasons Prague.** In the early days of Prague tourism after 1989, this was *the* place to stay in Prague. Twenty years later, the Four Seasons has competition from the Augustine and Mandarin across the river. Still, the luxury chain is keeping up, with renovations to the modern wing of the hotel (there are three buildings in all; the modern structure is joined by a factory from 1846 and a house from 1737) kitting out rooms with flat-screen TVs, Eames desk chairs, a herringbone-patterned carpet and more. It's classic Four Seasons throughout: exceedingly comfortable beds and pillows, stellar views of the Castle and Charles Bridge, formal, conscientious service, Allegro, arguably Prague's best-reviewed restaurant, and a lavish (and expensive) breakfast spread. You know exactly what you're getting, which is to say there are no surprises: Rooms really are an upscale wash of neutral tones and, if you close

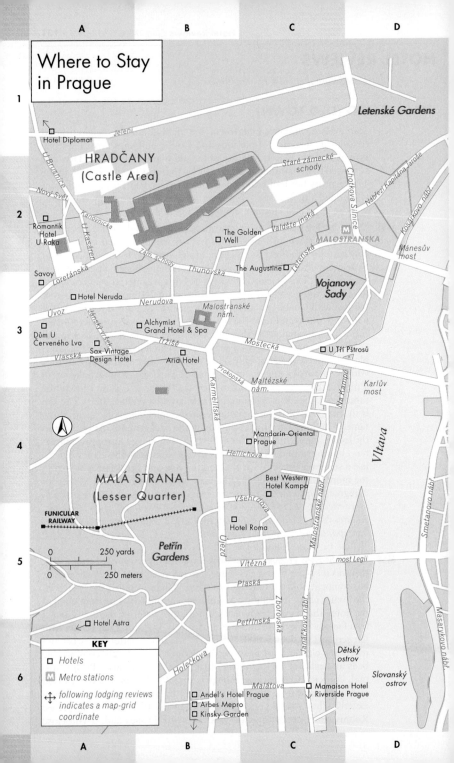

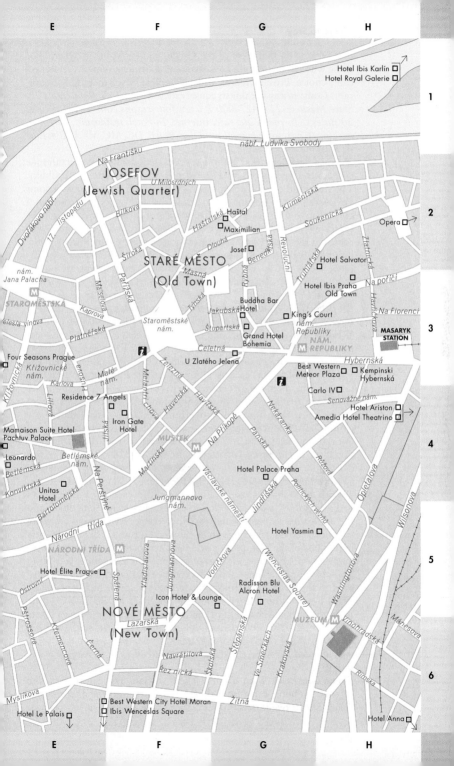

the curtains on that view of the Castle, you could be anywhere. For those who see the brand's consistency as a virtue, it remains an impeccable choice. **Pros:** incredible beds; incredible views; incredible restaurant. **Cons:** pricey breakfast; conservative styling. ⊠ *Veleslavinova 2a, Staré Město* ☎ *221–427–000* ⊕ *www.fourseasons.com* ⟿ *141 rooms, 20 suites* ♲ *In-room: a/c, safe, Internet. In-hotel: restaurant, bar, gym, parking (paid), some pets allowed (fee)* ▭ *AE, DC, MC, V* ⦺ *EP* Ⓜ *Line A: Staroměstská* ✛ *E3.*

$$$ ⊞ **Grand Hotel Bohemia.** This art nouveau *palais* dominates a picturesque corner near the Prašná brána (Powder Tower) and Náměstí Republiky. The clean and comfortable property has a warm, muted look. Rooms are decked out in elegant cream linens and dark-wood furniture for a conservative tone (save for some whimsical carpeting). Although the location is central, the rooms are a bit overpriced when compared with others in the area. **Pros:** city-center location; interesting history to the building; flat-screen televisions. **Cons:** nickel and dime charges (Ethernet access and breakfast are at additional cost); rooms are on the small side. ⊠ *Králodvorská 4, Staré Město* ☎ *234–608–111* ⊕ *www. grandhotelbohemia.cz* ⟿ *73 rooms, 5 suites* ♲ *In-room: a/c, safe, Internet (fee), Wi-Fi (some, fee). In-hotel: restaurant, bar, some pets allowed (fee)* ▭ *AE, DC, MC, V* ⦺ *BP* Ⓜ *Line B: Nám. Republiky* ✛ *G3.*

$$ ⊞ **Haštal.** The main selling point is the price, which is great for this location—in a quiet spot just a few minutes from Old Town Square and next door to the more modernist (and more pricy) Maximilian hotel. The Haštal's building was used as a brewery until the turn of the 20th century, and the room design comes from the same era—wooden desk and chairs, sea-foam duvets and white-linen drapes. Service and amenities can be hit or miss, however. **Pros:** great location on a quiet street; very clean rooms; free Wi-Fi in rooms. **Cons:** elevator goes only to the fourth floor; the pocket park across the street can attract some loud conversationalists. ⊠ *Haštalská 16, Staré Město* ☎ *222–314–335* ⟿ *31 rooms* ♲ *In-room: a/c, Wi-Fi. In-hotel: restaurant, parking (paid), some pets allowed (fee)* ▭ *AE, DC, MC, V* ⦺ *BP* Ⓜ *Line A: Staroměstská* ✛ *G2.*

$$ ⊞ **Hotel Ibis Praha Old Town.** A hint of mod decorates the public spaces here: the lobby is dotted with '60s-style chairs in key-lime hues, and the bar features a flamboyant red-poppy theme. Alas, rooms are more subdued in standard beige with blond-wood furniture. But the location here is one of the best, putting you right across the street from Obecní dům. Reasonable rates, clean rooms with a modern touch, and Wi-Fi available in public areas and in rooms give this hotel its appeal. **Pros:** next to the Municipal House, the location is ideal; buffet breakfast (€10) is served until noon. **Cons:** the enormity of the hotel detracts from any intimate charm; staff can be uninviting. ⊠ *Na Poříčí 5, Staré Město* ☎ *266–000–999* ⊕ *www.ibishotel.com* ⟿ *271 rooms* ♲ *In-room: a/c, safe, Wi-Fi (fee). In-hotel: restaurant, bar, parking (paid), some pets allowed (fee)* ▭ *AE, DC, MC, V* ⦺ *BP* Ⓜ *Line B: Nám. Republiky* ✛ *H3.*

$$$$ ⊞ **Iron Gate Hotel.** Want history? The Iron Gate has it in spades. The original building dates from the 14th century, and the architectural details still prove it. (Ask to see a room with painted ceiling beams.)

During the 16th century it underwent a major renovation, adding balconies and terraces. In 2003 it was restored yet again, exposing the original frescoes that had been hidden for years. The sleigh beds, tasteful antique touches, and fluffy terry bathrobes are nice details, but note that the amenities come up a bit short compared to other luxury properties in this price range. The prime location and a peaceful courtyard don't come cheap. **Pros:** history galore; each room is unique; located on one of the most precious cobblestone streets in the city; free cable Internet in rooms. **Cons:** firm beds; outgunned in the amenities department by new competitor hotels. ⊠ *Michalská 19, Staré Město* ☎ *225–777–777* ⊕ *www. irongate.cz* ⤴ *44 suites* ☊ *In-room: a/c, safe, kitchen, Internet. In-hotel: restaurant, room service, Wi-Fi hotspot* ⊟ *AE, MC, V* ⊺⊚⊺ *BP* Ⓜ *Line A: Staroměstská* ✛ *F4.*

DROP ANCHOR

One lodging alternative is "botels": boats moored to the banks of the Vltava converted into hotels. Prague has several, and what they lack in comfort, they compensate for in uniqueness. One plus is that you'll probably save a little money over standard hotels. On the downside, you may find yourself walking more, as the boats tend to be outside the city center. The Admirál (⊕ *www.admiral-botel. cz*) is the leading botel for the upmarket crowd. Budget travelers should take a look at the Racek (⊕ *www.botelracek.cz*). Always be sure to ask for a room facing the river, rather than the road.

$$$ ⊡ **Josef.** Cool, clean, white lines dominate the decor of this ultra-hip modern boutique hotel designed by London-based Czech architect Eva Jiricna. There are no suites, only single and double rooms, so the sizes range from small to smaller, but Jiricna knows how to manipulate space, glass, and color to make even the smallest space breathable. If you can book it, go for Room 801, which has an exquisite view of Prague's Old Town. Wi-Fi is in public areas. **Pros:** large patio for breakfast in the courtyard; just a few minutes' walk from Old Town Square. **Cons:** the minimalist design might be cold for some; some rooms have glass dividers for the bathroom and could lack privacy for some. ⊠ *Rybná 20, Staré Město* ☎ *221–700–111* ⊕ *www.hoteljosef.com* ⤴ *109 rooms* ☊ *In-room: a/c, safe, DVD, Internet. In-hotel: restaurant, bar, spa, laundry service, Wi-Fi hotspot, parking (paid), some pets allowed (fee)* ⊟ *AE, DC, MC, V* ⊺⊚⊺ *BP* Ⓜ *Line B: Nám. Republiky* ✛ *G2.*

$$$$ ⊡ **Kempinski Hybernská.** The vaunted Kempinski brand's first foray into the Prague market, this hotel—steps from Náměstí Republiky—brings a high-level of service and attention to detail to a scruffier part of Old Town. After renovating this 15th century palace, Kempinski Hybernská kept its original baroque exterior and supplemented it with modern amenities on the inside. Handsome, if staid rooms in a burgundy-and-brown palette feature wooden floors, a small desk area, and some of Prague's best beds. Suites have kitchenettes, a separate sitting area, nifty Czech modern art pieces like pendant chandeliers. All rooms have excellent bathrooms, with deep bathtubs or glass-box rainfall showers, or one of each. Guests appreciate the little extras like free overnight shoeshine service and a pretty courtyard garden. The hotel restaurant,

Le Grill, feels grand but overly formal, even at breakfast. **Pros:** great bathrooms; comfy beds. **Cons:** slow Wi-Fi (Ethernet is faster but not free); lobby not smoke-free. ⊠ *Hybernská 12, Staré Město* ☎ *226–226–111* ⊕ *www.kempinski.com* ↗ *75 rooms* ⚭ *In-room: a/c, safe, kitchen (some), refrigerator (some), Internet, Wi-Fi. In-hotel: restaurant, room service, spa, laundry service, Wi-Fi hotspot, parking (paid)* ⊟ *AE, D, DC, MC, V* ⊺○⏑ *EP* Ⓜ *Line B: Nám. Republiky* ✛ *H3.*

$$ ⛫ **King's Court.** Think of the King's Court as a discount version of the luxe Kempinski hotel—which is a good comparison, especially given Kempi's price. Steps from the exit of the Náměstí Republiky metro, they share more than a subway stop. The sleek 133 rooms of the King's Court straddle the line between modern design and functionality. Rooms are outfitted with art nouveau–inspired carpeting, orange velvet chairs, and oversized leather headboards for flair. That's bolstered by handsome dark-wood cabinetry, heated marble bathroom floors, rainfall showerheads, and large flat-screen televisions. The downstairs (M)eatingpoint restaurant may have a silly name, but it serves passably good international cuisine and has outdoor seating on the square. (It's also where you'll have breakfast in the morning.) The ostentatiously beautiful chandeliers and marble floors of the lobby make it a nice place to pass the time even without a drink. **Pros:** handsome room decorations; convenient location. **Cons:** street noise on weekend nights from the square; rooms aren't that big. ⊠ *U Obecního domu 3, Staré Město* ☎ *224–222–888* ⊕ *www.hotelkingscourt.cz* ↗ *133 rooms* ⚭ *In-room: a/c, safe, Wi-Fi. In-hotel: restaurant, bar, spa, Wi-Fi hotspot* ⊟ *AE, D, DC, MC, V* ⊺○⏑ *EP* Ⓜ *Line B: Nám. Republiky* ✛ *G3.*

$$$–$$$$ ⛫ **Leonardo.** Along with the usual singles, doubles, and suites, apartments are offered here at this enviable location: a quiet street near the Vltava River. Rooms are modern with art-deco flourishes (bentwood armchairs, ornate sconces), in a brown and orange palette. The upbeat and helpful staff is a huge plus in a city not known for quality service. The four top-floor junior suites look out on the river, Prague Castle, and the Charles Bridge, but note that other top-floor rooms have smaller windows with limited views. **Pros:** great location adjacent to the National Theater; extremely friendly, available, and helpful staff; Wi-Fi on ground floor, including the courtyard. **Cons:** the breakfast room is small, and tables fill quickly; busy with street life around the clock. ⊠ *Karolíny Světlé 27, Staré Město* ☎ *239–009–239* ⊕ *www.hotelleonardo.cz* ↗ *50 rooms, 11 suites* ⚭ *In-room: a/c, safe, Wi-Fi (free). In-hotel: restaurant, Wi-Fi hotspot, some pets allowed (fee)* ⊟ *AE, DC, MC, V* ⊺○⏑ *BP* Ⓜ *Line A: Staroměstská* ✛ *E4.*

$$$$ ⛫ **Mamaison Suite Hotel Pachtuv Palace.** Made from four structures—a
Fodor's Choice   baroque palace, two medieval houses, and a neoclassical building from
★   1836—the Pachtuv Palace can't really be matched for authenticity. The 50-room, all-suite hotel sits next to the river, just a (very old) stone's throw from the Charles Bridge near Karlové Lazne, right at the edge of the Old Town fray. That hum of humanity can seep into the rooms, thanks to the tram and foot traffic along the quay. Still, with springy two-poster beds, views of Prague Castle, Malá Strana, and the river, decadent chandeliers, and hardwood floors, the rooms are spacious and

Mamaison Suite Hotel Pachtuv Palace

The Augustine

opulent. Mozart, though, may not have agreed: legend has it that he was locked inside a room until he wrote six sonatas for the owner. **Pros:** lavish breakfast spread; friendly service; giant rooms. **Cons:** tetchy HVAC; street noise. ⊠ *Karolíny Světlé 34, Staré Město* ☎ *234–705–111* ⊕ *www. mamaison.com/pachtuvpalace* ➪ *50 rooms* ⋀ *In-room: a/c, safe, DVD, Internet. In-hotel: room service, gym, parking (paid)* ⊟ *AE, DC, MC, V* ⎮⊚⎮ *BP* Ⓜ *Line A: Staroměstská* ✢ *E4.*

$$$ 🔟 **Maximilian.** Architect Eva Jiricna spearheaded a rehab of this property in 2005, and the end result was an extreme Czech-ification (design-wise, at least). The hotel is chockablock with Modernist details like chrome lamps and graphically square armchairs. Downstairs, the lounge spaces are practically furniture showrooms of '20 s and '30 s style, with Czech graphic artists represented on the walls. Rooms continue the masculine, streamlined look to period perfection. But between the browns, blacks, and blues, it can get a bit dark; the tired, harshly lit bathrooms certainly don't lift the mood. What is mood lifting is the Zen Wellness spa in the hotel. A gym and sauna are at the Josef, a sister hotel around the way. The location can't be beat, either, next to two of the city's best restaurants and a five-minute walk from Old Town Square or the Náměstí Republiky metro station. **Pros:** a must-see for design aficionados; great breakfast spread; prime location. **Cons:** tired bathrooms; no restaurant in the hotel. ⊠ *Haštalská 14, Staré Město* ☎ *225–303–118* ⊕ *www. maximilianhotel.com* ➪ *70 rooms, 1 suite* ⋀ *In-room: a/c, safe, DVD, Internet. In-hotel: restaurant, room service, laundry service, parking (paid), some pets allowed (fee)* ⊟ *AE, DC, MC, V* ⎮⊚⎮ *BP* Ⓜ *Line A: Staroměstská* ✢ *G2.*

$$$ 🔟 **Residence 7 Angels.** In a residence that originally dates from 1411, this hotel offers a great location, not far from Old Town Square's Astronomical Clock. Rooms are divided between those with baroque details (massive wood headboards, brocaded curtains, gilt-framed mirrors), and those with a more modern look (glass coffee tables and white-leather couches). An adorable restaurant on-site serves Czech food paired with Moravian wines and live Gypsy music. Out of season you can sometimes find tremendous deals. **Pros:** spacious rooms, some with frescoes; charming restaurant. **Cons:** the courtyard is unattractive; rooms can be difficult to get to, especially for those with disabilities. ⊠ *Jilská 20, Staré Město* ☎ *224–234–381* ⊕ *www.7angels.cz* ➪ *6 rooms, 4 suites* ⋀ *In-room: no a/c, kitchen (some). In-hotel: restaurant, laundry service* ⊟ *AE, MC, V* ⎮⊚⎮ *BP* Ⓜ *Line A: Můstek* ✢ *F4.*

$ 🔟 **Unitas Hotel.** The rooms of this former convent, now operated by the Christian charity Unitas, once served as interrogation cells for the communist secret police. (Václav Havel was once a "guest.") Until recently, the property was also used as a prison hostel, and guests could actually stay in Havel's old room (there are plans in place to make this part of the building into a museum). But rooms betray nothing of this gloomy past; they're now cleaned, buffed, and looking somewhat airy, light, and modern, with pine furniture and beige linens. **Pros:** clean rooms; friendly staff; great location on a quiet street. **Cons:** some guests might find the decor too simple and uninspiring. ⊠ *Bartolomějská 9, Staré Město* ☎ *224–230–533* ⊕ *www.unitas.cz* ➪ *22* ⋀ *In-room: a/c,* *safe, DVD, Wi-Fi. In-hotel: restaurant, bar* ⊟ *AE, DC, MC, V* ⵔ *BP* Ⓜ *Line A: Staroměstská* ✛ *E4.*

$$ Ⓣ **U Zlatého Jelena.** Authentically austere, what U Zlatého Jelena lacks in personality and amenities it makes up for with a killer location off Old Town Square. With parquet floors, wooden furniture, and metal bed frames, rooms are not so much warm as functional, but the staff is honest and helpful, and these are probably the largest rooms you will find in the city center without spending a fortune at

a four-star hotel. (Online booking is recommended for better rates.) **Pros:** excellent location; large rooms. **Cons:** no air-conditioning; street noise in non-courtyard rooms. ⊠ *Celetná 11, Staré Město* ☎ *222–317–237* ⊕ *www.beetle-tour.cz* ⟳ *19 rooms* ⅋ *In-room: no a/c, safe, DVD (some), Wi-Fi. In-hotel: restaurant, some pets allowed (fee)* ⊟ *AE, DC, MC, V* ⵔ *CP* Ⓜ *Line A: Staroměstská* ✛ *G3.*

MALÁ STRANA (LESSER QUARTER)

With a bewitching storybook suite of baroque palaces and Renaissance façades, the Lesser Quarter—at the other end of the Charles Bridge from the Old Town—is the darling of Prague. Mostly a quiet area, removed from the bustle across the river, it's also filled with great restaurants and music clubs. Malá Strana provides an excellent location for visiting Prague Castle just up the hill, but may not be the best choice for people with mobility problems. Other cons: Car access on the narrow cobblestone streets is restricted, parking is difficult, and you'll spend a lot of your time walking on the Charles Bridge to get to the Old Town.

$$$$ Ⓣ **Alchymist Grand Hotel and Spa.** A baroque fever dream of Prague
Fodor'sChoice masterminded by an Italian developer, the Alchymist doesn't go the
★ understated route. With filigreed designs; a front courtyard with a koi pond and a bridge; room after room of intricate, gilded designs stitched together by a 500-year-old staircase; and topped off with a UNESCO-protected façade, it's the living definition of *de trop*. Thankfully, that's what makes it so darn fun. And the little extras just embellish all that glamour, including bedding that looks and feels as if it's fit for a Renaissance queen, wood floors and ceilings with painted designs, and a small but excellent spa. Downstairs, the lobby is a warren of rooms, which can be particularly frustrating when you want to find the complimentary afternoon wine tastings. The bathrooms are big, but they are combination shower/tubs, a bit of a disappointment at this price. **Pros:** unique design; high-quality spa. **Cons:** steep uphill walk from the tram; loud a/c. ⊠ *Tržiště 19, Malá Strana* ☎ *257–286–011-016* ⊕ *www. alchymisthotelresidence.com* ⟳ *26 rooms, 20 suites* ⅋ *In-room: a/c, safe, DVD, Internet. In-hotel: restaurant, gym, spa, laundry service* ⊟ *AE, DC, MC, V* ⵔ *BP* Ⓜ *Line A: Malostranská* ✛ *B3.*

Lodging Alternatives

APARTMENT RENTALS

Apartment rentals are a fantastic—and cheaper—option for those traveling in a group, or simply for those who prefer to have their own space and actually eat a few meals at home. Gorgeous apartment rentals can be found, from modern with a swimming pool to a more local decor (read: Ikea bric-a-brac and a dash of communist kitsch). As a fact, many rentals tend to be in the center and remarkably less expensive than surrounding hotels, but you don't get the *International Herald Tribune* brought with your breakfast or someone to turn down your bed in the evening. A longer stay usually guarantees some kind of discount.

If you're looking for an apartment, consider the following agencies:

Mary's Travel & Tourist Services. Agents have been known to go beyond the call of duty to ensure a safe landing for guests—especially after planes have been delayed past work hours. Their extra efforts have earned this company one of the best reputations in town. Arranging mostly stays in hotels, guesthouses, and apartments, they have a great selection in Old Town, many of which come with cleaning services. They also can arrange out-of-town stays. ⊠ *Italská 31, Vinohrady* ☎ *222–254–007* ⊕ *www.marys.cz.*

Myway Rentals. Focusing on an intimate neighborhood in Malá Strana, this young owner has frequent contact with the area's inventory, and ensures top service. ⊠ *Jánsky vršek 8, Malá Strana* ☎ *257–941–766* ⊕ *www. mywayrentals.com.*

Prague Accommodation Service. A frankly named agency that can help you find a reasonably priced apartment in the center of town for even a short stay. The prices are some of the cheapest around, but note that many of their apartments are somewhat simple when it comes to design. ⊠ *Platnerská 4, Staré Město* ☎ *224–933–257* ⊕ *www. accommodation-prague-centre.cz.*

Residence Belgicka. For luxury and comfort, you cannot beat this Vinohrady-based apartment complex managed by the same folks as the Riverside and the Pachtuv Palace, excellent for those staying for an extended period of time. The amenities are absolutely first-rate compared with other apartments, with DVD players, cable TV, high-speed Internet, Wi-Fi, access to a swimming pool, sauna, and gym in another residence, and the list goes on. ⊠ *Belgická 12, Vinohrady* ☎ *221–401–800* ⊕ *www. mamaison.com.*

Stop City. From rooms to apartments to hotels, this company in Prague 2 can score cheap deals for you in the city center. Nothing fancy for the most part, but the rates are some of the best. ⊠ *Vinohradská 24, Vinohrady* ☎ *222–521–233* ⊕ *www.stopcity.com.*

HOSTELS

No matter what your age, you can save on lodging costs by staying at hostels. In some 4,500 locations in more than 70 countries around the world, Hostelling International (HI), the umbrella group for a number of national youth-hostel associations, offers single-sex, dorm-style beds and, at many hostels, rooms for couples or family accommodations. Membership in any HI national hostel association, open to travelers of all ages, allows you to stay in HI-affiliated hostels at member rates; one-year membership is about $28 for adults (C$35 for a two-year minimum membership in Canada, £16 in U.K., A$32 in Australia, and NZ$40 in New Zealand); hostels charge about $10–$30 per night. Members have priority if the hostel is full; they're also eligible for discounts around the world, even on rail and bus travel in some countries. For more information about hosteling, contact your local youth hostel office.

Hostelling International—USA (✉ 8401 Colesville Rd., Suite 600, Silver Spring, MD ☎ 301/495-1240 ⊕ www.hiusa.org).

In the Czech Republic hostels are geared to the college crowd. For further information, visit the Web site ⊕ Backpackers.cz.

The **Clown & Bard** (✉ Bořivojova 102, Žižkov ☎ 222-716-453 ⊕ www. clownandbard.com) is a perfect choice if you want to meet other up-all-night travelers. The rates go from 250 Kč for a dorm room to 1,400 Kč for a two-person double with private bathroom.

A central favorite close to all the bars and shopping is the **Golden Sickle** (✉ Vodičkova 12, Nové Město ☎ 222-230-773 ⊕ www. golden-sickle.prague-hostels.cz). Rates range from 420 Kč for a bed in a dormitory-style room to 2,000 Kč for a four-bed apartment. At the Internet-equipped **Travellers' Hostel** (✉ Dlouhá 33, Staré Město ☎ 224-826-662 ⊕ www. travellers.cz) rates range from 350 Kč for a bed in a dormitory-style room to 1,190 Kč for a single room with a shower.

HOME SWAPPING

If you would like to exchange your home for someone else's, join a home-exchange organization.

There are two major U.S.-based home exchange organizations.**HomeLink International** (✉ 2937 N.W. 9th Terrace, Fort Lauderdale, FL ☎ 954/566-2687 or 800/638-3841 ⊕ www. homelink.org); $115 yearly for a listing and online access. **Intervac U.S** (✉ 30 Corte San Fernando, Tiburon, CA ☎ 800/756-4663 ⊕ www.intervacus. com); $99 yearly for a listing and online access.

PRIVATE ROOMS

A private room can be a cheaper and more interesting alternative to a hotel. You can find agencies offering such accommodations all over Prague, including at the main train station Hlavní nádraží), Holešovice Station (Nádraží Holešovice), and at Ruzyně Airport. These bureaus usually are staffed with people who speak some English, and most can book rooms in hotels and pensions as well as private accommodations. Rates for private rooms start at around 400 Kč per person per night, but can go much higher for better-quality rooms. In general, there's no fee, but you may need to try several bureaus to find the accommodation you want. Ask to see a photo of the room before accepting it, and be sure to pinpoint its location on a map—you don't want to wind up in an inconvenient location. If you're approached by someone in the stations hawking rooms with a deal, you should be wary of them. **Prague Information Service** arranges lodging from all its central offices, including the branch in the main train station, which is in the booth marked TURISTICKÉ INFORMACE on the left side of the main hall as you exit the station.

$$$$ ⬚ **Aria Hotel.** Back in the early 2000s, this property kicked off Prague's hotel boom, and it still holds up well today against the (considerably more expensive) competition. Sure, the music theme is really an excuse to give guests their own iPods—a detail that isn't as glitzy today as it was 10 years ago—but that's quite forgivable considering that the hotel also hosts live concerts and even has an on-site music librarian. Rooms are sleek, done up in sandy tones with red punctuations, flat-screens TVs, and spacious, well-lit bathrooms. But the star attractions here are the restaurant's rooftop terrace, which has some of the best views of Prague in the city, and the courtyard with steps leading up to the Castle Area. (A close runner-up is the plush mini–movie theater.) Though it's at the base of the street leading to the American embassy, there are still plenty of bars and restaurants at hand. **Pros:** gorgeous gardens make for a quiet escape; excellent breakfast; LCD televisions in all rooms, along with killer sound systems. **Cons:** proximity to the embassy can lead to tiresome security checks; iPods are begging to be lost. ⊠ *Tržiště 9, Malá Strana* ☎ *225–334–111* ⊕ *www.ariahotel.net* ⟿ *52 rooms, 7 suites* ⌂ *In-room: a/c, safe, DVD, Internet. In-hotel: restaurant, room service, gym, parking (paid)* ⊟ *AE, DC, MC, V* |⊙| *BP* Ⓜ *Line A: Malostranská* ⊹ *B3.*

$$$$
Fodor's Choice
★
⬚ **The Augustine.** There's plenty of competition in Prague's high-end hotel market, but Rocco Forte's Augustine has vaulted to the top. How did they pull it off? First, there's the historic location, converted from a 13th-century monastery, with several monks still living on the grounds. Then there's the impeccable service. And finally, the rooms themselves: designed by Olga Polizzi, they incorporate modernist and cubist furniture designs—chaises, dressers—and art from '20s and '30s Czechoslovakia, splashes of color on the unfinished wood floors. Bathrooms are spacious, with polished marble floors, rainfall showers, and expansive tubs. (Check out those television sets in the wall.) Some rooms even incorporate old bits of the monastery, like a 300-year-old door and doorframe. The spa isn't left out of this Czech theme, with treatments that involve beer brewed by the monks; there's a bar in the cellar where the monks used to do exactly that, as well as a more formal continental restaurant upstairs. There may be other five-star hotels in the city, but the Augustine is the first to reflect Prague's own beauty back. **Pros:** impeccable service; clever design; impressive spa. **Cons:** outrageously expensive Internet fees; noisy floors. ⊠ *Letenská 12, Malá Strana* ☎ *266–112–233* ⊕ *www.theaugustine.com* ⟿ *101 rooms, 16 suites* ⌂ *In-room: a/c, DVD, Internet (fee). In-hotel: 2 restaurants, room service, bars, gym, spa, laundry service, Wi-Fi hotspot, parking (paid)* ⊟ *AE, D, DC, MC, V* |⊙| *EP* Ⓜ *Line A: Malostranská* ⊹ *C2.*

$$ ⬚ **Best Western Hotel Kampa.** This early-baroque armory-turned-hotel is tucked away on an abundantly picturesque street at the southern end of Malá Strana, just off Kampa Island. Rooms offer the standard comforts you'd expect from a European Best Western, and the building features a few nice period details. (Note the late-Gothic vaulting in the massive dining room.) At one time the bucolic setting and proximity to the city center made this lodging option a comparative bargain; now hotels within blocks offer superior service at more competitive prices. It's a good fallback option if you absolutely must stay on Kampa. **Pros:** location is gorgeously positioned by Kampa Park; buffet breakfast is satisfying. **Cons:** indifferent staff; some rooms are cramped. ⊠ *Všehrdova 16, Malá Strana* ☎ *257–404–444 or 257–404–333* ⊕ *www.bestwestern-ce. com* ⇨ *85 rooms* ⌂ *In-room: no a/c. In-hotel: restaurant* ☰ *AE, MC, V* ⎟⊘⎟ *BP* Ⓜ *Line A: Malostranská* ✛ *C4.*

$$ 🏨 **Dům U Červeného Lva** *(House at the Red Lion).* An intimate, immaculately kept baroque building dating from the 15th century, this hotel is right on the main thoroughfare in the Lesser Quarter, a five-minute walk from Prague Castle's front gates. Guest rooms have parquet floors and 17th-century painted-beam ceilings. But a workout is included: there is no elevator, and the stairs are steep. **Pros:** the rooms are unique and intimate. **Cons:** no elevator—and no air-conditioning. ⊠ *Nerudova 41, Malá Strana* ☎ *257–533–833* ⊕ *www.hotelredlion.com* ⇨ *6 rooms* ⌂ *In-room: no a/c, safe. In-hotel: 2 restaurants, bar, some pets allowed* ☰ *AE, DC, MC, V* ⎟⊘⎟ *BP* Ⓜ *Line A: Malostranská* ✛ *A3.*

$$$ 🏨 **Golden Well.** Consistently rated one of Prague's best hotels, the Golden
Fodor's Choice Well is hidden away at the top of a narrow side street in Malá Strana.
★ Effectively built into the side of the hill below Prague Castle, the location makes for some spectacular views of the city. Rooms are done in a classic Renaissance style, some with original ceiling beams, although the age of the building means that electrical outlets are in short supply. Bathrooms are spacious—some rooms even come with Jacuzzis—and Molton Brown toiletries are a treat. Upstairs, the eponymous restaurant has a beautiful terrace for afternoon cocktails; in the morning, breakfast is served here with a panoramic view of Prague. But what most distinguishes the Golden Well is its staff; it's easily the best, and friendliest, in Prague, no small accomplishment in a city renown for surly service. **Pros:** great views; friendly service; spacious rooms. **Cons:** outlet shortage; slow Internet; far from the subway and tram stop. ⊠ *U Zlate Studne 4, Malá Strana* ☎ *257–011–213* ⊕ *www.goldenwell.cz* ⇨ *17 rooms, 2 suites* ⌂ *In-room: a/c, safe, Wi-Fi. In-hotel: restaurant, laundry service, Internet terminal, Wi-Fi hotspot* ☰ *AE, D, DC, MC, V* ⎟⊘⎟ *EP* Ⓜ *Line A: Malostranská* ✛ *B2.*

$$$–$$$$ 🏨 **Hotel Neruda.** Built in 1348, this landmark—now a small and modern hotel—is where the author Jan Neruda and his mother lived in 1860. As a tribute, lines from Neruda's *Povidky malostranske (Malá Strana Stories)* are painted in the stone hallways. The building supposedly has a ghost—you might hear her and her jingling keys in the hallway. Designed by Bořek Šipek, many of the rooms have splashes of color and flashy designer touches like a bathtub enclosed in glass in the center of the room. Try to see a couple of rooms before choosing one, as some rooms look out onto a wall. **Pros:** designer rooms have lots of character; historic location. **Cons:** design impinges on the livability and functionality of the hotel; street noise from rooms facing outward. ⊠ *Nerudova 44, Malá Strana* ☎ *257–535–557* ⊕ *www.hotelneruda. cz* ⇨ *20 rooms* ⌂ *In-room: a/c, safe, Wi-Fi (fee). In-hotel: restaurant, parking (paid), some pets allowed (fee)* ☰ *AE, DC, MC, V* ⎟⊘⎟ *BP* Ⓜ *Line A: Malostranská* ✛ *A3.*

Golden Well

Mandarin Oriental Prague

$$$ ⛼ **Hotel Roma**. Down the hill from Prague Castle, across the street from Petřín hill, and around the corner from Kampa Island, this hotel is nestled in the middle of some star attractions. The atrium lobby is a bit bland, but a few funky details, including an aquarium window in the lobby wall, give the place some character. Most rooms are simple and spare, with blond-wood furnishings and parquet floors. The Roma also offers suites, eight with real antiques—unfortunately, that also means two single beds with bumping headboards are pushed together; if desired, ensure that you are getting a proper double bed when booking your room. **Pros:** even though the hotel is situated on a street with a tram, it is surprisingly quiet; large bathrooms with bathtubs; friendly staff; free Internet in rooms; sauna. **Cons:** rooms with tiled floors are cold and make for noisy neighbors; pillows could be fluffier. ⊠ *Újezd 24, Malá Strana* ☎ *257–326–890* ⊕ *www.hotelroma.cz* ⇥ *62 rooms, 25 suites* ⟨ *In-room: a/c, safe, Internet, Wi-Fi (some). In-hotel: restaurant, bar, gym, laundry service, Internet terminal, parking (paid), some pets allowed (fee)* ▭ *AE, DC, MC, V* ⊙ *BP* Ⓜ *Line A: Malostranská* ✛ *B5.*

$$$$ ⛼ **Mandarin Oriental Prague**. A huge win for the city when it opened in
⟳ 2006, the Mandarin remains a top choice for Prague. Wisely, the hotel
Fodor's Choice steps outside the Mandarin brand, incorporating the site's history and
★ "Czech-ness." Housed in a former monastery just off Maltese Square, it retains a peaceful, meditative quality. Touches of what used to be remain. Take a look at the glass floor en route to the spa that displays the ruins of a Gothic church. Rooms are swathed in rich navy linens, and beds are among Prague's best; alas, the space is a bit cramped for the price, and the small (or rather, authentically small) windows don't help. But you'll find breathing room in the spa, which incorporates local botanicals (like linden blossoms) in treatments. Another highlight is the hotel's restaurant, Essensia, which splits its menu between locally sourced Czech dishes and Asian fare. Parents take note: children are given a toy on arrival, as well as special toiletries (including a rubber ducky). **Pros:** boffo spa; attentive service; comfy beds. **Cons:** some rooms are small or dark; pricey Internet is wired only; big breakfast spread is expensive. ⊠ *Nebovidská 459, Malá Strana* ☎ *233–088–888* ⊕ *www.mandarinoriental.com* ⇥ *99 rooms, 22 suites* ⟨ *In-room: a/c, safe, DVD, Internet. In-hotel: restaurant, bars, gym, spa, laundry service, Wi-Fi hotspot, parking (paid)* ▭ *AE, DC, MC, V* ⊙ *EP* Ⓜ *Line A: Malostranská* ✛ *C4.*

$$–$$$ ⛼ **Sax Vintage Design Hotel**. It is almost impossible to capture the ambi-
Fodor's Choice ence of this hotel in words without ingesting some sort of hallucino-
★ gen. The interior design is an explosion, and celebration, of all things excellent during the 1950s, '60s, and '70s—and everything, from the lamps to the bar stools, is original, believe it or not. Rooms keep the cheerfully retro vibes going with mushroom lamps and copious amounts of orange. The hotel staff even goes the extra mile and offers happy hour between 4 and 6 PM every day, including free wine, beer, and homemade pastries (also, in true '70s style, a bowl of salty snacks is always available in the lounge). The design is loud, intrusive, and wrong, which is what makes it oh so right. **Pros:** punchy and fun; free happy hour; hotel sits on a quiet street; friendly staff. **Cons:** this

4

might be too much for those with more conservative tastes; for those in Prague for the nightlife, this side of the river might be less than ideal. ⊠ *Jánský vršek 3, Malá Strana* ☎ *257–531–268* ⊕ *www.sax.cz* ⤳ *22 rooms* ⟁ *In-room: a/c, safe, DVD, Internet, Wi-Fi. In-hotel: restaurant, bar, parking (paid), some pets allowed (fee)* ⊟ *AE, DC, MC, V* ⌶⃝ *EP* Ⓜ *Line A: Staroměstská* ✛ *A3.*

$$$ ⌷ **U Tří Pštrosů.** This inviting inn has taken a couple of licks—first it was flooded, then burned to the ground, and then rebuilt, only to be taken by the communists, and finally restituted to the family owners. The location is so close to the Charles Bridge that you could barter with one of the street vendors from your window; it's beautiful, but busy out there. Rooms are spacious, and feature ornate ceilings and antique furniture. Sadly, there is no air-conditioning, but the rooms do have Wi-Fi, so it's behind the times in some ways and ahead in others. **Pros:** location, location, location. **Cons:** small rooms up top; no elevator or a/c. ⊠ *Dražického nám. 12, Malá Strana* ☎ *257–288–888* ⊕ *www.utripstrosu.cz* ⤳ *14 rooms, 4 suites* ⟁ *In-room: no a/c, Wi-Fi. In-hotel: restaurant, laundry service* ⊟ *AE, DC, MC, V* ⌶⃝ *BP* Ⓜ *Line A: Malostranská* ✛ *C3.*

HRADČANY

For some, Prague Castle is the romantic capital in this city. Though it is a hectic spot during the day with a lot of foot traffic, it is quiet and even spacious in the evening; the starlit castle grounds open onto hilly parks perfect for long strolls while drinking in a breathtaking panoramic view of the city.

$$$ ⌷ **Romantik Hotel U Raka.** With the quaint look of a woodsman's cottage from a bedtime story, this private guesthouse has a quiet location on the ancient, winding street of Nový Svět, just behind the Loreto Church and a 10-minute walk from Prague Castle. As the name says, the site is saturated with romance. One side of the 18th-century building presents a rare example of half-timbering, and the rooms sustain the country feel. A little luck is needed reserving one of the six rooms, but it does make a wonderful base for exploring Prague. **Pros:** near Prague Castle, but secluded for those who truly want to get away; in-room fireplaces in some rooms; free Wi-Fi throughout. **Cons:** tiny size makes rooms hard to come by; cramped breakfast area. ⊠ *Černínská 10/93, Hradčany* ☎ *220–511–100* ⊕ *www.romantikhotel-uraka.cz* ⤳ *5 rooms, 1 suite* ⟁ *In-room: a/c, Internet. In-hotel: Wi-Fi hotspot, parking (paid), no kids under 10* ⊟ *AE, MC, V* ⌶⃝ *BP* Ⓜ *Line A: Hradčanská* ✛ *A2.*

$$$–$$$$ ⌷ **Savoy.** A modest yellow Jugendstil façade conceals one of the city's most luxurious small hotels. Once a budget hotel, the building was gutted and lavishly refurbished in the mid-1990s. Today the rooms are a palette of primary colors: blue carpeting, pale yellow walls, and red bedspreads anchor traditional furnishings. A tram stop is practically at the front door, making trips into the center quick and easy, or you can walk downhill through the vineyards surrounding the Castle. **Pros:** peaceful location above it all; chipper lobby bar. **Cons:** long (uphill) walk home as it's away from the center; indifferent staff at times. ⊠ *Keplerova 6,*

Hradčany ☎ *224–302–430* ⊕ *www.hotel-savoy.cz* ➴ *55 rooms, 6 suites* ⚹ *In-room: a/c, safe, DVD, Wi-Fi. In-hotel: restaurant, gym, some pets allowed (fee)* ▭ *AE, DC, MC, V* |◎| *BP* Ⓜ *Line A: Hradčanská* ⊹ *A3.*

NOVÉ MĚSTO (NEW TOWN)

Not exactly "new," this district dates back to the 14th century, and includes the bustling Wenceslas Square. New Town isn't as clean and architecturally fragile as Old Town, but what it loses in baroque curls it makes up for in good location at slightly cheaper prices.

$$ ⌂ **Best Western City Hotel Moran.** This renovated 19th-century town house is a comfortable choice for those who want consistency in the quality of their accommodations. A bright, inviting lobby leads to equally bright, clean rooms, with some good views of Prague Castle if you're on an upper floor. **Pros:** comfortable beds in spacious rooms. **Cons:** rooms facing the tram street can be noisy for lighter sleepers; though in the city center, the location is in New Town, and can be considered a far walk from Old Town Square for the less active. ⊠ *Na Moráni 15, Nové Město* ☎ *224–915–208* ⊕ *www.bestwestern-ce.com/moran* ➴ *57 rooms* ⚹ *In-room: a/c, Wi-Fi. In-hotel: restaurant, some pets allowed* ▭ *AE, DC, MC, V* |◎| *BP* Ⓜ *Line B: Karlovo nám* ⊹ *E6.*

$$$ ⌂ **Best Western Meteor Plaza.** This hotel is a meeting of two times: Modern conveniences in a blue-blooded historic building (Empress Maria Theresa's son, Joseph II, stayed here when he was passing through in the 18th century). The baroque building is five minutes on foot from downtown. Renovations and generic room decor have masked much of the hotel's history behind a modern look. To get a sense of its age, visit the original 14th-century wine cellar. **Pros:** just a few steps from the Municipal House; clean rooms. **Cons:** interior is a bit drab for some tastes; breakfast room can fill up quickly. ⊠ *Hybernská 6, Nové Město* ☎ *224–192–559 or 224–192–111* ⊕ *www.hotel-meteor.cz* ➴ *90 rooms, 6 suites* ⚹ *In-room: a/c, Wi-Fi. In-hotel: restaurant, gym, parking (paid)* ▭ *AE, DC, MC, V* |◎| *BP* Ⓜ *Line B: Nám. Republiky* ⊹ *H3.*

$$$$ ⌂ **Carlo IV.** Dripping with glamour, this Italian-owned hotel has an imperial beauty. High ceilings present space for towering palm trees, and playful design touches like gargantuan floor lamps and an enormous umbrella lend it an Alice in Wonderland quality. Unfortunately, on closer inspection some of the details are more real world than wonderland, with carpeting in the rooms in need of repair and indifferent service. Still, there are plenty of luxe touches, particularly the excellent bedding, a cigar bar, and one of the oldest cognac vaults in Europe. The rooms in the original building are more antique in style, while modern rooms are available in the adjoining building. **Pros:** luxurious feel; cushy linens. **Cons:** a sometimes rude staff; breakfast is €25, and is not included in the room rate; tired carpeting and wallpaper. ⊠ *Senovážné nám. 13, Nové Město* ☎ *224–593–090* ⊕ *www.boscolohotels.com* ➴ *130 rooms, 22 suites* ⚹ *In-room: a/c, safe, Internet. In-hotel: restaurant, bars, pool, gym, laundry service, parking (paid), some pets allowed (fee)* ▭ *AE, DC, MC, V* |◎| *EP* Ⓜ *Line B: Nám. Republiky* ⊹ *H4.*

$$$ ⊡**Hotel Élite Prague.** A 14th-century Gothic façade and many poetic architectural details have been preserved in this hotel, thanks to an extensive renovation. Rooms are furnished with antiques, and many have decorated Renaissance-style wooden beams. One of the suites is even adorned with a frescoed ceiling. But rest assured that they did not forsake modern comforts: this is also a Wi-Fi hotspot. **Pros:** near the National Theater and a nice walk along the river from the Charles Bridge; free Wi-Fi. **Cons:** two rooms don't have air-conditioning, make note of this when booking; breakfast room can be cumbersome. ⊠ *Ostrovní 32, Nové Město* ☎ *224–932–250* ⊕ *www.hotelelite.cz* ⟿ *77 rooms, 2 suites* ⅙ *In-room: a/c, safe, Wi-Fi. In-hotel: restaurant, room service, bar, laundry service, parking (paid), some pets allowed (fee)* ▭ *AE, DC, MC, V* ⦿⧘ *BP* Ⓜ *Line B: Národní Třída* ✚ *E5.*

$$$$ ⊡**Hotel Palace Praha.** Perched on a busy corner in the city center, this pistachio-green art nouveau building trumpets its Victorian origins. Inside, rooms add to the ice-cream parlor color scheme with icy white marble bathrooms, pale yellow walls, and red velvet beds with canopies. The hotel restaurant is similarly lush: think saddle of venison and well-constructed cream sauces. A block from Wenceslas Square and adjacent to the shopping bonanza of Na Příkopě, the advantage here is location, which puts it ahead of other hotels in its class. **Pros:** helpful and knowledgeable staff; hotel sits in a great location only a short walk away from Wenceslas Square. **Cons:** wonky HVAC; gilded European style not for everyone. ⊠ *Panská 12, Nové Město* ☎ *224–093–111* ⊕ *www.palacehotel.cz* ⟿ *114 rooms, 10 suites* ⅙ *In-room: a/c, safe, Internet. In-hotel: 2 restaurants, laundry service* ▭ *AE, DC, MC, V* ⦿⧘ *BP* Ⓜ *Line A: Můstek* ✚ *G4.*

$–$$ ⊡**Hotel Salvator.** This efficiently run establishment just outside the Old
Fodor'sChoice Town offers more comforts than most in its class, including flat-screen
★   TVs and minibars in some rooms. Couple that with a prime location and low, low prices, and overall it's a good value. Rooms face either the street or the interior garden, and while the amenities are limited, they do offer free Wi-Fi, which is better than many top-tier hotels. Two rooms on the top floor have air-conditioning; however, there are portable air-conditioners that can be requested from the front desk. **Pros:** delicious and reasonably priced restaurant; large rooms; pool table and salon in the basement. **Cons:** rooms face the courtyard, where restaurant seating is available, so noise can be a problem at mealtimes; more discerning guests might find the furnishings dated. ⊠ *Truhlářská 10, Nové Město* ☎ *222–312–234* ⊕ *www.salvator.cz* ⟿ *28 rooms, 16 with bath; 7 suites* ⅙ *In-room: no a/c (some). In-hotel: restaurant, bar, parking (paid), some pets allowed (fee)* ▭ *AE, MC, V* ⦿⧘ *BP* Ⓜ *Line B: Nám. Republiky* ✚ *H2.*

$$$ ⊡**Hotel Yasmin.** A sprightly presence on a imperious street (it's just up the road from the Communist Party Headquarters), the Yasmin offers modern design at good prices. The rooms are decked out in a white and sage-green color scheme, which is cheerful, though neither color holds up well to wear and tear. Even the smaller rooms come with a table to sit at, and all boast a flat-screen TV, spacious black-tile bathroom, and view of the courtyard. Downstairs the snack-filled breakfast area teems with life in the morning, only to turn into a globally themed pasta restaurant called Noodles in the evening. Though this street is quiet, the location is a stone's throw to Wencelsas Square's attractions. **Pros:** Wenceslas Square adjacent; tasty breakfast spread; free access to sauna and gym. **Cons:** small rooms; slow, overworked elevator; carpeting in need of replacement. ⊠ *Politickych Veznu 12/913, Nové Město* ☏ *221–427–000* ⊕ *www.hotel-yasmin.cz* ⟿ *187 rooms, 11 suites* ⌂ *In-room: a/c, safe, Internet. In-hotel: restaurant, bar, gym, parking (paid), some pets allowed* ⊟ *AE, DC, MC, V* ⟡|*CP* Ⓜ *Line A: Můstek* ✛ *H5.*

$$$–$$$$ ⊡ **Icon Hotel & Lounge.** From its Diesel-clad and hair-gelled staff to its marshmallow-like Hästens beds, this hotel is dressed to impress, and has been attracting a lot of attention since it entered the hotel scene in 2007. The motto is "service with a sense of fun," but the real pleasure of the hotel is not so much the fun as its attention to detail—from Skype phones in rooms to biometric (yes, fingerprint) safes that fit laptops to hip furniture that's all made locally. Rooms have touches of gold and purple that would make Prince proud. Needless to say, this property is for the type of traveler that would embrace its Eurodisco trimmings. **Pros:** cushy beds; all-day breakfast spread; near expat hangout Jama. **Cons:** spa a bit too technofied; surly restaurant staff. ⊠ *V jámě 6, Nové Město* ☏ *221–634–100* ⊕ *www.iconhotel.eu* ⟿ *29 rooms, 2 suites* ⌂ *In-room: a/c, safe, DVD, Wi-Fi. In-hotel: restaurant, bar, spa, parking (paid), some pets allowed (fee)* ⊟ *AE, DC, MC, V* ⟡|*EP* Ⓜ *Line A: Můstek* ✛ *G5.*

$$$ ⊡ **Opera.** This hotel rejuvenated its grand fin-de-siècle façade with a perky pink-and-white exterior paint job. Inside, the rooms are done in the traditional Czech style, with blond-wood cabinetry, floral-patterned wooden chairs, and old-school red carpeting. Near the Florenc metro, it's not the best location, though it's convenient to trams and two subway lines. **Pros:** clean rooms; large bathrooms. **Cons:** some top-floor rooms have an obstructed view; a long walk to Old Town Square—it could take 15 minutes. ⊠ *Těšnov 13, Nové Město* ☏ *222–315–609* ⊕ *www.hotel-opera.cz* ⟿ *65 rooms, 2 suites* ⌂ *In-room: a/c, safe, Internet, Wi-Fi. In-hotel: restaurant, bar, gym, parking (paid), some pets allowed (fee)* ⊟ *AE, DC, MC, V* ⟡|*BP* Ⓜ *Line C: Florenc* ✛ *H2.*

$$$ ⊡ **Radisson Blu Alcron Hotel.** Opened in 1932, the Alcron was one of Prague's first luxury hotels; a major renovation of the building in 1998 modernized the look but restored the art deco building and the crystal chandeliers. The dramatic white-marble staircase front and center is bound to impress. The hotel is no longer the luxury leader it was twelve years ago, but that's just fine—it occupies the business niche quite well, outfitting rooms with flat-screen TVs, offering express dry cleaning service, and even placing Villeroy & Boch china and Zenga bath amenities en suite. The restaurant remains one of Prague's best, though it is not cheap in the slightest, but that's not a concern if you can expense it. **Pros:** free Wi-Fi; helpful staff; sweet restaurant. **Cons:** rooms vary in size; conservatively styled rooms compared to the public spaces. ⊠ *Štěpánská 40, Nové Město* ☏ *222–820–000* ⊕ *www.radissonblu.com* ⟿ *192 rooms, 19 suites* ⌂ *In-room: a/c, safe, Wi-Fi. In-hotel: 2 restaurants, bar, gym, laundry service* ⊟ *AE, MC, V* ⟡|*BP* Ⓜ *Line A: Můstek* ✛ *G5.*

VINOHRADY

Literally translated as "vineyards," as this area was many centuries ago, you can still find vestiges of grapevines in parks like Havlíčkovy sady in Prague 10. Today it's home to some of the city's wealthiest residents, and the values of the town houses here have tripled in value in the last decade. For visitors, the wealth means excellent restaurants and pleasant tree-lined streets, perfect for meandering after an exhausting day in the center.

$$ ⊞ **Hotel Anna.** The bright neoclassical façade and art nouveau details have been lovingly restored on this 19th-century building on a quiet residential street. Rooms feature simple wooden furniture and chic black-and-white photos of Prague. Suites on the top floors offer a nice view of the historic district. In 2002 the hotel opened an annex, the Dependance Anna, in the central courtyard of the block with 12 cheaper rooms, but you must return to the main hotel for breakfast. In an effort to stay competitive, the hotel has Wi-Fi in its recently updated rooms and encourages Internet users to call with questions via Skype. **Pros:** staff is helpful, with an excellent command of English; free Internet. **Cons:** some guests find walls to be too thin; though peaceful, the neighborhood is outside the city center. ⊠ *Budečská 17, Vinohrady* ☎ *222–513–111* ⊕ *www.hotelanna.cz* ⤴ *22 rooms, 2 suites, 12 annex rooms* ⌂ *In-room: no a/c, Wi-Fi (some). In-hotel: Wi-Fi hotspot, some pets allowed (fee)* ⊟ *AE, MC, V* �◎| *BP* Ⓜ *Line A: Nám. Míru* ⊹ *H6.*

$$$$
Fodor's Choice
★ ⊞ **Hotel Le Palais.** Built in 1841, this venerable building served as the home and shop of Prague's main butcher (one of the front rooms was used to produce and sell sausage until 1991). Today you will find sausage only in the distinctive hotel's restaurant. Rooms have original frescoes painted by Bohemian artist Ludek Marold, and a hallway has a mosaic floor from 1897. Some rooms have fireplaces, and all have heated bathroom floors and free access to the gym. **Pros:** divinely gorgeous hotel; wonderfully helpful, courteous staff. **Cons:** nice neighborhood but requires public transit to get anywhere; pricey Internet; small beds in basic rooms. ⊠ *U Zvonařky 1, Vinohrady* ☎ *234–634–111* ⊕ *www.palaishotel.cz* ⤴ *60 rooms, 12 suites* ⌂ *In-room: a/c, DVD, Internet, Wi-Fi (some). In-hotel: restaurant, bar, gym, parking (paid), some pets allowed (fee)* ⊟ *AE, DC, MC, V* ◎| *BP* Ⓜ *Line A: Nám. Míru* ⊹ *E6.*

$ ⊞ **Ibis Wenceslas Square.** The price and the location make this hotel a solid pick. A few minutes' walking distance from Wenceslas Square (despite its name, this is not *on* the square), this is the cheapest air-conditioned place you can find so close to the center. Rooms are without frills, but have everything you would expect from an international chain hotel, including Wi-Fi (€25 per day). If you are looking for a reasonably priced place to sleep but little else, it fits the bill quite nicely. **Pros:** clean rooms; air-conditioning; friendly staff. **Cons:** very little nightlife in the area; except for corner locations, rooms are rather small; price does not include breakfast, which is an additional €10. ⊠ *Kateřinská 36, Vinohrady* ☎ *222–865–777* ⊕ *www.ibishotel.com* ⤴ *181 rooms* ⌂ *In-room: a/c, Wi-Fi (fee). In-hotel: restaurant, some pets allowed (fee)* ⊟ *AE, DC, MC, V* ◎| *EP* Ⓜ *Line C: I. P. Pavlova* ⊹ *E6.*

Hotel Le Palais

ŽIŽKOV

Though Prague is an unbelievably safe city for anyone to amble about in alone, this is one of the seedier parts. It's a bit grittier and louder than other sections. With that said, it is a great neighborhood for extroverts who like student bars, music clubs, and hangouts where a fashion parade of people with piercings, tattoos, dreadlocks, or a dog (and sometimes all of the above) come to socialize. Being an eclectic and punk hood, it may come as little surprise that Žižkov is a popular spot for students or backpackers to stay at a hostel.

$$–$$$ **Amedia Hotel Theatrino.** The keys to this building have passed through many hands—in 1910 it was Žižkov's city hall, then a theater, and under the communists a bar (rumor has it, the upstairs rooms were used as a rendezvous point for couples). Today this hotel, which was rebuilt in 2000, is the nicest spot in this gritty neighborhood. The original art nouveau design was kept and paired with modern accoutrements and clean Scandinavian style; each room comes with its own individual design. **Pros:** Prague's best breakfast; sweet rooms have individual style. **Cons:** long walk into the city center; no a/c (save for the fifth floor); sketchy neighborhood. ⊠ *Bořivojova 53, Žižkov* ☎ *221–422–111* ⊕ *www.amediahotels.com* ✏ *73 rooms* ⚘ *In-room: no a/c (some), safe, Internet, Wi-Fi (some). In-hotel: restaurant, gym, parking (paid), some pets allowed (fee)* ▤ *AE, DC, MC, V* ⧉ *BP* Ⓜ *Line A: Jiřího z Poděbrad* ✛ *H4.*

SMÍCHOV

Smíchov means "mixed neighborhood." When the city had walls, the neighborhood was on the outside, and all manner of people could live there. Although it's still a colorful, working-class area, lots of new construction has made it a shopping and entertainment hub as well, with relatively easy access—via tram, metro, or on foot—to the city's historical center.

$$ **Andel's Hotel Prague.** Right next to one of the city's best shopping malls, this simple, modernist property is where many of the young, up-and-coming British trendsetters stay. And they should feel right at home, considering that the hotel was designed by Britain's Jestico + Whiles. It's popular with the stylish business traveler, too, with airy rooms decorated in a sleek style, glass-walled meeting and conference rooms, and luxury apartments for longer-term stays. **Pros:** great water pressure in showers; wide choice of foods for breakfast. **Cons:** a business hotel, so the breakfast room can be busy in the morning; mall area is long on shopping but short on personality ⊠ *Stroupežnického 21, Smíchov* ☎ *296–889–688* ⊕ *www.andelshotel.com* ✏ *231 rooms, 8 suites* ⚘ *In-room: a/c, safe, DVD, Internet. In-hotel: restaurant, room service, bar, gym, laundry service, parking (paid)* ▤ *AE, DC, MC, V* ⧉ *BP* Ⓜ *Line B: Anděl* ✛ *B6.*

$$ **Arbes Mepro.** For those travelers who like to stay in more "local" spots, this is for you. Smíchov is more of a self-contained neighborhood now than ever before, with sleek Czech restaurants, and the shopping and movie theaters of the Nový Smíchov mall a few shorts steps away.

As a hotel, it's clean, but doesn't go beyond what is necessary to make it outstanding—renovations were completed in 2002, adding new furniture and room safes. The wine cellar serves as a breakfast room, and can be booked for group dinners. It's a 10-minute walk to the historic center; trams are a block away. **Pros:** rooms are airy; the front desk sells metro and tram tickets. **Cons:** still a walk to Old Town; rooms are clean but not especially interesting. ⊠ *Viktora Huga 3, Smíchov* ☎ *257–210–410* ⊕ *www.arbes-mepro.cz* ↩ *27 rooms* ⚫ *In-room: no a/c, safe. In-hotel: bar, parking (paid), some pets allowed (fee)* ⊟ *AE, MC, V* ⫴ *BP* Ⓜ *Line B: Anděl* ⊹ *B6.*

$$ ⌕ **Kinsky Garden.** You could walk the mile from this hotel to Prague Castle entirely on the tree-lined paths of Petřín, the hilly park that starts across the street. Opened in 1997, the hotel takes its name from a garden established by Count Rudolf Kinsky in 1825. The Kinsky is nicer than most hotels at this price, with hardwood floors and flat-screen TVs in every one of its bright rooms. Alas, the beds are on the firm side. Aim for a room on one of the upper floors for a view of the park. **Pros:** great location for runners, as Petřín hill is right across the street; near a tram stop; free Wi-Fi in rooms. **Cons:** at least a 15-minute walk to the Charles Bridge; dysfunctional a/c and street noise make it hard to rest at night. ⊠ *Holečkova 7, Smíchov* ☎ *257–311–173* ⊕ *www. hotelkinskygarden.cz* ↩ *62 rooms* ⚫ *In-room: a/c, Wi-Fi. In-hotel: restaurant, bar, parking (paid), some pets allowed* ⊟ *AE, DC, MC, V* ⫴ *BP* Ⓜ *Line B: Anděl* ⊹ *B6.*

$$$$ ⌕ **Mamaison Hotel Riverside Prague.** True to its name, the Riverside is situated right above the Vltava across from Frank Gehry's Dancing House. The location, just below Malá Strana in Smíchov, makes for unobstructed views of the National Theater as well as of Prague Castle itself; courtyard-facing rooms get balconies as a consolation prize. The look here, designed by Frenchman Pascale de Montremy, differs from the strict modern or overstuffed baroque of many Czech hotels, with a theme of preppy stripes on the curtains and headboards, hardwood floors, and organically shaped bathroom fixtures. (Sometimes things get a bit too wacky; see the confusing shower controls.) There's no fitness center or restaurant, but breakfast is served in a nook in the basement and a mix of European tourists and businesspeople lingers in the houndstooth-patterned chairs by the lobby bar depending on the time of day. **Pros:** clever design; incredible views. **Cons:** no gym; interior rooms are dark. ⊠ *Janáčovo nabř. 15, Smíchov* ☎ *225–994–611* ⊕ *www.mamaison.com/riverside* ↩ *32 rooms, 13 suites* ⚫ *In-room: a/c, safe, Internet. In-hotel: restaurant, room service, bar, laundry service* ⊟ *AE, DC, MC, V* ⫴ *BP* Ⓜ *Line B: Anděl* ⊹ *C6.*

EASTERN SUBURBS

$$ ⌕ **Hotel Astra.** This modern hotel is best for drivers coming into town from the east, although it's also at the very end of the A metro line. The neighborhood is quiet, if ordinary, and the rooms are more comfortable than most in this price range, but unless you absolutely need to be this far out of town, there are better options for the same price. **Pros:** clean hotel; quiet neighborhood (you won't encounter any rowdy stag

parties). **Cons:** very far from the city center; guests are always at the mercy of public transportation or taxi services. ✉ *Mukařovská 1740/18, Stodůlky* ☎ *274–813–595* ⊕ *www.hotelastra.cz* ⤵ *43 rooms, 10 suites* ☄ *In-room: no a/c, Wi-Fi. In-hotel: restaurant, parking (paid), some pets allowed* ▭ *AE, DC, MC, V* ❘O❘ *BP* Ⓜ *Line A: Skalka; then walk south on Na padesátém about 5 min to Mukařovská* ✛ *A6.*

$ 🖭 **Hotel Ibis Karlín.** Minutes from the city center in a peaceful neighborhood with cheap restaurants—not to mention a great wine bar—this hotel offers an excellent way to save money without sacrificing location or cleanliness. **Pros:** it takes a bit of time, but walking to the city center is not out of the question; neighborhood restaurants are good and much cheaper than those in the city center. **Cons:** though clean, rooms could use an update; lighter sleepers might want to request a room away from the tram street; breakfast is an additional €10. ✉ *Šaldova 54, Karlín* ☎ *222–332–800* ⊕ *www.ibishotel.com* ⤵ *226 rooms* ☄ *In-room: a/c, safe. In-hotel: restaurant, parking (paid), some pets allowed* ▭ *AE, DC, MC, V* ❘O❘ *BP* Ⓜ *Line B: Křiříkova* ✛ *H1.*

$$ 🖭 **Hotel Royal Galerie.** A decidedly friendly staff will go out of their way to answer any questions you might have regarding your stay in Prague. Rooms are bland, but the atrium restaurant is relaxing. The neighborhood, which has made a tremendous comeback after the 2002 floods, is laid-back while being only a few tram stops from the center. Though the hotel charges for Wi-Fi in its rooms, it is practically free at 50 Kč for 24 hours. **Pros:** friendly staff; near tram stop, metro stop, and within a healthy walking distance of the city center; sauna available. **Cons:** rooms lack a modern touch; outside the nightlife of Prague. ✉ *Křiříkova 87, Karlín* ☎ *222–323–340* ⊕ *www.royalgalerie.com* ⤵ *22 rooms* ☄ *In-room: no a/c, Wi-Fi (fee)* ▭ *AE, DC, MC, V* ❘O❘ *BP* Ⓜ *Line B: Křiříkova* ✛ *H1.*

WESTERN SUBURBS

$$$$ 🖭 **Hotel Diplomat.** This hotel is a popular choice with business travelers, thanks to its location between the airport and downtown. From the hotel you can easily reach the city center by metro. Dejvice neighborhood is residential, but with plenty of restaurants and bars, it's also quite livable for visitors. Rooms are modern, with flat-screen TVs and high-speed Internet **Pros:** though far outside the city center, the hotel is near both metro and tram stops; quiet hotel. **Cons:** giant number of rooms makes it feel eerie when empty; fee for Internet use in rooms. ✉ *Evropská 15, Dejvice* ☎ *296–559–111* ⊕ *www.diplomatpraha.cz* ⤵ *369 rooms, 13 suites* ☄ *In-room: a/c, Internet. In-hotel: 2 restaurants, bar, gym, parking (paid)* ▭ *AE, DC, MC, V* ❘O❘ *BP* Ⓜ *Line A: Dejvická* ✛ *A1.*

5

The Performing Arts

WORD OF MOUTH

"Prague has an incredible music scene—everything from grand opera to the biggest pop stars to street corner entertainers of all kinds. The prices are generally very low and the quality high. Go to the town hall and get a list of events; there will be many each day. They are often held in churches or municipal buildings; most of which are worth your time."

—nytraveler

PERFORMING ARTS PLANNER

What to Wear

When getting dressed for a night of culture, take your cue from the city locals. You'll note that it is still common for people to dress up for performances, especially at the larger, traditional venues. Most women will be in cocktail dresses, and most men will don at least a shirt and tie (if not a full suit).

Concerts to Avoid

Experiencing classical music in a church setting can be an uplifting experience. Unfortunately in Prague, standards vary widely for church concerts. Low-quality shows are advertised in Old Town Square and Malá Strana and rely on nonrepeat tourists patrons to stay in business. To avoid disappointment, choose a bigger, better-known church like the ones listed here, and make sure the performance features a professional chamber group.

Word of Mouth

"I have to put in a plug for Don Giovanni performed in the Marionette Theatre. It was so funny and [we] absolutely loved it. Very LARGE marionettes . . . it was extremely charming. [We] would do it again."   —southeastern

Where to Get Tickets

The concierge at your hotel may be able to reserve tickets for you. Otherwise, for the cheapest tickets go directly to the theater box office a few days in advance or immediately before a performance. If all else fails, try one of the ticket agencies below. If you are interested in seeing a specific festival, like Prague Spring, definitely purchase tickets in advance directly from the organizer or one of these listed agencies.

Bohemia Ticket International. This agency specializes in mostly classical music, theater, and black-light theater. ⊠ *Na Příkopě 16, Nové Město* ☎ *224–215–031* ⊕ *www.ticketsbti. cz* ⊠ *Malé nám. 13, Staré Město* ☎ *224–227–832.*

Sazka Ticket. Sazka Ticket is the exclusive seller of tickets to events at O2 Arena. Major concerts and sporting events are held here. You can purchase tickets online or at betting shops and street newspaper stands throughout town. The O2 Arena box office is only open on the day of the event, so purchasing your tickets there is not recommended. ⊠ *Ocelářská 10 (O2 Arena), Vysočansky* ☎ *266–121–122 Sazka head ticket office* ⊕ *www.sazkaticket.cz.*

Ticketportal. Tickets for major classical music and theater venues are for sale through this agency; they also provide tickets through some travel agents. On rare occasion, they have exclusive rights to a show. ⊠ *Politických vězňů 15, Nové Město* ☎ *222–246–283* ⊕ *www.ticketportal. cz.* ⊠ *At Prague Information Desk inside Old Town Hall, Staroměstské nám. 1, Staré Město* ☎ *No phone.*

Ticketpro. This is the main outlet for tickets to all shows and clubs, especially stadium concerts, with several branches across the city. Ticketpro also has an easy search engine that allows you to search what's on by date. ⊠ *Rytířská 12, Staré Město* ⊠ *Václavské nám. 38, Nové Město* ⊕ *www. ticketpro.cz.*

Ticketstream. Hotel desks and some restaurants carry tickets for classical music and other events via this agency. ⊠ *Koubkova 8, Nové Město* ☎ *224–263–049* ⊕ *www. ticketstream.cz.*

By Jacy Meyer World-class culture, stunning venues, and affordable ticket prices: Prague is a performing-arts triple threat. It's almost criminal to come to this city and not take in a performance when they are so accessible. And the city is home to excellent ballet, opera, orchestra, and theater companies that offer their talents nearly every night of the week.

Prague's musical history is a rich and varied one, from hometown composers like Antonín Dvořák or Bedřich Smetana to expat composers like Mozart who took inspiration from the city. And the classical music scene in Prague is still thriving today. Most orchestras will include at least one Czech composer in their evening program, and Mozart's Don Giovanni is still performed regularly, as it made its debut here back in 1787. Other popular non-native, but adopted sons include Beethoven, Chopin, and Haydn. Modern Czech composers do exist, and while they aren't played as often as the biggies, you'll be in for a treat if you can find something by Bohuslav Martinů, Leoš Janáček, or Josef Suk.

But it's not all about the past; Czech dance companies produce vibrant work, and if you're looking for something avant-garde you won't be disappointed. And both the National Theater and State Opera have their own ballet companies staging a mix of classic and contemporary pieces.

As for theater, you can't escape its overwhelming popularity. Locals are avid theatergoers and there's a plethora of companies and venues. Unfortunately, while high-quality, it's usually performed in Czech, and English-language theater is a hit-or-miss affair. The solution? Opera. The productions are year-round, the performers are outstanding, and English subtitles are usually provided. The State Opera House and the Estates Theater are two of the best venues.

Even if you aren't a culture vulture at home, consider taking in a symphony or other performance while you are in town. Many of the concert halls are historic, gorgeous, and fairly well maintained. Most big theaters and concert halls go dark in July and August. Fortunately, entrepreneurial directors have stepped in and filled the cultural void with some sweet festivals.

One of the largest film festivals in Central Europe, **Febiofest** (⊕ *www. febiofest.cz*) runs for about a week at the end of March and beginning of April. Films—both premieres and retrospectives—come from virtually all over the world, and a number of directors and stars, including Claude Lelouch and Hal Hartley,have come to introduce their work. As a side to the festival, world-music bands also perform for free in the garage of the multiplex where the festival is held.

☾ Theater takes to the street every July thanks to **Teatrotoc** (⊕ *www. teatrotoc.eu*) on Kampa Island. Jugglers, stilt walkers, puppeteers, musicians, and mimes come out in full force to entertain all. Lots of amusements for kids, like puppet making and storytelling, but really a fun afternoon for everyone.

Fans of foreign films have a chance to catch up on recent English-subtitled efforts in **Days of European Film** (⊕ *www.eurofilmfest.cz*), which happens every April in Prague and Brno. Nearly 10 days of films play at two cinemas; there are also some panel discussions. Tickets are inexpensive, and the theaters used for screenings are beautiful and historic.

Fans of documentary films look forward to the **One World Human Rights Film Festival** (*Jeden svět* ⊕ *www.oneworld.cz*). Showcasing films dedicated to human rights and other social and political issues, One World offers a glimpse of global issues through a filmmaker's eye. The festival runs in March at various theaters, usually including Lucerna and Archa. Nearly all films are in English or with English subtitles.

Modern physical theater from performance companies around the world is showcased in the **4+4 Days in Motion** (*4+4 dny v pohybu* ⊕ *www. ctyridny.cz*), which often has shows in unusual venues like an old brickworks or disused factories as well as mainstream theaters. The festival usually takes place in the fall, and is one of the more creative festivals on the Prague circuit.

Celebrating Roma culture and diversity, the **Khamoro Festival** (⊕ *www. khamoro.cz*) offers music, dance, and film. Romany (Gypsy) bands have become a hot item in the world-music scene, and groups from all over Europe gather in Prague at the end of May for a week of merrymaking. Check out contemporary Roma music, Gypsy Jazz, exhibitions, and dance performances.

From amateur to professional, entertainers of all kinds descend on the grounds of a mental health institution for **Mezi ploty** (⊠ *Ústavní ulice, Bohnice* ⊕ *www.meziploty.cz*). The two-day festival has some of the best local bands, plus theater acts and art workshops, but be aware that only nonalcoholic beer can be sold on the grounds. The festival takes place at the beginning of June and functions to raise awareness of issues concerning mental illness.

The islands in the Vltava are one of the most underutilized aspects of the city. **United Islands of Prague** (⊕ *www.unitedislands.cz*) brings international rock, blues, and world-music acts to several waterside venues for a weekend at the end of June. In the evenings performances by additional bands take place in nearby clubs.

Since 1946 **Prague Spring** (*Pražské jaro* ⊕ *www.festival.cz*) has been the main event of the classical season, and usually runs from the end of May to the start of June. Conductors such as Leonard Bernstein and Sir Charles Mackerras have been among the guests. Important anniversaries of major composers, especially Czech ones, are marked with special concerts. Orchestra concerts, operas, and church recitals make up the bulk of the schedule. The competition element gives attendees the opportunity to see the next big star. Typically around 60 concerts are spread over more than 10 venues during the nearly three-week run. Bedřich Smetana's *Ma vlást* usually opens the festival. Major events can sell out months in advance; tickets usually go on sale mid-December.

There isn't much English-language theater in Prague. An exception is the annual **Prague Fringe Festival** (⊕ *www.praguefringe.com*), which began in 2002 and has visiting acts from Scotland, New Zealand, Australia, and the United States. The venues are scattered around Malá Strana; and performances are staggered so that you could conceivably see five a day. The Fringe takes place in late May.

European contemporary dance and movement is celebrated at **Tanec Praha** (⊕ *www.tanecpha.cz*) Lasting for about a month every June, renowned companies from all over the world strut their stuff in two Prague 8 venues.

The most important film festival in the Czech Republic is in the spa town of Karlovy Vary. The **Karlovy Vary International Film Festival** (⊕ *www. kviff.com*) ranks with Cannes, Berlin, and Venice among important European festivals. Visitors to the festival, which happens at the start of July, have included Lauren Bacall, Morgan Freeman, Michael Douglas, and Sharon Stone. This is one of the most publicly accessible film festivals around.

The lovely organ in Bazilika sv. Jakuba attracts noted international musicians for the annual **International Organ Festival** (✉ *Malá Štuparská, Staré Město* ⊕ *www.auditeorganum.cz/festival.html*), which runs from August to September with weekly concerts.

CLASSICAL MUSIC

Considering the Czech people's love of classical music, it seems like music should be ringing in the streets—and actually you will find street musicians throughout the city. But it's worth it to seek out the professionals that perform in historic venues from massive concert halls to baroque churches. Pick one of the better chamber ensembles (we've listed some here), as the programs are usually more adventurous and you're likely to hear little-known composers. Or get tickets to see a professional orchestra; the program may not take many risks, but you're practically guaranteed an evening of virtuoso playing, and often international guest musicians will take the stage. Steer clear of lesser-known ensembles or venues that cater to tourists, which can be subpar.

Agon Orchestra. Bucking the trend for classical, this group specializes in contemporary music, ranging from John Cage to Frank Zappa. Most often they play at Archa Theatre, but they have been in other venues

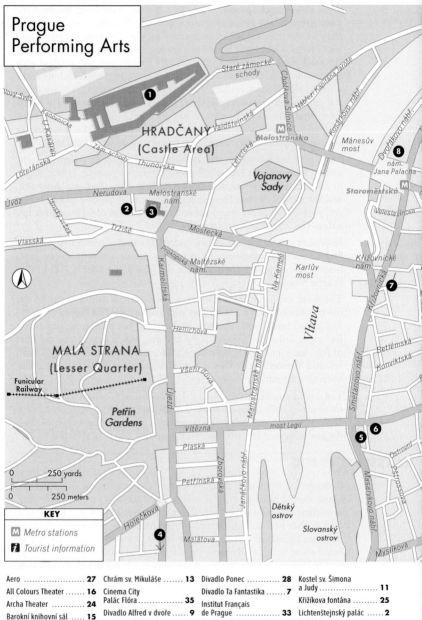

Prague Performing Arts

KEY

🅼 Metro stations

ℹ️ Tourist information

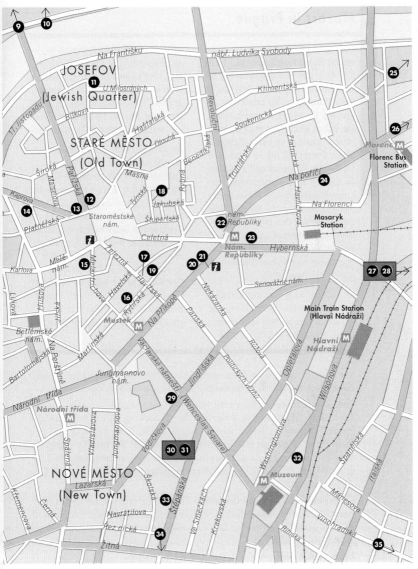

Mozart in Prague

Considering that Wolfgang Amadeus Mozart visited Prague only four times, it's impressive how deeply he left his stamp on the city. On his first trip, in early 1787, he visited Count Thun and his wife. They lived in what is now the British Embassy in Malá Strana. Mozart stayed at an inn on Celetná Street. During this trip he conducted his *Prague Symphony* and a day later, on January 20, a performance of his opera *The Marriage of Figaro*, which had a more successful run in Prague than in Vienna. One legend from this time has the host of a party inviting him an hour before all the other guests and making him compose new dances for the evening.

His second trip is the most famous. The maestro came to visit composer F.X. Dušek and his new wife, opera singer Josephine, in 1787 at their rural villa, Bertramka (although he also kept rooms at the Uhelný třída Inn). After several missed deadlines, he conducted the world premiere of *Don Giovanni* on October 29 at Stavovské divadlo. He tried out a number of church organs in his spare time.

His third visit was just a pass-through, but the fourth and final trip came just months before he died in 1791. He promised to write a new opera to mark the coronation of Leopold II as king of Bohemia. Unfortunately, *La Clemenza di Tito*, which premiered at the Stavovské divadlo on September 6, was written quickly, and was not as well received as *Don Giovanni*. Once news of his death on December 5 reached Prague, his friends staged a memorial service that ended with church bells ringing all over town.

---

including Národní divadlo. Agon also offers a great chance to hear contemporary Czech composers. ⊕ *www.petrkofron.com.*

Collegium Marianum. One of the most well-respected ensembles in town, Collegium Marianum is your best bet if looking to explore baroque music. They often revive seldom-heard works from archives and perform them on period instruments. Performances are usually organized around a historical or geographical theme. ⊠ *Melantrichova 971/19, Staré Město* ☎ *224–229–462* ⊕ *www.collegiummarianum.cz* Ⓜ *Line A: Staroměstská.*

Czech National Symphony Orchestra. This major full-size orchestra plays most often at the Rudolfinum. The orchestra has attracted some well-known guest conductors, and has also done some film sound-track work. ⊕ *www.cnso.cz.*

Czech Philharmonic. Antonín Dvořák conducted the orchestra's first performance back in 1896. Guest conductors have included Gustav Mahler and Leonard Bernstein. Since 1990 there has been a rapid turnover in chief conductors, but the performances have been of consistently high quality. Most programs include some works by Czech composers. ⊠ *Rudolfinum, nám. Jana Palacha, Staré Město* ☎ *227–059–227* ⊕ *www. czechphilharmonic.cz* Ⓜ *Line A: Staroměstská.*

Czech Radio Symphony Orchestra. As the name implies, this group started playing live on the radio in 1927. Since the 1960s it hasn't been directly

DID YOU KNOW?

Classical music has deep roots in Prague, and compared to other European cities, performances are very inexpensive...(sometimes even free!).

associated with the national radio system, and has fewer concerts than its main rivals. You can usually see them perform at the Rudolfinum. Besides Czech composers, the orchestra excels in Brahms and Mahler. ⊕ *www.rozhlas.cz/socr/portal.*

Ensemble Martinů. Domestic and international radio performances and film scores have kept this piano quartet in the spotlight. Formed in 1978 and re-formed in 1993, the group majors in music by the Czech composer Martinů, but also has a wide repertoire of other composers. This ensemble is an excellent choice for classical music lovers. ⊕ *www. ensemblemartinu.com.*

Nostitz Quartet. Named after a famous 18th-century patron of the arts, this youthful ensemble has won a few prestigious awards. They give excellent performances of works by Mozart and Czech composers, and are one of the better groups to appear in various church concerts around town. ⊕ *www.nostitzquartet.com.*

Prague Chamber Orchestra without Conductor. Famous for playing often (but not always) without a conductor, this ensemble covers the classics up through 20th-century composers. Usually they play about four concerts a year in the Rudolfinum. ⊕ *www.pko.cz.*

Prague Philharmonia. Founded in 1994, this orchestra is youthful in more ways than one. The average age of the members is 34, and conductor Jakub Hrůša was born in 1981. This fresh spirit can be felt in their work, which ranges from classic and romantic to contemporary composers. The group usually plays about six times a year in the Czech Republic at either the Rudolfinum or the Church of Saints Simon and Jude. ⊕ *www.pkf.cz.*

Prague Symphony Orchestra *(FOK).* The group's nickname stands for Film-Opera-Koncert. They started in 1934, but it wasn't until 1952 that they became the official city orchestra. In the 1930s they did music for many Czech films, although they don't do much opera and film anymore. The ensemble tours extensively, and has a large back catalog of recordings. Programs tend to be quite diverse, from Beethoven to Bruckner. They also offer public rehearsals for a mere 100 Kč. ⊠ *Obecní dům, Nám. Republiky 5, Staré Město* ☎ *222–002–336* ⊕ *www.fok.cz* Ⓜ *Line B: Nám. Republiky.*

Stamic Quartet. Two members of the quartet were born in the same town as composer J. V. Stamic, so they chose this name. The group often plays some Britten and Bártok along with the usual classics and Czech composers. ⊕ *www.stamicquartet.cz.*

Wihan Quartet. Many quartets borrow names from composers, but few choose the name of a musician. Wihan was a cellist who knew Dvořák. The quartet has won numerous awards since it started in 1985, and has participated in international broadcasts. Most of their sets include at least one Czech composer. ⊕ *www.wihanquartet.com.*

CHURCH CONCERTS

Church concerts have become a staple of the Prague classical music scene. The concerts help churches to raise money, and also give visitors more of an opportunity to hear classical music, often in an opulent setting. Banners or signs at the churches announce when there's a concert. Listings can also be found in English on the Web site ⊕ *www.pis.cz*.

■**TIP➔** Many churches aren't heated; ask before buying your ticket and dress appropriately.

Barokní knihovní sál *(Baroque Library Hall).* Impressive 18th-century frescoes and colorful stuccowork in a monastery library hall make for one of the more charming, though lesser-used, concert halls. This is usually a good bet for a quality performance, often by the Collegium Marianum ensemble. ⊠ *Melantrichova 971/19, Staré Město* ☎ *224–229–462* ⊕ *www.tynska.cuni.cz* Ⓜ *Line A: Staroměstská.*

Bazilika sv. Jakuba *(Basilica of St. James).* This is an excellent venue for organ concerts thanks to the church's organ, which was finished in 1709 and restored in the early 1980s to its original tone structure. Now it's one of the best in town. ⊠ *Malá Štupartská 6, Staré Město* ☎ *604–208–490* ⊕ *www.auditeorganum.cz/organ.html* Ⓜ *Line A: Staroměstská.*

Bazilika sv. Jiří *(Basilica of St. George).* Listen to small ensembles playing well-known Mozart tunes and Verdi's *Four Seasons* in a Romanesque setting. Located in Prague Castle, the building dates to the 11th century, and holds the tombs of some very early princes. ⊠ *Nám. U sv. Jiří, Pražský Hrad* ☎ *224–373–368* ⊕ *www.kulturanahrade.cz* Ⓜ *Line A: Hradčandská.*

Chrám sv. Mikuláše *(Church of St. Nicholas, Staré Město).* The chandelier inside this baroque landmark is based on the design for the Czar's crown. Private companies rent out the church for concerts by professional ensembles and visiting amateur choirs and orchestras. The quality and prices vary greatly. ⊠ *Staroměstské nám., Staré Město* ☎ *774–178–774* ⊕ *www.svmikulas.cz* Ⓜ *Line A: Staroměstská.*

Kostel sv. Mikuláše *(Church of St. Nicholas, Malá Strana).* Ballroom scenes in the movie *Van Helsing* used the interior of this beautiful baroque church. The building's dome was one of the last works finished by architect Kilian Ignatz Dientzenhofer before his death in 1751, and a memorial service to Mozart was held here after his death. Local ensembles play concerts of popular classics here throughout the year. ⊠ *Malostranské nám., Malá Strana* ☎ *257–534–215* ⊕ *www. psalterium.cz* Ⓜ *Line A: Malostranská.*

Kostel sv. Šimona a Judy *(Church of Sts. Simon and Jude).* This decommissioned church with a restored organ and frescoes is used by the Prague Symphony Orchestra for chamber concerts and recitals and it's also a popular venue for music festivals. The baroque altar is actually an elaborate painting on the wall. ⊠ *Dušní ulice, Josefov* ☎ *222–321–352* Ⓜ *Line A: Staroměstská.*

FILM

Hollywood descended on Prague en masse in the early 1990s, using its beauty as a stand-in for nearly every conceivable European city from Paris to Amsterdam. And it helped that Prague was far more affordable than any of those Western European capitals. It's still common to run into a film crew on the streets, although it's less likely to be a blockbuster now. The country's film industry has declined dramatically in the last five years, mainly because competing Central and Eastern European countries offer producers more bang for their buck. Movie watchers, however, are easily found. Multiplexes are the dominant force, and locals fill them regularly. For something indie, foreign, or Czech with subtitles, head to Prague's many independent and well-run art cinemas. Most films are shown in their original-language versions, but it pays to check. If a film was made in the United States or Britain, the chances are good that it will be shown with Czech subtitles rather than dubbed (the exception being cartoons).

> ## PRAGUE'S CLOSE UP
>
> Does Prague feel a little familiar? The late '90s and early 2000s saw a plethora of Hollywood blockbusters filmed in Prague. *The League of Extraordinary Gentleman, The Brothers Grimm, Mission Impossible, The Bourne Identity,* and *Casino Royale* all owe some scenography to Prague. Art-house fanatics may also recognize moments in Czech cinema around town from Oscar-award-winning *Kolya* that featured the Velvet Revolution taking place in Wenceslas Square or the Jiří Menzel classic, *Closely Watched Trains.*

Film titles, however, are usually translated into Czech. Movies in the original language are normally indicated with the note *českými titulky* (with Czech subtitles). Prague's English-language publications carry film reviews and full timetables.

■**TIP→** You can reserve tickets in advance at all movie theaters and multiplexes. Also note: unlike movie tickets in the U.S., your ticket has an assigned seat number.

Aero. Film junkies make the trek to this out-of-the-way gem of a theater knowing it's worth the trip. The tiny cinema is hidden in the middle of a residential block, and keeps an ambitious schedule of two or three different films a day: festivals, retrospectives, oldies but goodies (think *Clockwork Orange* and *Jailhouse Rock*) plus feature films with English subtitles. Czech translations are done through headphones. Visiting guests have included Terry Gilliam, Godfrey Reggio, and Paul Morrisey. The theater also has an outdoor beer garden in the summer months and a lively indoor bar year-round. ⊠ *Biskupcova 31, Žižkov* ☎ *271–771–349* ⊕ *www.kinoaero.cz* Ⓜ *Line A: Želivského.*

Bio Oko. Bargain ticket prices, an improved interior, and a schedule that offers greater variety and more "big name" films are just a few reasons to check out this theater outside the city center. New international releases as well as Czech films (sometimes with subtitles) and festival series give Oko a varied line-up. There's a refurbished bar and café here outfitted with Wi-Fi. ⊠ *Františka Křížka 15, Holešovice* ☎ *233–382–606* ⊕ *www.biooko.net* Ⓜ *Line C: Vltavská.*

Cinema City Palác Flóra. This venue has "Oskar-IMAX," a large-format theater that shows many short films in 3-D and the occasional feature on a very large screen. Most IMAX shows are dubbed. Other screens offer the standard multiplex experience. ⊠ *Vinohradská 151, Vinohrady* ☎ *255–742–021* ⊕ *www.cinemacity.cz* Ⓜ *Line A: Flora.*

Institut Français de Prague. A full-size movie theater is hidden away in the basement here, and most of the programming consists of recent French films and retrospectives of classics (also French). Some of the films have English subtitles, and the admission fee is usually nominal (80 Kč). They also host an annual French Film Festival in November. No food or drinks allowed (but on the ground floor there's an excellent café). "Serious" film watching only. ⊠ *Štěpanská 35, Nové Město* ☎ *221–401–011* ⊕ *www.ifp.cz* Ⓜ *Line A or B: Můstek.*

Lucerna. The city's handsomest old movie palace was designed by former President Václav Havel's grandfather and built in 1916. An art nouveau interior harks back to cinema's glory days, but it could use a little more maintenance. The programming tends toward a mix of new releases, foreign films, and festivals. The café leading to the theater proper sometimes features a live piano player. ⊠ *Vodičkova 36, Nové Město* ☎ *224–216–972* ⊕ *www.lucerna.cz* Ⓜ *Line A or B: Můstek.*

Palace Cinemas Slovanský dům. Probably the best multiplex in town—certainly the most convenient to downtown—runs about 10 movies at once, most of these being the latest Hollywood films in English (with Czech subtitles). It occasionally runs Czech films with English subtitles. ⊠ *Na Příkopé 22, Nové Město* ☎ *840–200–240 reservations* ⊕ *www.palacecinemas.cz* Ⓜ *Line B: Nám. Republiky.*

★ **Světozor.** Prague's central art-house cinema has a great location near the Lucerna shopping passage and an excellent selection of offbeat American films, classic European cinema, and the best of new Czech films. Many films are subtitled in English. The place was renovated in 2008, and local patrons now sponsor individual seats in the main hall. ⊠ *Vodičkova 41, Nové Město* ☎ *224–946–824* ⊕ *www.kinosvetozor.cz* Ⓜ *Line A or B: Můstek.*

OPERA

Opera has a long and strong tradition in the Czech Republic, and fans of it are rewarded with quality productions almost every night of the week. Operas are usually sung in their original language, and Czech ones are supertitled in English, while Italian and other languages are given Czech and English supertitles. The State Opera and the Estates Theater are two of the best venues. The State Opera company is a bit more inventive, and often features guest performances. Branch out from the usual composers with a Czech composer like Janaček, Dvořák or Smetana. The major opera houses also often stage ballets.

Národní divadlo *(National Theater).* A slightly bigger budget and three different venues for operas give the National Theater's resident opera company a bit more flexibility than its rival, the Statní opera Praha. Large, ambitious productions are at the main Národní divadlo. Stavovské divadlo runs more mainstream works; it's where Mozart premiered Don Giovanni, which is still regularly shown here. Truly experimental or chamber operas wind up in Kolowrat. The productions run from excellent to slightly misconceived, but they are always professional. ⊠ *Národní 2, Nové Město* ☎ *224–901–448* ⊕ *www.narodni-divadlo.cz* Ⓜ *Line B: Národní třída.*

Statní opera Praha *(Prague State Opera).* With fewer resources than the National Theater, the State Opera is forced to be a bit more creative to compete. The result? More new works and more challenging interpretations of obscure works along with the standard crowd-pleasers. They also have a ballet company. ⊠ *Wilsonova 4, Nové Město* ☎ *224–227–266* ⊕ *www.opera.cz* Ⓜ *Line A or C: Muzeum.*

PERFORMANCE ARTS CENTERS AND MAJOR VENUES

Divadlo Hybernia. The only Empire-style building in the city, a former military barracks, was turned into a theater in 2006. The program is not very adventurous, wavering between nonverbal theater for tourists and middle-of-the-road musicals. It is across the street from Obecní dům. ⊠ *Nám. Republiky 4* ☎ *221–419–420* ⊕ *www.divadlo-hybernia. cz/* Ⓜ *Line B: Nám. Republiky.*

Divadlo Kolowrat. Less significant compared with other National Theater stages; this small venue features more experimental works and chamber operas. The basement has a discreet and cheap restaurant heavily populated by Czech actors. ⊠ *Ovocný trh 6, Staré Město* ☎ *224–901–487* ⊕ *www.narodni-divadlo.cz* Ⓜ *Line A or B: Můstek.*

Kongresové centrum Praha *(Congress Center).* The former Palace of Culture, built in 1981, has never found a place in people's hearts. The large, functionalist, multipurpose building has several performance spaces that can seat thousands, but overall it has a very sterile feel. Plays—usually musicals—and special events come here. As the largest venue in the city, it also hosts the majority of conferences. ⊠ *5 kvetna 65, Nusle* ⊕ *www.kcp.cz* Ⓜ *Line C: Vyšehrad.*

Lichtenštejnský palác *(Lichtenstein Palace).* Home to the Czech music academy (HAMU), this baroque palace from the 1790s has the large Martinů Hall for professional concerts and a smaller gallery occasionally used for student recitals. The courtyard sometimes has music in the summer months. ⊠ *Malostranské nám. 13, Malá Strana* ☎ *257–534–206* Ⓜ *Line A: Malostranská.*

Fodor's Choice
★
Národní divadlo *(National Theater).* This is the main stage in the Czech Republic for drama and dance. Most of the theater performances are in Czech, but some operas have English supertitles. The interior—with its ornate and etched ceilings—is worth the visit alone. ⊠ *Národní 2, Nové Město* ☎ *224–901–448* ⊕ *www.narodni-divadlo. cz* Ⓜ *Line B: Národní třída.*

O2 Arena. Formerly the Sazka Arena (tickets are still sold through Sazka Ticket), this indoor sports venue often houses big-time rock and pop concerts, like Pink and Green Day.

CRAZY FOR YOU

Madonna has truly been cherished the two times she's visited Prague. Her first concert in the capital city came as recently as 2006, when her two shows sold out in record time, filling the 17,000 seat O2 Arena both nights. In 2009 an experimental "venue" was created in a field next to a city highway. The location wasn't well received, but the Material Girl was—more than 40,000 people attended the outdoor concert.

Opera performances draw large crowds at the Národní divadlo (National Theater).

The security level is very high, and almost airport-like. A small nail file or pocket scissors can delay your entrance. ⊠ *Očelářská 2, Vysočany* ☎ *266–771–000* ⊕ *www.o2arena.cz* Ⓜ *Line B: Českomoravská.*

★ **Obecní dům** *(Municipal House)*. The main concert hall, a true art nouveau gem named after composer Bedřich Smetana, is home to the Prague Symphony Orchestra and many music festivals. A few smaller halls, all named for famous figures, host chamber concerts. Tours of the building are also offered. ⊠ *Nám. Republiky 5, Staré Město* ☎ *222–002–101* ⊕ *www.obecnidum.cz* Ⓜ *Line B: Nám. Republiky.*

Fodor's Choice **Rudolfinum**. Austrian Crown Prince Rudolf lent his name to this neo-★ Renaissance concert space and exhibition gallery built in 1884. The large concert hall, named for Antonín Dvořák, who conducted here, hosts concerts by the Czech Philharmonic. The smaller Josef Suk Hall, on the opposite side of the building, is used for chamber concerts. Rivals may have richer interiors, but the acoustics here are excellent. ⊠ *Nám. Jana Palacha, Staré Město* ☎ *227–059–227* ⊕ *www.ceskafilharmonie. cz* Ⓜ *Line A: Staroměstská.*

★ **Statní opera Praha** *(State Opera House)*. With the most ornate interior of any venue in Prague, this theater has more than a touch of *Phantom of the Opera*. Marble sculptures support the loges, and a fresco in need of a good cleaning adorns the ceiling. The building started life as the German Theater in 1887, and has undergone several name changes since. A rotating stage offers directors a chance to experiment, although the stage can be a bit cramped. ⊠ *Wilsonova 4, Nové Město* ☎ *224–227–266* ⊕ *www.opera.cz* Ⓜ *Line A or C: Muzeum.*

If you find yourself taken by the marionettes for sale in Prague, take in a performance at one of the puppet shows and watch them come to life.

Stavovské divadlo *(Estates Theater)*. It's impossible to visit Prague without knowing that Mozart conducted the world premiere of *Don Giovanni* on this stage way back in 1787. Fittingly, the interior was used for scenes in Miloš Forman's movie *Amadeus*. It's stylish and refined without being distracting. This is a branch of the National Theater, and high-quality productions of Mozart are usually in the repertoire together with other classic operas, plays and the occasional smaller ballet. ⊠ *Ovocný trh 6, Nové Město* ☎ *224–901–448* ⊕ *www.narodni-divadlo.cz* Ⓜ *Line A or B: Můstek.*

Tesla Arena. Compared with other arenas, this communist-era relic is greatly in need of renovation. Even so, the acts coming through are fairly well known. When it is not hosting rock legends, the Sparta ice hockey team plays here. ⊠ *Za elektrárnou 419* ☎ *266–727–443 (Sparta-Customer Care Center) Bubeneč* ⊕ *www.tesla-arena.cz* Ⓜ *Nádraží Holešovice.*

Velký sál, Lucerna *(Great Hall, Lucerna)*. Part of the fascinating Lucerna complex, the Velký sál is a beautiful art nouveau ballroom with a big main floor and some loges. They host medium-size rock and pop bands like Blackmore's Night, Chuck Berry, and Kraftwerk. Swing orchestras also make use of it, and the occasional ball is held here as well. When open, it's one of the more impressive venues. It sometimes serves as a space for touring exhibits, such as items from the *Titanic*. ⊠ *Štěpánská 61, Nové Město* ☎ *296–333–333* ⊕ *www.lucerna.cz* Ⓜ *Line A or B: Můstek.*

PUPPET SHOWS AND BLACK-LIGHT THEATER

Black-light theater, a form of nonverbal theater—melding live acting, mime, video, and stage trickery—made a global splash when Czechoslovakia premiered it at Expo '58. The name comes from ultraviolet light, which is used to illuminate special makeup and details on the sets, creating optical illusions. Some black-light shows have been running for thousands of performances. Tickets can be pricey compared to other art options in town, and it is probably an acquired taste. Puppetry also has a long tradition, but most of the shows are dialogue-intensive and aimed at a young audience.

All Colours Theater. Since 1993 this small theater has been presenting a small repertoire of nonverbal shows. Faust is their main performance, although they occasionally revive other works. Some legends claim that the real Faust lived in Prague, which gives the show some local significance. ✉ *Rytiřská 31, Staré Město* ☎ *221–610–114* ⊕ *www. blacktheatre.cz* Ⓜ *Line A or B: Můstek.*

Divadlo Broadway. Right off one of the busiest tourist and shopping streets, this former movie theater—the first one to fall victim to the wave of multiplexes—is now home to black-light presentations and musicals performed in Czech. ✉ *Na Příkopě 31, Staré Město* ☎ *225–113–311* ⊕ *www.divadlo-broadway.cz/* Ⓜ *Line B: Nám. Republiky.*

Divadlo Image. This is the home of a black-light and pantomime company that has a repertoire of long-running classics of the genre and a "best of" show. ✉ *Pařížská 4, Josefov* ☎ *222–329–191* ⊕ *www. imagetheatre.cz* Ⓜ *Line A: Staroměstská.*

Divadlo Ta Fantastika. A black-light show called *Aspects of Alice*, based loosely on *Alice in Wonderland*, has run here almost daily for more than 2,000 performances. The theater was established in Florida in 1981, and moved to Prague after the Velvet Revolution. It's been running at its current address, a minor baroque palace, since 1993. ✉ *Karlova 8, Staré Město* ☎ *222–221–366* ⊕ *www.tafantastika.cz* Ⓜ *Line A: Staroměstská.*

Křižíkova fontána. Pressurized water and colored lights keep pace with recorded music that ranges from recent film scores to a tribute to Freddie Mercury and selections of classical music. Live acts share the stage on occasion. Tickets are available at the venue. ✉ *Výstaviště Holešovice* ☎ *723–665–694* ⊕ *www.krizikovafontana.cz* Ⓜ *Nádraži Holešovice.*

Národní divadlo marionet *(The National Marionette Theater).* This puppet company has been presenting Mozart's *Don Giovanni* with string puppets set to recorded music sung in Italian since 1991. The opera is slightly tongue-in-cheek, and Mozart himself makes a guest appearance. A new production of *The Magic Flute*, in German, is occasionally shown as well. ✉ *Žatecká 1, Staré Město* ☎ *224–819–322* ⊕ *www. mozart.cz* Ⓜ *Line A: Staroměstská.*

★ **Nová Scená.** The glass-block façade of the Nová scena (New Stage), which opened in 1983, stands out among the ornate 19th-century buildings in the area. Black-light theater company Laterna Magika (which takes its name from the original black-light presentation at Expo '58) performs here, and the rest of the program schedule is handled through

Národní divadlo. Contemporary dance pieces and other language-free performances dominate the calendar. ⊠ *Národní 4, Nové Město* ☎ *224–931–482* ⊕ *www.novascena.cz* Ⓜ *Line B: Národní třída.*

THEATER AND DANCE

Theater in Czech can be a bit inaccessible—plays in English, or plays available to non-Czech speakers are sporadic—but a variety of dance companies bring that theatricality to visitors without the language barrier. For complete listings, pick up a copy of the *Prague Post.*

Fodor's Choice
★ **Archa Theater.** Both for its central location and eclectic programming, Archa is the main venue for modern theater, dance, and avant-garde music. Some visiting troupes perform in English, and other shows are designated as English-friendly in the program. The theater opened in 1994, and is often referred to as the Alternative National Theater. ⊠ *Na Poříčí 26, Nové Město* ☎ *221–716–333* ⊕ *www.archatheatre.cz* Ⓜ *Line B: Nám. Republiky.*

Divadlo Alfred v dvoře. Most of the programming for this small, out-of-the-way theater is physical, nonverbal theater and dance. Visiting companies come often and take a more modern approach than can be seen in many of the more tourist-oriented nonverbal theaters. Best place to see cutting edge, unconventional productions. ⊠ *Fr. Křížka 36, Bubeneč* ☎ *233–376–997* ⊕ *www.alfredvedvore.cz* Ⓜ *Line C: Vltavská.*

Divadlo Ponec. A former cylinder factory, then a movie theater, this neo-classical building was renovated into a modern dance venue in 2001. The house presents a lot of premieres, and is the main "dance" theater in town. Several dance festivals are based here. ⊠ *Husitská 24/a, Žižkov* ☎ *224–817–886* ⊕ *www.divadloponec.cz* Ⓜ *Line B or C: Florenc.*

Švandovo divadlo. If you want to join the theater-loving masses and there's nothing on in English, Švandovo is your best bet. Plays, a rotating mix that ranges from Shakespeare to Ibsen to contemporary showings, are subtitled above the stage in English. Sit in the balcony, on the right side, facing the stage for the best view. ⊠ *Štefánikova 57, Smíchov* ☎ *257–318–666* ⊕ *www.svandovodivadlo.cz* Ⓜ *Line B: Anděl.*

Nightlife

WORD OF MOUTH

"On the way back down from visiting Prague Castle we found Wallenstein Palace and gardens and then fell into the nearest cafe to have a well-deserved beer. Just a note, the dark beer in Prague is really good and I'm not usually a beer drinker!"

—joode

NIGHTLIFE PLANNER

Top 5 Nightlife Picks

1. **AghaRTA.** Professional jazz acts in a historic vaulted basement.

2. **Pivovarský dům.** If you're coming to Prague for the beer, the best is at a microbrewery that doesn't employ gimmicks.

3. **Roxy.** One of the larger downtown clubs also gets some of the best live acts and DJs.

4. **U Zlatého Tygra.** The last of its kind downtown, this surly and smoky pub was a favorite hangout for writers and dissidents in the 1970s and '80s.

5. **Cloud 9** The recent trend has been for cocktail bars, and this one has rooftop views and exclusive drinks.

Scenic Boat Trips

A popular addition to the evening entertainment scene is a scenic boat trip on the Vltava. Several operators now offer two- to three-hour evening floats, usually complete with music and plenty of food and drink. Tickets can usually be purchased near the dock or reserved online through the boat operators' Web sites (see the Evening Boat Trips section in the chapter). This is sometimes cheaper than getting them through agencies.

Hours

Pubs used to all close by 10 PM in the communist era. For many old-fashioned pubs, the action does certainly wind down early, and many still close by 11 PM or midnight. The new breed of cocktail bars, however, tends to get going much later, picking up at midnight. For any bar with live music it's best to check, as a lot of shows have to start early and end by 10 PM so as to keep down noise levels down at night. Outdoor seating closes by 10 PM for the same reason.

Stag Parties and Safety

Stag parties used to be the curse of the city's nightlife scene for anyone looking for a quiet and pleasant evening with a few friends. There are still a few groups out and about on any given night in matching tacky outfits singing songs on the street, but just a fraction of what it used to be. Many of the pubs that used to cater to them have shifted their focus to better service and quality food in an attempt to make up for the loss of stag business, which is good news for the average visitor and downtown resident.

In an effort to control street rowdiness associated with stag parties in the touristy center, Prague adopted a ban on street drinking in certain main areas, but it does not apply to restaurants with sidewalk seating or beer gardens in parks.

A word of caution about adult entertainment: thanks to the former popularity of Prague as a stag destination, several dance and strip clubs have sprung up on the side streets at the upper end of Wenceslas Square. With the downturn in stag parties, many of the establishments have become quite aggressive in attracting clients, and have people on the nearby streets offering to show passersby a place for a "good time."

Although these places are legal, they aren't always safe or cheap. Some establishments charge large sums of money for every quarter-hour you stay or have other hidden fees; others simply charge outrageous fees for drinks. Around these areas, be sure to watch your wallet. Professional thieves frequent the same areas, and target those who have had too much to drink.

DID YOU KNOW?

Prague offers the rare opportunity to try unpasteurized beer, which can only be served fresh, not bottled.

PRAGUE'S BEER CULTURE

If there's one thing people associate with the Czech Republic, it's beer. And with good reason: The Czechs brew some of the world's best lagers. Whether it's the water, Czech hops, or simply that Pilsner was invented here is up for debate, but the golden liquid is central to Czech culture.

Accordingly, don't be surprised to see beer consumed in all manner of social situations, from construction workers cracking a can with their breakfast roll to high-schoolers meeting for some suds after class. It's simply central to most of the country's interactions; the Czechs drink more beer per capita than any other nation in the world. More than that, however, the Czechs take pride in the quality of their beer, so even if it's not normally your thing, don't be afraid to try a pint during a visit here.

A RARE BREW

Only a select few restaurants and pubs serve unpasteurized beer, called *tankové pivo.* You'll see it advertised prominently on the menu outside. The breweries bring it only to pubs they select, picking those that move a high volume of beer and adhere to their strict standards. The beer is kept in pressurized tanks and pumped in fresh by trucks weekly. The benefit? Unpasteurized beers retain their "spicy" characteristics from the Czech hops, yielding a more complex set of tastes than the beers that are exported.

A PUB PRIMER

A *Pivnice* is a Czech beer hall named after *pivo*, meaning "beer." Expect a range of beer, usually drunk in high quantities along with simple snacks. And one Czech phrase you'll learn very quickly here is "pivo, prosím," Or "beer, please."

ETIQUETTE

Don't be intimidated by Prague pubs: They're happy to host you and show off their wares, so to speak. Ordering a beer is quite easy: Ask for a pivo when the waiter comes by (it may take a minute or two, but they'll get to you). Though most pubs serve beers from a single brewer, you might have options between a 10- or 12-degree quaff; if you're not sure and just ask for a beer, you'll probably end up with the lighter 10-degree stuff. If you don't want another round, when the waiter comes by and asks, say no thanks (ne, dekuju).

As for the check itself (which will get tallied around 10:30 or 11 PM on weeknights if you don't finish first), it's a strip of paper on the table. Each mark on the paper represents a beer that you've had. The waiter will count them up and tell you how much you owe, though do try and keep your own count, and be mindful how much the beers cost if you want to be absolutely sure not to get overcharged.

A small tip is the norm here, essentially rounding up to the nearest large number (usually coming to a few extra dollars) and handing it to server, or another server who will come by with a money pouch to handle the transaction. There's no need to tip an additional 15% unless you think you've received exceptional service.

PRAGUE'S MUST-TASTE

Czech beers are rightfully famous for their quality. While it's easy to find beers from big brewers like Staropramen or Gambrinus on tap most anywhere, more and more pubs are utilizing a "fourth pipe" (or tap) to showcase a local, independent brew that you might not have seen before. Here are a few to keep an eye out for:
Bernard Lager: This Bohemian pilsner stands up well to the famous Pilsner Urquell thanks to its intense hoppiness.
Opat Kvasničák Nefiltrovaný: A tasty unfiltered brew with sweet and sour notes.
Primátor Stout: Great example of a darker beer from one of the more beloved independent breweries in the Czech Republic.
U Medvíku X-33: Available only at the famed traditional pub of the same name, the X-33 sounds like a secret government project, but is actually one of the stronger beers in the country, at 12% alcohol.

6

By Raymond Johnston

Before 1989, bar offerings were fairly limited to beer and shots of domestic rum or *slivovice* (plum brandy), and most bars closed by 10 PM or so. Decorations were a few pages torn from calendars and some stray sports trophies.

Now Western-style cocktail bars have come to dominate the downtown area, and traditional Czech pubs, with long wooden tables, early closing hours, and menus that look like they've been run off on mimeograph machines, are being pushed out. That's a shame, because nothing beats a good night at the pub for a true Czech experience. (But you can find a few of these relics these in the outlying residential neighborhoods.)

Bars in the center have grown closer to their Western rivals in international liquor selection—and price. But Czech beer on tap is still king in the majority of pubs. And outdoor seating at pubs and restaurants and beer gardens in parks in the summer offers a relaxed way to unwind after a day of trudging around the city's seven hills.

Recent entries to the cocktail-bar trend offer panoramic rooftop views of the skyline or trendy interior designs and lighting schemes, but these are clearly modeled on similar bars in Western Europe and the U.S.

For those who want to look beyond the bar there are evening cruises on the Vltava that show off a waterfront that is quickly being developed into prime real estate after decades of neglect.

And while Prague isn't Monte Carlo, gambling is legal, and there is a range of establishments from exclusive high-class casinos to all-night bars with slot machines and video-gaming terminals. Most gamers, though, say the venues are a bit lacking in luster and ambience.

The music club scene has been growing since the early 1990s, and many clubs now have long-standing theme nights and, often, visiting DJs from across Europe as well as resident DJs with committed followings.

The city also has an increasingly visible gay scene, as the local attitude of minding one's own business at all costs means that gays and lesbians, while not always welcomed with open arms, are tolerated without objections.

BARS AND PUBS

Bar and Books. Aggressively chasing the cigar set, this sister establishment of two New York bars stocks top-shelf brandies, whiskies, and port wines. Some have rather eye-popping price tags per shot, but they're worth it for those in the know. The dark-wood interior has a formal air suited to whispered discussions of high finance. ⊠ *Tynská 19, Staré Město* ☎ *224–808–250* ⊕ *www.barandbooks.cz* Ⓜ *Line A: Staroměstská.*

Baráčnická rychta. One of the city's few no-smoking bars is not too far from the Castle Area, but far enough so that it isn't overly packed. The upstairs has a pleasant beer garden with decent prices for the area. ⊠ *Tržiště 23, Malá Strana* ☎ *257–532–461* Ⓜ *Line A: Malostranská.*

Bugsy's. Modern steel-and-glass, lights-in-the-bar design gives this popular American-style cocktail bar a modern look. The list of drinks has all the expected favorites, and sometimes there's live music. Check out the curio rack showing off one of the last Bacardi rum bottles to come from pre-Castro Cuba. ⊠ *Pařížská 10, enter on Kostečna, Josefov* ☎ *224–810–287* ⊕ *www.bugsysbar.com* Ⓜ *Line A: Staroměstská.*

Caffrey's Irish Bar. Caffrey's is one of the Irish bars that has "rebranded" since the downturn in stag parties. The menu now offers modern Irish cooking with imported ingredients, and, of course, imported Irish beer. Unlike many pubs near Old Town Square, it offers a polite and professional staff. During the week surrounding St. Patrick's Day this bar turns into the main headquarters for organized celebrations. ⊠ *Staroměstské nám., Staré Město* ☎ *224–828–031* ⊕ *www.caffreys.cz* Ⓜ *Line A: Staroměstská.*

Hard Rock Cafe. The heavily decorated façade of the historical V.J. Rott Building is worth a look on its own just to see the frescoes. The venue opened in 2009, even though bootleg Hard Rock Café Prague T-shirts have been sold for two decades. A key talking point of the three-level interior is the giant guitar-shape chandelier. ⊠ *Malé náměstí 3, Staré Město* ☎ *224–229–529* ⊕ *www.hardrock.com/prague* Ⓜ *Line A: Staroměstská.*

Jáma *(The Hollow)*. An outdoor beer garden hidden from passersby on the street provides a refuge from the noisy downtown crowds. The indoor bar is decorated with old rock-and-roll posters. Beer and hard cider on tap go with Mexican food and some pretty good burgers. Internet access is available here for a reasonable price, and Wi-Fi access is free. ⊠ *V Jámě 7, Nové Město* ☎ *224–222–383* ⊕ *www.jamapub.cz* Ⓜ *Line A or B: Můstek.*

Manesová Bar and Books. The sister establishment to Bar and Books, this out-of-the-city-center lounge adds a touch of class to the trendy Vinohrady neighborhood with a velvet-and-brass look. It may be just the ticket for people who want to shake off the Old Town crowds. Just one drawback: The food menu is rather limited for a so-called bistro. ⊠ *Mánesova 64, Vinohrady* ☎ *22–724–581* ⊕ *www.barandbooks.cz* Ⓜ *Line A: Nám. Míru.*

6

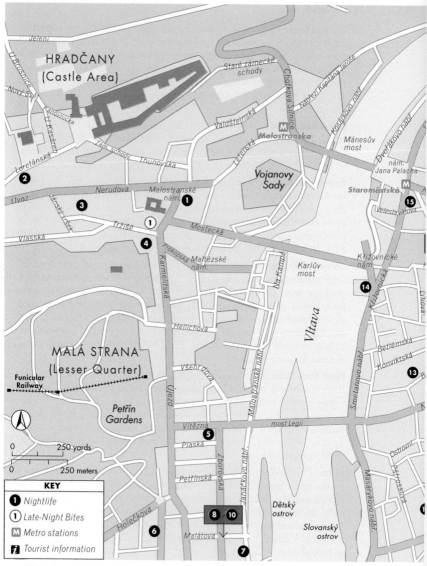

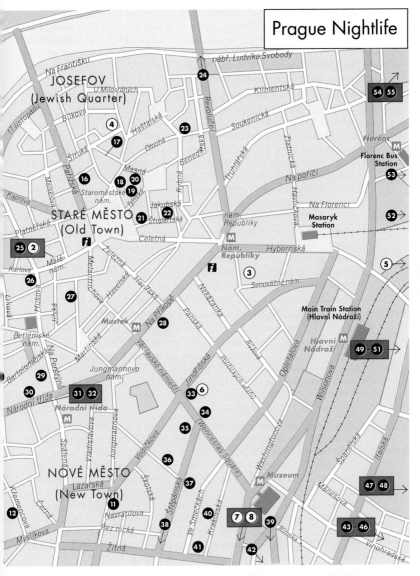

Prague Nightlife

M1 Secret Lounge. Movie stars in town for a shoot have been known to stop by this slightly hidden lounge on a side street in Old Town. But even if you don't spot a famous face, you'll see plenty of fashionistas who like to pose in the sleek, science fiction–esque location while sipping their cocktails. ✉ *Masná 1, Staré Město* ☎ *221–874–256* ⊕ *www. m1lounge.com* Ⓜ *Line A: Staroměstská.*

Mlekárna. In the middle of Reigrovy sady, one of the city's more pleasant parks, sits this renovated bar and café built at the start of the 20th century. In the summer, seating is available on the roof, which is always crowded. From the benches next to the building you can see the most spectacular view, particularly when the sun is setting over the Castle Area. After a long day, it can be the perfect place to relax and gaze at the city, especially for those on a budget. Seating is limited inside the small building, and it can be aggressively smoky. The park has a larger, but less romantic, fenced-in beer garden as well. ✉ *Reigrovy sady, Vinohrady* ☎ *No phone* Ⓜ *Line A: Nám. Jiřího z Poděbrad.*

Olympia. A hot spot from the 1930s returned to its former glory provides a somewhat romanticized but enjoyable take on a Czech pub. The interior is quite large, with 250 seats, but still the place gets very busy. Special unpasteurized Pilsner Urquell beer is served. But service, especially when the place is crowded, can be slow. ✉ *Vitežná 7, Malá Strana* ☎ *251–511–079* ⊕ *www.olympia-restaurant.cz* Ⓜ *Line B: Anděl.*

Fodor's Choice ★ **Pivovarský dům**. This brewpub—which opened in 1998—may be short on history, but it makes up for that with outstanding beer. The dark, light, and seasonal microbrew beers are stellar. (Fermenting beer can be viewed through a window.) A small menu of routine pub fare is printed on the place mats. The food is good, but a slight letdown when compared with the drinks. Take heed: there is often a line to get in. ✉ *Lípová 15, Nové Město* ☎ *296–216–666* ⊕ *www.gastroinfo.cz/ pivodum* Ⓜ *Line A or B: Můstek.*

★ **Pivovary Staropramen** *(Staropramen Brewery)*. The slogan for this place could be "for beer, go directly to the source." *Staropramen* means "old source," and it's one of the most ubiquitous beers in the city. Two venues inside the brewery, the Pivní bar and the larger Potrefená Husa Na Verandách Smíchov restaurant, serve several varieties of beer from the company's portfolio. With advance reservations tours are available. The brewery runs a chain of Potrefená Husa restaurants, with classic Czech food and beer, across the country as well. ✉ *Nádražní 84, Smíchov* ☎ *257–191–200 restaurant, 257–191–300 tours* ⊕ *navstevnicke-centrum.pivovarystaropramen.cz (tour), www. pivovary-staropramen.cz (restaurant)* Ⓜ *Line B: Anděl.*

Rocky O'Reillys Irish Pub. Stag parties are still welcome—if they keep it down to a roar—at Prague's largest Irish pub, which also shows soccer matches on TV. In the cooler months there's a burning fireplace. Unless you're a soccer fan, though, it's best not to go when games are being shown on TV; it's mellower at other times. Weekday lunches are also quiet. The bar does employ people to roam the surrounding area looking for potential patrons. ✉ *Štepanská 32, Nové Město* ☎ *222–231–060* ⊕ *www.rockyoreillys.cz* Ⓜ *Line A or B: Můstek.*

Sportbar Zlatá hvězda *(The Gold Star)*. Soccer and ice hockey are the big draws, although on occasion a U.S. football or baseball championship makes it onto the plasma screens. There are several sports bars in the area, but this one is the most popular with locals. Keep in mind the time difference if you are looking for U.S. games. ☒ *Ve Smečkách 12, Nové Město* ☎ *296–222–292* ⊕ *www.sportbar.cz* Ⓜ *Line A or B: Můstek.*

Tretter's. The lost elegance of the 1930s, with clean lines on dark wood, is re-created in a bar that serves Manhattans, martinis, and other classic cocktails, sometimes with live jazz in the background. This was a trend-setter in Prague when it first opened for classic cocktails. ☒ *V Kolkovně 3, Josefov* ☎ *224–811–165* ⊕ *www.tretters.cz* Ⓜ *Line A: Staroměstská.*

U Černého vola *(At the Black Ox)*. The last old-fashioned pub in the Castle Area, this place has cheap beer and the classic long tables. It's almost impossible to find many seats together at any time, though. Terry Jones, of Monty Python fame, is known to be a fan. The place is a bit run-down on the outside, and is sometimes mistaken for being closed. ☒ *Loretánské nám. 1, Hradčany* ☎ *220–513–481* Ⓜ *Line A: Hradčanská.*

U Fleků. The oldest brewpub in Europe—open since 1499—makes a tasty, if overpriced, dark beer. But the steady stream of tours means it's hard to find a seat. A brewery museum (phone for reservations) opened in 1999. Cabaret shows have been added to the entertainment. Beware of waiters putting unordered shots of liquor on your table. If you don't insist they remove them right away, they'll be on your bill, and service can be indifferent to rude. ☒ *Křemencova 11, Nové Město* ☎ *224–934–019* ⊕ *www.ufleku.cz* Ⓜ *Line B: Karlovo nám.*

U Medvídků. A former brewery dating as far back as the 15th century, U Medvídků now serves draft Budvar shipped directly from České Budějovice. Reservations are recommended, as organized tours often fill the entire bar. The interior, including the tap, have a turn-of-the-20th-century flavor. At times the bar offers exclusive Budvar brews available only at this location. ☒ *Na Perštýně 7, Staré Město* ☎ *224–211–916* ⊕ *www.umedvidku.cz* Ⓜ *Line B: Národní třída.*

U Rudolfina. Some people claim that the way the beer is tapped here makes it the best in town, which probably explains the constant crowds. This was one of the first places in the world to offer unpasteurized beer from tanks, rather than kegs. And the place still retains its old-fashioned charm, making it one of the best authentic Czech pubs in a heavily tourlisted area. Groups should make reservations—the free table is a rarity. ☒ *Křižovnická 10, Josefov* ☎ *222–313–088* Ⓜ *Line A: Staroměstská.*

Fodor's Choice **U Zlatého Tygra.** The last of the old, smoky, surly pubs in the Old Town is
★ famous for being one of the three best Prague pubs for Pilsner Urquell. It is also renowned as a former hangout of one of the country's best-known and beloved writers, Bohumil Hrabal, who died in 1997. Reservations are not accepted; one option is to show up at 3 PM, when the pub opens, with the rest of the early birds. ☒ *Husova 17, Staré Město* ☎ *222–221–111* ⊕ *www.uzlatehotygra.cz* Ⓜ *Line A: Staroměstská.*

Vinárna U Sudu. Although Prague is beer territory, this pays homage to that other camp: wine. A mazelike, multilevel cellar forms the large wine bar in a baroque building. This is usually one of the first places during the year to crack open *burčák*, new wine served shortly after harvest. ⊠ *Vodičkova 10, Nové Město* ☎ *222–232–207* Ⓜ *Line B: Karlovo nám.*

CASINOS

Gambling is legal in Prague. Many bars, especially those open around the clock, have a few slot machines and are marked with a sign that says *herna bar*. For those who want a little more action, most of the big hotels provide some sort of gaming room. A few casinos downtown stand out from the rest.

Casino Palais. Old-world charm and high betting limits are the trademarks of this gambling hall in a historic rococo palace. For those who wish to go incognito, a private room is also available. Games include roulette and poker, plus slot machines. This one is the destination of choice for local high rollers. ⊠ *Na Příkopě 10, Nové Město* ☎ *224–221–636* ⊕ *www.casinopalais.cz* Ⓜ *Line A or B: Můstek.*

Casino Royale Pershing. One of the less forbidding, more casual casinos has outdoor seating for food and drinks in nice weather, and a few large windows facing a pleasant Vinohrady square. The name is in an awkward effort to cash in on the James Bond film that was shot in Prague. The bar is open really late as well, to 6 AM for people who want to get out of the center. ⊠ *Nám. Jiřího z Poděbrad 16, Vinohrady* ☎ *No phone* ⊕ *ccbcz.eu/pershing.html* Ⓜ *Line A: Nám. Jiřího z Poděbrad.*

Happy Day Casino. A little piece of Las Vegas lost in the center of Prague, this casino has dozens of slot machines, a few tables, plus blinking lights and lots of bling-bling. ⊠ *Václavské nám. 35, Nové Město* ☎ *224–233–506* Ⓜ *Line A or B: Můstek.*

CLUBBING

The number of clubs in Prague is ever-growing, and the party shows no sign of letting up. Local house, techno, jungle, and trip-hop DJs—not to mention fairly well-known visitors—have made a home in some clubs. Other places specialize in campy Czech pop songs, which are often cheesy Western tunes from the '70s and '80s with Czech lyrics. Most dance spots open at 9 or 10 PM, but things don't heat up until after midnight, and then keep going until 4 or 5 AM. Unless there's a particularly well-known DJ, the cover charge is usually fairly nominal—30 Kč to 150 Kč.

Buddha Bar Prague. A giant statue of Buddha is an unmissable main feature of this split-level upscale restaurant/dance-club-with-a-DJ combo. Decorated in an Asian theme with dark tones, this dark club attracts a young, upscale clientele. The bar is attached to a hotel of the same name but has its own entrance, and the whole complex is part of a Paris-based chain that is in Asia, South America, and Europe. Everything in the club and hotel is tied to the concept of "Buddha attitude," for exotic relaxation. The drinks and meals are on the pricey side, but that goes along with the high-tone atmosphere.*Jakubská 8, Staré Město* ☎ *221–776–400* ⊕ *www.buddha-bar.cz.*

True to its name, Cloud 9 pairs cocktails with a bird's eye view of Prague.

Fodor'sChoice
★ **Cloud 9 Sky Bar & Lounge.** Opened in late 2008, the rooftop bar of the Hilton offers a spectacular view, with drink prices to match. The bar measures approximately 200 feet, and the lighting used more than 1,000 yards of wire. A small area now serves as a relaxed "exclusive" zone behind a beaded curtain that can be reserved for a per-person consumption minimum, easily met with a few top-shelf drinks. The bar also boasts its own elevator running exclusively from lobby to rooftop. Live music and DJs perform Thursday through Saturday. Check out some of the temporary art exhibits. In the winter there's an outdoor bar made of blocks of ice. ⊠ *Pobřežní 1, Karlín* ☎ *224–842–999* ⊕ *www. hiltonprague.cz* Ⓜ *Line B: Florenc.*

Duplex. Mick Jagger booked this multilevel penthouse nightclub for his 60th birthday party. On weekend evenings there's dancing and DJs with music that varies widely. Because of the location and aggressive marketing on the street level, the crowd is heavy with tourists who like to travel in packs, and prices are above the norm. In late 2009 the lower part became a restaurant called Duplex Kogo to cater to both day-time diners and late-night revelers. ⊠ *Václavské nám. 21, Nové Město* ☎ *732–221–111* ⊕ *www.duplex.cz* Ⓜ *Line A or B: Můstek.*

Face to Face. The break-dancing scenes from the film *Everything Is Illuminated* were shot in this trendy club located on a noisy island. Music varies, usually based on a party of some kind or a theme night. The club, formerly called Face to Face and renovated in 2007, has adopted a policy of including drinks with the admission fee. ⊠ *Ostrov Stvanice1125, Štvanice ostrov* ☎ *242–498–353* ⊕ *www.klubfacetoface.cz* Ⓜ *Line C: Vltavská.*

Karlovy Lázně. Inside a former bathhouse next to the Charles Bridge, this club claims to be the biggest in central Europe. We're not sure about that, but it is pretty big, with four levels of music ranging from house to soul and even old-school disco. The crowd tends to be a mix of young locals and tourists. Lines can be long on weekends. Recently the venue introduced an all-inclusive VIP area that can be booked by small groups. ✉ *Smetanovo nábř. 198, Staré Město* ☎ *222–220–502* ⊕ *www.karlovylazne.cz* Ⓜ *Line A: Staroměstská.*

Le Clan. Keep your eyes peeled: the entry here is easy to miss, as this venue bills itself as a private club. It opens around 10 PM, but the action seldom gets going until very late. There are several downstairs levels, but some are only for VIPs. Note, in keeping with its elitist image, sometimes poorly dressed or otherwise uncool people are denied entry. ✉ *Balbínova 23, Vinohrady* ☎ *222–251–226* ⊕ *www.leclan.cz* Ⓜ *Line A: Nám. Míru.*

★ **Mecca**. Show off your expensive designer jeans here. This converted factory is *the* place to get down with the überhip. However, if you're not a night owl, be aware that the DJ doesn't usually get going until after midnight. Live acts tend to start around 10 PM. The club has great lighting, a mirrored disco ball, and a downstairs lounge. They now have a VIP Hummer to pick up guests who meet certain "minimum requirements." ✉ *U Průhonu 3, Holešovice* ☎ *283–870–522* ⊕ *www.mecca. cz* Ⓜ *Line C: Vltavská.*

Radost FX. A clubbing institution dating from the early '90s, this place still draws a loyal following. The dance floor can be kind of cramped, but other rooms offer lots of seats and couches for hanging out. Those with two left feet can chill upstairs with a drink or eat food late in the vegetarian restaurant. ✉ *Bělehradská 120, Nové Město* ☎ *603–193– 711* ⊕ *www.radostfx.cz* Ⓜ *Line C: I. P. Pavlova.*

Retro. With a location just a bit out of the center, this club provides exodus from the hassle of downtown. The street-level part is a pleasant functionalist-style café with outdoor seating, and the lower level houses a club with a big dance floor. The name is a bit misleading. Although there are some '80s nights and other "retro" music events, the bulk of the schedule is hip-hop and other more contemporary sounds. It's also been increasing the number of live acts, ranging from John Mayall to heavy metal bands on reunion tours. ✉ *Francouzská 4, Vinohrady* ☎ *604–956–272 bar–restaurant* Ⓜ *Line A: Nám. Míru.*

EVENING BOAT TRIPS

Dinner Cruise with Music. This "dinner cruise" usually degenerates into a sing-along once the beer kicks in, so be prepared for boisterous merriment. The boat is heated, and this cruise runs in both winter and summer. The relatively early departure hour—7 PM—means you can catch the sunset in summertime. Entry price includes a buffet dinner and welcome drink, but no additional beverages. ✉ *Na Františku, under Čechův most, Josefov* ☎ *224–810–030* ⊕ *www.evd.cz.*

Evening boat trips show another side to the Vltava river.

Evening cruise. Significantly cheaper than trips with live music, the cruises offer some fun pop music, a dance floor, and a bar. After a three-hour cruise, the boat anchors until 2 AM for more partying. Tickets are available at the boats, with departures at 8 PM in the summer. ✉ *Rašínovo na'břeží, near Palackého bridge* ☎ *224–931–013* ⊕ *www. paroplavba.cz.*

Jazzboat. The Russian-made riverboat *Kotva* was refitted in 2001, and claims to be the fastest on the Vltava. Its bands are usually local. Be on time for the shows, as the ship normally leaves at the appointed 8:30 PM departure time. You can also buy food during the cruise, but take cash, since credit cards are not accepted. ✉ *Usually takes off from pier No. 5, under Čechův most, Josefov* ☎ *731–183–180* ⊕ *www.jazzboat. cz* Ⓜ *Line A: Staroměstská.*

U Bukanýra. The name works out to "At the Buccaneer," but the logo bears more than a passing resemblance to Humphrey Bogart in *The African Queen*. This anchored "house-boat music bar" gives you the feeling of being on the river without having to commit to a three-hour tour. Besides a few life preservers, the nautical theme isn't taken too far. Beware that the boat sometimes does change its "permanent" location. ✉ *Nábř. L. Svobody, Josefov* ☎ *608–973–582* ⊕ *www.bukanyr.cz* Ⓜ *Line A: Staroměstská.*

GAY AND LESBIAN

There are a number of good clubs for gay men, though the scene changes regularly. Several clubs have recently opened up in the Vinohrady area, but they are still vastly outnumbered by straight clubs in the area. Clubs—at least on the street level—are fairly discreet, and a rainbow-color sign might be the only clue that a bar caters to a gay clientele. Unfortunately, lesbians have fewer establishments to choose from, but some clubs host a ladies' night. For more information, check out the Web sites at ⊕ *prague.gayguide.net* and ⊕ *come2prague.com*.

Boudoir U sta rán. An old restaurant sign with a few missing letters creates the name of this discreet, gay-friendly bar with a backyard beer garden. There is no Web site, but it does have a Facebook page. ⊠ *Francouzská 50, Vinohrady*.

Bum Bum Club. The name works out to "boom boom," but the pun is probably intended. A nondescript residential building hides two levels of lounge chairs, flashy lighting, two bars, and a dance floor. Drinks are cheaper here than at other clubs. ⊠ *Ondříčkova 15, Vinohrady* ☎ *725–122–323* ⊕ *www.club-bumbum.cz*.

Drakes. The admission price allows for multiple visits over 24 hours to this club, which is owned by a gay porn director. Theme parties take place on a regular basis, so be sure to check the schedule. The drinks and admission are pricey, so most of the patrons are tourists. ⊠ *Zborovaská 50, Smíchov* ☎ *257–326–828* ⊕ *www.drakes.cz* Ⓜ *Line B: Anděl*.

Friends. This friendly bar in Old Town serves reasonably priced beer—and Western-priced mixed drinks—in a roomy cellar space. There's plenty of seating most weeknights, but it does get busy on weekends. Videos play every night, and a DJ spins after 10 on weekends, luring people onto a small dance floor. There's no cover. ⊠ *Bartolomějská 11, Nové Město* ☎ *224–236–772* ⊕ *www.friendsprague.cz* Ⓜ *Line A or B: Můstek*.

JampaDampa. One of the city's few lesbian clubs has a karaoke night and an occasional drag king show. The two-level space, including a vaulted basement, is a little less flashy than most other clubs. Drinks are quite reasonable considering it is close to Wenceslas Square. ⊠ *V Tůních 10, Nové Město* ☎ *739–592–099* ⊕ *www.jampadampa.cz*.

The Saints. This small British-owned pub and cocktail bar is centrally located near several other gay and gay-friendly establishments in Vinohrady. The owners also run a gay-friendly travel and accommodation service. ⊠ *Polská 32, Vinohrady* ☎ *222–250–326* ⊕ *www.praguesaints. cz* Ⓜ *Line C: Nám. Míru*.

Termix. Borders on claustrophobic on weekends, this club has precious little standing room—especially with the decorative automobile sticking out of the bar wall. The music themes vary from night to night. It's closed Monday and Tuesday. Note: The street-level door is easy to miss. ⊠ *Třebízského 4a, Vinohrady* ☎ *222–710–462* ⊕ *www.club-termix.cz* Ⓜ *Line C: Nám. Míru*.

Valentino. It claims to be the largest gay club in Prague, and with three floors that's probably right. There's a disco, several bars, and other attractions for a male crowd. Catch dancing every night, special parties on weekends, and the occasional fashion show. ⊠ *Vinohradská 40, Vinohrady* ☎ *222–513–491* ⊕ *www.club-valentino.cz.*

JAZZ CLUBS

Jazz gained notoriety under the Communists as a subtle form of protest, and the city still has some great jazz clubs, featuring everything from swing to blues and modern. All listed clubs have a cover charge, usually around 100 Kč to 250 Kč, but tickets can be substantially higher for visiting acts.

Fodor'sChoice ★ **AghaRTA.** Bearing the name of an old Miles Davis album, this small but charming vaulted basement is home base for many local jazz acts. The management also runs a jazz record label and sells their CDs at the club's store. The place can't handle big acts, so the club's ongoing jazz festival often puts name acts into Lucerna Music Bar *(⇨ Rock and Live Music Clubs, below).* Music starts around 9 PM, but come an hour earlier to get a seat. ⊠ *Železná 16, Staré Město* ☎ *222–211–275* ⊕ *www.agharta.cz* Ⓜ *Line A or C: Můstek.*

★ **Jazz Club U staré paní** *(USP Jazz Lounge).* This club, in a small hotel, hosts some of the better jazz acts in town, and DJs play after midnight. Like most of the other clubs, it's too small to handle the business. (Read: Show up early to get a decent seat.) The club also serves a late dinner. ⊠ *Michalská 9, Staré Město* ☎ *603–551–680* ⊕ *www.jazzlounge. cz* Ⓜ *Line A: Staroměstská.*

Jazz Dock. If you missed your boat tour, don't despair. The waterfront is becoming a trendy place, with modern-design entertainment venues popping up. This glass-enclosed nightclub built on a dock offers a view of the passing boat traffic and lit-up landmark buildings like the National Theater. Inside are a 30-foot-long bar and two concerts per night. ⊠ *Janáčkovo nábř. 2, Smíchov* ☎ *774–058–838* ⊕ *www.jazzdock. cz* Ⓜ *Line A: Anděl.*

Reduta. This is where President Bill Clinton jammed with Czech President Václav Havel in 1994, and lots of pictures of that night are still hanging around the joint. Reduta was one of the bigger clubs in the '60s and '70s, and still feels a little like a dated museum of those glory days. The coat-check person can be pretty aggressive, which is another throwback to the pre-1989 era. ⊠ *Národní 20, Nové Město* ☎ *224–912–246* ⊕ *www.redutajazzclub.cz* Ⓜ *Line B: Národní třída.*

U Malého Glena. Patrons are willing to cram into "Little Glen," where solid house bands and visiting acts come to jam. Get there early to stake out a seat near the stage; the tunnel-shape vault can be crowded. Upstairs they serve food until midnight. ⊠ *Karmelitská 23, Malá Strana* ☎ *257–531–717* ⊕ *www.malyglen.cz* Ⓜ *Line A: Malostranská.*

Ungelt. Hidden in the side streets behind Old Town Square, this basement has been around since the 15th century, and has been a club since 2000. The house bands are decent, and play jazz, blues, or fusion,

6

Take a break from the classical music scene with a performance at a local jazz club.

depending on the night. You won't be among locals, however. The touristy location and the price keep them at bay. ✉ *Týn 2, Staré Město* ☎ *224–895–748* ⊕ *www.jazzungelt.cz* Ⓜ *Line A: Staroměstská.*

ROCK AND LIVE MUSIC CLUBS

Prague's rock, alternative, and world music scene is thriving. Rock bands on reunion tours find enthusiastic crowds in clubs and arenas. Cover bands are pretty good (Lou Reed once mistook a recording by the local Velvet Underground's cover band for the real thing). World music, especially Romany bands, often sells out.

Futurum. Video parties and punk or Goth bands dominate the lineup at this out-of-the-way club with 1950s sci-fi decor, a solid video and sound system, and lots of beer-stained couches. ✉ *Zborovská 7, Smíchov* ☎ *257–328–571* ⊕ *www.musicbar.cz* Ⓜ *Line B: Anděl.*

Lucerna Music Bar. Rock bands on the comeback trail, touring bluesmen, plus Beatles and Rolling Stones cover bands make up the live schedule. Another big draw are the nights of 1980s or '90s music videos. ✉ *Vodičkova 36, Nové Město* ☎ *224–217–108* ⊕ *www.musicbar. cz* Ⓜ *Line A or B: Můstek.*

Malostranská Beseda. Back after several years of renovation, a now-spruced-up complex offers something different on every level—from an art gallery under the roof to a "video café," to a live music bar, restaurant, café, and basement beer pub. The live acts are mostly popular Czech bands. The building itself has quite a history as the former town hall and then a mecca for writers and artists. ✉ *Malostranské nám. 21,*

CLOSE UP

Late-Night Bites

Prague is getting better at catering to midnight munchies. During the last few years several places have opened up with late hours, and some are rather upscale, too. You can also find fast-food branches with late-night windows near major tram stops, and a few pubs serve really late as well. Václavské náměstí is lined with all-night food stands selling sausages on paper plates, but a planned renovation of the square may see many of these closing over the coming years.

Buddha Bar Prague. The lower level of this bar and nightclub serves a Pacific Rim inspired menu deep into the night. The prices are quite high, but the establishment brings a bit of class to late-night dining that had been missing. The restaurant is open to at least 3 AM. ⊠ *Jakubská 8, Staré Město* ☎ *221–776–400* ⊕ *www. buddha-bar.cz* Ⓜ *Line B: Náměstí Republiky.*

Duplex Kogo. Mediterranean-style food is served up in a rooftop restaurant above Wenceslas Square and below a popular dance club. Early in the week it closes at 11 PM, but Wednesday through Saturday it is open to 4 AM, with food available until 2 AM. ⊠ *Václavské nám. 21, Nové Město* ☎ *732–221–111* ⊕ *www.kogo. cz.* Ⓜ *Line A or B: Můstek.*

J.J. Murphy's Irish Bar. Decent burgers, pork chops, steaks, and shepherd's pie are served in this Irish sports bar a bit later than most places. Closing time varies, depending on how busy it is. ⊠ *Tržiště 4, Malá Strana* ☎ *257–535–575* ⊕ *www. jjmurphys.cz* Ⓜ *Line A: Malostranská.*

Luna di Notte. The Tuscan owners of "Moon of the Night" hope to fill the void for after-theater and late-night

fine dining, long popular in Italy and other Mediterranean countries. The menu ventures far beyond pasta, making it a night-owl scene with some culinary ambition. It's open until 2 AM. ⊠ *Vězeňská 3, Staré Město* ☎ *222– 312–999* ⊕ *www.lunadinotte.cz* Ⓜ *Line A: Staroměstská.*

Palác Akropolis. Tucked into the corner of a nightclub, this restaurant serves a variety of reasonably priced meals, including a few vegetarian selections, until midnight. ⊠ *Kubelíkova 27, Žižkov* ☎ *299–330– 913* Ⓜ *Line A: Nám. Jiřího z Poděbrad.*

Radost FX. The restaurant upstairs from the nightclub of the same name serves international vegetarian food to at least midnight, often much later, but seating is limited. ⊠ *Bělehradská 120, Nové Město* ☎ *224–254–776* ⊕ *www.radostfx.cz* Ⓜ *Line C: I.P. Pavlova.*

Restaurace Tlustá Koala. The Victorian flair may be puzzling, but originally the "Fat Koala" was part of the John Bull Brit-pub chain. The menu has a few attempts at international dishes, and it's all quite reasonably priced considering the area. The restaurant is open until at least 2 AM. ⊠ *Senovážná 8, Nové Město* ☎ *222–245–401* ⊕ *www.tlustakoala. cz* Ⓜ *Line B: Nám. Republiky.*

U Havrana (The Raven). This is a typical old-school Czech pub with *guláš* (goulash) and fried cheese. Although the atmosphere is a bit smoky, it's the only one of its kind to cook really late. U Havrana used to be open around the clock, but now it's open until 5 AM. ⊠ *Hálkova 6, Nové Město* ☎ *296– 200–020* ⊕ *www.restauraceuhavrana. cz* Ⓜ *Line C: I.P. Pavlova.*

6

Malá Strana ☎ 257–409–112 ⊕ *www. malostranska-beseda.cz* Ⓜ *Line A: Malostranská.*

★ **Palác Akropolis**. This is the city's best live music club, and home to an ongoing world-music festival called United Colors of Akropolis. When shows are sold out, though, this place can be pretty packed. The main room closes at 10 PM due to noise concerns. DJs play in the two side bars until late in the evening. ⊠ *Kubelíkova 27, Žižkov* ☎ *299–330–913* Ⓜ *Line A: Nám. Jiřího z Poděbrad.*

Rock Café. This little club hosts punk and alternative rock acts with the occasional screening of a movie on video or some avant-garde theater. The interior was rebuilt in 2006, making it a bit warmer and more inviting. ⊠ *Národní 20, Nové Město* ☎ *224–914–416* ⊕ *www.rockcafe.cz* Ⓜ *Line B: Národní třída.*

Fodor's Choice **Roxy**. Part nightclub, part performance space, the Roxy doubles as a
★ residence for DJs and a popular venue for electronica and touring cult bands. The large former theater has a comfortable, lived-in feel. The fun usually ends around 10 PM or so owing to complaints from the neighbors about noise. All exits from the club are final, and patrons are encouraged not to hang around the area. Upstairs, the NoD space has all manner of bizarre acts. Monday is free. ⊠ *Dlouhá 33, Staré Město* ☎ *224–826–296* ⊕ *www.roxy.cz* Ⓜ *Line B: Nám. Republiky.*

Švandovo divadlo Na Smichove. This popular Smíchov nightspot does double duty as a concert venue on some nights and a drama stage on others. Interesting avant-garde bands occasionally fill gaps in the schedule. ⊠ *Štefánikova 57, Smíchov* ☎ *234–651–111* ⊕ *www.svandovodivadlo. cz* Ⓜ *Line B: Anděl.*

Vagon. When it fills up, this long and narrow room offers only a few good spots to actually see the band that's playing, so video projectors also show the action on the walls toward the back. The emphasis is on Czech rock acts, with concerts starting at 9 and DJs weekends at midnight. ⊠ *Národní 25, Staré Město* ☎ *221–085–599* ⊕ *www.vagon. cz* Ⓜ *Line B: Národní třída.*

Shopping

WORD OF MOUTH

"Bohemia crystal is everywhere and I got tired of seeing it in all those tourist shops, you couldn't get away from it. If I were to buy a vase in Prague, I'd go to the flagship Moser store (a fab building, to boot) for something traditional or Blue Praha or Artel for something modern."

—MLF611

SHOPPING PLANNER

Top Buys in Prague

Maps of Prague's art deco and cubist architecture from Kubista

Organic body products, made with Czech produce and herbs, from Botanicus

A unique Bohemian crystal vase from Material

A linden-wood marionette from Truhlar Marionety

An innovative piece of jewelry from Czech-owned Belda Shop

An antique printing block with textile drawing from Traditional

V.A.T. Know-How

When making a purchase, ask for a V.A.T. refund form, and find out whether the merchant gives refunds (not all stores are required to do so). Have the form stamped by customs officials when you leave the country and drop it off at the refund-service counter to receive 20% back on all your purchases (10% back on books or food from grocery stores). Consult the Travel Smart chapter at the back of the book for more information.

Major Shopping Districts

Tree-lined **Pařížská ulice** is Prague's swankiest shopping street. Exclusive designers like Gucci, Louis Vuitton, and Hermès, to name a few, draw steady streams of luxury shoppers—and gaping tourists—all day long.

Stroll **Dlouhá třída**, extending off Old Town Square, for Czech fashion and design. Hipster favorite Klára Nademlýnská has a boutique here.

In the shadow of Prašné brány, **Na Příkopě** overflows with popular clothing chains like Zara and H&M. Crowded, and rife with sales, this street can feel overwhelming.

A handsome boulevard extending from the National Museum to Na Příkopě, **Václavské náměstí** has an energy level on a par with Times Square. Prague's megabookstore and two British department stores are all crammed in.

Street Markets

Havelská is a charming open-air market, centrally located in Staré Město, featuring touristy kitsch, seasonal trinkets, and handmade jewelry alongside fresh fruits and vegetables. The market is open daily.

River Town market, also known as Prazska or Holešovice, presents a veritable collage of wares along the Vltava. Devote most of your time to the farm-fresh produce and foods. Take the metro Line C (red line) to Vltavská station, and then catch any tram heading east. Exit at the first stop, Prazska tržnice. The market is closed Sunday.

Prague's annual **Easter Market** lends frivolity to the city. For two weeks before and after the holiday, stalls in Old Town and Wenceslas Squares sell traditional foods and assorted wooden items, like hand-painted eggs. Pomlázka, braided whips, are a traditional fixture.

December is arguably the prettiest time of year to visit Prague, thanks to the **Christmas Market** in the city's main squares. From December 5 (St. Nicholas' Day), wooden booths sell Czech handicrafts, piping-hot snacks, and spicy mulled wine. Performances by choirs and musical ensembles are held in Old Town Square throughout the month, all in the glow of the towering spruce tree.

By Sarah
Amandolare

Like the city itself, shopping in Prague presents a clash of old and new. Case in point: Although world-renowned crystal and glassware is still made by hand, the designs are often wildly modern.

Shops throughout the city are alternately exuberant and solemn, tending toward over-the-top or elegantly minimalist styles. Prague may eschew the middle of the road, but seesawing between these extremes in the city's historic center is great fun.

Endearing traditional crafts are available on every cobblestoned street. Each region of the Czech Republic has its own specialty, and many are represented in Prague. Wooden toys and carvings, ceramic dishes, delicate lace, and embroidered textiles all make perfect "I got it in Prague" gifts. The Czechs are also masterful herbalists, and put plants to good use in fragrant soaps and bath products made on local farms.

That said, every city has its kitsch, and Prague is no different. Marionettes have been a favorite Czech handicraft and storytelling vehicle since the late 18th century, and they are ubiquitous here. The trick is avoiding mass-produced versions at tourist kiosks. Trusty artisan shops sell a mishmash of sinister and cutesy marionettes made by skilled craftsmen. With a little digging, you can even find intricate antique puppets.

And speaking of antiques, art galleries and antiques stores seem to dot every street, and can range from pristine to dusty and cluttered. Either way, the unpredictable jumbles of merchandise offer a fun day of flea market–like spelunking—you may pick through purses from the 1930s in one shop and find cubist office chairs or porcelain figurines in the next. Meanwhile, the city's enchanting antiquarian bookshops fill shelves with Shakespearean sonnets translated into Czech, alongside old maps of Asia and the Middle East.

If you like your souvenirs to sparkle, garnet peddlers abound. But take heed: all that glitters isn't garnet—many are not the real deal. True Czech garnets are intensely dark red. Also known as pyrope or Bohemian garnet, these precious stones have been mined here for centuries. Tight clusters of garnets are found on antique pieces, while modern baubles are often sleeker and set in gold or silver. Stick to our recommended

Christmas markets in Prague show off the regional handicrafts.

shops for quality gems, and inquire about the setting—if a low-priced bauble seems too good to be true, it could be set in low-quality pot metal.

Fashionistas aren't forgotten either. You may not recognize Czech designers from glossy magazines, but their unknown status only makes them more of a true find. Expect clothes that are youthful, quirky, brightly colored, and patterned to the hilt. If you crave big luxury labels, the aptly named Paris street (aka Pařížská ulice) will give you your dose of runway glam. Do not expect any steals, unless you're willing to frequent the city's impressive selection of chain stores. Mango and Zara, for example, are on-trend but also sell affordable classic pieces.

Most of Prague's shops are open from 10 AM until 6 or 7 PM, and malls tend to stay open until 9 or 10 PM.

If shopkeepers in Prague seem aloof, don't be dissuaded—try greeting them with "dobry den" when entering a store, and you may be surprised by their warmth.

ANTIQUES

The post-communist glory days of antiquing may have passed, but Prague still presents an attractive assortment of heirlooms for collectors. Most shops stick to a jumble of art nouveau, art deco, and cubist items, as the vast majority of baroque pieces were snagged in the early 1990s. Nearly every antiques shop, or *starožitnosti*, in Prague also peddles clusters of dusty knickknacks, Czech glass, and porcelain.

Art Deco Galerie. The quintessential vintage shop just off Old Town Square is pleasantly cluttered with art deco–era sculptures and furnishings. Those with eclectic style will love the intricate brooches, turban-style headbands, and silk scarves here. Leather gloves and tea sets are suitably ladylike. ⊠ *Michalská 21, Staré Město* ☎ *224–223–076* ⊕ *www.artdecogalerie-mili.com* Ⓜ *Line A or B: Můstek.*

Fodor's Choice **Bric a Brac.** If you like the sensation of unearthing your treasure, this
★ antiques store is the ticket. About the size of a closet, this shop uses every nook to display a mix of vintage handbags, tin *Pilsner Urquell* signs, charming old typewriters, weighty pocket watches, and more. Memorable gifts can be found among the clutter—that colorful Turkish-Macedonian tobacco tin could make a great jewelry box. Ask the friendly English-speaking shopkeeper for tips. ⊠ *Týnská 7, Staré Město* ☎ *222–326–484* Ⓜ *Line A: Staroměstská.*

Dorotheum. Central Europe's answer to Sotheby's, this world-renowned auction house was founded in Austria in the early 1700s, and set up shop in Prague in 1992. Prices are quite steep, and items are appropriately opulent. Naturally the antique dishes and sculptures, 19th century paintings, ornate furniture, jewelry, and watches are worthy investments. ⊠ *Ovocný trh 2, Nové Město* ☎ *224–222–001* ⊕ *www. dorotheum.cz* Ⓜ *Line B: Nám. Republiky.*

JHB Starožitnosti. This shop has beautiful art deco and art nouveau diamond rings, porcelain and brass decorative objects, and furniture. But the company's specialty is clocks from the 18th- and 19th centuries hailing from Austria, the Czech Republic, France, and Germany. Antique wristwatches featured in the window displays also draw longing stares from knowing collectors. ⊠ *Panská 1, Nové Město* ⊕ *www.jhbantique. cz* ☎ *222–245–836* Ⓜ *Line A: Staroměstská.*

Starožitnosti Ungelt. Tucked away beneath an archway behind Týn Church, this elegant shop features a selection of art nouveau and art deco items. Beautiful glass vases from Bohemia-based companies Loetz and Harachov, and Meissen porcelain figurines, are standouts. ⊠ *Týn 1, Staré Město* ☎ *224–895–454* ⊕ *www.antiqueungelt.cz* Ⓜ *Line A: Staroměstská.*

ART GALLERIES

There is no mistaking Prague's creative energy, particularly inside the city's free-spirited galleries. The best are refreshingly quiet, devoid of tourists, and anything but stuffy, inviting visitors to peer closely at framed works or rifle through stacks of prints.

Galerie NoD. Above the Roxy music club on Dlouhá street, this gallery space is filled with youthful energy. Exhibits feature edgy work by up-and-coming artists like Josef Zacek. The gallery also hosts experimental theater, music, and comedy nights, and touts an adjacent bar and Internet café sprinkled with twentysomethings on laptops. The space is funded by the Linhart Foundation, which backs much of Prague's offbeat culture. ⊠ *Dlouhá 33, Staré Město* ☎ *224–826–296* ⊕ *nod.roxy. cz* Ⓜ *Line B: Nám. Republiky.*

Painted egg ornaments are just one of the handmade items for sale around the city.

★ **Galerie Peithner-Lichtenfels**. Jam-packed with paintings and drawings, this gallery is overseen by an approachable owner perched behind a cluttered desk. Among the wares are works by both famous and lesser-known Czech artists. A glass-covered table near the front of the store is crowded with small original drawings. ⊠ *Michalská 12, Staré Město* ☎ *224–227–680* ⊕ *www.gplc.cz* Ⓜ *Line A: Staroměstská.*

Galerie UBK. Specializing in postwar surrealism, this airy gallery features ongoing exhibits of work by Czech artists, such as filmmaker and mixed media artist Jan Švankmajer. If artwork prices are too many koruny for your comfort, a good alternative is picking up a book on the artist's exhibition, also for sale here. ⊠ *Betlémské nám. 8, Staré Město* ☎ *222–220–689* Ⓜ *Line B: Národní třída.*

BAGS, SCARVES, AND ACCESSORIES

Prague offers a stellar mix of high and low fashion: Glamorous boutiques peddle status purses and trendy chain stores offer of-the-moment fun pieces. If you crave something original, the city's open-air markets and antiques stores often hold surprises.

★ **Antique Újezd**. This dimly lit antiques shop fills bureau drawers with vintage accessories that will add a touch of luster to any outfit. A selection of dainty 1930s pocketbooks, clutches, and bejeweled coin purses should not be missed. Clusters of rings, bracelets, and charms awaiting chains are fun to rifle through. Check out the glass cases housing a pricey supply of diamonds, pearls, and gems. ⊠ *Újezd 37* ☎ *257–217–*

177 ⊕ *www.antique-ujezd.cz* ⊗ *Weekdays 10–6, Sat. noon–6. Closed Sun.* Ⓜ *Line A: Malostranská.*

Coccinelle Accessories. Girly is the name of the game inside this quaint boutique filled with Italian leather bags in soft shades of rose and blue, many with delicate ruching. Displays coordinate bags and wallets, perfect for women who like things pulled together and polished. Bureau drawers are stuffed with soft, floral-patterned scarves to top off each look. ⊠ *Náměstí Republiky 5, Staré Město* ☎ *222–002–340* ⊕ *www. coccinelle.cz* Ⓜ *Line B: Nám. Republiky.*

Decastello. Grandma's attic never smelled this good. In addition to colorful translucent soaps providing that flowery aroma, you'll find displays of long necklaces strung with oversized beads, and shelves of tiny wooden owls with jewels for eyes. A bit of everything is found here, and low prices mean you can pick and choose your favorites and even scoop up a pretty wooden jewelry box for storage. ⊠ *Karmelitská 26* ☎ *257–532–515* ⊕ *www.aa.cz/decastellodarky* ⊗ *Weekdays 10–7, weekends 10–6* Ⓜ *Line A: Malostranská.*

Francesco Biasia. These impossibly plush leather bags and wallets are given just enough adornment to be memorable—think silver zippers of a substantial weight, chain-link handles, and touches of shimmering metallic thread. The large black-and-white photographs of Roman ruins and the Tuscan countryside adorning the space add to the Italian air. ⊠ *Pařížská 24, Staré Město* ☎ *224–815–846* ⊕ *www.biasia.com* Ⓜ *Line A: Staroměstská.*

Hermès. Those iconic silk scarves that embody Parisian chic can be found here arranged in perfect rows in a glass display case among the other equestrian-inspired accessories. Racks of gem-color silk ties are on display upstairs, but it's the lush leather goods on the first floor that are the main attraction. ⊠ *Pařížská 12, Staré Město* ☎ *224–817–545* ⊕ *www.hermes.com* Ⓜ *Line A: Staroměstská.*

Louis Vuitton. A statuesque blonde tries a platinum watch on for size, and turns to her male companion for a kiss of approval—it's all part of the luxurious scene at this boutique on the corner of *Pařížská* and Siroka. Here you'll find a fleet of scarves, luggage, and of course, bags, all bearing the famous LV logo. ⊠ *Pařížská 13, Staré Město* ☎ *224–812–774* ⊕ *www.louisvuitton.com* Ⓜ *Line A: Staroměstská.*

BOOKS AND PRINTS

Known as *antikvariáts,* rare-book shops are freckled throughout the city, and hold some of the most beguiling souvenirs. Alongside handsomely worn academic texts and hardcover literary classics (mostly in Czech), there are often maps and advertisements steeped in Czechoslovak history. Prague also has excellent English-language bookstores, a few with charming cafés should you crave a quiet place to sit and read.

Anagram Books. Laid-back staff and a pretty view of Týn Square are part of the appeal here. In addition to a wide selection of fiction and non-fiction, there is a center table with a motley assortment of cookbooks, fashion, and architecture titles, and a few literary journals.

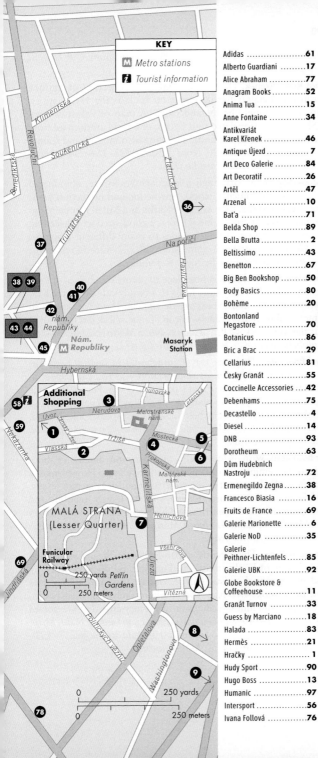

Additional
Shopping

Úvoz

Vlašská

MALÁ STRANA
(Lesser Quarter)

Funicular
Railway

0   250 yards *Petřín*
                     Gardens
0   250 meters

0   250 yards

0   250 meters

Nám.
Republiky

nám.
Republiky

Masaryk
Station

✉ *Týn 4, Staré Město* ☎ *224–895–737* ⊕ *www.anagram.cz* Ⓜ *Line B: Nám. Republiky.*

★ **Antikvariát Karel Křenek**. Despite the extensive collection of antique maps, prints, and engravings dating as far back as the 16th century, this shop is refreshingly bright and clean. A map of Pakistan from 1540, a Shakespeare translated into Czech, or a vivid art deco ad from 1900 are among some of the finds. The shop also mounts and frames works on request. ✉ *Národní 20, Nové Město* ☎ *222–314–734* ⊕ *www. karelkrenek.com* Ⓜ *Line B: Národní třída.*

Big Ben Bookshop. This cozy English-language bookstore, illuminated by a large wooden chandelier, stocks new fiction and nonfiction titles. Works by Czech authors, such as Franz Kafka and Milan Kundera, figure prominently on the front table. There is a good-sized sci-fi selection, and a thorough offering of travel guides to many different countries as well. ✉ *Malá Štupartská 5, Staré Město* ☎ *224–826–565* ⊕ *www. bigbenbookshop.com* Ⓜ *Line B: Nám. Republiky.*

Globe Bookstore & Coffeehouse. A fine place to peruse the shelves of English-language titles, this cozy store leads to a trendy café down the hall, where lattes, laptops, and expats are de rigueur. If you're hoping to attend literary, film, or arts events while in Prague, check out the wall of fliers near the front desk. ✉ *Pštrossova 6, Nové Město* ☎ *224–934–203* ⊕ *www.globebookstore.cz* Ⓜ *Line B: Národní třída.*

Kiwi Travel Bookshop. There are travel guidebooks in English here, but they are not organized into a separate section—so you can expect to do a bit of poking around, but that's part of the fun. Peruse the huge assortment of maps if you are planning to do any traveling outside of Prague. Sales associates are quite helpful, and most speak some English. ✉ *Jungmannova 23, Nové Město* ☎ *224–948–455* ⊕ *www.mapykiwi. cz* Ⓜ *Line B: Národní třída.*

Neoluxor Bookstore. With its four floors, music section, and coffee shop, this bookstore is reminiscent of major American chains. However, only a small area in the basement is set aside for English-language books. The store is an excellent source for maps of the Czech Republic and other European cities and countries, and has some travel guidebooks in English. ✉ *Václavské nám. 41, Nové Město* ☎ *296–110–351* ⊕ *www. neoluxor.cz* Ⓜ *Line A: Muzeum.*

Shakespeare & Sons. The recently expanded Malá Strana store now boasts two floors of books, mostly in English, and displays work by local and international artists. Farther out in Vršovice, a cozy café is flanked by a smoke-free back room, where shelves of used books, weekly readings, and film screenings draw literary crowds. ✉ *Krymská 12, Vršovice* ☎ *271–740–839* ⊕ *www.shakes.cz* Ⓜ *Line A: Nám. Míru, Tram 4, 22, 23* ✉ *U Lužického semináře 10, Malá Strana* ☎ *257–531–894* ⊕ *www.shakes.cz* Ⓜ *Line A: Malostranská.*

CHILDREN'S CLOTHING

Benetton. The preppy line downsizes its colorful polo shirts and crew-neck sweaters, adding a few sequins and cartoon character prints for fun, inside this small shop on the hectic fringe of Old Town Square. The huge Na Příkopě store has children's clothes downstairs. ⊠ *Železna 1, Staré Město* ☎ *224–221–910* ☺ *Daily 10:30–7* Ⓜ *Line A or B: Můstek* ⊠ *Na Příkopě 4, Staré Město* ☎ *224–236–744* Ⓜ *Line A or B: Můstek.*

Malá Ela. Little ones are indulged with big style here. Bohemian dresses by French label Catimini, and happy-go-lucky play clothes by Dutch brand Cakewalk are among the most adorable offerings. ⊠ *Karolíny Svetlé 18, Staré Město* ☎ *572–695–476* ⊕ *www.malaela.cz* ☺ *Weekdays 10–2, Sat. 11–3* Ⓜ *Line B: Národní třída.*

CLOTHING: MEN'S AND WOMEN'S

Diesel. Tough jeans, slinky dresses, and edgy accessories by the Italian label occupy two floors of this glitzy new store. If your pristine wardrobe needs a few gritty updates, anything here will do the trick. ⊠ *Pařížská 28* ☎ *222–317–647* Ⓜ *Line A or B: Můstek.*

Guess by Marciano. A jolt of rock and roll characterizes clothing here. Displays combine preppy classics, such as trench coats, with edgy basics like neon T-shirts for a casual yet energetic vibe. Calvin Klein and Pinko are on the first floor of this location; walk downstairs for Guess. ⊠ *Pařížská 22, Staré Město* ☎ *222–328–649* Ⓜ *Line A: Staroměstská.*

Kenvelo. A teen's dream, this shop is cluttered with affordable jeans, hooded sweatshirts, and T-shirts in various cuts. Be ready to sort through the somewhat messy displays to find the right size and color. It could be that a great simple sundress is in there, but rhinestone-encrusted or logo-adorned apparel might be hiding it. ⊠ *Václavské nám. 11, Nové Město* ☎ *251–011–028* Ⓜ *Line A or B: Můstek.*

Kenzo. The French fashion house, now led by Antonio Marras, makes clothing with a relaxed, bohemian feel. Nothing is too constricting or finished, particularly the billowy dresses and tops in lightweight fabrics, printed with smudgy tribal and floral patterns. Menswear is light-hearted and casual. Even the formal suits feature loose-fitting pants and long cardigans. ⊠ *U Prašné brány* ☎ *222–002–302* ⊕ *www.kenzo.com* ☺ *Weekdays 10–7, Sat. 10–6, Sun. 11–6* Ⓜ *Line B: Nám. Republiky.*

Marks & Spencer. This Czech flagship location of the popular British department store is housed inside the historic Melantrich building on Wenceslas Square. Browse four floors of stylish yet practical clothing, and trendy accessories that won't break the bank. Food items, such as coffees and teas, are also here. ⊠ *Václavské nám. 36, Nové Město* ☎ *224–237–503* ⊕ *www.marks-and-spencer.cz* Ⓜ *Line A or B: Můstek.*

Pietro Filipi. Taking its inspiration from the elegance and quality of Italian couture, this Czech brand makes timeless clothing for style-conscious professionals. Simple lines and understated prints result in classic pieces, like sailor-theme tops and floral silk dresses. ⊠ *Národní 31, Nové Město* ☎ *222–365–239* ⊕ *www.pietro-filipi.com* Ⓜ *Line B: Národní třída.*

Pour Pour. Can't bear the thought of leaving Prague without something completely unique? Stop by this little shop filled with eclectic creations by young, up-and-coming Czech designers. The Hedush label, for example, touts colorful knits with creative cutouts and unexpected patterns, while the voluminous dresses by Chatty tend toward neutral grays. The options will remind you why getting dressed can be an adventure. ⊠ *Vinohradská 74, Vinohrady* ⊕ *www.pourpour.com* ⊙ *Weekdays 11–7* Ⓜ *Line A: Jihiro Z Podebrad.*

Wilvorst. Boasting various urbane brands and occupying several residences on a posh street, Wilvorst is great fun to browse in. The young and svelte snag True Religion jeans and casual wear by Jean Paul Gautier, while chic preppies pick up hand-tailored suits by Eduard Dressler. Wealthy weekend warriors are covered, too, with yacht-ready clothing by Italian brand Paul and Shark. ⊠ *U Prašné brány 1, Nové Město* ☎ *222–323–573* Ⓜ *Line B: Nám. Republiky.*

CLOTHING: MEN'S ONLY

Shopping options are limited for men in Prague when compared with the overwhelming number of women's boutiques. But there are several international designers with men's stores around the city, and some have recently expanded their selection.

Ermenegildo Zegna. Men in the market for finely tailored suits (made-to-measure services are available) and posh basics like zip-front jackets and striped polos, will relish the atmosphere here. Signature colognes scent the store, which also sells stylish aviator and round-frame sunglasses to complete the pulled-together look. ⊠ *U Prašné brány 3, Staré Město* ☎ *224–810–018* ⊕ *www.zegna.com* Ⓜ *Line B: Nám. Republiky.*

Hugo Boss. For modern menswear, whether formal or casual, the German designer's gorgeously tailored pieces are unmatched. This store, stretching grandly around a Pařižská street corner, also stocks a fine selection of luggage and accessories. ⊠ *Pařížská 19, Staré Město* ☎ *222–327–260* ⊕ *www.hugoboss.com* Ⓜ *Line A: Staroměstská.*

Report's. High quality and the prices to match sum up this shop's selection of sleek Italian suits and country club–ready weekend wear. Crystal chandeliers illuminate display cases of crisp button-up shirts and silk ties, many in bright colors that add pop to those dashing suits. Touches of humor can be found in the fun pieces, like navy blazers with bright yellow stitching, or purple woven belts. ⊠ *V kolkovné 5, Staré Město* ☎ *222–329–823* Ⓜ *Line B: Nám. Republiky.*

CLOTHING: WOMEN'S ONLY

Trends tend to reach Prague after filtering through the world's runway capitals. But regardless of fads, Czech women prefer conspicuous clothing that's overtly feminine and often edgy. Certain designers have begun to pare things down, however, with beautifully refreshing results.

Alice Abraham. Inside her eye-catching boutique, the Czech designer shows off her flashy line. Clearly fond of animal prints and daring cuts,

Abraham is unafraid of pushing the fashion envelope, and her styles are anything but demure. ⊠ *Vodičkova 34, EGAP Building Nové Město* ☎ *604–846–462* ⊕ *www.aliceabraham.com* ◷ *Weekdays 10–7* Ⓜ *Line A or B: Můstek.*

Anima Tua. Not a single article of clothing is left without a touch of sparkle, courtesy of Italian brands like Pin Up and Love Sex Money. Even denim and bikinis come studded with gold or strung with chains, perfect for the girl on the prowl. ⊠ *Elišky Krásnohorské 13/3, Staré Město* ☎ *222–313–534* ⊕ *www.animatua.com* Ⓜ *Line A or B: Můstek.*

Anne Fontaine. There's something about the stormy gray wallpaper and white chandeliers that make this French designer's boutique feel as inviting as a walk-in closet. There are some feminine sweaters, mostly in black, but white blouses take center stage. Short or long-sleeved, lacy or sleek, they are nothing short of elegant, and remain the designer's signature item. ⊠ *Masna 12, Staré Město* ☎ *224–808–306* ⊕ *www. annefontaine.com* Ⓜ *Line A or B: Můstek.*

Bella Brutta. Spanish brands like Desigual and Melissa are the foundation of this youthful boutique. Led by two women with unconventional taste, the store holds some of the most modern and interesting clothing in Prague; unique prints and unexpected silhouettes are arresting, but not glaringly so. The store itself is set apart, located beside a teahouse up the hill from the American Embassy. ⊠ *Vlašská 13, Malá Strana* ☎ *776–867–124* ⊕ *www.bellabrutta.cz* Ⓜ *Line A: Malostranská.*

Bohème. The understated clothes and decor here tend toward creamy tones, muted grays, and warm browns. Great for work or brunch with friends, these garments by Czech designer Hana Stocklassa are classics with unexpected elements—a herringbone silk skirt with a few gentle pleats or a soft cardigan closed with asymmetrical buttons. Trying things on is a pleasure beneath the golden lighting from round overhead lamps. ⊠ *Dušní 8, Staré Město* ☎ *224–813–840* ⊕ *www.boheme. cz* Ⓜ *Line B: Nám. Republiky.*

DNB. Inside her chic studio close to the river, Czech designer Denisa Nova shows off carelessly sexy clothing that is both wearable and luxurious. Ruffles are left artfully unfinished, extra-long sweaters are torn in all the right places, and slick jackets lend just enough polish. ⊠ *Naprstkova 4* ☎ *222–221–342* ⊕ *www.denisanova.cz* ◷ *Weekdays 10–7, weekends 10–6* Ⓜ *Line B: Národní třída.*

Ivana Follová. Ms. Follová specializes in silk, which she dyes in bold patterns and shapes into gauzy, graffitied garments. You'll find bright statement pieces here, too, like bejeweled ballet flats and patterned trench coats and some distinctive accessories like chunky costume jewelry by other Czech designers. ⊠ *Vodičkova 36, Nové Město* ☎ *296–236–497* ⊕ *www.ivanafollova.cz* Ⓜ *Line A or B: Můstek.*

Fodor's Choice ★ Klára Nademlýnská. Catering to carefree hipsters, this Czech designer's style is trendy but comfortable. A close look at the original pieces inside this boutique off Old Town Square reveals a wealth of details: unusual draping, fantastically fun prints, or unexpected buttons. The views of Dlouhá Street out the front window don't hurt either. ⊠ *Dlouhá 3,*

DID YOU KNOW?

Part of the shopping experience in Prague is to enjoy the architecture. So act like a local and enjoy your day, don't rush it. And don't forget to look up to spot art nouveau details or old house signs that grace the contemporary stores.

Staré Město ☎ *224–818–769* ⊕ *www.klaranademlynska.cz* Ⓜ *Line B: Nám. Republiky.*

Leeda. This artistic-minded shop collaborates with graphic designers, photographers, and musicians. Clothes with whimsical touches—like pom-poms and bows in candy-colored pastels and neon shades—prove that grown-up dressing doesn't have to mean sacrificing fun. ✉ *Bartolomějská 1* ⊕ *www.leeda.cz* ⊙ *Weekdays and Sat. 11–7* ☎ *224–234–056* Ⓜ *Line B: Národní třída.*

Mango. The latest trends are presented with a bit more refinement by this Spanish brand, which grounds flirty dresses with sophisticated structured jackets and classic leather satchels. The size of the store will make your jaw drop—it could very well host rock concerts, for all the space is offers. ✉ *Na Příkopě 8, Nové Město* ☎ *224–218–884* ⊕ *www.mango.com* Ⓜ *Line A or B: Můstek.*

Marella. Stylish and versatile clothes suitable for the office, dining in sidewalk cafés, or lazing at a resort are made by this Italian brand affiliated with designer Max Mara. Recently opened in Prague, this spacious store features body-conscious knit dresses and menswear-inspired separates that are current but timeless. ✉ *Zelezná 22, Staré Město* ☎ *224–228–203* ⊕ *www.marella.it* Ⓜ *Line A or B: Můstek.*

Marina Rinaldi. Understated feminine clothing from this Italian label can be found in its pretty Prague shop, opened in October 2009. Curve-skimming dresses, wide-leg pants, and draped blouses in earth tones, black, and white epitomize comfortable elegance. ✉ *Siroka 10, Staré Město* ☎ *224–234–636* ⊕ *www.maxpraga.cz* ⊙ *Mon. noon–7, Tues.–Sat. 10–7, Sun. noon–6* Ⓜ *Line A or B: Můstek.*

Navarila. Relaxed and cozy knitwear by Czech designer Martina Nevarilova is organized by color inside her boutique and showroom. You might imagine lounging around at a beachside resort or ski lodge in these roomy pullover sweaters, chunky cardigans, and shawls. Each piece is class, yet easy to personalize with accessories. ✉ *Elišky Krásno-horske 4/11* ☎ *271–742–091* ⊕ *www.navarila.cz* ⊙ *Daily 10–7* Ⓜ *Line B: Národní třída.*

Nový Svět. A quietly feminine shop, Nový Svět peddles business-casual wear for women who enjoy a bit of pizzazz. Racks of clothes are neatly arranged, but browsing reveals a charming mix of textures and prints, like a pretty polka-dot blouse or fringed suede jacket. ✉ *V kolkovné 5, Staré Město* ☎ *602–238–456* Ⓜ *Line A: Staroměstská.*

Fodor's Choice
★ **Tatiana**. Expect a dose of glamour and lots of eveningwear inside this bright boutique. Simple sheaths in basic black, or gray laced with shimmering thread, are dressed up with statement belts. Sleeveless high-necked blouses work equally well for meetings or cocktails. The Czech label also does wedding dresses, and much of the apparel is appropriate for a reception or formal dinner. ✉ *Dušní 1, Staré Město* ☎ *224–813–723* ⊕ *www.tatiana.cz* Ⓜ *Line A: Staroměstská.*

Timoure et Group. Led by two Czech designers, this label churns out sleek, minimalist career and casual wear like wrap dresses and trenches. Colors and prints are used sparingly, and tend toward classic red or navy, checked or striped. Women seeking effortless style and comfort should find these clothes endlessly appealing. ⊠ *V kolkovné 6, Staré Město* ☎ *222–327–358* ⊕ *www.timoure. cz* Ⓜ *Line A: Staroměstská.*

Versace. Perched on a pretty corner of U Prasne Brany within view of the sprawling Hotel Paris, this shop has all the trappings you'd expect from Versace. Window displays feature neon touches and mannequins in loud prints. Inside, marble floors and ornate paisley curtains complete the opulent scene. ⊠ *U Prašné brány 3, Staré Město* ☎ *224– 810–016* ⊕ *www.versace.com* Ⓜ *Line B: Nám. Republiky.*

Yanny. If you've got it and like to flaunt it, this shop is for you. Join Prague's nightclub-inclined ladies as they peruse racks of stretchy jeans, leopard-print lingerie, and revealing tops by edgy designers like Dolce and Gabanna. ⊠ *Na Příkopě 27, Nové Město* ☎ *224–228–196* Ⓜ *Line B: Nám. Republiky.*

COSMETICS AND PERFUME

7

Body Basics. All things fresh and fragrant for hands, feet, and body are offered by this Czech brand. Natural ingredients—mostly fruits, soothing herbs, and healing oils like bergamot—are emphasized. After a long day of pounding the pavement in Prague, try unwinding with a Bath Fizzer Ball filled with rejuvenating natural salts. ⊠ *Václavské nám.* 40, *Nové Město* ☎ *246–063–317* Ⓜ *Line A or B: Můstek.*

Botanicus. Organic body and bath products here, like "Lettuce and Olive Oil" soap, are crafted from fresh fruits, vegetables, and herbs on a rural Czech farm. Inside the spacious and fragrant store there are myriad other all-natural products that make charming gifts for those back home, including tempting chutneys and condiments. ⊠ *Týnsky Dvůr 3, Staré Město* ☎ *224–895–446* ⊕ *www.botanicus.cz* Ⓜ *Line B: Nám. Republiky.*

L'Occitane. Never too sweet, these products for body and home are always fresh and clean-smelling. Scents by this French brand are appropriately inspired by the countryside of Provence, resulting in simple citrus combinations and olive-based lotions made from all natural ingredients. ⊠ *Na Příkopě 15* ☎ *224–240–884* ⊕ *www.loccitane.cz* ☉ *Mon.– Sat. 10–8, Sun. 10–7.*

Lush. This happy little shop, with branches across Europe, smells delightfully sweet and stocks a tempting array of fruit- and vegetable-based soaps and body products. Organic ingredients and few or no preservatives ensure freshness of swirling pink and orange "Karma" soaps and cellulite-attacking Sugar Scrubs. ⊠ *Nám. Republiky 1, Staré Město* ☎ *603–164–362* Ⓜ *Line B: Nám. Republiky.*

Sephora. The makeup mainstay remains a dependable source for high-quality cosmetics and skin-care products from international brands. This location is not overwhelmingly large, like some of the chain's other stores, so you should have no trouble finding your favorite Clinique moisturizer or Dior mascara if you've run out. ⊠ *Václavské náměstí 19, Nové Město* ☏ *234–656–101* Ⓜ *Line A or B: Můstek.*

FOOD AND WINE

Cellarius. Try out acclaimed Moravian wines, or pick up a select imported bottle at one of two locations: in the Lucerna Passage or at the Budecska Street store, which also features a wine cellar and garden restaurant. Both stores offer tastings. ⊠ *Lucerna Passage, Stepanska 61, Nové Město* ☏ *224–210–979* ⊕ *www.cellarius.cz* ⊗ *Mon.–Sat. 9:30–9, Sun. 3–8* Ⓜ *Line A or B: Můstek* ⊠ *Budecska 29, Vinohrady* ☏ *222–515–243* ⊕ *www.cellarius.cz* ⊗ *Weekdays 10:30–9, Sat. noon–9* Ⓜ *Line A: Nám. Míru.*

Fruits de France. A posh array of French foods and wines, with some Italian and Greek items for good measure, await shoppers here. Grab fresh fruits and vegetables, a block of cheese or terrine, and enjoy a picnic in one of Vinohrady's leafy parks. ⊠ *Bělehradská 94, Vinohrady* ☏ *222–511–261* ⊕ *www.fdf.cz* Ⓜ *Line C: I.P. Pavlova.*

Monarch. Vintages from countries around the world are represented inside this discreet wine bar, situated just far enough away from the Old Town Square hubbub. Snag bottles of Cotes du Rhone or Grüner Veltliner, or enjoy a glass of wine and plates of tapas or fondue on-site. ⊠ *Na Perštýně 15* ☏ *224–239–602* ⊕ *www.monarch.cz* ⊗ *Fri. and Sat. noon–midnight* ⊠ *Radlická 110, Smíchov* ☏ *266–710–499* ⊗ *Weekdays 8:30–6* Ⓜ *Line B: Radlická.*

GLASS

Czechs are renowned for their glassmaking, a traditional skill that took root in North Bohemia centuries ago and remained active and inventive even through communism. There are exquisite finds in Prague today, so long as you seek Bohemian crystal from established brands rather than touristy shops.

Fodor's Choice **Artěl**. This American company, led by designer Karen Feldman, merges
★ modern style with traditional Czech techniques using mouth-blown molten crystal and hand-painted glassware, for instance. Items are so painstakingly crafted that they're bound to become family heirlooms, but all are far from prim. The shop also stocks a playful mix of

toys and accessories, including charming greeting cards by indie artists. ✉ *Celetná 29 (entrance on Rybna), Staré Město* ☎ *224–815–085* ⊕ *www.artelglass.com* Ⓜ *Line B: Nám. Republiky.*

★ **Material.** This elegant boutique prides itself on supplying Bohemian crystal wares by the most exciting and innovative Czech designers. Tomas Kysela, for instance, adds silver or gold metal finish to his "Chemical" collection of minimalist vases. Glistening stemware with clean lines, textures, or colored adornments catches the eye. Gently curved chandeliers are strikingly sleek, illuminating the shop's deep gray walls and wood plank floors. ✉ *U Lužického semináře 7, Malá Strana* ☎ *775–568–667* Ⓜ *Line A: Malostranská.*

Moser. Elegant glass stemware and decorative bowls and candlesticks are mouth-blown or hand-cut, and gorgeous enough to outfit the dining tables of Europe's aristocratic elite. This historic Czech company, established in Karlovy Vary in 1857, maintains two Prague locations. Both stores are breathtaking, boasting chandeliers, tea sets, and porcelain figurines on multiple floors, in addition to all that graceful glass. ✉ *Na Příkopě 12, Nové Město* ☎ *224–211–293* ⊕ *www.moser-glass. com* Ⓜ *Line B: Nám. Republiky.*

HOME DESIGN

Often wildly imaginative or tongue-in-cheek, Czech design is always a conversation piece. Traditional craftsmanship ensures the quality of each decorative object and piece of furniture.

Arzenal. Peruse glass creations and furniture by Czech designer and architect Borek Sipek, whose talents have been called upon by President Havel for Prague Castle restorations. You'll find unusual pieces, like glass vases with red spikes or yellow calla lilies emerging from all sides. Sipek helped design the Kyoto opera house, and his work appears in the Museum of Modern Art. Whether or not the extravagant items housed in his sleek showroom fit your aesthetic, you will certainly remember them. ✉ *Valentinská 11, Staré Město* ☎ *224–814–099* ⊕ *www.arzenal. cz* Ⓜ *Line A: Staroměstská.*

Fodor's Choice **Kubista.** On the ground floor of the stunning House at the Black ★ Madonna, this museum shop brings original and replica cubist and art deco pieces into the real world. Marvel at angular black-and-white vases by Vlastislav Hofman, and let your eyes linger on the lines of a 1930s tubular armchair. Maps of Prague's art deco, cubist, and modern architecture are also sold here. ✉ *Ovocný trh 19* ☎ *224–236–378* ⊕ *www. kubista.cz* ⊙ *Tues.–Sun. 10–6* Ⓜ *Line B: Nám. Republiky.*

Modernista. Innovation is revered at this store, a magnet for fans of cubist and modernist furniture and decor. Originals, reproductions, and work by new Czech designers are available, making it nearly impossible to leave without something distinctive—a streamlined steel liquor cabinet or vintage reclinable lounge chair, perhaps. ✉ *Celetná 12, Staré Město* ☎ *224–241–300* Ⓜ *Line A or B: Můstek.*

★ **Qubus Design.** Tucked away on narrow stretch of Rámová, this small modernist shop is filled with knickknacks and home accessories by

For a more modern take on Prague handicrafts, Kubista offers gifts with a cubist bent

nonconformist Czech designers. Pick up a translucent pink hippo or candleholder disguised as a baby's head, or stick to less conspicuous wine glasses. This design studio also does interiors, graphic, and product design. ⊠ *Rámová 3, Staré Město* ☎ *222–313–151* ⊕ *www.qubus. cz* Ⓜ *Line B: Nám. Republiky.*

Fodor's Choice **Traditional.** Like a cozy cottage, this shop has something to see in each
★ nook, cranny, and corner. Of particular interest are the hand-carved, antique print blocks from the 1800s, which can be purchased in sets of three along with an original drawing used for textile prints. Antique coffee grinders, irons, and cooking utensils make equally enchanting gifts. ⊠ *Haštalská 7* ☎ *222–316–661* ⊕ *www.traditional.cz* ☯ *Daily 10–8* Ⓜ *Line B: Nám. Republiky.*

JEWELRY

With their good looks and rich history, Czech garnets are hard to resist and make a classic Prague souvenir. Amber is also ubiquitous, but be aware that amber sold in Prague is not usually mined in the Czech Republic. Golden yellow and deep red glimmer inside countless shops throughout the city, so compare prices before purchasing. A pretty silver necklace with garnet or amber setting costs the equivalent of about $100, but simple rings and other small pieces are usually $50 or less.

Fodor's Choice **Art Decoratif.** Fans of Czech art nouveau painter Alfons Mucha can snag ·
★ jewelry inspired by his swirling bohemian designs. Focusing on Mucha's works from 1905–1925, designers make silver necklaces, bracelets, and earrings unlike anything you'll find in a typical jewelry store. A selection

of antique watches and pocket watches is also on offer. ⊠ *U Obecního domu 2, Staré Město* ☎ *222–002–350* ⊕ *www.artdecoratif.cz* Ⓜ *Line A or B: Nám. Republiky.*

Belda Shop. Jewelry shops are typically quiet places, and this family-run business is no exception. But the wares, overseen by University of Applied Arts in Prague graduate Jiří Belda Jr., defy their setting. Bold, yet minimalist, the designs are jolted with colorful precious stones and tiny pearls. ⊠ *Mikulandská 10* ☎ *224–933–052* ⊕ *www.belda.cz* ⊙ *Mon.–Thurs. 10–6, Fri. 10–5* Ⓜ *Line B: Národní třída.*

WORD OF MOUTH

"Most garnets are mined near Prague and only one company mines and sets them. It is Granát Turnov and you should get a certificate of authenticity when you purchase. The store in Prague also had a store in Cesky Krumlov and I purchased a few gifts there."
—violetduck

Česky Granát. This shop's friendly staff is eager to answer any questions about their stock of gorgeous garnets and amber jewelry. Delicate necklaces and dangling earrings may set you back up to $500, but some pieces in the gleaming selection of charms and rings cost only one-tenth as much. ⊠ *Celetná 4, Staré Město* ☎ *224–228–281* Ⓜ *Line A or B: Můstek.*

Granát Turnov. This store is part of the Granát Co-op, the world's most prolific producer of Bohemian garnet jewelry. The elegant Dlouhá branch has two separate rooms. Gold and silver jewelry, including an especially nice selection of brooches, is to the right. Pricier diamond-clad pieces are to the left. ⊠ *Dlouhá 30, Staré Město* ☎ *222–315–612* ⊕ *www.granat.eu* Ⓜ *Line B: Nám. Republiky.*

Halada. With three stores in Prague, this German jewelry company supplys trinkets by carefully chosen brands. Stunning pearls in different shades, as well as gold, silver, and platinum pieces are fixtures. Lia Halada on Pařížská offers the most varied selection, while the serene shop on Na Příkopě focuses on pearls. ⊠ *Pařížská 7, Staré Město* ☎ *224–311–868* Ⓜ *Line A: Staroměstská* ⊠ *Na Příkopě 16, Nové Město* ☎ *224–218–643* Ⓜ *Line B: Nám. Republiky* ⊠ *Václavské náměstí 28, Nové Město* ☎ *224–248–748* Ⓜ *Line A or B: Můstek.*

Swarovksi Bohemia. There's no avoiding the allure of this brand's crystal, and the store itself is an attractive complement, outfitted with dangling crystals and sleek sliding doors. Pick up a playful key-ring charm or glittering bauble at relatively affordable prices. It's worth spending some time reveling in the window-filled space, as shoppers outside point excitedly at the displays. ⊠ *Celetná 7, Staré Město* ☎ *222–315–585* ⊕ *www.swarovski.com* Ⓜ *Line A or B: Můstek.*

MARIONETTES

Puppetry is one of many endearing Czech traditions, but it's also a respected artistic endeavor. Initially used for storytelling by roving ensembles, marionettes provided entertainment and were passed from generation to generation. Today regional artisans' kooky creations

Kids and adults alike enjoy shopping for handmade marionettes.

inhabit shelves and hang from the rafters of several esteemed stores in Prague. But be aware that many shops hawk chintzy knock-offs, so stick to our recommendations for quality crafts.

Galerie Marionette. You may feel as if you've stepped into a fairy tale here. Bug-eyed little witches and crinkly old creatures with walking sticks sway back and forth from their perches around the shop. Familiar favorites like Pinocchio and Raggedy Ann are also available, and there is a colorful stock of porcelain masks near the front window. ⊠ *U Lužického semináře 7, Malá Strana* ☎ *257–535–091* Ⓜ *Line A: Malostranská.*

Marionety. A fresh wooded scent greets visitors to this pleasant puppet shop on steep Nerudova Street. Discover a spellbinding array of linden-wood marionettes, including classic characters like Tinkerbell and Charlie Chaplin, eerily reptilian wizards, and princesses in pink. Artist biographies are found alongside a few displays, and plaster puppets—cheaper but not quite as charming—are also on offer. ⊠ *Nerudova 51, Malá Strana* ☎ *257–533–035* Ⓜ *Line A: Malostranská.*

Fodor's Choice
★

Truhlář Marionety. Among Prague's many marionette peddlers, this shop below the Charles Bridge stands out for its selection of unadorned linden-wood marionettes handmade by local and regional artisans. There's also a quirky stock of decorative wooden toys, such as rocking horses and giant mermaids, fit for a child's bedroom. A second location sits in Týn Square. ⊠ *U Lužického semináře 5, Malá Strana* ☎ *602–689–918* ⊕ *www.marionety.com* Ⓜ *Line A: Malostranská* ⊠ *Týn 1 Staré Město* ☎ *224–895–437* Ⓜ *Line A: Staroměstská.*

MUSIC AND MUSICAL INSTRUMENTS

Bontonland Megastore. This behemoth of a music store is situated underground, somewhere between the Metro station and the street, affording it a cavelike atmosphere. This is the best place to purchase Czech music and films, and there is a limited supply of English-language media, too. ⊠ *Palác Koruna, Václavské nám. 1, Nové Město* ☎ *224–473–080* ⊕ *www.bontonland.cz* Ⓜ *Line A or B: Můstek.*

Dům Hudebnich Nastroju. In addition to shiny new guitars, pianos, brass, and wind instruments, this four-story outlet in quaint Jungmann Square also sells unusual items like bongos and harmonicas. ⊠ *Jungmannovo nám. 17, Nové Město* ☎ *224–236–303* Ⓜ *Line A or B: Můstek.*

SHOES

Alberto Guardiani. For shoes that turn heads, get to this narrow shop festively lined with purple carpeting. Italian glamour is apparent even in the sneakers, some in plush suede and dotted with rhinestones. Strappy metallic sandals for women are surefire conversation starters, while men's styles combine athleticism with a distinctly sleek, European sensibility. ⊠ *Pařížská 24, Staré Město* ☎ *224–815–976* ⊕ *www. albertoguardiani.it* Ⓜ *Line A: Staroměstská.*

Bať'a. This venerable shoe giant has locations around the world, but got its start in what is now the Czech Republic. Although this store stretches five floors, the well-planned layout makes the massive selection of shoes less overwhelming. Sneakers in every shade of the rainbow and rows of sandals, platform heels, and clogs are made from high quality products sourced from international suppliers. ⊠ *Václavské nám. 6, Nové Město* ☎ *224–218–133* Ⓜ *Line A or B: Můstek* ⊠ *Nový Smíchov, Plzeňská 8, Smíchov* ☎ *251–512–847* Ⓜ *Line B: Anděl.*

Beltissimo. Styles for men and women here are classic but sleek. The shop stocks high-end labels—quirky/sophisticated heels by Marc Jacobs, and understated-but-elegant loafers by Emporio Armani—alongside its own brand. Supermodel Kate Moss designed a line of Longchamp bags that found their way into the shop, whose wide windows look out onto the street. ⊠ *U Prašné brány 1, Staré Město* ☎ *222–002–320* Ⓜ *Line B: Nám. Republiky.*

Humanic. The latest trends in shoes—wooden platform clogs, ankle-strap sandals, and dominatrix heels heralded by glossy magazines—are the bread and butter of this affordable Austrian chain. Located next to Nový Smíchov, this is Prague's version of DSW Shoes, where you can try things on without having to wait for sales help. ⊠ *OC Nový Smíchov, Plzenská 8, Staré Město* ☎ *257–289–490* Ⓜ *Line B: Anděl.*

Sergio Rossi. Architecturally stunning heels get interesting touches like swirling cutouts and subtle peep toes from the Italian designer. Like the shoes, the store is a tad wild, with its glossy black furnishings and giggling staff. ⊠ *Pařížská 18, Staré Město* ☎ *224–216–407* Ⓜ *Line A: Staroměstská.*

7

SPORTING GOODS

Adidas. Three stripes and Samba sneakers, the emblems of the brand, are found inside this unusually spacious Concept Store on a crowded stretch of Na Příkopě. The back room is devoted to athletic and casual shoes, which European tourists seem to flock to, while apparel and swimsuits fill the front space. ⊠ *Na Příkopě 12, Nové Město* ☎ *224–210–160* Ⓜ *Line A or B: Můstek.*

Hudy Sport. The two floors here overflow with hiking, camping, and rock-climbing equipment from top brands like North Face. This store is also a good place to pick up a backpack, laptop bag, or Nalgene water bottle. Look for end-of-season sale bins. ⊠ *Na Perštýně 14, Nové Město* ☎ *224–218–600* ⊕ *www.hudy.cz/praha.perstyn* Ⓜ *Line B: Nám. Republiky.*

Intersport. The megastore inside Galerie Myslbek spans two enormous floors, and supplies gear for every sport under the sun. Less mainstream pursuits like roller hockey and rock climbing are covered, but you'll also see basic necessities for runners and tennis players. There is a selection of backpacks for day trips or lengthy hikes, which could come in handy for day trips out of Prague. ⊠ *Na Příkopě 19, Nové Město* ☎ *221–088–094* ⊕ *www.intersport.cz* Ⓜ *Line A or B: Můstek.*

Nike. Relentless pop music, with bass to spare, pulses through a dizzying array of athletic wear here. Zip-front jackets complete with the famous Swoosh logo, neon tennis outfits, and even Nike Prague T-shirts can be yours if you have the patience to deal with crowds of teenagers. A wall of casual shoes and athletic footwear is all the way in the back of the store. ⊠ *Václavské nám. 18, Nové Město* ☎ *224–237–921* ⊕ *www.praguestore.cz* Ⓜ *Line A or B: Můstek.*

TOYS AND GIFTS FOR CHILDREN

There are certainly puzzles and stuffed animals available, but you'd be remiss to leave Prague's toy stores without something special. Hand-carved wooden figurines, beautifully illustrated books, and watercolor sets are but a few of the delights to be had.

Hračky. Take a trip back in time to when toys were made from wood and model cars were cherished. Everything about this store will make you smile, from the kind owner's greeting to the stock of cheerful wind-up music boxes and animal figurines. Look closely at those wood-carved motorcycles and three-headed dragons—many items are handmade by Czech craftsmen. The shop even sells kits with colored pencils and pastels for budding young artists. ⊠ *Loretánské nám. 3, Hradčany* ☎ *603–515–745* Ⓜ *Line A: Hradčanská.*

★ **Pohádka**. Easy to spot on a street strewn with tiny tourist shops, this two-floor toy store is a child's haven. Hand puppets make a softer, friendlier alternative to those mischievous marionettes, and the shop stocks plenty of both styles. Shelves of Russian dolls line a tiny back room, while the second floor is reserved for all manner of wooden toys, like carved animals and airplanes, puzzles and even mangers. ⊠ *Celetná*

Merchants along the Charles Bridge have to apply for special permits to sell their wares along this high-traffic area. Only original handicrafts are selected.

32, Nové Město ☎ 224–239–469 ⊕ www.czechtoys.cz Ⓜ Line B: Nám. Republiky ✉ Zlatá ulička 16, Hradčany ☎ 224–372–292 ⊕ www. czechtoys.cz Ⓜ Line A: Malostranská.

Sparkys. This is Prague's preeminent toy store, with goodies for babies, toddlers and older children. Let the little ones run wild among three floors of Lego, puzzles, and games. Sparkys also stocks an adorable array of stuffed animals. ✉ Havířská 2, Nové Město ☎ 224–239–309 Ⓜ Line B: Nám. Republiky.

SHOPPING MALLS AND DEPARTMENT STORES

Prague still lacks the pristine department stores characteristic of other major cities like New York and London. Czech chains are mainly kiosks selling a motley assortment of apparel, home goods, and flea market–type items. The selection is more expansive and reliable at British department stores around the city, but don't expect too many bells and whistles.

On the flipside, Prague boasts a rather impressive lineup of malls within close range of the center. Although the ambience is nothing to write home about, these four plazas are convenient if you want to hit several chain stores in a limited amount of time. Each mall also has its own cinema, often with new releases in English.

Debenhams. If you need an extra pair of socks or a seasonal item, like a beach towel, this U.K. department store is a dependable choice. Relatively affordable selections of apparel and accessories for men and women are current but not overly trendy. The upstairs coffee bar has free Wi-Fi access. ⊠ *Václavské nám. 21, Nové Město* ☎ *221–015–026* Ⓜ *Line A or B: Můstek.*

Kotva. A veritable flea market of finds awaits shoppers at kiosk after kiosk inside this Czech-run department store, located across tram tracks from the massive Palladium. Combined with the standard apparel and household goods on offer, the odd mix of electronics, beauty products, and luggage amounts to a jumbled treasure trove of possibilities, whether you're seeking a specific item or just browsing. ⊠ *Nám. Republiky 8, Nové Město* ☎ *224–801–111* ⊕ *www.od-kotva.cz* Ⓜ *Line B: Nám. Republiky.*

☼ **Nový Smíchov.** This bright and airy mall is manageably sized, with a convenient mix of shops and an indoor playground. Zara, H&M, Levi's, Clinique, and a two-floor Tesco are in the mix. The second floor of the mall also connects to a lovely new park with great views of the city. ⊠ *Plzeňská 8, Smíchov* ☎ *251–511–151* ⊕ *www.novysmichov.eu* Ⓜ *Line B: Anděl.*

Palace Flora. Towering and easy to reach on the A Line, this mall has Prague's only IMAX movie theater. Certain apparel options like Lacoste and Miss Sixty, and sporting goods stores like Puma and Rock Point, are not found at Nový Smíchov—but the atmosphere here is more hectic. ⊠ *Vinohradská 151, Žižkov* ☎ *255–741–712* ⊕ *www.palacflora. cz* Ⓜ *Line A: Flora.*

Palladium. Since its opening in 2007, this gigantic mall has drawn hordes of shoppers to its four floors, one of which is all bars and restaurants serving everything from sushi to Indian food. Amid the hordes of teenagers and 200 shops, including U.K. favorite Top Shop and a two-floor H&M, keep in mind that this historic building served as the city's army barracks in the 19th century. ⊠ *Nám. Republiky 1* ☎ *225–770–250* ⊕ *www.palladiumpraha.cz* ☉ *Mon.–Sat. 9 AM–10 PM, Sun. 9–9.*

Slovanský dům. A bit classier than the average mall, this collection of shops is flanked by a shady courtyard and features a few decent restaurants. Stores include big names like Armani and Calvin Klein, but it's the chic little boutiques, like Camper shoes, that set this mall apart. There's also a movie theater showing new releases, sometimes in English. ⊠ *Na Příkopě 22, Nové Město* ☎ *257–451–400* ⊕ *www.slovanskydum.com* Ⓜ *Line B: Nám. Republiky.*

Tesco. A one-stop wonder, this U.K. department store stocks clothing for the whole family, plus home goods, cosmetics, and a full basement floor of groceries. There is a pleasant coffee bar on the ground floor, perfect for fueling up before you delve into the selection of English-language magazines or try on some shoes. ⊠ *Národní třída 26, Nové Město* ☎ *222–003–111* Ⓜ *Line B: Národní třída.*

Day Trips from Prague

WORD OF MOUTH

"Kutna Hora is a lovely small town with typical Czech architecture and architectural embellishments of pastel painted buildings, arches and curlicues, and corner niches with religious sculptures. It's an hour and a half from Prague and would make a delightful day trip or a stopover en route to other places in the Czech Republic."

—Adrienne

DAY TRIPS FROM PRAGUE

TOP REASONS TO GO

★ **Visit spooky Sedlec:** The Kostnice outside of Kutná Hora is a mesmerizing church full of bones.

★ **Find a storybook come to life:** A true medieval castle, babbling brook and all, sits in Karlštejn.

★ **Take a historic tour:** The home of Archduke Franz Ferdinand, whose assassination started World War I, is remarkably well preserved in Konopiště.

★ **Pay remembrance to the past:** In Terezín, a baroque fortress turned into a concentration camp is both powerful and chilling.

★ **Keep it all in the family:** Since 1241 Český Šternberk's castle has sheltered various branches of the same family.

1 Kutná Hora. From the downright macabre to the simply lovely; in Kutná Hora you can see a church of bones, a cathedral of majesty, and an adorable town.

2 Karlštejn. The quickest castle excursion from Prague; plus a chance to escape into nature away from city air.

3 Křivoklát. Balance that peace and quiet with a side tour of a castle torture chamber.

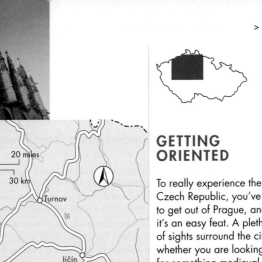

GETTING ORIENTED

To really experience the Czech Republic, you've got to get out of Prague, and it's an easy feat. A plethora of sights surround the city, whether you are looking for something medieval, macabre, or rural. In a couple of hours you'll have forgotten the cramped city and be lost in the rolling countryside or admiring the glorious castles and cathedrals outside the capital. Prague's public transport system can deliver you to any of these destinations any day of the week. Car rentals are easy to come by, or make it easy on yourself and book a day tour. Any way you choose, a side trip into Bohemia is a worthy addition to any Prague itinerary.

8

4 Český Šternberk. Go way out of Prague and be impressed by the massive hulk of stone perched over the river.

5 Konopiště. With a moat of bears, a hall of horns, and an untamed park, this is one sprawling estate.

6 Lidice. A chance to reflect upon the tragedy of World War II.

7 Terezín. Emotional and educational—a glimpse into a former WWII Jewish ghetto and concentration camp.

DAY TRIPS FROM PRAGUE PLANNER

When to Go

Many of the Czech Republic's castles and monuments are closed November through March. Some, especially those closer to Prague, are staying open year-round, although with shortened hours. Busiest times for a visit are June through August; April and October will be less crowded. When school is in session, expect school groups during the week.

Getting Here

In general, buses are faster and cheaper, while trains are easier to navigate and a bit more comfortable. Bus drivers don't typically announce the stops, so when boarding, ask the driver to let you know when you should get off. If you are planning a trip, it's worth it to know your options ahead of time; visit ⊕ www.idos.cz for an online timetable. If you are taking a bus from Florenc, go to the station a day or two before your trip and purchase your tickets. People with tickets board first, and you'll get an assigned seat (and not have to stand). The ticket will be printed with the platform number. There's a computer in the Florenc station where you can check bus times as well.

Guided Tours from Prague

Guided bus tours are available from several companies for Karlštejn, Konopiště, Kutná Hora, Český Šternberk, and Terezín. The ease of booking and traveling (compared with figuring out the train and bus schedules or renting a car) are often worth the time constraints and extra cost. Wittmann Tours specializes in tours to Terezín as well as to Jewish sites all over the country. If you are looking for something more specialized, Prague Day Trips arranges custom tours.

Martin Tour (⊠ Nám. Republiky 3, a booth across from Municipal House, Nové Město ☎ 224–212–473 ⊕ www. martintour.cz). **Prague Day Trips** (⊠ V Olsinach 992, Vršovice ☎ 775–714–440 ⊕ www.praguedaytrips. com).**Premiant City Tour** (⊠ Nekázanka 11, Nové Město ☎ 224–946–922 ⊕ www.premiant.cz). **Wittmann Tours** (⊠ Novotného lávka 5, Staré Město ☎ 222–252–472 ⊕ www.wittmann-tours.com).

Restaurants and Hotels

In general, food and lodging should be cheaper than in Prague, but some restaurants, especially those close to the center or near a tourist attraction, can be just as pricey. You won't find the same range of options either, and be prepared for fewer English speakers.

WHAT IT COSTS IN KORUNA AND EUROS

	¢	$	$$	$$$	$$$$
Restaurants in Koruna	under 100 Kč	100 Kč–150 Kč	150 Kč–300 Kč	300 Kč–500 Kč	over 500 Kč
Hotels in Koruna	under 1,500 Kč	1,500 Kč–3,500 Kč	3,500 Kč–5,000 Kč	5,000 Kč–7,000 Kč	over 7,000 Kč
Hotels in Euros	under €65	€65–€150	€150–€218	€218–€305	over €305

Hotel prices are for two people in a double room with a private bath and breakfast during peak season (April through October) and generally include tax. Restaurant prices are per person for a main course at dinner and include tax.

By Jacy Meyer   The phrase "Something for Everyone" sounds like a marketing tool, but when it comes to things to do outside Prague it feels pretty darn accurate. Still more than 60% of all tourists to the Czech Republic only visit Prague, and that's a real shame. To truly experience a country, you need to get out of the capital and go to where the locals live.

You can stay overnight, or for the weekend, but it's not required. There's plenty to do with just a few hours set aside.

Castles your thing? You have tons to choose from. Karlštejn offers a medieval castle, and it's the quickest and easiest place to reach. Křivoklát is more distant, quieter, and, in a way, more interesting. Český Šternberk is even more remote; however it has an impressive interior and amazingly it's still lived in by a descendant of the original owners.

Feel the need for something green? The regions around Křivoklát and Karlštejn are popular with hikers. Another close destination is Konopiště, which in addition to a well-preserved chateau offers a huge, lovely, and unkempt park with lots of easy walking paths.

History buffs will want to explore Lidice and Terezín, two sites that resonate with the fatalities of World War II. Lidice was the city completely destroyed by the Nazis in retaliation for the assassination of their German leader in Bohemia. Terezín is a former military fortress that was seized by the Nazis and turned into a Jewish ghetto and concentration camp. Both sites are powerfully moving.

If a night out of Prague is what you are after, look no farther than the charming towns of Kutná Hora and Litoměřice, next door to Terezín. UNESCO listed Kutná Hora offers a variety of attractions, while Litoměřice's riverside setting is appealing and relaxing.

Things may not come as easy as in Prague—fewer tourist facilities, fewer English speakers, and fewer nightlife and entertainment options. But the trade-off will be more bang for your buck and a genuine feel for the country and its people.

8

KUTNÁ HORA

70 km (44 mi) east of Prague.

For a little macabre fun, as well as the chance to see a beautiful Czech village, head to Kutná Hora. There are a number of interesting sights in this historic silver mining town about 70 kilometers from Prague. In the city proper, a must-see is the Cathedral of St. Barbara. This magnificent building was built in 1388, and reflects the majesty and importance of the town back then. For a more in-depth look at life in the mines; visit the Czech Silver Museum, which includes a tour of a medieval mine.

The city is a UNESCO World Heritage Site, and proudly boasts of its "10 centuries of architecture" covering the gamut from gothic to Cubism.

But the most famous site in Kutná Hora is the Sedlec Ossuary. Less than 2 km outside of Kutná Hora, the ossuary, aka "Bone Church," is a morbid *memento mori*. More than 40,000 human bones have been arranged into fantastic shapes, chandeliers, and other decorative arrangements.

The city holds a couple of annual festivals. In spring, around the beginning of April, Awakening Kutná Hora is celebrated, marking the beginning of the "tourist" season, when castles and other monuments are open to the public. Period peddlers, dancers, and fencers celebrate the city's mining history at the Royal Silver Festival held every June.

GETTING HERE

Both buses and trains make the short trip to Kutná Hora, but the train is your better bet. A train ticket will cost about 100 Kč, and you will most likely be dropped off at the Kutná Hora main station, which is in the suburb of Sedlec, about 2 km (1¼ mi) away. (About half the trains are direct; half involve a change in Kolín.) If you are given a ticket that says *město* (city), that means you'll be going to the train station in town. However, since you are in Sedlec anyway, take advantage of the fact and walk about 10 minutes (signs point you the way and there's a map in the station) to the Bone Church. You can then walk into town—about 25 minutes. It's an easy straight shot, but not the most scenic. Buses leave from either Prague's Florenc main station or Černý Most in the outskirts of town, off the yellow (B line) metro. Direct ones are not frequent; the ride takes about 20 minutes longer than the train, and the cost is about 100 Kč. By car, Highway 333, the westward extension of Vinohradská třída, goes all the way to Kutná Hora. The drive takes about an hour.

Information Info-Centre Kutná Hora (✉ *Palackého nám. 377* ☎ *327–512–378* ⊕ *www.kutnahora.cz*)

EXPLORING

České Muzeum Stříbra *(Czech Museum of Silver).* All manner of medieval mining and minting equipment can be discovered at this museum housed in the Hrádek (Little Castle), once a part of the town's fortification. Information on the town's history, geology, and archaeology are on display. The real reason for a visit, though, is the chance to tour a medieval mine. Something to note if you're claustrophobic: the tunnel is a bit tight, and the tour lasts for about 30 minutes. You'll follow the

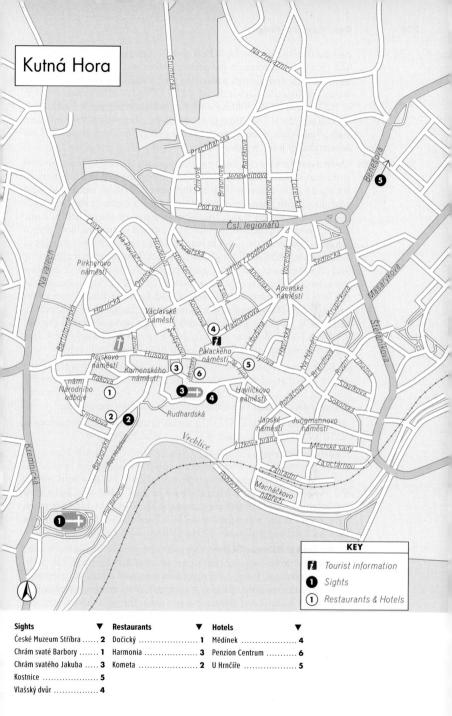

Kutná Hora

KEY

i *Tourist information*

1 *Sights*

① *Restaurants & Hotels*

Sights ▼	Restaurants ▼	Hotels ▼
Ćeské Muzeum Stříbra **2**	Dočický **1**	Mědínek **4**
Chrám svaté Barbory **1**	Harmonia **3**	Penzion Centrum **6**
Chrám svatého Jakuba **3**	Kometa **2**	U Hrnčíře **5**
Kostnice **5**		
Vlašský dvůr **4**		

process of silver mining from how to find it all the way to the minting. The city boasted some of the deepest mines in the world back in the 16th century, and the trek nowadays will probably make you glad you weren't a miner. ⊠ *Barborská ul. 28* ☎ *327–512–159* ⊕ *www.cms-kh. cz* 🖢 *70 Kč–140 Kč, 400 Kč with English-speaking guide* ⊙ *Apr. and Oct., Tues.–Sun. 9–5; May, June, and Sept., Tues.–Sun. 9–6; July and Aug., Tues.–Sun. 10–6; Nov., weekdays: Prior booking required. Last admission 90 mins before closing.*

Fodor'sChoice
★
Chrám svaté Barbory *(St. Barbara's Cathedral).* Getting to this beautiful cathedral is nearly as pleasurable as a visit to the Gothic church itself. It's about a 10-minute walk from the main Palackého náměstí along a road lined with baroque statues where you can gaze at the surrounding countryside and watch the massive shape of the cathedral come closer. From afar, the church resembles a grand circus tent more than a religious center. As the jewel in Kutná Hora's crown, it's a highpoint of Gothic style, although through the centuries there have been alterations and improvements. Barbara's was started in the late 1300s; it drew on the talents of the Peter Parler workshop as well as two luminaries of the late 15th century, Matyáš Rejsek and Benedikt Ried. Upon entering, look up. The soaring ceiling is one of the church's most impressive features. It was added in 1558, and replaced and restored in the late 1800s. If you walk to the western façade, you'll see a lovely view over the town and the visibly leaning tower of St. James's Church.

St. Barbara is the patron saint of miners, and glimpses of this profession can be seen throughout the interior, including Gothic frescoes of angels carrying shields with mining symbols. There's also a special Mintner's Chapel, which holds a statue of a miner, a novelty for its time.

⊠ *Barborská ul.* ☎ *327–512–115 parish* ⊕ *www.chramsvatebarbory.cz* 🖢 *50 Kč* ⊙ *Apr.–Oct., daily 9–6; Nov.–Mar., daily 10–4.*

Chrám svatého Jakuba *(St. James's Church).* If you've already been to St. Barbara's, you'll have seen the tilting tower of this church next to the old mint. It doesn't keep normal operating hours, but go ahead and try the door anyway. It was originally built in the Gothic style, but a massive baroque transformation occurred in the 17th and 18th centuries. (The onion dome was added in 1737.) The baroque paintings on the wall are Czech masterpieces. ⊠ *Havlíčkovo nám.* ☎ *No phone.*

Gasko Central Bohemia Gallery. Opposite the parade of Gothic statues leading you down into town sits this massive gallery housed inside a former Jesuit college. Long, long open corridors and a certain reverential vibe make this an ideal space to display art. A series of rotating collections, both historic and contemporary, come through these floors, but the biggest draw for a visitor is the reproduction of a rare illuminated manuscript depicting Kutná Hora's mining process. Acquired at auction, this illustration captures in amazing detail the daily life that took place around the area, all with picture-book like cross-sections. Don't miss the gift shop with its collection of artsy books and avant garde handbags. The shelving alone is a work of art. ⊠ *Barborská ul. 51–53* ⊕ *www.gask.cz* ☎ *725–607–388* 🖢 *90 Kč* ⊙ *Daily 10–6.*

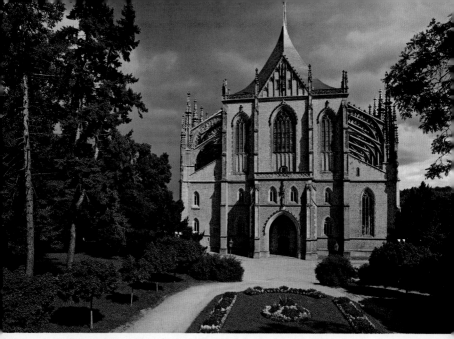

The looming St. Barbara's Cathedral is a tribute to Kutná Hora's miners.

Kostnice *(ossuary)*. This is the reason many people outside the Czech Republic have heard of, and make the trip to, Kutná Hora. Forget all that beautiful baroque architecture and descend into the darkness with some bones. Thousands of bones to be exact; all lovingly arranged in the Kaple Všech svatých (All Saints Chapel), more commonly called the Bone Church. Built in the 16th century, this church forced the movement of a nearby graveyard. Monks from the nearby Sedlec Monastery decided to use the displaced cemetery bones to decorate the church, because, why not? The recently renovated **Church of the Assumption of the Virgin** (✉ *Vítězná, Sedlec* ☎ *327–561–143 parish* 🎫 *30 Kč, prior booking needed*) across the street from the ossuary at the former Sedlec Monastery exemplifies the work of Giovanni Santini (1667–1723). A master of expressive line and delicate proportion, this one-of-a-kind architect fathered a bravura hybrid of Gothic and baroque. ✉ *Zámecká 127, Sedlec* ☎ *607–743–770* ⊕ *www.kostnice.cz* 🎫 *50 Kč, 70 Kč for ossuary and church* ⊙ *Apr.–Sept., daily 8–6; Oct. and Mar., daily, 9–5; Nov.–Feb., daily 9–4.*

Vlašský dvůr *(Italian Court)*. Coins were first minted here in 1300, made by Italian artisans brought in from Florence—hence the mint's odd name. The Italian Court was where the Prague groschen, one of the most widely circulated coins of the Middle Ages, was minted until 1726. There's a **coin museum,** where you can see the small, silvery groschen being struck and buy replicas. ✉ *Havlíčkovo nám. 552* ☎ *327–512–873* 🎫 *100 Kč* ⊙ *Apr.–Sept., daily 9–6; Oct. and Mar., daily 10–5; Nov.–Feb., daily 10–4. Last admission 30 mins before closing.*

8

WHERE TO EAT

$$ **✕ Dačický.** A medieval tavern feel
CZECH and big plates of Czech food make
Dačický a warm, authentic experi-
ence. The painted walls and long
shared wooden tables are barely lit
by candles hanging from the walls
and a massive chandelier. With a
long menu of Czech specialties and
six different beers on tap, it's a good
dinner choice. ⊠ *Rakova 8* ☎ *327–
512–248* ▭ *AE, DC, MC, V.*

$$ **✕ Harmonia.** A charming spot just
CZECH off Komenského náměstí near St.
James's, Harmonia serves good food at good prices. The small back
patio is relatively secluded and the perfect place for an espresso and
quiet conversation. Food, like chicken cutlets and steaks, is simple and
hearty. No-smoking to boot. ⊠ *Husova 104* ☎ *327–512–275* ▭ *AE,
MC, V.*

$$ **✕ Kometa.** Heading toward, or coming back from St. Barbara's, plan
CZECH a lunch or coffee break on the beautiful Kometa terrace under the
shade of a huge tree and looking over the Jesuit College. The food is
acceptable, offering Czech staples, but it's more of an atmospheric stop.
⊠ *Barborská 29* ☎ *327–515–515* ▭ *AE, DC, MC, V.*

WHERE TO STAY

$ **⛉ Medínek.** Don't let the front 1960s façade scare you, this is the city's
largest and most modern hotel, located right on the city's main square.
It has all the basic amenities you could need for a night, along with a
restaurant that serves solid Czech cooking. Rooms are actually quite
spacious and clean, making this a decent overnight option. **Pros:** spa-
cious rooms on the main square. **Cons:** a night bar with a disco is not
everybody's taste; staff can run a bit hot and cold. ⊠ *Palackého nám.
316* ☎ *327–512–741* ⊕ *www.medinek.cz* ↜ *50 rooms* ☖ *In-room: no
a/c. In-hotel: restaurant, gym, some pets allowed (fee)* ▭ *AE, MC, V*
¶○¶ *BP.*

¢ **⛉ Penzion Centrum.** An excellent location and lovely garden make this
your best bet in central Kutná Hora. You won't be taking pictures of
the rooms, which are little more than spartan beds and teensy bath-
rooms, or raving about the amenities to your friends, but it's a decent
place to lay your head, with restaurants and bars at your doorstep.
Bottom line: the property is clean, the staff is friendly, and the price is
a great value. **Pros:** location is terrific; parking space in the courtyard.
Cons: basic rooms and basic services. ⊠ *Jakubská 57* ☎ *327–514–218*
⊕ *www.penzioncentrum.com* ↜ *7 rooms* ☖ *In-room: no a/c. In-hotel:
restaurant, some pets allowed* ▭ *No credit cards* ¶○¶ *EP.*

$ **⛉ U Hrnčíře.** If you are looking for a more rustic stay, head over to U
Hrnčíře. Thanks to a friendly staff, the place feels homey, even if the
decor leaves a bit to be desired (older furnishings, lots of tablecloths,
and a lack of art make it serviceable, but not too warm). Guests, and
even those not staying overnight, will appreciate the restaurant and its

8

back garden. It serves up a great meal with a lovely view of St. James's Church. **Pros:** old picturesque building; good restaurant on the spot. **Cons:** steep stairs and no elevator. ✉ *Barborská 24* 🕾 *327–512–113* ⊕ *www.hoteluhrncire.cz* 🛏 *5 rooms* ♿ *In-room: no a/c. In-hotel: restaurant, some pets allowed (fee)* ▭ *MC, V* ¹⊚¹ *BP.*

KARLŠTEJN

29 km (18 mi) southwest of Prague.

If you've only a few hours to spend outside of Prague, going to Karlštejn, an easy and delightful day trip, might make the most sense. The town itself seems to exist mainly to support visitors to the castle, so if you are looking for some Czech authenticity this probably isn't the town to choose. But for castle lovers and nature lovers, it's a lovely outing.

GETTING HERE

There's no bus service to Karlštejn from Prague, but it's an easy train journey (50 Kč). Many trains leave everyday from Hlavní nádraží—look on the schedule for trains heading to Beroun. When you arrive at the Karlštejn station, exit the station, turn right, and walk back along the small lane parallel to the railway tracks to find the town. Follow the signs reading "Hrad." After a few minutes, cross a bridge over the river, and turn right onto the main road, which resembles a small highway (the absence of a pedestrian sidewalk doesn't bother the locals). Be wary of traffic, but continue for another two or three minutes until you reach a road going up the hill to your left. This is the main road up to the village and castle.

A visit to Karlštejn can also be combined with a challenging 13-km (8-mi) hike through beautiful forests and along a small wooded waterfall from Beroun. Get off at the Beroun station, walk toward town and make a right just before an underpass. Follow the red-marked trail through the hills and dales, passing through the tiny village of Svatý Jan before arriving in Karlštejn—just above the village—about three hours later. Don't set out without water, good shoes, and, above all, a decent local hiking map available at the visitor's center (✉ *Nad parkovištěm 334* 🕾 *311–681–370* ⊕ *www.karlstejnsko.cz*).

By car from Prague, take Highway 4—on the western side of the Vltava—to the edge of the city, then go right on Highway 115, southwest through Radotín. Take the Karlštejn exit, which puts you on Highway 116, and after a few more minutes you end up beside the Berounka River. You can find a large parking lot at the bottom of the hill below Karlštejn. No vehicles are allowed on the road up to the castle.

TIMING

December is actually a good time to come here, as the city hosts a number of Christmas concerts on weekends. In September a wine festival is held, complete with tastings, craft booths, artistic displays, and a visit from Charles IV himself.

EXPLORING

★ **Karlštejn castle.** Once Charles IV's summer palace, Karlštejn was originally built to hold and guard the crown jewels (which were moved to Prague Castle's St. Vitus's Cathedral in 1619). Sitting high up on the hillside, the stunning castle can't be missed from below. There is a fairly strenuous hike up to the castle—sadly lined with souvenir

WORD OF MOUTH

"I loved every minute of the Czech Republic. The trip out to Kutná Hora was the highlight. The Ossuary in Sedlec was incredible. I don't know why but I do have a morbid fascination about history.
—Colin

stands and overpriced snack bars—but worth the journey. Once you've reached the top, take time to walk the ramparts and drink in the panorama of the village and countryside below.

The interior tours are time-consuming—55 minutes for the first circuit and 75 minutes for the second. Opt for tour number two, which includes the castle's greatest treasure, the Chapel of the Holy Cross, which once held the crown jewels. One hundred and twenty-nine painted wooden panels and an arched canopy with semi-precious stones envelope the room. The rest of the tour covers the castle's picture gallery, library, and church. Tours of the chapel are limited (and more expensive than the other tour route), so be sure to book in advance. Tour 1 passes through a variety of rooms dating from the 14th to 19th centuries, plus you'll see some historic interiors from the imperial palace. If you're not a castle buff, stick to the (free) exterior courtyards of the castle. Because of its proximity to Prague, it is the most-visited site outside of the Czech capital, so be prepared for crowds, especially in the high summer months. ⊠ *Karlštejn 18, Karlštejn* ☎ *311–681–617 castle information, 274–008–154 tour reservations, tickets can also be booked online* ⊕ *www.hradkarlstejn.cz* ✉ *rezervace@stc.npu.cz for tour reservations* ☙ *Tour 1: 250 Kč; Tour 2: 300 Kč plus compulsory reservation fee 30 Kč, available only June–Oct., free admission to walk grounds* ☉ *Apr. and Oct., Tues.–Sun. 9–4; May, June, and Sept., Tues.–Sun. 9–5; July and Aug., Tues.–Sun. 9–6; Nov., Dec., Jan., Mar., Tues.–Sun. 9–3. Closed Mon. and Feb.*

WHERE TO EAT AND STAY

$–$$$ ✕**Restaurace a Penzion Pod dračí skálou.** This traditional hunting lodge–
CZECH style restaurant is the most rustic and fun of Karlštejn's eateries. To find it, follow the main road uphill out of the village about 1,650 feet from town. If you've visited the castle, take the path to your left when you leave; or if walking from Beroun, you'll pass by before reaching the Castle. The portions of pork, chicken, beef, and game are massive. A small terrace is popular with cyclists in nice weather. ⊠ *Karlštejn 130* ☎ *311–681–177* ▤ *MC, V.*

¢–$$ ✕**U Janů.** The best of the many touristy restaurants in the town proper,
CZECH this spot is just on the upper edge of the village, not far from where the castle path starts. It also offers a nice big terrace with slight views of the castle. Decent Czech-style food, including some game and fish options, is offered on the menu. The pension can also be a comfortable place to stay if you feel like being outside of Prague for a night but close to

the action at Karlštejn. ⊠ *Karlštejn 28* ☎ *311–681–210* ⊕ *www.ujanu. cz* ⊟ *AE, V.*

¢ 🔟 **Hotel Karlštejn.** The newest hotel in town, the Karlštjn offers 11 modern but pared-down rooms. All rooms are touted as eco-friendly, with recycling bins and automatic lighting,and some offer castle views. Room 8 is deluxe; in other words, a little bigger and with a huge bathtub. Decor is very basic: wood furnishings and white linens paired with satellite and a LCD TV. **Pros:** inexpensive, clean, modern rooms for the area. **Cons:** no design to speak of; no elevator. ⊠ *Pod hradem 7* ☎ *311–600–900* ⊕ *www.hotel-karlstejn.cz* ↰ *11 rooms* ⌂ *In-room: no a/c. In-hotel: Wi-Fi (free)* ⊟ *No credit cards.*

KŘIVOKLÁT

43 km (27 mi) west of Prague.

GETTING HERE

A train is the best way to reach Křivoklát. Trains depart from Hlavní nádraží, and a change in Beroun is required. The scenic ride will take about 1½ hours and cost around 100 Kč. Trains aren't all that regular, so check your return options before setting off.

If you're driving, the fastest way to Křivoklát is to follow Route 6 from Prague toward Karlovy Vary and after Jeneč turn onto Route 201 via Unhoště to Křivoklát. The trip is about an hour. For a beautifully scenic drive—and an extra 15 minutes—take the E50 Highway from Prague toward Plzeň, then exit at Křivoklát to Route 116. Follow this highway, which goes along a river before veering up into the hills, to Route 201, which winds back south toward Křivoklát. Parking is just beneath the castle.

VISITOR INFORMATION There's no information center in Křivoklát, but the castle can provide some basic tourist information. Further information on the region is available from the tourist office in the nearby town of Rakovník.

Information Rakovník Tourist Information (⊠ *Husovo nám. 114, Rakovník* ☎ *313–512–270*)

TIMING

Křivoklát holds an Advent fair, complete with musicians, performances, and lots of crafts.

EXPLORING

Křivoklát. For those in search of charm, nature, and peace, Křivoklát delivers. Its distance from Prague is actually a bonus to hardy travelers. It's a less crowded and more authentic castle experience. There's not much in the way of a town; so only those truly interested in Gothic beauty or nature outings should make a visit. Circled by dense forest (the name Křivoklát means "twisted branches"), among the rolling green hills above the Berounka River, the castle enjoys a peaceful setting. And it's a favorite of Czechs, thanks to its many romantic references in Czech literature, so you'll mostly be competing with locals for a visit. The river area is popular with hikers and cyclists, so you'll also see a lot of them stopping off for a break.

Not surprisingly, when you look at the lush forests surrounding the castle, the structure was used as a humble hunting lodge back in the 12th century. Greater things were to come, thanks to King Wenceslas I, who commissioned the first castle here. Future inhabitants expanded and beautified the place, including Charles IV and his son, Wenceslas IV. A number of fires significantly damaged the buildings, and toward the end of the 16th century it lost its importance and fell into disrepair.

After the Thirty Years' War the Schwarzenbergs took over and revived it. It's been in state hands since 1929.

A walk around the castle walls is one of the most enjoyable reasons to visit. Take a tour and you'll pass through the Great Hall (one of the largest Gothic hall in Central Europe, second only to one in Prague Castle) plus another hall, both loaded with Gothic paintings and sculpture; a beautiful chapel (another highlight of the interior tour), the castle library, a castle prison complete with torture instruments, and lots of hunting trophies. It's truly one of the more interesting castle tours around. One-hour tours are offered regularly in Czech, and tours in English must be requested in advance. ✉ *Křivoklát* ☎ *313–558–440 castle information and tour reservations* ⊕ *www.krivoklat.cz* ✉ *200 Kč, tower 100 Kč* ✆ *Nov.–Mar., weekdays 10–3; Apr., Tues.–Sun. 9–4; May, June, and Sept., Tues.–Sun. 9–5; July and Aug., daily 9–6; Oct., Tues.–Sun. 10–4; Nov. and Dec., weekends, 10–3. Tower May–Oct.*

WHERE TO EAT

¢ ✕ **U Jelena.** Considering that hunting was a popular pastime in this village, this hotel's restaurant (¢–$$$) fits in with the theme. Game dishes are the house specialty, and relatively upscale meals are served in a genteel European setting, from the familiar *svíčková* (slices of beef loin in cream sauce) to more elaborate dishes such as venison steak with Cumberland sauce. If you'd like to stay overnight, there are a few rooms upstairs, outfitted simply but with a cozy feeling thanks to wooden furnishings and pleasant lighting. Most have good views of the woodsy surroundings. ✉ *Hradní 53* ☎ *313–558–529* ⊕ *wwww.ujelena. eu* ▭ *AE, MC, V.*

ČESKÝ ŠTERNBERK

48 km (30 mi) southeast of Prague.

GETTING HERE

Both trains and buses go daily to Český Šternberk, but it's not the easiest trip. (If you are willing to do an arranged tour with a company, that's certainly the simplest way to arrive.) Buses depart from Prague's southernmost bus station, Roztyly, which is about 15 minutes by metro from the city center on Line C (red line). There's an information office outside the metro station, and the bus platforms stretch to your left and down the hill. Purchase tickets (about 65 Kč) directly from the driver, and be prepared to change buses, usually in Benešov.

Trains leave from Hlavní nádraží and stop in many small towns on the way; you will have to change trains in Čerčany, about one hour out of Prague. Though the train ride is about 20 minutes longer than the trip by bus, it's a bit more scenic and easier to figure out. The trip takes about two hours. In summer you may be lucky enough to score a ride on an old-fashioned steam train. Ask at the main station for the *parní vlak* (steam train). If you're driving, take the D1 highway out of Prague (the main highway to Brno) and take the turnoff to Český Šternberk, following Route 111 to the castle, which perches over the highway. The drive takes just under an hour.

VISITOR
INFORMATION
A small tourist office is below the castle near the main parking lot, and can help to prebook castle tours. Their opening hours are quite haphazard, but there's not much reason to need them.

Information Český Šternberk Information (✉ *Český Šternberk* ☎ *317–855–101* ⊕ *www.hradceskysternberk.cz*).

TIMING

In winter, late autumn, and early spring the castle is either closed or has restricted opening hours. Summers see the most tourists, so May and September are your calmest bets. There's a falconer display most summer days and a historical festival held every October that features "live" characters from the castle's history.

EXPLORING

Fodor's Choice
★
Český Šternberk. Dramatic Český Šternberk lords over the Sázava River and surrounding countryside, and looks positively forbidding at night. Šternberk roughly translates to "star on the hill." Perched on an outcropping of rock, this 13th-century castle is striking from the exterior, and it has the period interiors to match.

Founded in 1241 by Zdeslav of Divišov, it was originally built as a fortress. Amazingly, descendants of Zdeslav have remained in the castle, making it their residence through the centuries and up to the present day. The Šternberk name comes from the custom of using German names at the time. The exterior retains a late Gothic look, while the interiors were mainly redone in a baroque style. The latest major work was done in 1911, when electricity and water were added. Tours are required to see the interior, approximately 45 minutes in length, but the rooms are gorgeous and the guides are excellent. (Best to reserve online in advance.) Furnishings date back to the Renaissance, and are either original from the castle or brought from other Šternberk properties around Europe. Beautiful frescoed walls and stucco ceilings can be found throughout, including the Knight's Hall lined with paintings. You'll see items in the rococo and Czech baroque style, Louis XVI furnishings, portraits of generations of Šternberks, and an amazing collection of copper engravings dating back to the 17th century. Guides will also explain the connections between the family history and the country, while a timeline strings the rooms together. Members of the Šternberk family included scientists, bishops, officers, and government employees, all of whom left their mark on aspects of the country's history. One even helped found the National Museum in Prague. During the nationalization period under communism, the castle was seized and became government property; however Jiří Šternberk agreed to stay on as caretaker and guide, thus keeping the family's connection to the

Český Šternberk or the "Star on the Hill" lives up to its name.

castle. The Šternberks received the property back in 1992, and Jiří's son Zdeněk still lives in four rooms on the second floor.

Also on the property is a "small" tower you can climb (10 Kč) for a view of the castle, river, and surrounding forest. ⊠ *Český Šternberk 1, Česky Šternberk* ☎ *317–855–101* ⊕ *www.hradceskysternberk.cz* ☒ *Guided tour 170 Kč, night tour 250 Kč* ☉ *Apr. and Oct., weekends 9–5; May and Sept., Tues.–Sun. 9–5; June–Aug., Tues.–Sun. 9–6; Nov.–Mar. by appointment only.*

WHERE TO EAT AND STAY

¢–$$ ✕ **Hradní Restaurace.** There's not much in the way of dining in Český
CZECH   Šternberk, so one of the best options is the castle restaurant (even the castle guides eat here). The prices are bargain-basement, and some harder-to-find traditional Czech dishes, such as potato dumplings with smoked meat, and yeast-raised pancakes with blueberries, are humble but satisfying. ⊠ *Český Šternberk 1* ☎ *317–855–101* ▭ *No credit cards* ☉ *Closed Mon.*

¢   ▥ **Parkhotel Český Šternberk.** The Parkhotel—on the opposite side of the river from the castle—doesn't have much competition; it's the only game in town for lodging. But you can find clean and cozy rooms and beautiful views of the castle. Even if you're not spending the night, the restaurant makes a plesant stop, especially its terrace. **Pros:** magnificent view of the castle. **Cons:** only eight rooms are turned in that direction. ⊠ *Český Šternberk 46* ☎ *317–855–168* ⊕ *www.parkhoteldt.cz* ⇖ *18 rooms* ⌂ *In-room: no a/c. In-hotel: restaurant, some pets allowed* ▭ *No credit cards* ⊙ *EP.*

KONOPIŠTĚ

45 km (27 mi) southeast of Prague.

GETTING HERE

For being so close, Konopiště can sure feel remote. Buses leave mainly from the Roztyly metro station, on Line C (red line), and occasionally from the main Florenc bus station. The trip will take about an hour, and requires a change in Benešov to the Benešov, Konopiště stop. Tickets cost around 50 Kč. Alternatively, you can follow the signs from the bus station and walk about 2½ km. Trains leave from the main train station; they also take about an hour and cost 70 Kč. The same walk will be required. Or you can take a taxi. By car, take the D1 highway southwest toward Brno, and exit following the signs to Benešov. Signs on this road lead you to Konopiště.

Information Konopiště Tourist Information (✉ *Malé nám. 1700, Benešov* ☎ *317–726–004*). There's also a small tourist info booth in the castle parking lot.

EXPLORING

Zámek Konopiště *(Konopiště Castle)*. World War I buffs, take note: Konopiště Castle could be your favorite day trip. The castle dates from the 14th century, but is best known as the hunting lodge of Archduke Franz Ferdinand. Ferdinand's hunting prowess is clearly on display with the extensive collection of weapons and animal trophies. The interior of Konopiště has been carefully preserved, and visitors can see Ferdinand's collection of Italian cabinets, Meissen porcelain, the archduke's private rooms, and the chapel. There's also a huge park surrounding the grounds, so even if you have no interest in the ill-fated heir to the Austrian throne or the "Great War," you can still enjoy the gardens, lakes, and woodland paths that make this a peaceful half-day excursion.

Getting to the castle usually involves a ⅓-mi walk through the woods. At first glimpse the castle makes a strong impression; the rounded, neo-Gothic towers appear through the trees, and then you reach the formal garden with its mystical circle of classical statues. Although the structure was built as a late 13th-century Gothic fortress, it began to take on more of a castlelike appearance in the 15th century, and was completed as a baroque residence in the 18th century. But it was Archduke Ferdinand who turned the place into the magnificent residence you can see today. Much of the interior and furnishings are original, and reflect Ferdinand's incredible opulence. A valuable collection of weapons from the 16th through 19th centuries can be seen in the Weapons Hall.

The castle can only be seen on a guided tour; book in advance for an English-speaking guide. If one isn't available, ask for an English text to accompany the tour. ✉ *Zámek Konopiště, Benešov* ☎ *317–721–366 castle information, 274–008–154 reservations* ⊕ *www.zamek-konopiste. cz* 🖃 *Tours 200 Kč–300 Kč* ☉ *Apr. and Oct., Tues.–Fri. 9–3, weekends 9–4; May–Aug., Tues.–Sun. 9–5; Sept., Tues.–Fri. 9–4, weekends 9–5.*

WHERE TO STAY

$ 🏨 **Amber Hotel Konopiště**. Konopiště is so close to Prague that it's easy to do in a day trip, but if you're looking for a sporty weekend with a bit of relaxation at the end, Amber Hotel should satisfy. This modern and well-maintained motel is about a 15-minute walk through the woods from the castle. The tennis court, pool, fitness center, sauna—not to mention brisk walks thought the forest—should have you working up an appetite. Thank goodness for the hotel's restaurant Stodola ($$–$$$; open for lunch and dinner), which serves up a variety of meat and fish entrées. Rooms are small but adequate. **Pros:** many sport facilities and gorgeous woodlands to walk in. **Cons:** The remoteness may be too isolated for some. ⊠ *Benešov* ☎ *317–722–732* ⊕ *www.amberhotels.cz* ↪ *44 rooms, 1 apartment* ⅋ *In-room: no a/c. In-hotel: 2 restaurants, tennis court, pool, gym, some pets allowed (fee), parking* ⊟ *AE, DC, MC, V* ⫮⧵ *BP*.

THE MYSTERIOUS FRANZ FERDINAND

Visiting Konopiště Castle, you may find yourself wondering about Franz Ferdinand. He clearly loved travel and hunting. The numbers speak for themselves—his home is covered with almost 100,000 hunting trophies. His other great love was his wife, whom he courted in secret for two years. Against the wishes of Emperor Franz Joseph and the criticism of the court, he married his secret sweetheart. The slander that followed drove them out of Austria to Konopiště.

LIDICE

18 km (11 mi) northwest of Prague.

No more than a speck on the map to the northwest of Prague, this tiny village became a part of the tragic history of World War II. Adolf Hitler ordered Lidice to be razed to the ground as a lesson to the Czechs and a representation of what would happen to anyone that opposed his rule. The act was a retaliation for the assassination of the Nazi leader Reinhard Heydrich by Czech patriots. On the night of June 9, 1942, a Gestapo unit entered Lidice. The entire adult male population was shot, nearly 200 men; about the same number of women was sent to the Ravensbrück concentration camp. The children were either sent to Germany to be "Aryanized" or accompanied the women to the death camp. By June 10 the entire village was wiped out.

The name Lidice soon became an example around the world of what the Nazis were capable of. A group of English miners from Birmingham took up the cause and formed "Lidice Must Live," an initiative to build a new village of Lidice. The city is adjacent to the memorial, which is an amazing and beautiful site, albeit one that is usually only visited by school groups. For most tourists, and even Czechs, Lidice still doesn't seem to be on the map. If you are driving and plan to go to Terezín, make Lidice a short stop on your way.

GETTING HERE

It's a shame that an important memorial so close to Prague is so difficult to reach by public transportation. There's no train service to Lidice, leaving only regular bus service from Evropska třída near the Dejvice metro station on Line A (green line). You'll want the bus stops across the street from the large Diplomat Hotel; look for coaches heading towards Kladno. Before getting on the bus, ask the driver if he stops in Lidice. (Buses heading to Kladno pass nearby, but often do not stop at Lidice.) Tickets (25 Kč) are purchased directly from the driver, and ask him to let you know when the stop comes up. The trip should take about 20 minutes, and when all goes well, you'll be let off at an intersection across from the memorial itself.

By car, Lidice is an easy 30-minute journey. From the Dejvice area, follow Evropská třída out of Prague past the airport, then continue west on Route 551 until you see the well-marked memorial, with a parking lot, beside the highway. If you're driving, it's ideal to combine this with a trip to Terezín, about 30 km (18 mi) farther along in the same direction from Prague.

A MONUMENT FOR THE CHILDREN

Heartbreaking but captivating, the memorial to the child victims of Lidice is a realistic tribute to the atrocities that took place. Marie Uchytilová, a sculpture professor, was so appalled by the assassination of these children that she began a monument that would take more than two decades to complete. After her death in 1989, her husband continued to finish the sculptures. The 82 lifelike sculptures of children ranging in age from 1 to 15 represent the real victims. The statues are even more chilling when covered with snow.

EXPLORING

Lidice Memorial. There is an eerie silence at Lidice. The lovely green rolling hills, small pond, babbling brook, and groves of trees are typical of the Czech countryside; but somehow the events that happened here remain in the air.

You'll first enter the colonnade that houses a small museum. Inside, you're introduced, through photographs, to the original inhabitants of the city. German documentation from the time describes the horror of the mass murder in a disturbingly straightforward fashion. The staff doesn't speak much English, but they can play a short film in English on request. The grounds of the memorial are free to wander. You can buy a map inside the museum for 10 Kč or book a guide to escort you around the entire area for 500 Kč. Heading straight from the museum you'll encounter a vast rose garden. At the opposite end of the garden from the memorial is a rose map with a history of the garden and detailing which roses are planted where and why. For example, the west portion of the garden is planted with light-colored roses to honor the children. Heading straight down the hill from the museum, at the end of the terrace, you'll come to a round building called In Memoriam. Here rotating thematic exhibitions are presented. Signs point out what used to be at that particular location, and you'll find the remains of a few foundations, such as a church and a school, scattered about.

Be sure to walk over toward the Children's War Victims Memorial. This life-size sculpture of the 82 children gassed by the Nazis is haunting in its detail, particularly the delicate facial expressions. On the opposite side of the path is a stark cross, which marks the place where the men were executed. You can continue walking to the end of the field to see the former location of the town's cemetery. ⊠ *Ul. 10 června 1942* ☎ *312–253–088* ⊕ *www.lidice-memorial.cz* ✉ *80 Kč, 500 Kč guided tour in English* ☉ *Apr.–Oct., daily 9–6; Nov.–Mar., daily 9–4.*

TEREZÍN

48 km (30 mi) northwest of Prague.

Just the word Terezín (Theresienstadt in German) immediately recalls the horrors of the Jewish Holocaust for Czechs. Originally built as a military city in the 18th century, Nazis quickly saw its potential, and removed the 7,000 original inhabitants to turn the city into a Jewish ghetto, and the fortress into a prison. Terezín was the main Nazi concentration camp in Bohemia; but it wasn't designed as a death camp, even though in the end more than 38,000 people died in either the ghetto or prison. The city was supposed to be a "model" Jewish settlement, part of a humane façade the Nazis presented to the Red Cross in 1944.

GETTING HERE

There's no train service directly to Terezín. Several buses leave the Nádraží Holešovice station daily, and weekends offer a bit more choice. The trip lasts almost an hour. To get a good overview of the city, ask the driver for a ticket to Terezín bioveta, the stop just outside the town proper, closer to the **Malá Pevnost** *(Small Fortress)*. Visiting here first and taking the guided tour (included in the ticket price; make an advance reservation online) will give you a good overview of not only the main prison camp but also the ghetto itself.

If you're driving, take the E55 north out of Prague (this is the main highway going to Dresden and Berlin) and head toward Lovosice. You can either take Exit 35 at Doksany and follow the country road straight to Terezín or continue to Lovosice, and from there, turn right; the road leads directly into Terezín. There's a large parking lot next to the **Malá Pevnost**. The trip takes about 50 minutes. To visit Střekov, follow the road signs from Terezín to Litoměřice, then take Highway 261 to Ústí nad Labem.

Information Terezín Tourist Information (⊠ *Nám.ČSA 179, Terezín* ☎ *416–782–616* ⊕ *www.terezin.cz*) is a small, friendly office that can help you with area information. There's also a more comprehensive tourist office in the neighboring town of Litoměřice. **Litoměřice Tourist Information** (⊠ *Mírové nám. 16, Litoměřice* ☎ *416–732–440* ⊕ *www.litomerice.cz*).

EXPLORING

Fodor's Choice **Terezín.** The most powerful aspect of Terezín is that you don't need much
★ imagination to visualize how it looked under Nazi rule. When it was a Jewish ghetto, more than 59,000 people were crammed into this camp. Terezín was actually an exception among the many Nazi concentration camps in Central Europe. The Germans, for a time, used it as a model city in order to deflect international criticism of Nazi policy toward the Jews. In the early years of the war—until as late as 1944—detainees had

a semblance of a normal life, with limited self-rule, schools, a theater, even a library. (Pictures drawn by the children at Terezín are on display in Prague's Jewish Museum.) These areas can be experienced in more detail through exhibitions in the Magdeburg Barracks. As the Nazi war effort soured, the conditions for the people in Terezín worsened. Transports to Auschwitz and other death camps were increased to several times a week, and eventually 87,000 Jews were murdered in this way. Another 35,000 died from starvation or disease.

The enormity of Terezín's role in history is difficult to grasp at first, but the **Památník Terezín** *(Terezín Memorial)* encompasses all the existing buildings that are open to the public and has produced an excellent guide to direct you around the city. Buildings include the **Magdeburg Barracks,** where the Jewish Council of Elders met, and the **Jewish cemetery's crematorium** just outside the town walls.

Told in words and pictures, the town's horrific story is depicted at the **Museum of the Terezín Ghetto** (⊠ *Komenského ul.* ☎ *416–782–577*), just off the central park in town. A short documentary is also shown in many languages. Tell the staff that you speak English; they'll let you roam the building and flag you down when the next English-language video is being shown.

The **Malá Pevnost** *(Small Fortress)* functioned as a jail, mainly for political prisoners and others resisting the German occupation, holding them in abject conditions. Around 30,000 prisoners came through here during the war. A tour through the fortress is chilling; you'll first visit the administrative area, where new prisoners were brought, and then glimpse their cells; crudely furnished with stone floors and long wooden beds. Not much has been done to spruce up the place for visitors, leaving the original atmosphere intact. As a military prison, 150 people could be held in the cells; under the Nazis, it was typical to have 1,500 prisoners held in the same space. There was no gas chamber here; but the appalling hygienic conditions led to many deaths, and about 300 prisoners were executed. Many of the juxtapositions are deeply cruel, such as the swimming pools for guards and their families, which prisoners would pass on their way to their execution.

Those who did not die in detention were shipped off to other concentration camps. Above the entrance to the main courtyard stands the horribly false motto ARBEIT MACHT FREI (Work Brings Freedom). At the far end of the fortress, opposite the main entrance, is the special wing built by the Nazis when space became tight. These windowless cells display a brutal captivity. ⊠ *Principova alej 304, Terezín* ☎ *416–782–225* ⊕ *www.pamatnik-terezin.cz.* ➩ *One unit 160 Kč; all units 200 Kč* ☉ *Small Fortress Apr.–Oct., daily 8–6; Nov.–Mar., daily 8–4:30. Ghetto Museum and Magdeburg Barracks Apr.–Oct., daily 9–6; Nov.–Mar., daily 9–5:30. Crematorium daily 9–5.*

The city's second museum is the **Magdeburg Barracks.** Under the Nazis, the building was primarily used as administration offices, but it's been reconstructed into an education facility. There's an excellent re-creation of how a former dormitory would have looked, plus exhibits detailing the arts in Terezín. Inspiring displays show how people in the ghetto

The gate of Terezín had the cruel and horribly false sign, "Work Brings Freedom" above the entrance.

continued to hold literary, musical, theatrical and artistic happenings. ✉ *Tyrsova 204, Terezín* ☎ *416–782–948* ⊕ *www.pamatnik-terezin.cz* 🎟 *One unit 160 Kč; all units 200 Kč* ☉ *Ghetto Museum and Magdeburg Barracks Apr.–Oct., daily 9–6; Nov.–Mar., daily 9–5:30. Small Fortress Apr.–Oct., daily 8–6; Nov.–Mar., daily 8–4:30. Crematorium daily 9–5.*

OFF THE BEATEN PATH

Střekov Castle. The Vltava River flows through a long, unspoiled, winding valley, packed in by surrounding hills north of Litoměřice. As you near heavily industrialized Ústí nad Labem, your vision is suddenly assaulted by the towering mass of Střekov Castle hanging precariously on huge cliffs and rising abruptly above the right bank. The fortress was built in 1319 by King John of Luxembourg to control the rebellious nobles of northern Bohemia. During the 16th century it became the residence of Wenceslas of Lobkowicz, who rebuilt the castle in the Renaissance style. These lonely ruins have inspired many German artists and poets, including Richard Wagner, who came here on a moonlit night in the summer of 1842 and was inspired to write his romantic opera *Tannhäuser*. If you arrive on a dark night, you may be reminded of another classic—Mary Shelley's *Frankenstein*. Inside is a small historical exhibit about the Lobkowicz family and wine making. Guides do not speak English, but will give you printed information in English, German, or Russian. The last admission is 30 minutes before closing time. This is an interesting-looking castle, and it's probably worth a stop if you happen to be driving by, but it's not a destination unto itself. Night tours (100 Kč) are occasionally offered in the summer, and there's a small gallery that hosts temporary exhibitions. ✉ *Na Zacházce, Ústí* *nad Labem* ☎ 475–530–682 ⊕ *www.hradstrekov.cz* ▤ 65 *Kč* ⊘ *Apr.– Oct., Tues.–Sun. 9:30–4:30; Nov., weekends 9:30–4:00.*

WHERE TO EAT

Terezín has very little in the way of services for visitors. There are a couple of depressing haunts, serving mostly inedible pub standards from menus run off on mimeograph machines. Duck out of town to nearby Litoměřice down the road about 2 km (1 mi). Buses run regularly from the main square, and it's barely a five-minute ride. After the heavy atmosphere of Terezín, it's refreshing to walk down the tree-lined main street between colorful buildings bustling with shops and people.

¢–$$ ✕ **Hotel Restaurant Salva Guarda.** Dating back to the 14th century, this
CZECH   stately old building is dolled up with arches and *sgraffito*. The interior is comparatively plain, but in nice weather you can relax on the patio. Game dishes and Czech food of the cutlet category are served. Do try the local white wine from the Žernoseky region. There are also a few rooms available, fairly simple and decorated in a hodge-podge of styles ranging from pink and flowery to muted with brass or cane furnishings. ⊠ *Mírové nám. 12, Litoměřice* ☎ 416–732–506 ⊕ *www.salva-guarda. cz* ⊟ *AE, MC, V.*

$$–$$$ ✕ **Radniční Sklípek.** This spot is local favorite, and it's easy to see why.
CZECH   Here the setting, a Gothic cellar with arched ceilings, is as pleasant as the food. The menu is heavy on Czech specialties and game, and service is attentive. If you're an oenophile, ask to see their historic wine cellars, or just order a bottle from the extensive wine list that includes regional Czech and French varieties. ⊠ *Mírové nám. 21, Litoměřice* ☎ 416–731–142 ⊕ *www.radnicni-sklipek.cz* ⊟ *AE, MC, V.*

Southern Bohemia

WORD OF MOUTH

"You might want to consider stopping overnight in Cesky Krumlov if
you have enough time; there's a lot to see there. We really enjoyed
touring the castle, especially seeing the amazing baroque theater
in the castle, and taking a raft trip on the river around the town.
(It doesn't take long, but it's fun and very scenic.) We spent two
nights and wished we could have stayed longer."

—Sara

WELCOME TO SOUTHERN BOHEMIA

TOP REASONS TO GO

★ **Sense the enchantment:** Feel like a storybook character strolling through Český Krumlov.

★ **Loop around little streets:** Get lost among the tiny streets of Tábor.

★ **Take the bike lane to lunch:** Bike around and eat the fresh carp caught from the fishponds of Třeboň.

★ **Go for baroque:** Experience rustic baroque with a visit to the 19th-century living-museum village of Holašovice.

★ **Sip the suds:** Drink the local brew in České Budějovice, Český Krumlov, or Třeboň.

GERMANY

| 0 | | 20 miles |
| 0 | 20 km | |

1 Český Krumlov. A fanciful city with a stunning castle and gardens: Český Krumlov is *the* must-see in Southern Bohemia

2 Tábor. With streets designed to thwart invading armies, Tábor will lose you in its beauty and friendliness.

3 Písek. Strung along the river, the city with the oldest Gothic bridge in the country is also home to some great museums.

4 Třeboň. The spas of Southern Bohemia can be found in Třeboň. Peat-moss bath anyone?

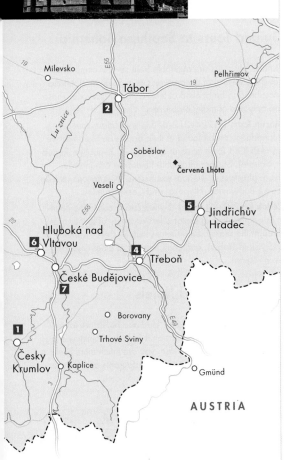

GETTING ORIENTED

Southern Bohemia is one of the most popular regions in the Czech Republic. Chock-full of castles and pretty cities with well-preserved squares, it's a favorite weekend getaway for many Prague locals. The well-marked hiking and biking trails encourage lots of sporty times, and it's easy for visitors to take part, since even some of the train stations rent bicycles. The towns themselves are active, too, and many hold a variety of festivals throughout the year. Being so close to Prague, several of these cities can be done in a day trip; but to get a true flavor of the town and its inhabitants, it's worth your time to stay over or spend a couple of days jumping between a few of the outer areas. The attractiveness of the landscape combined with cultural pursuits makes Southern Bohemia an amazing place to explore.

9

5 Jindřichův Hradec. Authentic and attractive, Jindřichův Hradec is the perfect example of a true Southern Bohemian town: interesting castle, beautiful architecture, and real people.

6 Hluboká nad Vltavou. A castle to die for. The fairy-tale hulk of turreted white can be seen for miles around.

7 České Budějovice. Southern Bohemia's largest city, with a beautiful medieval square and lots of outdoor activities.

SOUTHERN BOHEMIA PLANNER

When to Go

Southern Bohemia is an nature lover's paradise, and in nice weather it seems that the whole country heads here for cycling and hiking trips. Most of the main attractions are closed November through March, as well as Monday year-round, so winters will be quiet, but no less lovely in its snowy way. Many will do weekend Christmas markets, so December is a particularly pretty time. Note: roads get congested with weekenders on Friday and Sunday.

Guided Tours to Southern Bohemia

Guided bus tours are available from several companies covering several of the destinations in Southern Bohemia. Most need to be booked at least a day in advance. These are only two of many organizers.

Martin Tours (☎ 224–212–473 ⊕ www.martintour.cz). Information can be found at their booths on Staroměstské náměstí (Old Town Square) and náměstí Republiky (Republic Square). Southern Bohemia itineraries can include overnight stays or 10-hour excursions. Destinations include České Budějovice, Hluboká, and Český Krumlov.

Čedok (☎ 221–447–241 ⊕ www.cedok.com). The country's original tour operator offers a variety of longer trips through the region. Experiences include Český Krumlov, a spa visit in Třeboň, and combinations of other cities and even regions.

Getting Here

Trains normally depart from the Hlavní nádraží main station while buses leave from either the main Florenc station or the southern Roztyly station, accessible from a metro stop on the Red (C) Line. When exploring your transport options, look into the Student Agency. (It's just a name; services are for everyone.) They offer more direct routes, plus free hot drinks and a movie onboard. Tickets must be purchased ahead of time; they have a window at the Florenc station.

Restaurants and Hotels

Outside of Prague, prices for food and hotels are lower, but service—especially functional English—sometimes lags behind. With Austria so close, you are much more likely to find German-language menus in restaurants and German-speaking staff in both restaurants and hotels.

WHAT IT COSTS IN KORUNA AND EUROS

	¢	$	$$	$$$	$$$$
RESTAURANTS	under 100 Kč	100 Kč–150 Kč	150 Kč–350 Kč	350 Kč–500 Kč	over 500 Kč
HOTELS in koruna	under 1,200 Kč	1,200 Kč–2,200 Kč	2,200 Kč–4,000 Kč	4,000 Kč–6,500 Kč	over 6,500 Kč
HOTELS in euros	under €52	€52–€95	€95–€175	€175–€280	over €280

Hotel prices are for two people in a double room with a private bath and breakfast during peak season (April through October) and generally include tax. Restaurant prices are per person for a main course at dinner and include tax.

By Jacy Meyer   Southern Bohemia calls itself the "pearl of the Czech Republic," and it's not just a clever nickname. Huddled in the corner of the country bordering Germany and Austria, its richness and beauty are undisputable.

The natural landscape is lovely—soft rolling hills crisscrossed with rivers and dotted with ponds mark most of the territory, while the Šumava Mountains to the southwest are a popular ski destination. Coming from Prague, you'll cross the border somewhere north of Tábor, while heading east the indiscernible crossing to Moravia comes near to Telč. Forestry and fishing make up most of the area's important industry, with tourism and beer brewing more fun runner-ups.

The history of the cities is intertwined with many an aristocratic name. The Hapsburgs, Rosenbergs, and Schwarzenbergs all had a large influence on the region, and their nobility is reflected in the area's many castles and beautifully preserved historic squares. The 15th century saw the territory wrapped up in the religious wars sparked by Jan Hus; whose reformist ways angered the Catholic Church and eventually led to his martyrdom. Evidence of the Hussite Wars in the mid-1400s is visible in Tábor.

Český Krumlov is the one must-see destination and often the only stop for visitors. The castle here rivals any monument in Prague.

9

ČESKÝ KRUMLOV

48 km (29 mi) southwest of Třeboň; 186 km (112 mi) south of Prague.

It's rare that a place not only lives up to its hype but exceeds it. Český Krumlov, the official residence of the Rožmberk family for some 300 years, is such a place. It's the only must-see in Southern Bohemia, with a storybook landscape so perfect it resembles a movie set. Hordes of other tourists pass through, but if you stay overnight you can experience the city after the tour buses have departed, and in the evening when quiet descends, the town is twice as spellbinding.

Český Krumlov's lovely looks can be put down to a castle and a river. Krumlov castle is one of the most gorgeous in the country; perched on a hill watching over its quaint village with the Vltava River doing its picturesque winding best. The castle area offers plenty of sightseeing, and the extensive gardens are worth an hour or two. Down in the town, the medieval streets are beyond charming.

As in the rest of Southern Bohemia, outdoor activities are plentiful here. Check with the local tourist information office about places to rent bikes or rafts, or pick up an area hiking map.

GETTING HERE

A direct bus to Český Krumlov leaves Prague from both the Florenc and the Na Knížecí stations. The trip lasts a hair under three hours, and costs 150 Kč. There's no direct train; with a change at České Budějovice, a train trip clocks in at more than four hours and costs 250 Kč. Note that the train station is a 20-minute hike from the main square, while the bus station is much closer. Your best choice would be to purchase a bus ticket a day or two before travel; Český Krumlov is a popular destination.

Car travel from Prague is fairly straightforward and takes three hours. Simply follow the directions to České Budějovice, and once there follow the signs to Český Krumlov. When you arrive in Český Krumlov you'll be confronted by a confusing array of public parking areas, with no indication of how close the parking lot is to the Old Town. One safe bet is to use Parking Lot No. 2, which if you follow the tiny lanes as far as they go, will bring you to just behind the town brewery, and an easy 10-minute walk from the main square.

VISITOR INFORMATION Český Krumlov's tourist information office is on the main square. Well versed and extremely helpful, the staff can assist you in everything from what to see to where to go. They can recommend restaurants and hotels as well as book tickets and assist with bus and train schedules, or even boat and bike travel.

The Vltava travel agency is a solid bet if you're considering outdoor activities. They'll rent boats and bikes as well as arrange excursions.

Information **Český Krumlov Tourist Information** (✉ *Nám. Svornosti 2* ☎ *380–704–622* ⊕ *www.ckrumlov.cz*). **Vltava** (✉ *Kájovská 62* ☎ *380–711–988* ⊕ *www.ckvltava.cz*).

TIMING

Wintertime can be lonely in Český Krumlov, and most of the sites are closed, including the castle. On the flipside, avoid weekends in the summer; hordes of tourists, both Czech and German, flood the streets. Also, midday when the tour buses arrive can be a bit overwhelming. The city holds a Renaissance festival called the Five-Petaled Rose Celebration every June; an Early Music Festival and an International Music Festival in July; an Autumn Fair at the end of September; and a number of holiday events in December.

EXPLORING

Egon Schiele Center. A large and rambling former brewery now showcases the work of Schiele along with other modern and contemporary Czech and European artists. The Renaissance building itself is a wonder, with soaring ceilings in some places and wooden-beamed rooms in others. Schiele often painted landscapes of Český Krumlov from the

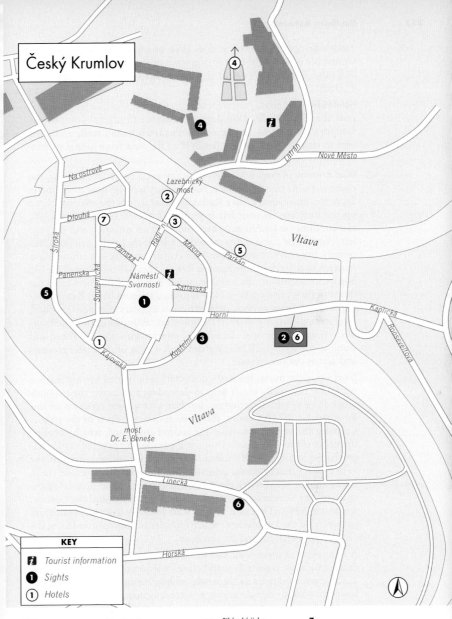

Český Krumlov

Na ostrově
Lazebnický most
Dlouhá
Široká
Panská
Radniční
Masná
Parkán
Vltava
Latrán
Nové Město
Panenská
Soukenická
Náměstí Svornosti
Šatlavská
Horní
Kaplická
Rooseveltova
Kájovská
Kostelní
Vltava
most Dr. E. Beneše
Linecká
Horská

KEY

🛈 Tourist information

1 Sights

① Hotels

castle's bridge. The museum does close unexpectedly on occasion in winter, but is one of the only sites in town normally opened year-round. ✉ *Široká 71* ☎ *380–704–011* ⊕ *www.schieleartcentrum.cz* 🎫 *120 Kč* ⊙ *Daily 10–6.*

Hotel Růže. Gorgeous *sgraffiti* façades decorate this former Jesuit school, now the Hotel Růže. Abundant Renaissance flourishes point to the fact that the city used to be on the Bavarian-Italian trade route. Be sure to visit the parking area (really!), as the view from here is perfect. ✉ *Horní 154.*

☽ **Hrad Krumlov** *(Krumlov Castle).* Like any good protective fortress, the castle is visible from a distance, but you may wonder how to get there. From the main square, take Radniční Street across the river and head up the staircase on your left from Latrán Street. (Alternatively, you can continue on Latrán and enter via the main gateway; also on your left.) You'll first come across the oldest part of the castle, a round 13th-century **tower** renovated in the 16th century to look something like a minaret, with its delicately arcaded Renaissance balcony. Part of the old border fortifications, the tower guarded Bohemian frontiers from the threat of Austrian incursion. Now repainted to resemble its Renaissance appearance, from various perspectives it appears pompous, absurd, astonishingly lovely—or all of these at once. From dungeon to bells, its inner secrets can be seen climbing the interior staircase. Go ahead and climb to the top, you'll be rewarded with a view of the castle grounds and across the countryside.

Next up is the moat, fearlessly protected by a pair of brown bears—truthfully not really much help in defending the castle; their moods range from playful to lethargic. But bears have been residents of this moat since 1707. In season, the castle rooms are open to the public. Crossing the bridge, you enter the second courtyard, which contains the ticket office. The Route 1 tour will parade you past the castle chapel, baroque suite, and Renaissance rooms. The highlights here are the 18th-century frescoes in the delightful **Maškarní Sál** (Masquerade Hall). Route 2 takes you through the portrait gallery and the seigneurial apartments of the Schwarzenbergs, who owned the castle until the Gestapo seized it in 1940. (The castle became state property in 1947.) In summer you can visit the Lapidarium, which includes statues removed from the castle for protection, and the dungeon.

A succession of owners all had the same thing in mind—upgrade the castle a bit more opulently than before. Vilém von Rožmberk oversaw a major refurbishment of the castle, adding buildings, heightening the tower, and adding rich decorations—generally making the place suitable for one of the grandest Bohemians of the day. The castle passed out of the Rožmberks' hands, however, when Vilém's brother and last of the line, the dissolute Petr Vok, sold both castle and town to Emperor Rudolf II in 1602 to pay off his debts. Under the succeeding Eggenbergs and Schwarzenbergs the castle continued to be transformed into an opulent palace. The Eggenbergs' prime addition was a **theater**, which was begun in the 1680s and completed in 1766 by Josef Adam of Schwarzenberg. Much of the theater and its accoutrements—sets, props, costumes, stage machinery—survive intact as a rare working display of period stagecraft. Theater buffs will appreciate a tour, and tickets should be reserved in advance.

Continuing along outside, the third courtyard bears some beautiful Renaissance frescoes, while the fourth contains the Upper Castle, whose rooms can be visited on the tours. From here you'll arrive at a wonderfully romantic elevated passageway with spectacular views of the huddled houses of the Old Town. The Austrian expressionist painter Egon Schiele often stayed in Český Krumlov in the early 1900s, and liked to paint this particular view over the river; he titled his Krumlov series *Dead City*. The middle level here is the **most Na plášti** (Cloaked Bridge), a massive construction spanning a deep ravine. Below the passageway are three levels of high arches, looking like a particularly elaborate Roman viaduct. At the end of the passageway you come to the theater, then to the nicely appointed **castle garden** dating from the 17th century. A cascade fountain, groomed walking paths, flowerbeds, and manicured lawns are a restful delight. The famed open-air **Revolving Theater** is here, as is the **Musical Pavilion**. If you continue walking away from the castle, the park grows a bit wilder and quieter. Unlike the castle, the courtyards and passageways are open to the public year-round. ⊠ *Český Krumlov* ☎ *380–704–711* ⛲ *Garden free, castle tours 240 Kč, tower 50 Kč, theater tours 380 Kč* ⊙ *Garden Apr.–Oct., Tues.–Sun. Castle interior Apr., May, Sept., and Oct., Tues.–Sun. 8:45–4; June–Aug., Tues.–Sun. 8:45–5. Tower Apr., May, Sept., and Oct., Tues.–Sun. 8:45–4; June–Aug., Tues.–Sun. 8:45–5. Theater May–Oct., Tues.–Sun. 10–4.*

Kostel svatého Víta *(St. Vitus's Church).* This neo-Gothic church with its octagonal tower provides a nice contrast with the castle's older tower across the river. Step inside to see the elaborate baptismal font. Much reconstruction took place in the 17th and 18th centuries, however the Gothic entrance portal dates from 1410. ⊠ *Kostelní ul.*

Náměstí Svornosti *(Unity Square).* A little odd-shape, yes, but a "square" nonetheless; Unity Square should be home base for your explorations. Pick a street and head off into the tiny alleys that fan out in all directions. There's no real sense in "planning" your route, simply choose a direction and go—you'll end up where you started eventually. Each turn seems to bring a new charming vista, and cute buildings and shops will amuse and keep shutterbugs busy. Don't forget to look up in the direction of the castle every once in a while; it pokes through in some amazing places. The actual square has a couple of notable buildings, including the Town Hall with its Renaissance friezes and Gothic arcades.

Seidel Photographic Studio Museum. Head across the other side of the river from the castle and explore a more lived-in side of the city. This refurbished home used to belong to photographer Josef Seidel, and is now a museum dedicated to his work and the history of photography. The exhibit is a fascinating mix of home and workplace, with period furnishings plus photographic studio. The building itself is lovely, including a picturesque garden, and photography lovers will enjoy the historic camera collection plus samples of Seidel's work. ⊠ *Linecká 272* ☎ *380–712–354* ⛲ *130 Kč* ⊙ *Daily 9–noon and 1–5, last tour 1 hour prior to closing.*

9

DID YOU KNOW?

The picturesque historic center of Česky Krumlov has been a UNESCO World Heritage Site since 1992.

WHERE TO EAT

¢–$ **✕ Na Louži.** Czech comfort food is
CZECH served up every night at Na Louži.
Fodor'sChoice Lovingly preserved wood furniture
★ and paneling lend a traditional
touch to this warm, inviting, family-
run pub. The food is unfussy yet satisfying. Look for the grilled *pstruh*
(trout) with potatoes and lemon.
Finish off with *ovocný knedliky*,
delicious, traditional Czech fruit

dumplings that are frustratingly hard to find on menus around the country. (The 11 country-style rooms upstairs [¢] are basic and cheap, perfect
for a one-night stay; breakfast is included.) ⊠ *Kájovská 66* 🏠🏠 *380–
711–280* ➡ *No credit cards.*

WHERE TO STAY

It seems you can't walk two blocks in Český Krumlov without stum-
bling over a pension or place offering private rooms. Even with this
plethora, you'll need to book ahead May through September, when
it's high season. Prices can be on a level with some Prague hotels, and
definitely more expensive than in neighboring cities.

$$ 🏨 **Bellevue.** Don't be confused; the recently renamed Bellevue hotel still
has its former name, Hotel U města Vídně scrolled across the front
façade. Located near the town gates, it's tucked away in a quiet corner.
Room decor is a bit dated, and ranges from baroque-ish to modern,
each different from the other, so you might want to ask to see a few
before choosing one. The restaurant Le Jardin is quite good and true to
its name, it has a beautiful garden. **Pros:** impressive restaurant; plenti-
ful services available through the hotel. **Cons:** limited complimentary
toiletries; small breakfast room. ⊠ *Latrán 77* 🏠 *380–720–177* ⊕ *www.
bellevuehotels.cz* ➡ *59 rooms* ⚴ *In-hotel: restaurant, laundry service,
Wi-Fi hotspot, parking (free)* ➡ *AE, MC, V* ⦿*CP.*

$$ 🏨 **Hotel Dvořák.** A bit more modern (and cheaper) than the neighboring Hotel Růže, this small hotel has three things going for it: location,
location, location. Rooms are bright and spacious, but excessively covered in floral patterns. Still, with friendly service and good amenities,
it's a solid choice. **Pros:** nice views; smack-dab central location. **Cons:**
dated interior design; the hotel restaurant could be better. ⊠ *Radniční
101* 🏠 *380–711–020* ⊕ *www.hoteldvorak.com* ➡ *22 rooms, 3 suites*
⚴ *In-room: no a/c, safe. In-hotel: restaurant, bar, laundry service, Wi-Fi*
➡ *AE, DC, MC, V* ⦿*BP.*

$$$–$$$$ 🏨 **Hotel Růže.** Converted from a Jesuit school, this excellent hotel is a
Fodor'sChoice two-minute walk from the main square. A good restaurant, spacious
★ rooms, and a central location are this hotel's selling points. The decor
is Ye Olde Bohemian, but tastefully done. A few rooms have drop-
dead views of the castle, so ask to see several before choosing. Note
that some double rooms have two narrow single beds, whereas some
singles have beds large enough for two. The restaurant offers top-notch
dining in a setting that's formal but not stuffy. **Pros:** central location;
great views; quality restaurant. **Cons:** inconsistent bed layouts; baroque

decorations are a bit overdone; pricey. ⊠ *Horní 154* ☎ *380–772–100* ⊕ *www.hotelruze.cz* ↩ *71 rooms* ⌂ *In-room: no a/c. In-hotel: 2 restaurants, pool, gym, bicycles, laundry service, some pets allowed (fee)* ☰ *AE, MC, V* ⦿ *BP.*

$-$$ 🔲 **Hotýlek & Hospoda u malého Vítka.** Between the castle and the main ★ square, this charming hotel has been tastefully renovated. Rooms are cleverly named after Czech fairy tales, with simple wooden furniture and fittings, and the folklore spirit extends throughout the hotel. There's also a petite terrace and wine room. **Pros:** whimsical spirit; great value for the money. **Cons:** limited in-room amenities; rooms are simple and paired down; cramped bathrooms. ⊠ *Radniční 27* ☎ *380–711–925* ⊕ *www.vitekhotel.cz* ↩ *20 rooms* ⌂ *In-room: no a/c. In-hotel: restaurant, bar, bicycles, some pets allowed (fee)* ☰ *AE, MC, V* ⦿ *BP.*

NIGHTLIFE

Cikánská jizba. If you're in town on a Friday night, head over to this tiny pub. The local gypsy band Cindži Renta plays and Czechs pack the place for cold beer and great live music. ⊠ *Dlouhá 31* ☎ *No phone.*

THE PERFORMING ARTS

Český Krumlov is a hotbed of cultural activity in summer. Events range from Renaissance fairs to music festivals. Activities to note include the International Music Festival held at the castle in July and August and summer performances at the open-air Revolving Theater. Opera and theater companies from České Budějovice perform here. Tickets can be prebooked (almost a necessity) by visiting *www.otacivehlediste.cz* or check with the tourist information offices in either Český Krumlov or České Budějovice. The Český Krumlov office can also tell you about any other concerts or events happening while you are in town.

OFF THE BEATEN PATH

Hrad Rožmberk *(Rosenberg Castle).* This darkened castle keeps a lonely vigil atop the hill overlooking the Vltava River, about 30 km (18 mi) south of Český Krumlov. Inside, you'll see a mix of Romantic and Renaissance interiors; portraits of crusaders; and the Rosenberg Hall, dedicated to the family's history. The English Tower is a 200-step climb, and rewards with beautiful vistas of the countryside. It's virtually impossible to reach the castle via public transport on weekends; weekdays offer more options. If you've a free day and good weather, rent bikes in Český Krumlov and follow the lightly traveled road about 90 minutes. ⊠ *Rožmberk nad Vltavou* ☎ *380–749–838* ⊕ *www.hrad-rozmberk.eu* ▤ *180 Kč, tower only 40 Kč, combined ticket 210 Kč* ⊙ *Oct. and Apr., weekends 9–4:15; May and Sept., Tues.–Sun. 9–4:15; June, Tues.–Sun. 9–5:15; July and Aug., Tues.–Sun. 9–5:45.*

TÁBOR

90 km (54 mi) south of Prague.

Looking at Tábor now, it's hard to believe that this was once a counter-culture utopia and fortress. Lucky for visitors a few centuries later, the town has retained all this turbulent history in its design and buildings.

In the 15th century the town began as an encampment for religious reformers centered on the teachings of the anti-Catholic firebrand preacher Jan Hus. After Hus was burned at the stake in Constance, his followers came here by the thousands to build a society opposed to the excesses of Rome and modeled on the primitive communities of the early Christians. Tábor quickly evolved into the Hussites' symbolic and spiritual center, and along with Prague served as the bulwark of the religious reform movement.

The 1420s in Tábor were heady days for the reformers. Private property was denounced, and the many poor who made the pilgrimage to Tábor were required to leave their possessions at the town gates. Some sects rejected the doctrine of transubstantiation (the belief that the Eucharistic elements become the body and blood of Christ), turning Holy Communion into a bawdy, secular feast of bread and wine. Other reformers considered themselves superior to Christ—who by dying had shown himself to be merely mortal.

War fever in Tábor ran high, and the town became one of the focal points of the Hussite Wars (1419–34), which pitted reformers against an array of foreign crusaders, Catholics, and noblemen. Military general Jan Žižka led the charge fairly successfully, but the Church proved to be stronger and wealthier. Many of the reformists' victories were assisted by the strategic location of Tábor, which with its hilltop position and river boundary made it virtually impregnable. And what nature didn't provide; the residents did. The town was well fortified and there was an ingenious system of underground tunnels (whether they were used to hide in or to store food in is disputed). The streets were purposely laid out in a crooked and confusing manner to thwart invaders. Glimpses of this past can still be seen, and make Tábor one of the more interesting places to visit.

GETTING HERE

Direct buses and trains to Tábor are available and both take about 1½ hours. Buses leave from the Florenc station and cost about 90 Kč, while the train will cost about 150 Kč and departs from Hlavní nádraží. By car, the distance is about 90 km (56 mi), and should take a little more than an hour. You'll take the E 55 heading south toward České Budějovice.

Information Tábor Tourist Information (✉ *Žižkovo nám. 2* ☎ *381–486–230* ⊕ *www.tabor.cz*).

TIMING

Tábor is rarely overrun with tourists, which makes it a relaxing place to see. It's a popular spot with cyclists, and summers always brings a few more people. The South Bohemian Music Festival is held each July. There's also a Christmas market in December. Their big event is the Tábor Meeting Days, held at the beginning of September. This fun medieval festival is incredibly popular. Crafts, music, entertainers, and food all pack into the main square; there's even a parade.

EXPLORING

Hrad Kotnov (*Kotnov Castle*). Rising above the river in the distance, this castle dates from the 13th century, and was part of Tábor's earliest fortifications. After a fire in the early 1600s the castle was rebuilt as a brewery. You can visit the tower, which the Hussites used for storing artillery, as well as Bechyňská brána (Bechyně Gate). This is the last city gate still standing, and has been preserved in its original High Gothic style. Inside is an exhibit "Life and Work of Medieval Society." ⊠ *Klokotská* ☎ *381–252–242* ⊕ *www.husmuzeum.cz* ⊠ *Castle 40 Kč, tower 20 Kč* ⊙ *May–Sept. 8:30–5; other times by appointment.*

Husitské muzeum *(Hussite Museum).* A newly opened exhibit will impart all you ever wanted to know about the Hussite movement and the founding and history of the city.

> ### WARRIOR, BODY AND SOUL
>
> Hussite military leader Jan Žižka was able to command his men despite his handicap—he was blind in one eye since childhood. Žižka's armies were made up of peasants, and their greatest victory came in Prague, where another statue of him stands today. When he died, Žižka commanded that his skin be made into drums, so that he could continue to urge on his troops.

The museum is housed in the Old Town Hall, a building that dates back to the early 1500s. You can also enter the extensive labyrinth of tunnels below the Old Town here. A tour of the tunnels takes about 20 minutes. ⊠ *Žižkovo nám. 1* ☎ *381–252–242* ⊕ *www.husmuzeum.cz* ⊠ *Museum and tunnel tours 40 Kč–60 Kč* ⊙ *Apr.–Oct., daily 8:30–5; Nov.–Mar., weekdays 8:30–5.*

Pražská ulice. The main route to the newer part of town, this street is delightfully lined with beautiful Renaissance façades. If you turn right at Divadelní and head to the Lužnice River, you can see the remaining walls and fortifications of the 15th century, evidence of the town's function as a vital stronghold.

Žižkovo náměstí *(Žižka Square).* There's no doubt who this square belongs to—a bronze statue of Jan Žižka dominates the area and clearly points to its Hussite past. The stone tables in front of the Gothic town hall and the house at No. 6 date from the 15th century, and were used by the Hussites to give daily communion to the faithful. Many fine houses that line the square bear plaques describing their architectural style and original purpose. Be sure to stroll the tiny streets around the square, as they curve around, branch off, and then stop; few lead back to the main square. This bemusing layout, created in the 15th century, was purposely created to thwart incoming invaders.

WHERE TO EAT

$ ✕ **Havana.** Right on the square, this café/bar has a superb atmosphere,
CAFÉ   if oddly resembling an English pub, and serves up tasty plates of Mexican and "American" specialties (think chicken wings and pork ribs). ⊠ *Žižkovo nám. 17* ☎ *381–253–383* ⊕ *www.kafehavana.cz* ⊟ *AE, MC, V.*

$ ✕ **Budvarka U Zlatého Lva.** For the best pizza in town or some choice
CAFÉ   Czech food, head to this spot right on the main square. With lots of Budvar beers on tap, you may not stray far. ⊠ *Žižkovo nám. 16* ☎ *381–252–397* ⊕ *www.budvarkatabor.cz* ⊟ *AE, MC, V.*

Side streets leading off Tábor's town square are purposely confusing in order to protect the center from incoming invasions.

WHERE TO STAY

$$ ☷ **Dvořák.** A bit outside the city center, this former brewery building has been thoroughly renovated into one of the nicest places in town. Upbeat—even slick—modern furnishings decorate this property. The rooms are a welcome change of pace from the puritan, standard-issue bed and nightstands of typical Czech hotels, and the "let's get down" attitude extends to the main lobby and café bar. Some rooms also have sofa beds, a great boon for larger families. It's clean, well run, and a great choice. The hotel's restaurant, La Cave ($$–$$$), is one of the nicest in town, offering creative Czech dishes. **Pros:** modern rooms; efficient, helpful staff. **Cons:** a bit pricey for outside of Prague. ⊠ *Hradební 3037* ☎ *381–207–211* ⊕ *www.orea.cz* ⇲ *72 rooms, 12 suites* ⚷ *In-hotel: restaurant, bar, Wi-Fi hotspot* ▭ *AE, DC, MC, V* ⦿*BP.*

$$ ☷ **Nautilus.** A tasteful boutique hotel in a tiny town? Surprisingly, yes. This tiny hotel right on the edge of Tábor's charming central square exhibits touches of Bohemian craftsmanship in the architecture, beautiful antiques in the rooms, and elegant, original art on the walls (think shells). The hotel's restaurant—Goldie—is an excellent place to dine. Very few central squares in the Czech Republic are blessed with such an elegant and comfortable place to stay. **Pros:** great eats; best address in town; rooms with genuine Bohemian flair. **Cons:** some rooms are a little dark; breakfast spread not as great as the food at the restaurant. ⊠ *Žižkovo nám. 20* ☎ *380–900–900* ⊕ *www.hotelnautilus.cz* ⇲ *22 rooms* ⚷ *In-room: Internet. In-hotel: restaurant, bar* ▭ *AE, DC, MC, V* ⦿*BP.*

Fodor's Choice
★

9

PÍSEK

44 km (28 mi) west of Tábor; 103 km (62 mi) south of Prague.

Písek is a bit of a surprise. It used to be that people came for one thing: Písek's 700-year-old **Gothic bridge** peopled with baroque statues. But a recent infusion of European Union funds has introduced some beautiful upgrades. The former mill cum power station is now a museum dedicated to electricity, and a former malt house is a cultural house and art museum. There's a new promenade that runs along the river beside the old city wall, and the square around the church is nothing short of lovely. They've changed the former Gothic moat into a tiny park, and even the city museum displays some interesting finds.

GETTING HERE

There's no direct train from Prague to Písek. Buses leave from the Na Knížecí station, and will take you there for around 110 Kč in approximately two hours. If you drive, the trip should take no more than 90 minutes.

Information Písek Tourist Information (⌧ *Heydukova 97* ☏ *382–213–592* ⊕ *www.icpisek.cz*).

TIMING

Písek means "sand," and back before the city was a city, people used to pan for gold in the river. From mid-May to the beginning of June the city has sand sculptures on display, honoring their namesake. There's a town festival every June and a folklore festival at the end of August.

EXPLORING

Gothic Bridge. Once the city's only claim to fame, this bridge is a site to see. It was built in the 1260s—making it the oldest bridge in the Czech Republic, surpassing Prague's Charles Bridge by 90 years. Not too shabby. Přemysl Otakar II commissioned it, seeking a secure crossing for his salt shipments over the difficult-to-ford Otava River. As early as the 9th century Písek stood at the center of one of the most important trade routes to the west, linking Prague to Passau and the rest of Bavaria. In the 15th century it became one of five major Hussite strongholds. The statues of saints weren't added to the bridge until the 18th century. During the devastating floods of 2002 one of the statues was damaged, and all the paving stones washed away, but divers recovered most of the lost pieces. The statues on the bridge are not the originals; there are plans to put those on display in the Sladovna cultural house.

Mariánský chrám *(Church of the Virgin).* Just off the main square, this church is the highlight of the recently renovated *Bakaláře Square.* You can't miss the 240-foot tower, *which is open for a climb.* Construction began in the late 1200s, about the time the bridge was built. The lone surviving tower was completed in 1487. On the inside, look for the *Madonna of Písek,* a 14th-century Gothic altar painting. On a middle pillar is a rare series of early-Gothic wall paintings dating from the end of the 13th century. ⌧ *Bakaláře at Leoše Janáčka.*

Prácheňské Museum. Inside a 13th-century castle's frescoed medieval halls, this museum documents the history of Písek and its surroundings, including the Czech fishing industry (with the additional original touch of live fish in large aquarium) and the history of local gold panning and mining in the nearby hills. There are two galleries devoted to temporary exhibits. Everything is in Czech, but ask for an info sheet in English. ☒ *Velké nám. 114* ☏ *382–201–111* ☒ *30 Kč* ☉ *Mar.–Sept., Tues.–Sun. 9–6; Oct.–Dec., Tues.–Sun. 9–5.*

Sladovna. Písek has a brewing history dating back to the Middle Ages. This malt house was built in the 19th century, and continued producing malt for 100 years. In 2008 the city opened Sladovna, a cultural facility that houses two permanent exhibitions and five showrooms for temporary ones. "In the Footsteps of Illustration" focuses on Czech children's book illustrators, and you can see some delightful designs by a variety of artists. There's a spot for inspired kids to color, a reading area, plus an igloo that shows fairy tales. It's all in Czech, but children should appreciate the bright colors and great graphics. ☒ *Velké nám. 113* ☏ *389–600–760* ☒ *60 Kč* ☉ *Tues.–Sun. 9–5.*

OFF THE BEATEN PATH

Zvíkov. In a country overrun with castles, Zvíkov lays claim to being the most famous early Gothic one. Everyone needs its marketing hook, but Zvíkov is interesting enough thanks to its location on two rivers and its authenticity. Unlike many other castles in Bohemia, this one survived the 18th and 19th centuries without renovation, and still looks exactly as it did 500 years ago. If you have the time, you can cycle here from Písek or jump on a boat and float downriver to another nearby castle, Orlík. ☒ *Rte. 138, 18 km (11 mi) north of Písek* ☏ *382–285–676* ☒ *70 Kč* ☉ *May and Sept., Tues.–Sun. 9:30–noon and 1–4; June, Tues.–Sat. 9–noon and 1–5; July and Aug., Tues.–Sun. 9–5; Apr. and Oct., weekends 9:30–noon and 1–3:30.*

WHERE TO STAY

$ 🖵 **Hotel Biograf.** A design-conscious hotel with an award-winning restaurant is a rare find in Písek. Don't be put off by the plain exterior, the interior is surprisingly modern. Rooms are decorated in boxy blond-wood furniture and neutral tones, and bathrooms are nicely spacious. The location, right across the street from the Church of the Virgin is perfect. **Pros:** large rooms, good location, all amenities. **Cons:** exterior low on charm, not a lot in the area to keep you overnight. ☒ *Gregorova 124* ☏ *380–425–510* ⊕ *www.hotelbiograf.com* ⇆ *44 rooms, 3 suites* ⌂ *In-room: a/c (some), Internet. In-hotel: restaurant, Wi-Fi* ▤ *AE, MC, V* ⦿ *CP.*

9

TŘEBOŇ

48 km (28 mi) south of Tábor; 138 km (83 mi) south of Prague.

Třeboň, like Tábor, is off the international tourist trail, but it's a favorite with cyclists. And the town offers an appealing mix of adorable old buildings and authentic work-a-day local life.

Třeboň itself is a charming jewel box of a town. It was settled during the 12th century by the Wittkowitzes (later called the Rožmberks, or Rosenbergs), once Bohemia's noblest family. You can see their emblem, a five-petal rose, on castles, doorways, and coats of arms all over the region. Their official residence was 40 km (25 mi) to the southwest, in Český Krumlov, but Třeboň was an important second residence and repository of the family archives, which still reside in the town's château. The main square, Masarykovo náměstí, is a pleasing arrangement of baroque and Renaissance structures. Various markets pop up here all through the summer, and the Town Hall has notable frescoes.

To Czechs, Třeboň and carp are almost synonymous. If you're in the area in late autumn, you may be lucky enough to witness the great carp harvests, when tens of thousands of the glittering fish are netted from ponds in the surrounding area. Traditionally, they are served breaded and fried as the centerpiece of Christmas Eve dinner. But regardless of the season, you'll find carp on every menu in town. Don't be afraid to order it; the carp here are not the notorious bottom feeders they are elsewhere, but are raised in clean ponds and served as a fresh catch with none of that dirt aftertaste.

One of the most pleasant activities here is a walk around the **Rybník Svět** (World Pond), an easy 12-km trail that takes you through grassy fields and forests. When taking the walk (or as a destination itself), visit the Schwarzenberg Family Vault. Built in English Gothic style; it's a bit startling at first, but then seems to blend into its woody environs. If you'd rather not walk, 45-minute boat tours go around the lake about once an hour, in season and weather permitting. There's a variety of other walks, and lots of cycle paths in the region; ask at the tourist information office for recommended routes and maps.

Along with the ponds, the region is known for its peat bogs. This has given rise to a local spa industry, and wellness weekends are popular attractions at the city's two main spas; **Bertiny Lázně** (☏ *384–754–111* ⊕ *www.berta.cz*) and **Lázně Aurora** (☏ *384–750–111* ⊕ *www.aurora.cz*). A variety of treatments are on offer; but both do peat massages. A dip in the iron-rich squishy substance is supposed to help with arthritis and other joint problems. But the sensation and smell are acquired tastes.

GETTING HERE

Direct buses leave from Prague's Florenc station, take about three hours, and cost around 135 Kč. Trains depart from the main station, and a change will be required in Veselí. Be sure to ask to go to the Třeboň lázné station versus the main Třeboň station, and save yourself a 20-minute walk into town. The train takes nearly three hours, and costs about 200 Kč.

Information Třeboň Tourist Information (✉ *Masarykovo nám. 103* ☏ *384–721–169* ⊕ *www.itrebon.cz*).

EXPLORING

Bílý Koníček *(Little White Horse).* Look for the *Little White Horse*, the best-preserved Renaissance house on the square, dating from 1544. It's now a modest hotel and restaurant—the perfect spot to enjoy some excellent local beer. ✉ *Masarykovo nám. 97* ☏ *384–721–213* ⊕ *www. hotelbilykonicek.cz*.

Zámek Třeboň *(Třeboň Château).* The entrance to this chateau lies at the southwest corner of the square. From the outside the white walls make it appear restrained, but the inner courtyard is covered with *sgraffito*. There's a variety of tours of the interior, which boasts sumptuous recreations of the Renaissance lifestyle enjoyed by the Rožmberks and apartments furnished in late-19th-century splendor. The gardens adjacent to the castle are well maintained and free to stroll in. The last of the Rožmberks died in 1611, and the castle eventually became the property of the Schwarzenberg family, who built their family tomb in a grand park on the other side of Svět Pond. It's now a monumental neo-Gothic destination for Sunday-afternoon picnickers. It's well worth the easy stroll along the lake to visit this tomb; summer concerts are held here occasionally. ⊠ *Masarykovo nám.* ☎ *384–721–193* ⚏ *Tour of family tomb 50 Kč, tour of apartments 160 Kč* ☉ *Apr., May, Sept., and Oct., Tues.–Sun. 9–4; June–Aug., Tues.–Sun. 9–5. Closed Mon. and 11:45–12:45.*

Kostel svatého Jiljí *(Church of St. Giles).* The Gothic style of South Bohemia is exemplified in this curious church. The unassuming exterior gives no clue to the vastness inside, nor the treasures it holds. Paintings in Czech Gothic style can be found by the main altar, also other artwork and frescoes dating as far back as the late 15th century. ⊠ *Husova.*

WHERE TO EAT

$–$$ ✕ **Šupinka**. In a city surrounded by fish; this is where the locals come to
CZECH   enjoy theirs. A stylish interior with floor-to-ceiling wooden arches and a small terrace serve as the backdrops to some creative cooking. There are some interesting variations on classic cuisine, including a *svíčková* (beef in cream sauce) made with pasta and mustard instead of cream. Still, the majority of the menu focuses on *kapr* (carp), including a "demon" carp filled with Dijon mustard and chilies. ⊠ *Valy 56* ☎ *384–721–149* ⊟ *AE, MC, V.*

WHERE TO STAY

The tourist information center on the square is very helpful when it comes to booking rooms. They also offer a catalog of hotel options that includes amenities and prices to help narrow your choice.

$ ⌶ **Romantick**. Flower power is the theme at this boutique hotel newly opened 2009. Each room is named and designed after a flower; so the "Violet" room is decked out in shades of lilac and airy scarves hanging from the walls. Request a room with a view of the city. You can also unplug in the whirlpool or sauna, or they can arrange procedures at nearby spas. **Pros:** new hotel, lots of amenities for this area. **Cons:** on the outskirts of the city, in an unattractive area. ⊠ *K Bertě* ☎ *725–135–888* ⊕ *www.romantick.cz* ⤏ *26 rooms* ⌂ *In-room: a/c (some), Wi-Fi. In-hotel: restaurant, parking* ⊟ *AE, MC, V.*

JINDŘICHŮV HRADEC

28 km (17 mi) southwest of Třeboň; 158 km (95 mi) south of Prague.

The ancient town of Jindřichův Hradec, which dates to the end of the 12th century, is mirrored in the reflective waters of the Vajgar Pond right in the town's center. Originally a market colony near the border between Bohemia and Moravia, the town acquired a castle to protect

Jindřichův Hradec has a cluster of historic buildings including a castle that features "European Mannerism" style.

it, and it's the main attraction here as the third largest castle in the country. (The interior, now an administrative center, is less interesting.) Other attractions include a town square with Gothic, Renaissance, and some baroque aspects, a regional museum, and excursions into the countryside.

Like other South Bohemian towns, this region is a popular spot for cyclists and hikers. If the countryside appeals to you but you're lacking the footpower to explore it, hitch a ride on the Narrow Gauge Railway (*www.jhmd.cz*). Trains depart daily in July and August from the city's main train station. The rails are a mere 760 millimeters apart, and the route winds south nearly to the border with Austria,

GETTING HERE

Jindřichův Hradec is about three hours from Prague by bus; buses leave from either the Florenc or Roztyly stations and cost about 155 Kč. The train from Hlavní nádraží (main station) will require a change at Veselí and takes 15 minutes longer than the bus. It also costs more, about 200 Kč.

Information **Jindřichův Hradec Tourist Information** (✉ *Panská 136* ☎ *384–363–546* ⊕ *www.jh.cz*).

TIMING

A laid-back vibe flows through Jindřichův Hradec. Winters feel isolated, but summers bring lots of cyclists to the area. The Day of the City festival is held at the castle every June, while the big summertime festivities happen during the Folk Rose Festival in mid-July.

EXPLORING

★ **Jindřichův Hradec's Castle.** As the third-largest castle in the Czech Republic, this is the dominant structure in town, holding 300 rooms and 10,000 pieces of art. Behind the courtyard and its elegant Italian arcades, the castle's core is pure Gothic splendor, reflected not only in its thick defensive walls and round tower but also in the **frescoes** covering interior corridors. Colorful examples of medieval coats of arms and a panorama depicting the legend of St. George date from 1338. Over the course of centuries, buildings of an adjoining Renaissance-era château were added to the early Gothic castle, together forming a large complex. There are three different marked routes through the castle for visitors to follow. Tour A is best for design lovers; you'll visit the Adam building, which includes glimpses of Renaissance, baroque, rococo, Empire, and classical styles, as well as see numerous paintings from a previous owner's vast collection. Tour B takes you to the castle's Gothic and medieval core the Chapel of the Holy Spirit, and the Royal Hall. Tour C offers the opportunity to visit the Rondel, a bit of an architectural oddity set in this Gothic scene, designed by an Italian in the 16th century. The official term for the decor is "European Mannerism," but it really resembles a big pink cake with confectionary images of aristocratic dancers and musicians. Built as a ballroom, this space still hosts the occasional concert. Wander the exterior courtyards for free, or simply climb the Black Tower for a view of the castle and surrounding area. ⊠ *Dobrovského 1* ⊕ *www.zamek-jindrichuvhradec. eu/* ☎ *384–321–279* 🖃 *Tour A: 180 Kč; Tours B and C 160 Kč; entire complex 360 Kč; Black Tower 25 Kč.* ☉ *Apr. and Oct., Tues.–Sun. 10–4; May and Sept., Tues.–Sun. 10–5; June–Aug., daily 9–5.*

Kostel svatého Jana Křtitele *(Church of St. John the Baptist).* The oldest church in town, built between the 13th and 16th centuries, this is an excellent example of Bohemian Gothic architecture. Inside, extensive frescoes in the clerestory date from the first half of the 14th century, and portray scenes from the lives of Christ, the Apostles, and various Czech saints. They also demonstrate the medieval necessity for pictorial narratives in educating the illiterate population. On the south side of the sanctuary you can see the Chapel of St. Nicholas, built in 1369. The vaulted ceiling is supported by a single central pillar; this is one of the earliest buildings using this construction in Bohemia. The church is not regularly open to the public, but in July and August or during an occasional concert you can sometimes catch a peek inside. The adjacent monastery is now part of the city museum, and hosts temporary exhibitions. ⊠ *Štítného* 🖃 *20 Kč* ☉ *July and Aug., daily 9–noon and 1–4.*

Kostel Nanebevzetí Panny Marie *(Church of the Ascension of Our Lady).* Dating from the second half of the 14th century, this church and its tower are the other dominating features of the city's skyline. It's a Gothic triple-nave church with some interesting elements, including a Gothic Madonna from the beginning of the 15th century. By coincidence, the church straddles the 15th meridian, and you'll see a line marking the point. The city tower is also open for those wishing to scale 157 steps for an extensive view of the surrounding area. ⊠ *Za kostelem*

9

⬛ *Tower 20 Kč ⊙ June–Aug., daily 10–noon and 1–4; Apr., May, and Sept.–Jan., weekends 10–noon and 1–4.*

Muzeum Jindřichohradecka. Founded in 1882, this museum's big draw is its impressive nativity scene. The huge, mechanical créche was built by one committed craftsman, Mr. Krýza, who dedicated more than 60 years to its creation in the latter part of the 19th century. The old mechanism has now been replaced with an electrical system, but the primitive charm of the moving figures remains. Amazingly, the scene contains 1,398 figures. Other exhibitions in the former Jesuit seminary include an apothecary. ⊠ *Balbínovo nám. 19* ☎ *384–363–660* ⊕ *www.mjh.cz* ⬛ *70 Kč ⊙ June–Aug., daily 8–noon and 1–5; Apr.–Dec., Tues.–Sun. 8–noon and 1–5.*

Národní muzeum fotografie *(National Photography Museum).* This former Jesuit college now houses the foremost photography institution in the country. Newly reconstructed interiors rival the photos on display—the wall and ceiling frescoes have been lovingly restored. The permanent collection includes more than 200 photos donated by Czech photographers. Attached to the museum is the Chapel of St. Mary Magdalene, which occasionally hosts concerts. ⊠ *Kostelní 20* ☎ *384–362–459* ⊕ *www.nmf.cz* ⬛ *60 Kč ⊙ June–Aug., Tues.–Sun., 10–5; Jan.–May and Sept.–Dec., Tues.–Sun. noon–5.*

WHERE TO STAY

¢   🔲 **Hotel Bílá paní.** Legend has it that the castle is haunted, and sightings
★ of a White Lady drifting around have been rumored for years. Situated next to the castle, this cozy hotel takes its name from that legend. Suitably comfortable—if not that stylish—the hotel's rooms are simple and extremely varied, from their layout to their furnishings. Ask to see a few before making your choice. The restaurant's front terrace is a popular people-watching spot. **Pros:** cheap and cheerful; castle views; ghost-free. **Cons:** rooms are sweet but spare; bathroom size and placement is a bit unorthodox. ⊠ *Dobrovského 5* ☎ *384–363–329* ⊕ *www.hotelbilapani.cz* ⥅ *10 rooms* ⟡ *In-room: no a/c. In-hotel: restaurant, Wi-Fi, some pets allowed* ⊟ *MC, V* ⦿*BP.*

\$–\$\$ 🔲 **Hotel Concertino.** Right on the town square, this hotel lets you spring directly into sightseeing action. The façade suggests a charming period conversion, but once inside, modernity is the name of the game. No two rooms are alike, and some feature particularly colorful bathrooms done up in blue-and-white tiles. Many rooms are interconnected, which is nice for families or large groups. **Pros:** near the town square; expressive furnishings; plentiful services for business travelers. **Cons:** a little pricey; decor is expressive but not necessarily cohesive; restaurant is hit or miss. ⊠ *Nám. Míru 141* ☎ *384–362–320* ⊕ *www.concertino.cz* ⥅ *31 rooms, 3 suites* ⟡ *In-room: no a/c, safe, Wi-Fi. In-hotel: restaurant, bar, bicycles, laundry service, parking (paid)* ⊟ *AE, DC, MC, V* ⦿*EP.*

Hluboka's Royal Castle has echoes of England's Windsor Castle.

HLUBOKÁ NAD VLTAVOU

17 km (10½ mi) southwest of Třeboň; 155 km (93½ mi) south of Prague.

Yes, Hluboká has a massive fairy-tale castle that can be seen for miles around. But active outdoorsy types should come here for the excellent sport center that offers tennis, golf, an adrenaline center, and more. Cycling is easy for a brief nature break.

GETTING HERE

The journey from Prague to Hluboká—either by train from the Hlavní nádraží (main station) or by bus from the Florenc station—is 2½ hours unless you get one of the local connections that stops in every small town (in which case the trip takes 3½ hours). The train ticket costs about 225 Kč, the bus ticket 160 Kč; both require a change in České Budějovice. You may find it more convenient to stay overnight in České Budějovice and see the castle in the morning after a 10-minute train trip. Alternatively, there's a 10-km cycle path.

Information Hluboká nad Vltavou **Tourist Center** (⊠ *Zborovská 80* ☎ *387–966-164* ⊕ *www.hluboka.cz).*

EXPLORING

⌘ **Lovecká chata Ohrada.** *(Ohrada Hunting Lodge).* Care for a brisk walk? Follow the yellow trail signs 2 km (1 mi) to the *Ohrada Hunting Lodge,* which houses a museum of hunting and fishing and is near a small children's zoo. ⊠ *Zamék Ohrada 1, off Rte. 105, Hluboká nad Vltavou* ☎ *387–965-340* ⊴ *60 Kč* ☉ *Apr.–Oct., Tues.–Sun. 9–5.*

Fodor's Choice
★
Royal Castle. Hluboká's main focus is its castle, with a cluster of white towers flanking its walls, and tour groups pop in and out regularly. Although the structure dates from the 13th century, what you see is pure 19th-century excess, perpetrated by the wealthy Schwarzenberg family attempting to prove their good taste. If you think you've seen this castle somewhere before, you're probably thinking of Windsor Castle, near London, which served as the template. Take a tour; the happy hodge-podge of styles in the interior reflects the no-holds-barred tastes of the time. On Tour A you'll see representative rooms, including the stunning morning salon and library. Tour B brings you into the private apartments and hunting salon, while Tour C takes in the kitchen. Tour D is available only in July and August, and shows off the tower and chapel. Check out the wooden Renaissance ceiling in the large dining room, which was removed by the Schwarzenbergs from the castle at Český Krumlov and brought here. Also look for the beautiful late-baroque bookshelves in the library. The gardens are free to wander in. **Galerie Mikoláše Alše** (*Aleš Art Gallery* ☎ *387–967–041* ⊕ *www.ajg.cz*) is the region's museum for art history, and displays a variety of works including sculpture, paintings and porcelain. It's one of the most extensive collections of Gothic art in the country, and temporary exhibitions range from modern to contemporary. ⊠ *Zamék 142, Hluboká nad Vltavou* ☎ *387–843–911* ⊕ *www.zamek-hluboka.eu* ⊠ *Castle Tour A: 220 Kč, Tour B: 230 Kč, Tour C: 170 Kč, Tour D: 40 Kč, Aleš Art Gallery 80 Kč; or combined with castle tour, add 20 Kč to visit gallery as well.* ⊙ *Castle: Jan.–Mar., Tues.–Sun. 10–noon and 12:30–4; Apr. and Sept., Tues.–Sun. 9–noon and 12:30–4:30; May and June, Tues.–Sun. 9–noon and 12:30–5; July and Aug., daily 9–noon and 12:30–5. Aleš Art Gallery: Apr.–Sept., daily 9–6; Oct.–Mar., daily 9–4.*

Sportovně relaxačni areál (*Sport-Relax Area*). Hluboká is working hard to offer visitors something beyond their castle, and this extensive sports complex is a complete change of pace. Here you can golf, play tennis or volleyball, rent rollerblades or other sports equipment, test your bravery (and fitness level) in the "adrenaline park," (think massive rope course, unicycles and a bungee trampoline), watch the local hockey team play in the stadium, or even catch a baseball game or soccer match. The park offers a playground for kids, plus a restaurant with a huge terrace. It backs up to the woods, so you can take off for a short hike as well. ⊠ *Sportovní 1276* ☎ *723–584–866* ⊕ *www.sport-hluboka.cz.*

ČESKÉ BUDĚJOVICE

26 km (16 mi) southwest of Třeboň; 164 km (99 mi) south of Prague.

České Budějovice is the largest city in Southern Bohemia, but it's more of a transportation hub and not nearly as charming as the neighboring towns. Still, a couple of interesting spots ensure that you won't be bored if you have a stopover, and you probably will. Schedule a couple of extra hours for a wander through the Old Town and a lunch break, and pause to sip the locally brewed Budvar.

The major attraction is the enormously proportioned main square named after King Přemysl Otakar II and lined with arcaded houses. It boasts a stunning Old Town Hall from the 16th century. Designed by an Italian, it has bells in the tower that chime old South Bohemian tunes at the top of every hour. Another attraction is the central fountain from the 18th century. Be sure to look for the "magic stone," the lone cobblestone in the brick-covered square. Legend has it that if you step on this stone after 10 PM, you'll become lost. But the town's real claim to fame is its beer—the slightly sweetish *Budvar*, which can be found across the country and around the world (you may know it as Czechvar, as it's branded in the U.S.). Unfortunately, you can't tour the Budvar brewery itself, but the beer easily found at pubs around town—simply look for the "Budvar" sign.

GETTING HERE

The trip to Česká Budějovice from Prague takes about two hours by either bus or train. Be careful to choose a *rychlík* (express train) not an *osobní* (passenger train), which would make your journey four hours. Trains leave from the Hlavní nádraží (main station) and cost about 220 Kč; buses leave from both Florenc and Na Knížecí and cost 170 Kč. Car travel affords the greatest ease and flexibility. Česká Budějovice lies on the main artery through the region, the two-lane E55 south from Prague, which, though often crowded, is in relatively good shape. The journey by car should take no more than about 2½ hours.

VISITOR INFORMATION **Česká Budějovice Tourist Center** (✉ *Přemysla Otakára II 2* ☎ *386–801–413* ⊕ *www.c-budejovice.cz).*

EXPLORING

Černá věž *(Black Tower)*. To get a good view over the city, climb the 225 steps up to the Renaissance gallery of the *Black Tower* at the northeast corner of the square next to St. Nicholas's Cathedral. Don't look for a Black Tower; it's actually white, but got the nickname after a fire left some charred marks. ✉ *Nám. Přemysla Otakara II* ☎ *30 Kč* ⊙ *Apr.–June, Sept., and Oct., Tues.–Sun. 10–6; July and Aug., daily 10–6.*

Jihočeské Museum. You can't miss the imposing neo-Renaissance building of the Museum of Southern Bohemia. It was originally founded in 1877 in a small building next to the town hall, but generous donors flooded the facility with so many artifacts that the space had to be expanded. The major exhibits include theme collections portraying the history of the town and the region through an extensive variety of artifacts including metalwork, ceramics, glass, and furniture. A fascinating large-scale model shows the Old Town and its picturesque medieval walls and towers. A regular series of temporary exhibits also runs alongside the permanent ones. ✉ *Dukelská 1* ☎ *387–929–311* ⊕ *www.muzeumcb.cz* ☎ *100 Kč* ⊙ *Tues.–Sun. 9–12:30 and 1–5.*

Koněspřežka. A source of pride for Česká Budějovice, Koněspřežka is the oldest railway station on the continent. Designed to transport salt to Bohemia from Linz in Austria, a horse-drawn railway was built between 1825 and 1832. One of the first major industrial developments in Europe, it reduced the journey between Linz and Česká Budějovice from two weeks to four days. Public transport was introduced soon

9

afterward. The station is now a part of the city museum, and houses an exhibit dedicated to the horse-drawn railroad. You can also pick-up a brochure from the tourist office that details other buildings throughout town that played a role in the transport. ⊠ *Mánesova 10* ☏ *386–354– 820* ⊕ *www.jiznicechy.org* 🖅 *20 Kč* ☉ *May–Oct., Tues.–Sun. 9–12:30 and 1–5.*

OFF THE BEATEN PATH

Holašovice. Peppered with small country homes and farmsteads, this traditional Czech village is so well preserved it's been designated a UNESCO Cultural Heritage Site. Hardly touched by reconstruction or modern meddling, some of the houses date back to the town's founding in the 13th century. Don't expect grand chateaus or extensive decoration; this is "rural baroque," but every bit as picturesque with custard-yellow façades. A small exhibit at No. 60 offers an insight into village life. Budget about an hour for a visit, or longer if you'd like to enjoy traditional fare at **Špejchar u Vojty** (⊠ *Holašovice 3* ☏ *777–621–221* ☉ *May–Oct.*). Every July a "peasant" festival, Selské slavnosti, is held with traditional crafts and entertainment. ☏ *387–982–145 Tourist Information Office open Apr.–Oct., Tues.–Sun. 9–5* ⊕ *www.holasovice. eu* ☏ *602–378–687 Rural Homestead Museum* 🖅 *40 Kč* ☉ *Daily 9–6.*

WHERE TO EAT

$

CZECH

✕ **Masné krámy.** This former butcher's market is now one of the best restaurants in town; specializing in great Czech food and serving unpasteurized Budvar beer. They offer fish and game as well. ⊠ *Krajinská 13* ☏ *387–201–301* ⊟ *AE, V.*

WHERE TO STAY

$$

🖬 **Hotel Budweis.** Situated next to the river in a former mill, this grand hotel was recently restored, and the results are beautiful: exposed wooden beams, polished floors, and loads of natural light. Rooms feature large arched windows with views of the river and park or historic cityscapes of the main square. The decor is tastefully modern in neutral tones and dark-wood accents. **Pros:** newest, nicest hotel in town. **Cons:** cheaper options available. ⊠ *Mlýnská 6* ☏ *389–822–111* ⊕ *www. hotelbudweis.cz* ⟿ *59 rooms, 1 suite* ⟐ *In-room: a/c, Wi-Fi. In-hotel: restaurant, café, parking (paid), some pets allowed (fee)* ⊟ *AE, MC, V.*

THE PERFORMING ARTS

If you stay overnight in České Budějovice, there are plenty of activities that don't circle around the pub. The city has its own theater, ballet, opera, and orchestra that put on a variety of performances throughout the year. The South Bohemian Theater is also the group that organizes the July and August performances at the Revolving Theater in Český Krumlov. Tickets sell out fast. You can reserve online at *www.cbsystem. cz.* ⊠ *Dr. Stejskala 23* ☏ *386–356–925* ⊕ *www.jihoceskedivadlo.cz.*

Western Bohemia

WORD OF MOUTH

"We arrived in Karlovy Vary around 1 PM. What an amazing town! . . . People buy cups with built-in straws & fill them with mineral water from faucets/springs. The water is different temperatures and tastes different from each spring; some are sweet & some are almost salty. We basically spent the afternoon walking around, acclimating ourselves, and drinking mineral water!!!"

—Kwoo

WELCOME TO WESTERN BOHEMIA

TOP REASONS TO GO

★ **Take the waters:** At the Vřídlo Colonnade adventurous souls here can sip from the mineral-rich springs.

★ **Book a Spa Day:** Both old-school heath-oriented treatments or more familiar pampering are available in these spa town.

★ **Stroll the "main streets":** Picturesque spa town Františkovy Lázně and Mariánské Lázně have quaint easy-to-cover town centers.

★ **Catch the stunning views:** Head up to "Stag's Leap" for a sweeping vista.

★ **Drink Pilsener where it was born:** Sip a Pilsener Urquell in its namesake town—Plzeň.

1 Karlovy Vary. Better known to many as Karlsbad, the largest of the spa towns also hosts the country's biggest film festival every July.

2 Cheb. Proximity to the German border brings many bargain hunters for shopping, while castle ruins and a historical center add some diversion.

3 Františkovy Lázně. The smallest of the spa towns in West Bohemia offers a quiet escape to hotels with mud baths and Old World pampering.

4 Mariánské Lázně. In the town's heyday, everyone from Thomas Edison to Czar Nicholas II came for the waters. Current visitors can also enjoy golf and hiking.

5 Plzeň. The only major Czech city to have been liberated by U.S. forces at the end of World War II, it's also home to the country's largest brewery.

GERMANY

Františkovy Lázně   Sokolov

3

Cheb

2

6

21

Tachov

E50

GERMANY

0   20 miles
0   30 km

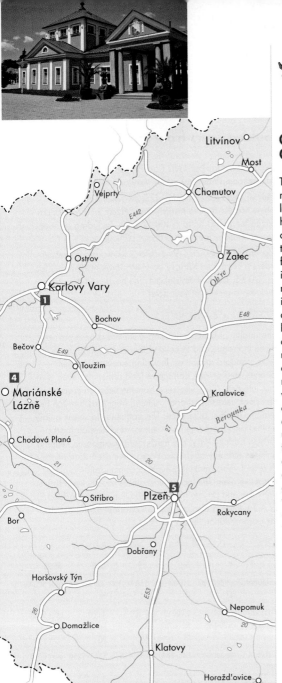

GETTING ORIENTED

The natural springs of hot mineral water that dot the lands of Western Bohemia have made this region one of Europe's most important spa centers. These facilities near neighboring Germany have been renovated inside to meet international expectations during the last 20 years, but the exteriors of the colonnades and pavilions still reflect the styles of the 19th century. Because access to much of the border area was highly restricted in the communist era, the hills and forests still provide unspoiled natural settings for hiking and biking. The area also has a rich history of manufacturing luxury glassware and porcelain, which can be seen in downtown shops and factory stores. Farther south is the city of Plzeň, famous for inventing Pilsner-style beer.

10

WESTERN BOHEMIA PLANNER

When to Go

The region's key cultural event is the Karlovy Vary International Film Festival, held in the first week in July. As strolling on the promenades of the spa towns is *de rigeur*, the summer months are the season. The winter months are fine if you want to spend all your time indoors getting massages and other luxury treatments. Most hotels do stay open during this season. But promenading around the colonnade will be a bit of a letdown in the cold, and there's less hobnobbing with fellow spa goers due to much smaller crowds.

Getting Here

By car, the D5 (E50) highway leads directly to Plzeň, while the R6 (E48) goes to Karlovy Vary and the spa towns in the northern part of the region. Some towns, even major ones like Karlovy Vary, lack direct train connections, making a dirct bus a better choice. Buses to major hubs such as Plzeň are also faster and less expensive than trains.

Guided Tours from Prague

Guided one-day bus tours from Prague are available from several companies to Karlovy Vary and Mariánské Lázně.
Martin Tours (☎ 224–212–473 ⊕ www.martintour.cz) offers regular trips to Karlovy Vary, Plzeň, and Mariánské Lázně for 1,300 Kč to 1,400 Kč each, including sightseeing and lunch. Tour time is about 10 hours.
Tip Top Travel (☎ 267–914–576 ⊕ www.tiptoptravel.cz) offers a combined Karlovy Vary–Mariánské Lázně tour for 2,100 Kč. The tour lasts about nine hours and the price includes a pickup at your hotel.

RESTAURANTS AND HOTELS

The quality of hotels in Western Bohemia is on a par with those in Prague and three- and four-star establishments have standard amenities, including satellite TV, room phones, and private bathrooms (and sometimes even wireless Internet). One difference from the hotels in Prague: The peak season is shorter, running from May through September. Another difference: The staff tends to speak a very limited amount of English—German and Russian (particularly in Karlovy Vary) are much more common, in keeping with the majority of visitors. Prices have risen dramatically in recent years, making private accommodation a more attractive offer. The local tourist offices usually keep lists of pensions and private rooms. In addition to value-added tax (V.A.T.), there is also a "spa tax" of about 15 Kč per day for accomodation in spa facilities.

WHAT IT COSTS IN KORUNA AND EUROS

	¢	$	$$	$$$	$$$$
RESTAURANTS	under 100 Kč	100 Kč–150 Kč	150 Kč–350 Kč	350 Kč–500 Kč	over 500 Kč
HOTELS in koruna	under 1,200 Kč	1,200 Kč–2,200 Kč	2,200 Kč–4,000 Kč	4,000 Kč–6,500 Kč	over 6,500 Kč
HOTELS in euros	under €46	€46–€84	€84–€153	€153–€250	over €250

Hotel prices are for two people in a double room with a private bath and breakfast during peak season (May through September). Restaurant prices are per person for a main course at dinner and include 20% V.A.T.

By Raymond Johnston

Once upon a time, Western Bohemia was known as the playground of Central Europe's rich and famous. Its three well-known spas, Karlovy Vary, Mariánské Lázně, and Františkovy Lázně (also known by their German names, Karlsbad, Marienbad, and Franzensbad, respectively), were the annual haunts of everybody who was anybody: Johann Wolfgang von Goethe, Ludwig van Beethoven, Karl Marx, and England's King Edward VII, to name but a few.

The spas suffered dramatically, however, in the decades after World War II. The concept of a luxurious health spa was anathema to the ruling communist government, and many of the spa facilities were transformed into hospitals—in fact, the idea that these towns are where the sick should recuperate remains today. Pre-1989, some of the nicest properties were transformed into recuperation centers for workers.

The years since 1989 have been kinder to the spa resorts, and now the cities are home to the rich and (in)famous once again. Karlovy Vary, as always, has the most recognition, and rebounded best of all. Helped by its annual international film festival and a heavy infusion of Russian private capital, Karlovy Vary is back on the map as an international spa destination. Františkovy Lázně, too, is on the comeback trail. The city officials have used bucketloads of Kaiser-yellow paint to spruce up those aging Empire façades, and the city's parks have gotten a much-needed makeover. Mariánské Lázně benefits from hordes of German day-trippers from just over the border.

In the Czech Republic spas are seen as serious health treatments first, complete with physical examinations, blood tests, and various infusions to complement the waters, relaxation, and massage. This means for many visitors that the local concept of a "spa" differs from what you are used to back home (and explains in part the large number of elderly tourists shuffling about). Many hotels have added treatments—from Thai massages to pedicures—that fit with the modern concept of a spa resort. For the moment, though, a "spa" primarily means doctors,

10

nurses, and lab coats. The best place to inquire is at your hotel or the tourist information center.

Aside from the spas, the area is full of historic features stemming from the wealth it accrued as the district's important trade route into Germany and Italy. A strong Germanic influence can still be seen, particularly in towns like Cheb and Mariánské Lázně. Everywhere in the region you'll see Germans, mostly pensioners on coach tours dropping by for a walk around town and a slice of apple strudel before hitting the road back to Deutschland.

KARLOVY VARY

132 km (79 mi) west of Prague on R6 (E48).

Karlovy Vary—often known outside the Czech Republic by its German name, Karlsbad—is the most famous of the Bohemian spas. It's named for the omnipresent Emperor Charles IV, who allegedly happened upon the springs in 1358 while on a hunting expedition. As the story goes, the emperor's hound fell into a boiling spring and was scalded. Charles had the water tested and, familiar with spas in Italy, ordered the village of Vary to be transformed into a haven for baths. The spa reached its golden age in the 19th century, when aristocrats from all over Europe came for treatments. The long list of those who "took the cure" includes Peter the Great, Goethe, Schiller, Beethoven, and Chopin. Even Karl Marx, when he wasn't decrying wealth and privilege, spent time at the wealthy and privileged resort; he wrote some of *Das Kapital* here between 1874 and 1876.

Pulling off an extraordinary comeback after decades of communist neglect that left many buildings crumbling into dust behind beautiful façades, Karlovy Vary drips with luxury once again. Much of the reconstruction was led not by Czechs, but by Russians. Since the days of Peter the Great, Karlovy Vary has held a deep fascination for Russians, and many of them poured their newly gained wealth into properties here—so much so that Karlovy Vary's sleepy airport boasts nonstop service from Moscow several times a week, and four-fifths of the properties are actually Russian-owned. Don't be surprised to hear Russian spoken widely in the streets or see it used as the second language, after Czech, on restaurant menus.

Karlovy Vary's other vehicle in luring attention and investment has been its international film festival, now in its fourth decade. Every year during the first week of July, international stars and film fans flock here. Recent attendees include Robert De Niro, Antonio Banderas, and John Malkovich. If you're planning on visiting during the festival, line up your hotel room well in advance. Unless you're a true film buff, you're better off coming in a different week.

Whether you're arriving by bus, train, or car, your first view of the town approaching from Prague will be of the run-down section on the banks of the Ohře River. Don't despair: continue along the main road, following the signs to the Grandhotel Pupp, until you are rewarded with a glimpse of the lovely main street in the older spa area, situated gently astride the banks of the little Teplá ("Warm") River. (Drivers, note that driving through or parking in the main spa area is allowed only with a permit obtained at your hotel.) The walk from the new town to the spa area is about 20 minutes.

The Historická čtvrt (Historic District) is still largely intact. Tall 19th-century houses, with decorative and often eccentric façades, line the spa's proud riverside streets. Throughout, you can see colonnades full of people sipping the spa's hot sulfuric water from funny drinking cups with piped spouts. At night the streets fill with steam escaping from cracks in the earth, giving the town a slightly macabre feel.

GETTING HERE

Frequent bus service between Prague and Karlovy Vary makes the journey only about two hours each way, and the ticket costs about 120 Kč. Avoid the train. The Prague–Karlovy Vary run takes far longer than it should—more than three hours by the shortest route—and costs more than double the price of a bus ticket. If you're driving, you can take the E48 directly from Prague to Karlovy Vary, a drive of about 1½ hours in light traffic.

Information Karlovy Vary Tourist Information (⊠ *Husovo nám. 2* ☎ *353–224–097* ⊕ *www.karlovy-vary.cz*).

EXPLORING

Elefant. On one of the town's main shopping streets is this resolutely old-fashioned, sophisticated coffeehouse, one of a dying breed. The apple strudel and coffee are quite good, and it's a prime location for people-watching. ⊠ *Stará louka 30* ☎ *353–222–544.*

Hotel Thermal. The 20th century raises its head in the form of this huge, bunker-like hotel, across the river from the historic district. Built in the late 1960s as the communist idea of luxury, the building is an aesthetic thumb in the eye compared with the rest of the town. The rooftop pool, however, is nothing short of spectacular. Even if you don't feel like a swim, it's worth taking the winding road up to the baths for the view—and, of course, you can't see the hotel if you're on top of it. Another reason to visit: the hotel is the main venue of the Karlovy Vary International Film Festival in early July. ⊠ *I. P. Pavlova 11* ☎ *359–001–111* ☏ *80 Kč per hour* ☉ *Pool daily 8:30* AM–*8* PM.

Fodor's Choice **Jelení skok** *(Stag's Leap)*. From Kostel svatého Lukáše, take a sharp right
★ uphill on a redbrick road, then turn left onto a footpath through the woods, following signs to Jelení skok (Stag's Leap). After a while, steps lead up to a bronze statue of a deer looking over the cliffs, the symbol of Karlovy Vary. From here a winding path threads toward a little red gazebo opening onto a mythical panorama that's worth the strenuous hike to the top. ⊠ *Sovava trail in Petrova Výšina park*.

★ **Kostel Maří Magdaleny** *(Church of Mary Magdalene).* To the right of the Vřídlo Colonnade, steps lead up to the white *Church of Mary Magdalene.* Designed by Kilian Ignaz Dientzenhofer (architect of the two churches of St. Nicholas in Prague), this is the best of the few baroque buildings still standing in Karlovy Vary. ⊠ *Moravská ul.* ☎ *No phone* ☉ *Daily 9–6.*

10

Like Prague, Karlovy Vary also has a central river—the swirling Teplá.

Kostel svatého Lukáše (*St. Luke's Church*). A five-minute walk up the steep Zámecký vrch from the Market Colonnade brings you to the red-brick Victorian *St. Luke's Church*, once a gathering point for the local English community. ☒ *Zámecký vrch at Petra Velikého.*

Kostel svatých Petra a Pavla (*Church of Sts. Peter and Paul*). Six domes top this splendid Russian Orthodox church. It dates from the end of the 19th century, and is decorated with paintings and icons donated by wealthy Russian visitors. ☒ *Třída Krále Jiřího.*

Mlýnská kolonáda (*Mill Colonnade*). This neo-Renaissance pillared hall, along the river, is the town's centerpiece. Built from 1871 to 1881, it has four springs: Rusalka, Libussa, Prince Wenceslas, and Millpond. ☒ *Mlýnské nábř.*

Sadová kolonáda (*Park Colonnade*). Laced with white wrought iron, this elegant colonnade was built in 1882 by the Viennese architectural duo Fellner and Helmer, who sprinkled the Austro-Hungarian Empire with many such edifices during the late 19th century. They also designed the town's theater, the quaint wooden Tržní kolonáda (Market Colonnade) next to the Vřídlo Colonnade, and one of the old bathhouses. ☒ *Zahradní.*

QUICK BITES

After reaching the summit of Stag's Leap, reward yourself with a light meal at the nearby restaurant **Jelení skok**. There may be an entrance fee if a live band is playing (prepare yourself for smooth rock by a synth-guitar duo). If you don't want to walk up, you can drive up a signposted road from the Victorian church.

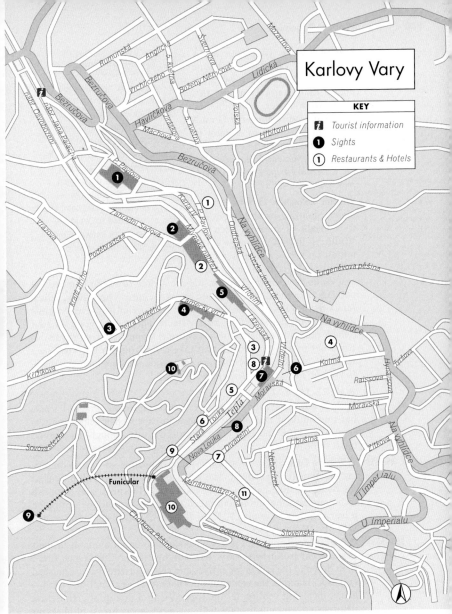

Karlovy Vary

KEY
- 🛈 Tourist information
- ❶ Sights
- ① Restaurants & Hotels

Funicular

Rozhledna Diana. Give your feet a rest. You won't need to walk to one of the best views of the town. Even higher than Stag's Leap sits this observation tower, accessible by funicular from behind the Grandhotel Pupp. There's an elevator to the top of the tower. ✉ *Výšina přátelství* 🚡 *Funicular 40 Kč one-way, 70 Kč round-trip; tower entry is free* ☉ *Daily 9–6.*

Vřídelní kolonáda *(Vřídlo Colonnade).* Shooting its scalding water to a height of some 40 feet, the Vřídlo is indeed Karlovy Vary's hottest and most dramatic gusher. Built around it is the jarringly modern *Vřídlo Colonnade.* Walk inside the arcade to watch hundreds of patients take the famed Karlsbad drinking cure. The waters, which range from 30°F to 72°F, are said to be especially effective against diseases of the digestive and urinary tracts. They're also good for gout (which probably explains the spa's former popularity with royals). If you want to join the crowds and take a sip, you can buy your own spouted cup from one of the souvenir vendors throughout the town. ✉ *Vřídelní ul., near Kosterní nám.*

> ### TO YOUR HEALTH
>
> Becherovka, an herbal alcoholic liqueur made with water from Karlovy Vary, is often referred to as the "The Thirteenth Spring." Many Czechs believe that this locally produced drink has medicinal properties (such as aiding in digestion, just like the waters), which is why they often travel with a bottle. The exact combination of herbs and spices in the recipe is a secret known to only two people in the company.

WHERE TO EAT

Little by little, the food in Karlovy Vary is improving. Prague it's not, but the influx of Russians with money to spend has helped matters somewhat. Pork and beer pubs are still the rule, though. Hotel food tends to be better.

\$\$–\$\$\$ ✗ **Pizzeria Capri.** This "riverfront" pizzeria became an institution during the annual film festival. The walls are decked out with photos of the owner smiling next to Hollywood stars. The pizza and fresh-fish dishes are passably good, and much improved by outdoor seating on a warm summer evening. ✉ *Stará Louka 42* ☎ *353–236–090* ▭ *AE, DC, MC, V.*

\$\$\$–\$\$\$\$ ✗ **Promenáda.** Though it's pricey, Promenáda is unquestionably the best place to eat in Karlovy Vary. The starchy vibe is '70s French fussy, right down to the sauces for entrées and crêpes suzette that are finished tableside. Happily, the emphasis on what's fresh, seasonal, and local—game, including venison terrine topped with a dollop of cranberries, pan-roasted wild mushrooms with a cheese sauce, breast of pheasant with onion confit and croquettes—bridges the gap to the 21st century. There's also an impressive selection of Moravian wines and a staff that's efficient without hovering. ✉ *Trziste 31* ☎ *353–225–648* ▭ *AE, MC, V.*

\$–\$\$ ✗ **U Švejka.** Usually when a restaurant has the name "Schweik" in it—from the novel *Good Soldier Schweik*—it means one thing: tourist trap. But this local Schweik incarnation is a cut above its brethren. If you're looking for a simple, decent Czech pub, with good local cooking

CZECH

CONTINENTAL

CZECH

and excellent beer, you've found it. ⊠ *Stará Louka 10* ☎ *353–232–276* ▣ *No credit cards*.

WHERE TO STAY

$$$–$$$$ 🛏 **Carlsbad Plaza**. A luxury hotel a stone's throw from the Grandhotel Pupp, Carlsbad Plaza is aimed at Karlovy Vary's wealthiest visitors. Everything here speaks refinement, down to the lunchtime dress code: "jacket and tie" for men. The staff tries hard to maintain the highest standards, but the overall effect can be fussy and distant. The rooms are tastefully furnished, with all modern conveniences. Reserve the "Moser Crystal Suite" if you've just cashed out your 401(k). The wellness center (a small pool and sauna complex), spa, and fitness centers offer every comfort and treatment yet invented. **Pros:** everything you could ever want. **Cons:** lots of things you probably don't—and you're paying for it all. ⊠ *Mariánskolázeňská 23* ☎ *352–441–111* ⊕ *www.carlsbadplaza. cz* ⤸ *146 rooms, 14 suites* ⚲ *In-room: a/c, safe, kitchen (some), Wi-Fi. In-hotel: 3 restaurants, bar, gym, spa, bicycles, laundry service, Wi-Fi hotspot, some pets allowed (fee)* ▣ *AE, MC, V* ⦿ *BP*.

$$$$ 🛏 **Grandhotel Pupp**. The granddaddy of them all, this is one of Central
Fodor's Choice Europe's most famous resorts, going back some 200 years. Under the
★ Communists, when the hotel was called "Grandhotel Moskva," standards and service slipped, but the highly professional management has more than made up for the decades of neglect. So much so, in fact, that it was the stand-in for the Montenegro casino in the Bond flick *Casino Royale*. The baroque-style rooms are quite large, and come well furnished with a big tub and a flat-screen TV. Be warned, though, that extras (like Internet access) don't come cheap. For much of the cost-no-object clientele, it's beside the point. Every July the Pupp houses international movie stars in town for the Karlovy Vary International Film Festival (you'll see their photos in the hallways). The hotel is split into two connected parts: five-star Grandhotel Pupp de Luxe and the slightly cheaper four-star Grandhotel Pupp First Class. **Pros:** large rooms; living history; a sleek casino. **Cons:** costly extras; rooms are opulent but not that modern. ⊠ *Mírové nám. 2* ☎ *353–109–631* ⊕ *www.pupp.cz* ⤸ *Grandhotel Pupp de Luxe: 76 rooms, 35 suites; Grandhotel Pupp First Class: 106 rooms, 11 suites* ⚲ *In-room: no a/c (some), safe, Internet. In-hotel: 4 restaurants, bar, gym, spa, bicycles, laundry service, Wi-Fi hotspot, parking (fee), some pets allowed (fee)* ▣ *AE, DC, MC, V* ⦿ *BP*.

$$$ 🛏 **Hotel Dvořák**. The Austrian-owned Dvořák opened in 1990. Despite the influx of new properties, it has managed to keep pace in the ensuing two decades. Rooms are decked out in cheery yellows and reds, whereas the bathrooms are more austere (yet impressively large). There's an excellent in-house restaurant, and there are full spa facilities. The hotel occupies three renovated houses; request a room with a bay-window view overlooking Nová louka and the Teplá River. The staff is invaluable for booking last-minute spa activities like massages. **Pros:** efficient staff; large spa for the price point. **Cons:** some rooms are cramped. ⊠ *Nová Louka 11* ☎ *353–224–145* ⊕ *www.hotel-dvorak.cz* ⤸ *111 rooms, 15 suites* ⚲ *In-room: a/c, safe, Internet, Wi-Fi. In-hotel: restaurant, pool, gym, spa, laundry services, parking (paid), some pets allowed* ▣ *AE, DC, MC, V* ⦿ *BP*.

10

$$ ⊡ **Hotel Embassy.** On a peaceful bend in the river, this family-run hotel
Fodor's Choice   includes spacious, well-appointed rooms. The Embassy is more intimate
★   and personal than the Carlsbad Plaza or Grandhotel Pupp—in fact, dol-
lar for dollar, the rooms are actually a bit nicer, some sporting period
furniture, wallpaper, and drapery not out of place in a 19th-century
chateaux. The hotel offers greens-fee discounts and starting times at
four local courses for the golf-obsessed, and massages and spa treat-
ments for those who are not. **Pros:** perfect for duffers; rooms offer a
great value. **Cons:** small; no spa. ⊠ *Nová Louka 21* ☎ *353–221–161*
⊕ *www.embassy.cz* ⊑ *24 rooms, 5 suites* ⌂ *In-room: no a/c, safe, Wi-Fi.
In-hotel: restaurant, bar, Wi-Fi hotspot, gym, bicycles, laundry service,
some pets allowed (fee)* ⊟ *AE, MC, V* ⊚ *BP.*

$$ ⊡ **Hotel Heluan.** A clean, safe bet if you've arrived in town without reservations and don't want to spend your savings on a room. The location,
smack dab in the main spa area, couldn't be better. The look—wood
flooring and fixtures with limited flourishes throughout—is more austere than other properties in town, but comes across as more restrained
than plain. The hotel can arrange spa services nearby, bit lacks its own
facilities. **Pros:** inexpensive; friendly staff, completely no-smoking hotel.
Cons: a bit of a hike uphill. ⊠ *Tržíště 41* ☎ *353–321–111* ⊕ *www.
heluan.cz* ⊑ *25 rooms* ⌂ *In-room: no a/c, safe. In-hotel: restaurant,
bar, laundry service, some pets allowed (fee), Wi-Fi hotspot, parking
(fee)* ⊟ *AE, MC, V* ⊚ *BP.*

$ ⊡ **Lázně III.** Neo-Gothic in style—on the outside, anyway—this spa
hotel serves the general public as well as patients of the facility. (Try
to ignore the "intestinal irrigation" signs by the entrance.) The rooms
themselves are spartan, but classical-music lovers may find it charming, as the Karlovy Vary Symphony Orchestra plays in a concert hall
located in the same building. **Pros:** beautiful building; great location.
Cons: austere rooms; limited amenities; medical feel. ⊠ *Mlýnské nábř.
5* ☎ *353–223–473* ⊕ *www.lazneiii.cz* ⊑ *32 rooms, 2 suites* ⌂ *In-room:
no a/c, refrigerator. In-hotel: restaurant, bar, spa* ⊟ *AE, MC, V* ⊚ *BP.*

$$ ⊡ **Promenáda.** Just down the street from the Heluan, the family-oper-
ated Promenáda is another good last-minute option right in the center
of town. Pastel yellow rooms are plain, though they're brightened by
the occasional exposed wooden beam or windowsill flower box. The
mosaic-tiled pool in the spa area is a keeper, as is the hotel's restaurant,
which is one of Karlovy Vary's best. **Pros:** beautiful pool; American-style
spa, great restaurant; large rooms. **Cons:** dated fixtures; street noise on
weekends. ⊠ *Trziste 31* ☎ *353–225–648* ⊕ *www.hotel-promenada.cz*
⊑ *21 rooms, 1 suite* ⌂ *In-room: no a/c, safe, kitchen (some), Wi-Fi.
In-hotel: restaurant, bar, pool, spa, laundry service, parking (paid),
some pets allowed (fee)* ⊟ *AE, DC, MC, V.*

$$ ⊡ **Růže Hotel.** More than adequately comfortable and well priced given
its location in the center of the spa district, the Růže also offers an array
of modern spa services like bubble baths and Thai massage. Many
of the rooms overlook the colonnade. The triples are a good deal if
you're traveling as a family or group. In the warmer months you can
enjoy the hotel restaurant's summer garden. **Pros:** nice views; good for
large groups; new rooms. **Cons:** the modern interior lacks character.

✉ *I. P. Pavlova 1* 🕿 *353–221–846 or 353–221–853* ⊕ *www.hotel-ruze.com* 🛏 *52 rooms, 2 suites* ♿ *In-room: a/c, safe, refrigerator. In-hotel: restaurant, spa, parking (paid)* ▭ *AE, V* |◎| *BP.*

$$ **Wellness Hotel Jean de Carro.** Framed on a hilltop off a side street above the spa, the Jean de Carro sits comfortably above the fray. The hotel is a warren of three interconnected properties; standard rooms are cramped compared with the suites, but every room in the hotel

> ### SIP WITH CAUTION
>
> The waters from natural springs are loaded with minerals, which mean they often have a sulfuric smell and taste. Not necessarily the most appetizing thing. What's more, many of the waters speed the digestive process. You may want to sip at first as you get used to the flavor, and plan your day accordingly.

offers views of the town. Grab a seat at one of the outdoor umbrella-covered tables to while away the hours picking out Karlovy Vary's landmarks and enjoying its lush, green surroundings; from this panoramic viewpoint it's worth the climb. The hotel's offers delicious-sounding chocolate massage, honey massage, and cinnamon packs among its treatments. **Pros:** great views; friendly staff. **Cons:** a bit of a hike; small rooms. ✉ *Stezka Jeana de Carro 4–6* 🕿 *353–365–190* ⊕ *www.premium-hotels.com* 🛏 *25 rooms, 7 suites* ♿ *In-room: no a/c, Internet. In-hotel: restaurant, bar, parking (paid), some pets allowed (fee)* ▭ *AE, MC, V* |◎| *BP.*

THE PERFORMING ARTS

Lázně III. If you're looking to get your high-culture fix, the Karlovy Vary Symphony Orchestra plays regularly at this hotel, a spa facility that doubles as an important cultural center for the town. Head to the Antonín Dvořák Music Hall on the first floor of the building to catch the concerts. ✉ *Mlýnské nábř. 5* 🕿 *353–242–500.*

NIGHTLIFE

California Club. There's enough space for you and 249 of your closest friends in this West Coast–theme club. DJs spin "oldies" (which usually means music from the 1970s on up) or disco, depending on the night. The kitchen is open late (until 3:30 AM, except for Sunday, when it closes at 12:30) for hungry night owls. There's no cover, and it's open from 1 PM until 5 AM. ✉ *Tyršova 1753/2* 🕿 *353–222–087.*

Grandhotel Pupp. This upscale funhouse consists of the two nightclubs and the casino of the biggest hotel in town. You don't have to be as smooth as Bond to get in, so gamble the night away within the mirrored walls and under the glass ceiling of the Pupp Casino Club, or settle into a cocktail and some cheesy live crooning at the English-theme Becher's Bar. ✉ *Mírové nám. 2* 🕿 *353–109–111.*

Pyramida Music Club. Dance contests and themes like Latino disco, r'n'b and '80s night make up the schedule at one of the few clubs targeting the younger crowd. On Friday and Saturday it's open to 5 AM. ✉ *Jugoslávská 3* 🕿 *353–815–543* ⊕ *www.pyramida-club.cz.*

SPORTS AND THE OUTDOORS

Karlovy Vary is a town made for staying active in the outdoors. Exercise was often part of the treatment during the heyday of the resort, and the air quality here is markedly superior to that of Prague or other industrialized towns in the Czech Republic. Hiking trails snake across the beech-and pine-covered hills that surround the town on three sides. If you walk past the Grandhotel Pupp, away from the center, and follow the paved walkway that runs alongside the river for about 10 minutes, you will discover a Japanese garden.

Karlovy Vary's warm, open-air public pool on top of the **Thermal Hotel** (⊠ *I. P. Pavlova*) offers the experience of swimming at a cozy bathtub temperature even in the coolest weather; the view over the town is outstanding. Even if you are not staying at the hotel, you can still take a dip in the waters for 80 Kč per hour. The **Karlovy Vary Golf Club** (⊠ *Pražská 125* ☎ *353–331–001* ⊕ *www.golfresort.cz*) is just out of town on the road to Prague; greens fees are 2,000 Kč for 18 holes.

SHOPPING

A cluster of exclusive stores huddles around the Grandhotel Pupp and back toward town along the river on Stará Louka. Lesser-known, high-quality makers of glass and porcelain can also be found on this street. If you're looking for an inexpensive but nonetheless singular gift from Karlovy Vary, consider a bottle of the bittersweet (and potent) Becherovka, a liqueur produced by the town's own Jan Becher distillery. Another thoughtful gift would be one of the pipe-shape ceramic drinking cups used to take the drinking cure at spas; you can find them along the colonnades. Boxes of tasty *oplatky* wafers, sometimes covered with chocolate, can be found at shops in all the spa towns. (The most famous, Kolonáda, is actually made in Mariánské Lázně). The challenge is stopping yourself from eating it all before you give it as a gift.

Kolonáda (⊠ *I. P. Pavlova 15*) sells boxes of heavenly spa wafers. Looking a bit like flattened-out manhole covers, the hazelnut- or chocolate-filled treats are the perfect confection on a sunny day. The store is generally closed from 12:30 to 1 PM for lunch.To glass enthusiasts, Karlovy Vary is best known as the home of **Moser** (⊠ *Tržíště 7* ☎ *353–235–303* ⊕ *www.moser.cz*), one of the world's leading producers of crystal and decorative glassware. For people who want to see more of the process of glassmaking, the Moser Visitors Center at (⊠ *Kapitána Jarose 19 7* ☎ *353–416–242* ⊕ *www.moser.cz*) has a museum and offers factory tours along with shopping.

10

CHEB

42 km (26 mi) southwest of Karlovy Vary; 174 km (105 mi) southwest of Prague.

Known for centuries by its German name of Eger, the old town of Cheb tickles the German border in the far west of the Czech Republic. The town has been a fixture of Bohemia since 1322 (when it was handed over to King Jan as thanks for his support of a Bavarian prince), but as you walk around the beautiful medieval square it's easy to forget you're not in Germany. The tall merchants' houses surrounding the main square, with their long, red-tile, sloping roofs dotted with windows like droopy eyelids, are more Germanic in style than anything else in Bohemia. You will also hear a lot of German on the streets from the day-trippers coming here from across the border.

Germany took possession of the town in 1938 under the terms of the notorious Munich Agreement. Following World War II, virtually the entire German population was expelled, and the Czech name of Cheb was officially adopted. During the Cold War, Cheb suffered as a communist outpost along the heavily fortified border with West Germany. Since then, thanks to German tourist dollars, Cheb has made an obvious economic comeback. The town center merits a few hours of strolling. A pedestrian zone with trees imported from Belgium is partly completed, and the final phase should be finished by July 2011.

GETTING HERE
The journey from Prague to Cheb is about 3½ hours each way, whether you are taking the bus or the train; expect to pay almost twice as much to ride the train. The price for the bus trip is 170 Kč, the price for the train ride 275 Kč to 350 Kč. If you're driving, you can take the E50 and then the 21 from Prague to Cheb, a drive of about 2½ hours, though traffic can sometimes be heavy.

Information **Tourist Info Cheb** (⊠ *Jateční 2* ☎ *354–440–302* ⊕ *www.tic. mestocheb.cz*).

EXPLORING
Chebské muzeum *(Cheb Museum)*. The building that houses this museum is just as interesting at its collection; it's known as the Pachelbel House, the setting for a Macbeth-like murder during the Thirty Years' War. In 1634 the great general Albrecht von Wallenstein was executed in this house on the orders of his own emperor. The Hapsburg emperor Ferdinand II, provoked by Wallenstein's increasing power and rumors of treason, ordered the deed done. According to legend, Wallenstein was on his way to the Saxon border to enlist support to fight the Swedes when his own officers barged into his room and stabbed him through the heart with a stave. In his memory, Wallenstein's stark bedroom has been left as it was with its four-poster bed and dark red velvet curtains. (The story also inspired playwright Friedrich Schiller to write the *Wallenstein* trilogy; he planned the work while living at the top of the square at No. 2.) Aside from preserving this scene, the museum is interesting in its own right, with a Wallenstein family picture gallery, a section on the history of Cheb, and a collection of minerals (including one discovered by Goethe). There's also the stuffed remains of Wallenstein's horse, who died in battle, and a rotating selection of temporary exhibits. ⊠ *Nám. Krále Jiřího z Poděbrad 4* ☎ *354–400–620* ⊕ *www. muzeumcheb.cz* 💰 *60 Kč* ☽ *Tues.–Sun. 9–12:30 and 1–5.*

Chebský hrad *(Cheb Castle)*. Built with blocks of lava taken from the nearby Komorní Hůrka volcano, *this castle* stands on a cliff overlooking the Ohře River, behind the Church of St. Nicholas. The castle—now a ruin—was built in the late 12th century for Holy Roman Emperor Frederick Barbarossa. Redbrick walls are 17th-century additions. Inside the castle grounds is the carefully restored double-decker **Romanesque chapel,** notable for the many lovely columns with heads carved into their capitals. The rather dark ground floor was used by commoners. A bright, ornate top floor was reserved for the emperor and his family, who entered via a wooden bridge leading to the royal palace. ⊠ *Dobrovského 21* ☎ *354–422–942* ⊕ *www.muzeumcheb.cz* ⊠ *40 Kč* ⊙ *Oct. and Nov., Tues.–Sun. 9–4; Apr., May, and Sept., Tues.–Sun. 9–5; June–Aug., Tues.–Sun. 9–6.*

Komorní Hůrka. Red markers indicate a path from Cheb's main square westward along the river and then north past this extinct volcano, now a tree-covered hill. Excavations on one side have laid bare the rock, and one tunnel remains open. Goethe instigated and took part in the excavations, and you can still—barely—make out a relief of the poet carved into the rock face.

Kostel svatého Mikuláše *(Church of St. Nicholas).* The plain but imposing *Church of St. Nicholas* was begun in 1230, when the church belonged to the Order of Teutonic Knights. You can still see Romanesque windows on the towers; tinkering throughout the centuries added an impressive Gothic portal and a baroque interior. Just inside the Gothic entrance is a wonderfully faded plaque commemorating the diamond jubilee of Hapsburg emperor Franz Joseph in 1908. ⊠ *Kostelní nám.* ☎ *354–422–458.*

"Roland" Statue. In the middle of the central square, náměstí Krále Jiřího z Poděbrad, this statue is similar to other Roland statues seen throughout Bohemia, attesting to the town's royal privileges. (Roland is a figure in medieval and Renaissance literature; his statues are found throughout Europe.) This one represents the town hero, Wastel of Eger. Look carefully at his right foot, and you can see a small man holding a sword and a head—this shows the town had its own judge and executioner.

Špalíček. In the lower part of náměstí Krále Jiřího z Poděbrad stand two rickety-looking groups of timbered medieval buildings (11 houses in all) divided by a narrow alley. The houses, forming the area known as Špalíček, date from the 13th century, and were once home to many Jewish merchants. **Židovská ulice** (Jews' Street), running uphill to the left of the Špalíček, served as the actual center of the ghetto. The small, unmarked alley running to the left off Židovská is called ulička Zavražděných (Lane of the Murdered); though not signposted, it was the scene of an outrageous act of violence in 1350. Pressures had been building for some time between Jews and Christians. Incited by an anti-Semitic bishop, the townspeople finally chased the Jews into the street, closed off both ends, and massacred them. Now only the name attests to the slaughter. ⊠ *Nám. Krále Jiřího z Poděbrad.*

WHERE TO EAT AND STAY

$
CZECH ✕ **Kavárna-Restaurace Špalíček.** The sameness of the restaurants lining the square can be a bit numbing, but this one offers a reasonably priced selection of standard pork and chicken dishes, with the added charm of being in the ancient Špalíček complex. ⊠ *Nám. Krále Jiřího z Poděbrad* ☎ *728–436–974* ▭ *No credit cards.*

10

$ ☰ **Barbarossa**. One block from the main square, this charming family-run hotel is a favorite among visiting Germans, so book ahead, especially on weekends. The clean, rather large rooms are simply furnished in modern style and get plenty of direct sunlight. Bathrooms are new. The front desk can also arrange hunting and fishing trips with guides. **Pros:** near the main square; friendly staff. **Cons:** gets crowded; few amenities. ☒ *Jateční 7* ☎ *354–423–446* ⊕ *www.hotel-barbarossa.cz* ↵ *21 rooms with bath* ⚭ *In-room: no a/c, Internet. In-hotel: restaurant, parking (paid), some pets allowed (fee)* ▤ *AE, MC, V* ⦿ *BP.*

FRANTIŠKOVY LÁZNĚ

6 km (4 mi) north of Cheb; 180 km (109 mi) southwest of Prague.

Františkovy Lázně, or Franzensbad, is the smallest of the three main Bohemian spas. It isn't really in the same league as Karlovy Vary. The main spa area is only a few blocks, and aside from a dozen or so cafés in which to enjoy an apple strudel or ice cream, there isn't much to see or do. That said, the charm of its uniform, Kaiser-yellow Empire architecture grows on you. Gardens surrounding the main spa area—both the manicured "French" gardens and the wilder "English"-style parks—grow on you, too. They're as perfect for strolling now as they were 200 years ago. Summer is particularly pleasant, when a small orchestra occupies the gazebo in the Městkské sady (city park) and locals and visitors sit in lawn chairs and listen.

The healing properties of the waters here were recognized as early as the 15th century, but Františkovy Lázně came into its own only at the start of the 19th century. Like Bohemia's other spas, Františkovy Lázně drew from the top drawer of European society, including one Ludwig Van Beethoven, who came here in 1812. But it remained in Cheb's shadow, and the spa stayed relatively small. In the years following World War II the spa declined. Most of the buildings were given over to factories and organizations to use as convalescent centers. Františkovy Lázně also developed a reputation for helping women with fertility problems, and Milan Kundera used it as the humorous, small-town backdrop for his novel *The Farewell Party*. Since 1989 the town has worked hard to restore the yellow façades to their former glory.

The best way to approach Františkovy Lázně is simply to find **Národní ulice,** the main street, and walk.

GETTING HERE

Expect to spend about four hours each way traveling between Prague and Františkovy Lázne via bus or train. As with other destinations, you'll pay almost double for riding the rails. Costs are about 170 Kč one-way for the bus, about 280 Kč to 360 Kč for the train. Frequent buses run to and from Cheb. If you're driving, you can take the E50 and then the 21 from Prague to Františkovy Lázne, a drive of about three hours.

Information **Františkovy Lázně Tourist Information** (☒ *Tři Lilie Hotel, Národní 3* ☎ *354–208–990* ⊕ *www.franzensbad.cz*).

10

EXPLORING

Františkův pramen. Under a little gazebo filled with brass pipes sits the town's main spring. The colonnade to the left once displayed a bust of Lenin that was replaced in 1990 by a memorial to the American liberation of the town in April 1945. To the right, in the garden, you'll see a statue of a small cherub holding a fish. The oval neoclassical temple just beyond the spring (amazingly, *not* painted yellow and white) is the **Glauberova dvorana** (Glauber Pavilion), where several springs bubble up into glass cases. ⊠ *Národní ul.*

> ### FISHING FOR A CHILD
>
> Františkovy Lázne has long been known as a refuge for women seeking help in fertility problems. Evidence of that can be seen in the main spring's statue of a small cherub holding a fish. In keeping with the fertility theme, women are encouraged to touch the fish (or, ahem, another part of the cherub) to ensure their own fertility. You'll notice the statue is shiny from so many years of being rubbed.

Mĕtské muzeum *(Town Museum).* A fascinating peek into spa culture is housed in this small museum, just off Národní ulice. There's a wonderful collection of spa-related antiques, including copper bathtubs and a turn-of-the-20th-century exercise bike called a Velotrab. The guest books provide insight into the cosmopolitan world of pre–World War I Central Europe. The book for 1812 contains the entry "Ludwig van Beethoven, composer from Vienna." ⊠ *Dlouhá 4* ☎ *354–542–344* ⊕ *web.telecom.cz/muzeum_fl* ☜ *30 Kč* ۞ *Tues.–Sun. 10–5; usually closed mid-Dec.–mid-Jan.*

WHERE TO STAY

Most of the lodging establishments in town depend on spa patients, who generally stay for several weeks. Spa treatments usually require a medical check and cost substantially more than the normal room charge. Walk-in treatment can be arranged at some hotels or at the information center. Signs around town advertise massage therapy and other treatments for casual visitors.

¢ 🏨 **Rossini.** An alternative to the upscale spa hotels in the center, this small family-operated pension is in a more residential area and offers nine rooms, two with balconies. While it lacks most spa services, it does offer bicycle rentals, and the house's backyard can be used for grilling. Microwave ovens and electric water kettles can be borrowed. **Pros:** affordable and clean; free coffee throughout the day. **Cons:** no spa; outside of the town's main area. ⊠ *Lidická 5* ☎ *603–156–760* ⊕ *www.rossini.cz* ➲ *9 rooms* ☖ *In-room: no a/c, Internet. In-hotel: restaurant, pool, bicycles* ☰ *AE, DC, MC, V* ⦿| *BP.*

$$ 🏨 **Tři Lilie.** "Three Lilies," which once accommodated the likes of
Fodor's Choice Goethe and Metternich, immediately reestablished itself as the most
★ comfortable spa hotel in town after an expensive renovation in 1995. (The building dates to 1793.) In the center of the spa quarter, this three-story yellow building has what many others lack—air-conditioning. Some rooms have balconies with French doors. It is thoroughly elegant, from guest rooms to brasserie. **Pros:** glorious a/c; rooms with balconies;

extremely efficient service. **Cons:** if you don't want spa services, much of its appeal is lost. ⊠ *Národní 3* ☎ *354–208–900* ⊷ *31 rooms* ⌂ *In-room: a/c. In-hotel: restaurant, spa, laundry service, Wi-Fi hotspot, some pets allowed (fee)* ▭ *AE, MC, V* ⦿ *BP.*

MARIÁNSKÉ LÁZNĚ

30 km (18 mi) southeast of Cheb; 47 km (29 mi) south of Karlovy Vary.

Once Bohemia's star spa town, Mariánské Lázně now plays second fiddle to Karlovy Vary. Whereas the latter, with its glitzy international film festival and wealthy "New Russian" residents, has succeeded in luring investors, Mariánské Lázně seems to survive largely on the decidedly less glamorous (and much older) crowd coming over from Germany. Busloads of German retirees arrive daily, discharging their passengers to walk the promenades and repair over ice cream and cake before boarding the coach to head back home. This trade keeps the properties in business, but hardly brings the capital influx needed to overhaul the spa facilities.

The grounds have remained lush and lovely, especially the upper part of the town's spa area near the Grandhotel Pacifik. Here you'll find the colonnades and fountains and river walks you expect from a once-world-famous spa. And the woods surrounding the town are magnificent.

A hundred years ago Mariánské Lázně, or Marienbad as it was known, was one of Europe's finest resorts. It was a favorite of Britain's King Edward VII. Goethe and Chopin also came. Mark Twain, on a visit in 1892, couldn't get over how new everything looked. Twain—who had a natural aversion to anything too salubrious—labeled the town a "health factory."

The best way to experience the spa—short of signing up for a weeklong treatment—is simply to buy a spouted drinking cup (available at the colonnades) and join the rest of the sippers taking the drinking cure. Be forewarned, though: the waters from the Rudolph, Ambrose, and Caroline springs, though harmless, all have a noticeable diuretic effect. For this reason they're used extensively in treating disorders of the kidney and bladder. Unlike Karlovy Vary, the springs here are all cold water, and may be easier to stomach.

Walking trails of varied difficulty surround the resort in all directions, and one of the country's best golf courses lies about 3 km (2 mi) to the east of town. Hotel staff can also help arrange activities such as tennis and horseback riding. For the less intrepid, a simple stroll around the gardens, with a few deep inhalations of the town's clean air, is enough to restore a healthy sense of perspective.

For information on spa treatments, inquire at the main **spa offices** (⊠ *Masarykova 22* ☎ *354–623–061* ⊕ *www.marienbad.cz*). Walk-in treatments can be arranged at the **Nové Lázně** (*New Spa* ⊠ *Reitenbergerova 53* ☎ *354–644–111*).

10

DID YOU KNOW?

Walking Marianske Lazně's colonnades, it's easy to picture the town as it was when Goethe and Chopin came to "take the waters."

GETTING HERE

Regular bus and train service between Prague and Mariánské Lázně makes the journey about three hours each way. Although similar in travel time, the train costs more than the bus. Expect to pay 155 Kč one-way for the bus, 240 Kč for the train. However, from Karlovy Vary, there is hourly train service for about 55 Kč. If you're driving, you can take the E50 and then the 21 from Prague to Mariánské Lázně, a drive of about two hours.

Information Mariánské Lázně Tourist Information (*Cultural and Information Center* ⊠ *Hlavní 47* ☎ *354–625–330* ⊕ *www.marianskelazne.cz*).

> ### MARIENBAD WITH A FRENCH TWIST
>
> If the name "Marienbad" rings a bell, you may be remembering the groundbreaking 1961 French Film *Last Year at Marienbad*. A collection of surreal vignettes, the movie explores the possible affair one French couple had in Marienbad using new-wave tricks like jarring jump cuts. But don't expect the manicured lawns and estates of this movie to reflect the landscape of the real Marienbad; it was shot in Southern Germany.

OFF THE BEATEN PATH

Chodová Planá. Need a break from the rigorous healthiness of spa life? The Pivovarská restaurace a muzeum ve skále (Brewery Restaurant & Museum in the Rock) is a few miles south of Mariánské Lázně in an underground complex of granite tunnels that have been used to age beer since the 1400s. Generous servings of Czech dishes—including a whole roast suckling pig—can be ordered to accompany the strong, fresh Chodovar beer tapped directly from granite storage vaults. Giant tanks of aging beer and brewing memorabilia can be seen through glass windows on the way in. You can tour the brewery, but tours are conducted in German only. The brewery also offers "beer spas," starting at 600 Kč. A beer-lover's fantasy, clients dip into a 20-minute soak in warm dark "bathing beer," followed by a 20-minute relaxation period and a glass of Chodovar, taken orally, of course. The brewery promises it will cause a mild and gradual rise in heart activity and "scour away any unhealthy substances that may have accumulated." A 20-minute "pack in hot grains," which will presumably cause you to ferment, is also available. ⊠ *Pivovarská 107, Chodová Planá* ☎ *374–794–181* ⊕ *www.chodovar. cz* ▦ *Museum free, tour 50 Kč* ⊙ *Daily 11–11; brewery tours daily at 2.*

WHERE TO EAT

$$–$$$
STEAK

✕ **Churchill's.** Dark-wood paneling, a serpentine bar, and a mixture of tables and booths give this restaurant a comfy British-pub vibe. It's in the same building as the Excelsior hotel, but with a separate entrance. British food isn't that far off from Czech—meat and potatoes are still front and center—but there are also decent pastas and salads to be had. ⊠ *Hlavní 121* ☎ *354–697–235* ▭ *AE, MC, V.*

$$–$$$
CZECH
★

✕ **Koliba.** An excellent alternative to the hotel restaurants in town, Koliba serves grilled meats and shish kebabs, plus tankards of Moravian wine (try the dry, cherry-red Rulandské červené), with traditional gusto. Occasionally fiddlers play rousing Moravian folk tunes. Exposed wooden ceiling beams add to the rustic charm of the inn's 15 rooms that

10

face the surrounding nature preserve. ⊠ *Dusíkova 592* ☏ *354–625–169* ▭ *MC, V.*

$–$$ ✕ **Maui Lounge.** Just off the main drag, near the Olympia hotel, the sleek
CONTINENTAL Maui Lounge offers an impressive variety of small nibbles, including a
rotating selection of Spanish-style tapas. A few classic Czech entrées,
including a mixed grill, are also on the menu. The extensive cocktail menu helps wash it all down. DJs play here on certain weekend
nights—hence the Maui's tagline "Tapas, Soul and More." ⊠ *Ruská
72* ☏ *607–879–813.*

WHERE TO STAY

Hotel prices have risen in recent years, and many properties are terribly overpriced for what is offered. Despite the glorious Empire and
neoclassical façacdes of many of the hotels and spas, the rooms are
a bit on the blah side—typical Central European bland for the most
part—with a few exceptions listed below. Most of the hotels have ready-
made packages with treatments, and if you plan to indulge in the spas
anyway, they can offer some level of savings. Check the hotel's Web
site for current offers. Private accommodations are usually cheaper than
hotels, although with more limited amenities. The best place to look for
a private room is along Paleckého ulice and Hlavní třída, south of the
main spa area, or look in the neighboring villages of Zádub and Závišín.

$$ ⬚ **Centrální Lázně.** Near the colonnade and Ambrose Spring, this egg-
shell-white spa hotel offers unusual treatments such as magnetotherapy
and peat packs. The wooden pavilion of the Mary Spring, used in
special "gaseous" therapy, stands opposite the entrance to the court-
yard. The rooms aren't anything exemplary, though the extensive use
of marble in the bathrooms is a nice touch. Judging by the number of
seniors sitting around the lobby, it's a favorite with the over-70 set.
Pros: extensive therapies; central location (hence the name). **Cons:** not
exactly a jumping scene; rooms are a bit spartan. ⊠ *Goethovo nám. 1*
☏ *354–634–111* ⊕ *www.marienbad.cz* ⤴ *98 rooms, 1 suite* ⬚ *In-room:
no a/c (some), safe, kitchen (some), Wi-Fi. In-hotel: restaurant, bar,
spa, laundry sevice, Wi-Fi hotspot, parking (fee)* ▭ *AE, MC, V* ⊺⊙⏐ *BP.*

$$$ ⬚ **Grandhotel Pacifik.** This regal hotel at the top of Hlavní Street has been
thoroughly renovated and now may be the best of the bunch. It has a
full range of spa and wellness facilities, including a pool and a sauna.
With commanding views of the main spa area, the rooms are toned
down and tastefully modern, in contrast to the over-exuberant balcony-
studded, yellow façade. Rooms with a view over the park are worth the
extra money. **Pros:** great views; prime location; extensive treatments.
Cons: pricey; common areas a bit down at the heels. ⊠ *Mírové nám.
84* ☏ *354–651–111* ⊕ *www.marienbad.cz* ⤴ *95 rooms, 7 suites* ⬚ *In-
room: no a/c, safe, Wi-Fi. In-hotel: restaurant, spa, laundry serices,
Wi-Fi hotspot, some pets allowed (fee)* ▭ *AE, MC, V* ⊺⊙⏐ *BP.*

$$ ⬚ **Hotel Bohemia.** As a cheaper alternative to some of the posher places
in town, this late-19th-century hotel feels pleasantly down-to-earth.
The crystal chandeliers in the lobby and graciously proportioned
rooms—some with balconies off the front—are like stepping into the
days of Goethe. Alas, the plain furnishings recall the communist era,
when the spas were used as recuperation centers for factory workers.

The helpful staff can arrange spa treatments and horseback riding. An annex, Dependence, features 12 additional suites. **Pros:** inexpensive compared with the other properties in town; friendly staff; beautiful fixtures. **Cons:** rooms a bit dark and grim; no spa. ✉ *Hlavní třída 100* ☎ *354–610–111* ⊕ *www.orea.cz* ⤴ *72 rooms, 4 suites, 12 additional suites in Dependence* ♿ *In-room: no a/c, safe, Wi-Fi. In-hotel: restaurant, bar, laundry service, some pets allowed (fee), parking (fee)* ▭ *AE, MC, V* ◎ *BP.*

$$ 🏨 **Hotel Grand Spa Marienbad.** The new kid on the block, this Austrian-owned hotel aims high. The hotel, made up of three interconnected buildings, boasts the most rooms and the biggest wellness center in Mariánské Lázně—it even pumps mineral water from its own spring in the center of town. The spa area is an impressive mix of medical treatments, including the ominous-sounding "gasbag therapy," as well as options for the more casual spa devotee. Rooms are Central European austere, though some have high ceilings and exposed wooden floors with views of the town. The bar area also boasts the occasional lounge act on weekends. **Pros:** huge spa; sleek rooms. **Cons:** officious staff; overly Teutonic vibe. ✉ *Ruska 123* ☎ *354–929–396* ⊕ *www. falkensteiner.com/en/hotel/marienbad* ⤴ *170 rooms, 4 suites* ♿ *In-room: no a/c, safe. In-hotel: restaurant, bar, gym, pool, spa, Wi-Fi hotspot* ▭ *AE, DC, MC, V* ◎ *MAP.*

$$$ 🏨 **Hotel Nové Lázně.** This neo-Renaissance hotel and spa—opened in
★ 1896—lines a large part of one side of the park. In the center of the building a cast-iron sculpture of the donor of health, Hygiea, is carried by the sea god Triton, the son of Neptune. He stands on top, stressing the importance of water in spa treatments. Inside, the complex of Roman baths is decorated with marble, and houses period frescoes. Alas, for all the gilt in the public areas, the rooms are rather ho-hum affairs, though the view of the park in some is unobstructed. Nonetheless, this is a serious spa, aimed at spa package devotees rather than overnight visitors. **Pros:** beautiful façade; ideal for spa-fiends. **Cons:** not so ideal for the casual visitor; maintains a slight institutional feel. ✉ *Reitenbergerova 53* ☎ *354–644–111* ⊕ *www.marienbad.cz* ⤴ *97 rooms, 1 suite* ♿ *In-room: no a/c (some), safe, Wi-Fi. In-hotel: restaurant, bar, gym, spa, laundry service, Wi-Fi hotspot, some pets allowed (fee), parking (fee)* ▭ *AE, MC, V* ◎ *BP.*

$ 🏨 **Koliba.** This is a perfect choice if you're here for just a day or two,
Fodor's Choice puttering around town without an interest in lavish spa treatments.
★ This hunting-style lodge is situated above and behind the main spa area, about a 15-minute walk from town. The exceptionally cute, clean, rustic rooms and the over-the-top friendliness of the staff are a literal breath of fresh air compared with some of Mariánské Lázně's stuffier hotels. The highly stylized romantic restaurant has the best Czech food in the area. **Pros:** authentic charm; friendly staff. **Cons:** outside the center of town; a bit rustic. ✉ *Dusíkova 592* ☎ *354–625–169* ⊕ *koliba.xercom. cz* ⤴ *12 rooms* ♿ *In-room: no a/c. In-hotel: restaurant, bicycles, some pets allowed (fee)* ▭ *AE, DC, MC, V* ◎ *BP.*

$$ 🏨 **Parkhotel Golf.** A room at this stately villa, 3½ km (2 mi) out of town on the road to Karlovy Vary, requires some advanced booking.

10

Marianske Lazně's "Singing Fountain" sets off its water jets to accompanying music every hour.

The large open rooms are cheery and modern. The restaurant on the main floor is excellent, but the main draw is the 18-hole golf course on the premises, one of the best in the Czech Republic, opened in 1905 by King Edward VII. The spa treatments are ideal for golfers, too, and including paraffin wraps for the hands and peat wraps. **Pros:** great greens; large rooms. **Cons:** far from town; requires significant forward planning to get a room and a tee time. ✉ *Zádub 580* ☎ *354–622–651* 🌐 *www.parkhotel-golf.cz* *28 rooms* *In-room: no a/c, safe, Internet. In-hotel: restaurants, golf course, tennis court, pool, spa, parking (paid), some pets allowed (fee)* *AE, DC, MC, V* *BP.*

$$ **Villa Butterfly.** Decorated with the works of some of the country's top artists, the interior and exterior of this modern, angular art nouveau–style hotel could almost double as a gallery. Female figurines stand on the roof, arms outspread like a butterfly's wings, seemingly about to take flight. Ask for a room in the front, as the view of the forested hills is outstanding. **Pros:** sweeping views; bright and airy rooms; snazzy "King Edward Club" restaurant—lounge a trip. **Cons:** lobby a tribute to early '90s style; standard rooms are cramped. ✉ *Hlavní třída 655* ☎ *354–654–111* 🌐 *www.marienbad.cz* *88 rooms, 8 suites* *In room: a/c, Wi-Fi. In-hotel: 2 restaurants, room service, bar, pool, spa, gym, laundry service, Wi-Fi hotspot, some pets allowed (fee), parking (fee)* *AE, MC, V* *BP.*

THE PERFORMING ARTS

The West Bohemian Symphony Orchestra performs regularly in the New Spa (Nové Lázně). The town's annual Chopin Festival each August brings in pianists from around Europe to perform the Polish composer's works.

NIGHTLIFE

Casino Bellevue (✉ *Anglická 281* ☎ *354–628–628*) is open to 3 or 4 AM for those who want to try their luck. It also caters to buses of tourists on shopping and gambling trips from Germany. For late-night drinks, try the **Parkhotel Golf** (✉ *Zádub 580* ☎ *354–622–651*), which has a good nightclub.

PLZEŇ

92 km (55 mi) southwest of Prague.

Plzeň—or Pilsen in German, as it's better known abroad—is the industrial heart of Western Bohemia and the region's biggest city. To most visitors the city is known as a beer mecca. Anyone who loves the stuff must pay homage to the enormous Pilsner Urquell brewery, where modern "Pils"-style beer was first developed more than 150 years ago. Brewery tours are available and highly recommended. There's even a brewing museum here for intellectual beer aficionados.

Another item of interest—particularly for Americans—is historical. Whereas most of the Czech Republic was liberated by Soviet troops at the end of World War II, Plzeň was liberated by the U.S. Army, led by General George S. Patton. Under the Communists this fact was not widely acknowledged. But since 1989 the liberation week celebrations held in May have gotten bigger and bigger each passing year. If you're traveling in the area at this time, it's worth stopping by to take part in the festivities. To this day Plzeň retains a certain "pro-American" feeling that other towns in the Czech Republic lack. There's even a big statue here emblazoned with an enthusiastic: "Thank You, America!" written in both English and Czech. You'll find it, naturally, at the top of Americká Street near the intersection with Klatovská. You can learn all about the liberation at the Patton Memorial Museum.

GETTING HERE

Frequent bus and train service between Prague and Plzeň makes the journey about 1 hour 15 minutes each way. Bus fares are significantly less than train fares. Expect to pay about 95 Kč for the bus, 150 Kč for the train. If you're driving, you can take the E50 directly to Plzeň, a drive of about one hour.

Information Plzeň City Information Centre (✉ *Nám. Republiky 41* ☎ *378–035–330* ⊕ *www.plzen.eu*).

EXPLORING

Náměstí Republiky *(Republic Square).* The city's architectural attractions center on this main square. Dominated by the enormous Gothic **Chrám svatého Bartoloměje** (Church of St. Bartholomew), the square is one of the largest in Bohemia. The church, at 335 feet, is among the tallest in the Czech Republic, and its height is rather accentuated by the emptiness of the square around it. There are a variety of other architectural jewels around the perimeter of the square, including the town hall, adorned with *sgraffiti* and built in the Renaissance style by Italian architects during the town's heyday in the 16th century. The

10

The Pilsner Urquell Brewery, a mecca for beer lovers.

Great Synagogue, which claims to be the second-largest in Europe, is a few blocks west of the square, just outside the green strip that circles the Old Town.

Fodor's Choice
★

Pilsner Urquell Brewery. This is a must-see for any beer lover. The first Pilsner beer was created in 1842 using the excellent Plzeň water, a special malt fermented on the premises, and hops grown in the region around Žatec. (Hops from this area remain in great demand today.) Guided tours of the brewery, complete with a visit to the brewhouse and beer tastings, are offered daily at 12:30 and 2. The brewery is east of the city near the railway station. ⊠ *U Prazdroje 7* ☎ *377–062–888* ⊕ *www. prazdroj.cz* 🖅 *150 Kč; 250 Kč with museum tour; photo permit 100 Kč, valid for brewery, museum, and underground* ☉ *Daily 10–6, tours in English at 12:45, 2:15, and 4:15.*

▌**QUICK
BITES**

If you visit the Pilsner Urquell Brewery, carry on drinking and find some cheap traditional grub at the large **Na Spilce** (⊠ *U Prazdroje 7*) beer hall just inside the brewery gates. The pub is open weekdays and Sunday from 11 AM to 10 PM, Friday and Saturday from 11 AM to 11 PM.

Pivovarské muzeum *(Brewery Museum).* In a late-Gothic malt house, this museum sits one block northeast of náměstí Republiky. All kinds of fascinating paraphernalia trace the region's brewing history, including the horse-drawn carts used to haul the kegs. ⊠ *Veleslavínova 6* ☎ *377–235–574* ⊕ *www.prazdroj.cz* 🖅 *120 Kč guided, 90 Kč unguided; 250 Kč with brewery tour; photo permit 100 Kč, valid for brewery, museum, and underground* ☉ *Apr.–Dec., daily 10–6; Jan.–Mar., daily 10–5.*

An old label of the local beer Pilsner Urquell, bottled in Plzeň.

★ **Plzeň Historical Underground.** Dating from the 13th century, this is a web of multilevel tunnels. Used for storing food and producing beer and wine, many of the labyrinthine passageways are dotted with wells and their accompanying wooden water-pipe systems. Tours last about 40 minutes. The entrance has been moved to the Brewery Museum. ⊠ *Veleslavínova 6* ☎ *377–225–214* 💷 *90 Kč; photo permit 100 Kč, valid for brewery, museum, and underground* ⊙ *Apr.–Dec., daily 10–6; Feb.–Mar., daily 10–5; closed in Jan.*

U.S. General George S. Patton Memorial. With exhibits and photos, this memorial tells the story of the liberation of Plzeň from the Nazis by U.S. soldiers on May 6, 1945. As the story goes, Patton wanted to press on from Plzeň to liberate Prague, but was prevented from doing so by the Yalta agreement between the United States and the Soviet Union that said Czechoslovakia was to remain under Soviet influence. The museum was dedicated in 2005 on the 60th anniversary of Plzeň's liberation. ⊠ *Pobřežní 10* ☎ *377–320–414* ⊕ *www.pattonmemorial.cz* 💷 *60 Kč* ⊙ *Tues.–Sun. 9–1 and 2–5.*

WHERE TO EAT

¢–$

VEGETARIAN ✕ **Anděl Café.** A fusion cuisine approach puts dishes like risotto with sundried tomatoes; rice noodles with asparagus, coconut, and fried tofu; and curry couscous with broccoli and cheese on the affordable menu here. The interior is pleasant with that stripped-down modern look. ⊠ *Bezručova 5* ☎ *777–022–235* ⊕ *www.andelcafe.cz.*

¢

CAFÉ ✕ **Caffe Fellini.** This dessert spot is right across from St. Bartholomew Church. With an outdoor patio overlooking the square, it's a great place to cool down. Order some ice cream or a piece of cake and take in the front-row views. ⊠ *Nám. Republiky* ☎ *377–423–965* ⊕ *www. caffefellini.cz* 🖃 *No credit cards.*

\$\$–\$\$\$
SPANISH

✕ **El Cid**. Strawberry-infused mojitos wash down excellent tapas dishes at this Spanish-style restaurant along the old town walls, just across from the Continental hotel. Pictures of bullfighters line the yellow walls, while a large patio overlooks the sprawling Křižíkovy Park. The menu also includes some high-end dishes like langosta with white-truffle sauce and beef Wellington. ⊠ *Křižíkovy sady 1* ☎ *377–224–595* ⊕ *www.elcid.cz* 🖃 *AE, MC, V.*

¢–\$
PIZZA

✕ **Pizzerie Paganini**. Just off the main square on Rooseveltova, this cheery spot with red-and-white checked tablecloths serves up rather impressive thin-crust pies and pastas for an industrial town outside of Prague. Still, you're better off sticking with the simpler menu items rather than getting too fancy. ⊠ *Rooseveltova 12* ☎ *377–326–022* ⊕ *pizza-paganini. cz* 🖃 *AE, MC, V.*

\$–\$\$
MEDITERRANEAN

✕ **Rango**. Part of a hotel of the same name, the interior of Rango is a mash-up of medieval, baroque, and modern style—think Gothic arched ceilings and '60s modern light fixtures. The food similarly ranges around Italy and Greece; in addition to pizzas and panini, they serve an excellent grilled flounder with lemon curd and roasted pasta with lamb ragout. ⊠ *Pražská 10* ☎ *377–329–969* ⊕ *www.rango.cz* 🖃 *AE, MC, V.*

¢
VEGETARIAN

✕ **Slunečnice**. The sunny interior here echoes its name, which means "sunflower." This vegetarian café is a good place to grab a ready-made sandwich or a cheap buffet meal of rice and fresh vegetables. Vegan products and "bio juices" are also available. ⊠ *Jungmannova 4* ☎ *377–236–093.*

\$–\$\$
CZECH

✕ **U Bílého lva**. A large stone pillar from the 16th century supports a vaulted ceiling illuminated by imitation torches, giving the dining room some drama. High dark-wood chairs further accent the old-fashioned feel. The wall opposite the entrance dates to the 12th century, and the first mention of the space being used as an eatery is in 1628. While the current menu does have some pasta dishes, the surroundings are more suited to the Czech traditional offerings like roasted duck, pork skewer, and grilled chicken breast with honey sauce. ⊠ *Perlová 2* ☎ *724–322–886* ⊕ *www.u-bileho-lva.cz* 🖃 *AE, MC, V.*

\$\$–\$\$\$
CZECH

✕ **U Mansfelda**. Fresh Pilsner Urquell and variations on classic Czech dishes draw diners to this Pilsner Urquell–sponsored restaurant. A gleaming copper hood floats above the taps in traditional pub style, and the patio invites visitors to spend the evening sipping cold beer and enjoying treats such as boar goulash with dumplings or roasted duck liver in red wine and almonds. ⊠ *Dřevěná 9* ☎ *377–333–844* ⊕ *umansfelda.cz* 🖃 *AE, MC, V* ☉ *Closed Sun. and Mon.*

WHERE TO STAY

\$\$

🛏 **Courtyard Pilsen**. A surprising addition to the hotel scene in Plzeň, this sleek new property offers all the amenities a visiting American could hope for, right down to the flat-screen televisions and ice machines in the hallways on each floor. Rooms that look onto the park are the quietest and have the best views; there's also an impressive fitness center. **Pros:** great amenities; a trusted name. **Cons:** doesn't feel especially local; extras, including Internet, are pricey. ⊠ *Sady 5. kvetna 57* 🕾 *373–370–100* ⊕ *www.marriott.com* ⤵ *171 rooms, 24 suites* ⚒ *In-room: a/c, safe, refrigerator, Internet. In-hotel: restaurant, bar, gym, Wi-Fi hotspot, parking (paid)* ▭ *AE, DC, MC, V.*

$ 🖵 **Hotel Central.** Czar Alexander of Russia once stayed here, when the hotel was a charming inn known as the Golden Eagle. Now an angular 1960s structure, this hotel is recommendable for its sunny blue-and-white rooms, friendly staff, and great location, right on the main square. Recent additions to the property include a small spa and a hairdresser on the second floor. **Pros:** superlative staff; beautiful views of the main square, no-smoking restaurant. **Cons:** the square can echo noise at night; very small bathrooms. ⊠ *Nám. Republiky 33* 🕾 *377–226–757* ⊕ *www.central-hotel.cz* ⤵ *77 rooms* ⚒ *In-room: no a/c (some), Wi-Fi. In-hotel: restaurant, bar, spa, some pets allowed (fee)* ▭ *AE, DC, MC, V* ⦿ *EP.*

$ 🖵 **Hotel Continental.** The Continental aims for a turn-of-the-20th-century feel, and for the most part, it succeeds. The furnishings, which include antique mirrors and armoires, make for historic but comfortable surroundings. Some of the rooms are named for famous people that stayed at the hotel, such as actor Gérard Depardieu, who was there in 2000, and Jack Benny, who stayed while visiting U.S. troops at the end of World War II. **Pros:** spacious rooms; period details. **Cons:** worn-down common areas; occasionally surly staff. ⊠ *Zbrojnická 8* 🕾 *377–235–292* ⤵ *21 rooms* ⚒ *In-room: no a/c, safe, Wi-Fi. In-hotel: restaurant, bar, laundry service, parking (free)* ▭ *AE, MC, V* ⦿ *BP.*

$ 🖵 ★ **Hotel Gondola.** A superb choice, the Gondola is clean and quiet with modern facilities, including air-conditioning—all just a few steps away from the central square, just across the street from a playground. The owners have gone out of their way to make it cozy—the brick-walled rooms have separate baths and showers, flat-screen TVs, and free high-speed Internet access. The innocuous exterior belies the quality of the hotel within. Check for weekend discounts. **Pros:** incredible value; chockablock with add-ons. **Cons:** slightly odd location; limited business facilities. ⊠ *Pallova 12* 🕾 *377–994–211* ⊕ *www.hotelgondola.cz* ⤵ *12 rooms* ⚒ *In-room: a/c, safe, refrigerator, Wi-Fi. In-hotel: restaurant, spa, laundry service, parking (free)* ▭ *AE, DC, MC, V* ⦿ *BP.*

$$ 🖵 **Parkhotel Plzeň.** A 10-minute tram ride from the center, this hotel built in 2004 near the Borský Park is perfect for anyone passing through town with a car. Rooms are modern with dark wood, large windows, and gigantic bathtubs, free Wi-Fi, and drinks in the room. There's also a passable fitness center, which includes a 9-hole golf course, a driving range, and tennis courts within the hotel complex. **Pros:** sleek new rooms; free Wi-Fi; golf course. **Cons:** outside the center; breakfast options rather limited. ⊠ *U Borského parku 31* 🕾 *378–772–977* ⊕ *www.parkhotel-plzen.cz* ⤵ *72 rooms, 4 suites* ⚒ *In-room: no a/c, safe, Wi-Fi. In-hotel: restaurant, bar, golf course, tennis, pool, gym, bicycles, parking (paid), laundry service* ▭ *AE, MC, V.*

10

NIGHTLIFE

House of Blues (✉ *Černická 10* ☎ *608–777–606*), related to the American chain in name only, showcases live blues and rock acts. Ignore the mirrored disco ball on the ceiling—ashtrays on every table let you know you're in a real joint. **Jazz Rock Cafe** (✉ *Sedláčkova 18* ☎ *377–224–294*) gives you a license to party. Drop by on Wednesday to catch some live blues or jazz music.

pLezir (✉ *Martinská 8* ☎ *No phone*) features an assortment of DJ nights and theme parties. Doors open at 5 PM; closing time varies between midnight and 5 AM. **Zach's pub** (✉ *Palackého nám.* ☎ *377–223–176*) highlights various live acts, including Latin and blues, outdoors on its summer patio.

Excursion to Moravia

WORD OF MOUTH

"Telč ranks high on my list of beautiful towns (possibly the most beautiful town square I've ever seen). You won't find much English spoken but many restaurants do have menus in English . . . June would be a great time to go as the weather will be mild—not too hot."

—Adrienne

WELCOME TO MORAVIA

TOP REASONS TO GO

★ **Circle the square:**
In a country full of town squares, Telč's is far and away the most impressive.

★ **Spot colossal columns:**
Olomouc's trinity column is so amazing it's under UNESCO protection.

★ **Tour chateau grounds:**
The Lednice Chateau has huge gardens and even a minaret out back.

★ **Uncover new history:** Třebíč and Mikulov are both renovating and promoting their Jewish quarters.

★ **See a classic castle:**
When people think of castles, they imagine something like Hrad Bouzov.

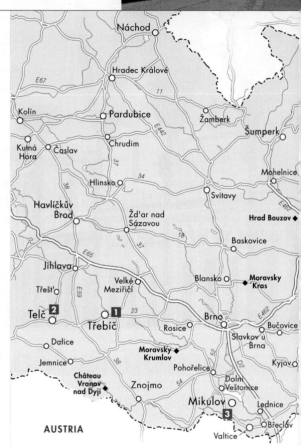

1 **Třebíč.** One of the best-preserved Jewish quarters in Central Europe, with a number of synagogues and a cemetery, puts this small town on the UNESCO World Heritage list. The city's dominant feature, however, is a looming Catholic basilica.

2 **Telč.** Time seems to have stopped several centuries ago in this town, almost unchanged since the Renaissance. Beautiful frescoes adorn the exteriors of most of the buildings in pastel colors or ornate black and white.

0   30 miles

0   30 km

Jeseník

POLAND

Krnov

Bruntál

Opava

Karviná

Ostrava

Český Těšín

Frýdek-Místek

♦ Hrad Šternberk

Olomouc

Nový Jičín

4

Přerov

Valašské Meziříčí

Prostějov

Kroměříž

Vsetín

Zlín

Otrokovice

Uherské Hradiště

Uherské Brod

Veselí

Hodonín

Skalica

SLOVAKIA

GETTING ORIENTED

The most obvious difference between Bohemia and Moravia is that the former is beer country and the latter is wine country. The divisions, while amicable, run much deeper. The people are also more in touch with their past, embracing folk costumes and music for celebrations. In smaller towns some older women still wear embroidered scarves and dresses, something you never see in Bohemia. The pace is also much slower, as agriculture and not industry has always been the driving force of life. The castles and chateaus attest to the fact that the area was once quite wealthy, but in recent times development has been limited, leaving many areas still unspoiled. And because it's so far off the beaten path of Prague, you'll see far fewer tourists.

3 **Mikulov.** Moravia is wine country, and Mikulov is at its center. Castles, chateaus, and sculpted parks dot the area, and vineyards cover many of the hills. Small wine cellars serve the best of the local beverages plus regional cuisine.

4 **Olomouc.** The central city of Moravia was a major base for occupying Russian soldiers. Parts still have an abandoned feel, but slowly the city is waking up. The main square offers a truly monumental baroque column not far from a curious socialist-realist town clock built after World War II.

MORAVIA PLANNER

When to Go

Wine harvest festivals, with the opportunity to taste the barely fermented young wine, hear folk songs and eat local delicacies, are mainly in September. For some towns it is the only time they are truly crowded. But the summer months offer pleasant relaxation at outdoor cafés in an unhurried atmosphere. For bikers, many trails have opened up in the wine region, with spring and early summer being ideal for a tour. Winter should be avoided, especially in smaller towns, as many sights are closed and many shops still close for the weekend throughout the year.

Getting Here

Bus and train service makes much of Moravia easily accessible. A high-speed train to Olomouc makes it possible to go to there as a day trip, in just over two hours each way. And while trains do serve the smaller towns and cities, buses are usually more direct and faster. The D1 highway from Prague also leads into South Moravia and loops back up to end near Olomouc, but it gets heavy traffic at the start and end of the weekend.

Guided Tours

Only a few tour providers offer day trips from Prague to Moravia. Guided tours are often available from the information centers in individual towns.

Wittmann Tours (☎ 222–252–472 ⊕ www.wittmann-tours.com) focuses on Jewish culture, and offers a trip to Třebíč and Telč as well as a trip to key Jewish sites in Moravia. Each trip is 2,800 Kč per person, plus entrance fees, in a group of five or more, or 9,100 Kč for one or two.

Travel agency Cesty za vínem (☎ 511–141–451 ⊕ www.wine-tours.cz) creates customized tours of the wine region, with transportation from Prague or Brno, accommodation, and add-ons like live music and wine tastings.

RESTAURANTS AND HOTELS

Change has been slow to arrive in Moravia, especially beyond the major towns. You're much more likely to find German-speaking staff in restaurants and hotels. Hotel and restaurant workers tend to be friendlier in Moravia and a bit more attentive than they are in Prague.

Cuisine tends to be heavy and old-fashioned. Choices are limited to pork, chicken, and duck, usually with lots of gravy. Pizza places are widespread, but the fare is a bit bland. In mountainous areas, inquire about the possibility of staying in a *chata* (cabin). These are abundant, and often carry a bit more of the Moravian spirit than modern hotels. Many lack modern amenities, so be prepared to rough it.

WHAT IT COSTS IN KORUNA AND EUROS

	¢	$	$$	$$$	$$$$
RESTAURANTS	under 100 Kč	100 Kč–150 Kč	150 Kč–350 Kč	350 Kč–500 Kč	over 500 Kč
HOTELS in koruna	under 1,200 Kč	1,200 Kč–2,200 Kč	2,200 Kč–4,000 Kč	4,000 Kč–6,500 Kč	over 6,500 Kč
HOTELS in euros	under €45	€45–€85	€85–€156	€156–€255	over €255

Hotel prices are for two people in a double room with a private bath and breakfast during peak season (March through October, excluding July and August) and generally include 10% V.A.T. Restaurant prices are per person for a main course at dinner and also include 20% V.A.T.

By Raymond
Johnston

The Czech Republic's other half, Moravia, is frequently overlooked by visitors. No cities here can compare with the noble beauty of Prague, and Moravia's gentle mountains suffer in comparison with the more rugged Tatras in Slovakia just to the east. Yet Moravia's colorful villages and rolling hills do merit a few days of exploration. Come here for the good wine, good folk music, friendly faces, and languid pace.

Despite sharing a common political union for more than 1,000 years with Bohemians, Moravians still consider themselves distinct from "Czechs" (though it must be said that those differences are not always apparent to visitors). The Moravian dialect of Czech is softer and—as Moravians insist—purer than that spoken in Bohemia. It's hard to generalize, but in a word the Moravians are "earthier" than their Bohemian cousins. They tend to prefer a glass of wine—or even better fiery *slivovice* (plum brandy)—to beer. Folk music, all but gone in Bohemia, is still very much alive in Moravia. And Catholicism is still a part of life here—particularly in cities like Olomouc—in a way that died out long ago in much of Bohemia.

Historically, Olomouc is one of its main centers. And it is still impressive today. Long a bastion of the Austro-Hungarian Empire—the city boasts two enormous central squares, a clock tower, and the country's largest Trinity column. In addition, southern Moravia has many small cities, including Mikulov, and a lovely wine region.

If your time is limited or you're just passing through, be sure to at least plan a stopover in the town of Telč in the south. Its enormous central square is like the backdrop of a film set.

TŘEBÍČ

(21 mi) east of Telč; 151 km (91 mi) southeast of Prague.

UNESCO declared the looping streets in the Jewish Quarter and an ornate basilica in Třebíč World Heritage Sites in 2003. The town is first mentioned in 1101, but it was almost completely destroyed in a war in 1468 and then rebuilt. Though known for its historic buildings, Třebíč also has a few modern ones in the art nouveau, cubist, and functionalist styles. Guided tours of the town are available in English from the information center at Karlovo náměstí 53. As in all small towns, very few shops are open on weekends.

If you arrive by bus or train from Prague, keep an eye out for the 19th-century windmill at the west edge of town. The town's tower **Městská věz** on Martinské Square provides a nice view of the whole city.

GETTING HERE

Ideally, you should combine Třebíč with a visit to Telč. Direct bus travel to Třebíč from Prague takes around 2½ hours and costs around 160 Kč. Train connections are not direct, and are more expensive. Bus travel with a change in Jihlava, which has a nice square and town wall, is also possible; from Telč the bus trip takes less than 45 minutes and costs less than 30 Kč.

Car travel from Telč is direct on Route 23 and takes about 20 minutes. From Prague it's fastest to get back on Highway E50 and go east to Velké Meziříčí. Then go south on Route 360; the trip should take less than three hours.

Information Třebíč Tourist information (✉ *Karlovo nám. 53* ☎ *568–847–070* ⊕ *www.visittrebic.eu*).

Out of respect for Jewish traditions, some sights are closed on Saturday.

EXPLORING

Bazilika sv. Prokupa *(St. Procopius Basilica).* The late Romanesque and early Gothic *St. Procopius Basilica* remains true to its original layout, begun in 1260. New sections were added up to the 1950s, but the oldest parts are easy to spot. Look for a very heavy style, with lots of stone and few windows. Two baroque towers at the front were added in the early 1700s by architect F.M. Kaňka. One of the oldest sections is the crypt, with Romanesque pillars and arches. The adjoining château houses the West Moravian Museum, and displays a collection of Nativity scenes, 250 tobacco pipes, folk-art items, and even some mineral samples. ✉ *Zámek 1* ☎ *568–840–518* 🖃 *Basilica 40 Kč; Museum 40 Kč (separate admission)* ☉ *Basilica: Apr.–Sept., Tues.–Fri. 8–11:30 and 1–5, weekends 1—5; Museum: May, June, and Sept., Tues.–Sun. 8–noon and 1–5; July and Aug., daily 8–noon and 1–5; Oct.–Apr., Tues.–Sun. 8–noon and 1–4.*

★ **Židovská čtvrť** *(Jewish Quarter).* A spiraling maze of winding streets, the *Jewish Quarter* has two synagogues and other buildings formerly used by the town's Jewish community. The **Front Synagogue** on Tiché náměstí is now used for Protestant services. The **Rear Synagogue** (✉ *Subakova 44* ☎ *568–823–005*) has an exhibition of Jewish religious items and a wooden model of the ghetto as it was in the 1800s. A touch screen attached to the model provides audio information about the various buildings, with English as an option. The **Jewish Cemetery** (✉ *Hrádek 14* ☎ 568–896–120) has 3,000 tombstones dating from the Renaissance up to the 20th century. It's free to enter, but guided tours can be arranged. The cemetery is closed on Saturday, but almost all of it can be seen from the gate and the low wall. Several houses in the district are intriguing, including a pink Renaissance house with an overhanging second floor at Pokorný 5. A trail of signs in English points out the remarkable spots. Remember your manners—most houses in this area are not museums, and people actually live in them. ✉ *Rear Synagogue 40 Kč, Jewish Cemetery free* ☉ *Rear Synagogue: June–Sept., weekdays 9–noon and 1–5, weekends 1–5; Oct.–May, weekends 1–5. Jewish Cemetery: daily, except Sat., 8–5.*

TELČ

35 km (21 mi) south of Třebič; 154 km (94 mi) southeast of Prague via Rte. 406.

Don't be fooled by the dusty approach to the little town of Telč or the unpromising, unkempt countryside surrounding the place. Telč is a knockout. What strikes the eye most here is not just its size but the unified style of the buildings. On the lowest levels are beautifully vaulted Gothic halls, just above are Renaissance floors and façades, and all the buildings are crowned with rich Renaissance and baroque gables.

GETTING HERE

A car is your best option, and makes it easy to combine a trip to Telč with a stop in Třebič. From Prague, take Highway E50 and E59 south to Route 23 and then west to Telč. The trip takes about two hours without stops. Třebič is east on Route 23.

Direct bus service leaves from Prague's Florenc bus station and takes just under three hours; the fare is approximately 130 Kč. From Třebič a direct bus can take 42 minutes, and costs around 40 Kč.

Train service from Prague requires several changes and takes more than four hours, so it isn't a practical option. It's recommended only for those who want the scenic route.

Information Telč Tourist Information (✉ *Nám. Zachariáše z Hradce 10* ☎ *567-112-407* ⊕ *www.telc-etc.cz*).

EXPLORING

Kostel svatého Ducha *(Church of the Holy Spirit).* A tiny street leading off the main square takes you to the 160-foot Romanesque tower of the *Church of the Holy Spirit*, a solid tower finished off in conical gray peaks. This is the oldest standing structure in Telč, dating from the first quarter of the 13th century. The interior, however, is a confused hodgepodge, as the style was fiddled with repeatedly, first in a late-Gothic makeover and then refashioned again because of fire damage. ✉ *Palackého ul.*

A unified style is what makes Telč so lovely.

Fodor's Choice **Náměstí Zachariáše z Hradce.** This main square is so perfect you feel like
★ you've stepped into a painting, not a living town. Zacharias of Neuhaus,
the square's namesake, allegedly created the architectural unity. During the 16th century, so the story goes, the wealthy Zacharias had the
castle—originally a small fort—rebuilt into a Renaissance château. But
the town's dull buildings clashed so badly that Zacharias had the square
rebuilt to match the castle's splendor. Luckily for architecture fans, the
Neuhaus dynasty died out shortly thereafter, and succeeding nobles had
no desire to outfit the town in the latest architectural fashions.

If you've come by car, park outside the main walls on the south side of
town and walk through the **Great Gate,** part of the original fortifications
dating to the 13th century. As you approach on Palackého ulice,
the square unfolds in front of you, graced with the château at the northern end and beautiful houses bathed in pastel ice-cream shades. Fans
of Renaissance reliefs should note the *sgraffito* corner house at No. 15,
etched like fine porcelain. The house at No. 61, across from the Černý
Orel Hotel, also bears intricate details.

Statní zámek Telč *(Telč château).* Credit the Italians for transforming
this château from a Gothic castle into a refined Renaissance château.
Grouped in a complex with the former **Jesuit college** and **Kostel svatého Jakuba** (Church of St. James), the castle was built during the 14th
century, perhaps by King John of Luxembourg, the father of Charles IV.
Renovation, overseen by Italian masters, took place between 1553 and
1568. In season you can tour the castle and admire the rich Renaissance
interiors. Given the reputation of nobles for lively, lengthy banquets,
the chastising *sgraffito* relief in the dining room depicting gluttony (in

addition to the six other deadly sins) seems odd indeed. Other interesting rooms with *sgraffiti* include the Treasury, the Armory, and the Blue and Gold chambers. A curious counterpoint to all this Renaissance splendor is the castle's permanent exhibit of paintings by leading Czech modernist Jan Zrzavý. There are two tours: the first goes through the Renaissance chambers; the second displays the rooms that were used as recently as 1945. The chateau gallery now houses a toy collection from the 1920s to 1980s. ⊠ *Nám. J. Kypty* ☎ *567–243–943* 🎫 *Tour A 210 Kč (110 Kč entry plus 100 Kč for English commentary); tour B, in Czech and available only May–Sept., 80 Kč; gallery 55 Kč* ⊙ *Apr. and Oct., Tues.–Sun. 9–4; May–Sept., Tues.–Sun. 9–5.*

QUICK BITES

Give in to your sweet tooth and indulge in good, freshly made cakes or an ice-cream cone at **Cukrárna u Matěje**, a little café and pastry shop at Na baště 2, on the street leading past the château to a small lake.

WHERE TO STAY

$ 🏨 **Celerin**. Occupying a tiny corner of the square on the opposite side from the castle, this is the nicest hotel in town. Room No. 5 features some bright, 19th-century period furnishings and a pretty view of the square. The attic rooms are larger, with modern furnishings. **Pros:** central location on square, Wi-Fi connections. **Cons:** some rooms have limited views due to small (but historically accurate) windows, no elevator. ⊠ *Nám. Zachariáše z Hradce 1/43* ☎ *567–243–477* 🛏 *12 rooms* ⊕ *www.hotelcelerin.cz* ⟲ *In-room: no a/c, Wi-Fi. In-hotel: some pets allowed, parking (free)* ⊟ *AE, MC, V* ¶⊙¶ *BP.*

$ 🏨 **Hotel U Černého orla**. In a lemon-yellow baroque house on the square, this is a decent older hotel that has nevertheless maintained suitably high standards. The public areas mix architectural details such as vaulted ceilings with plush, contemporary armchairs, but the basic rooms are inviting and well balanced. Ask for a room overlooking the square. Even if you don't stay here, take a meal at the very good hotel restaurant ($–$$$$), arguably the best place in town for straightforward beef and pork dishes. **Pros:** restored historic building right on the main square, free Wi-Fi access in rooms, pets can stay for free. **Cons:** it lacks modern features such as a/c. ⊠ *Nám. Zachariáše z Hradce 7* ☎ *731–556–644* ⊕ *www.cernyorel.cz* ⟲ *30 rooms, 25 with bath* ⟲ *In-room: no a/c, Wi-Fi. In-hotel: restaurant, bar, some pets allowed, parking (free)* ⊟ *AE, MC, V* ¶⊙¶ *BP.*

MIKULOV

60 km (37 mi) south of Brno; 283 km (174 mi) southeast of Prague.

In many ways, Mikulov is the quintessential Moravian town, with pastel pink-and-yellow buildings and green rolling hills. For centuries it was one of the most important towns in the region—the seat of the Liechtenstein family in the late Middle Ages and then later the home to the powerful Dietrichstein family. The castle's size and splendor demonstrate Mikulov's onetime crucial position astride the traditional border between Moravia and Austria.

But Mikulov began an extended decline in the 19th century, when the main railroad line from Vienna bypassed the town in favor of Břeclav. Historically, Mikulov was the center of Moravia's Jewish community, growing to a population of several thousand at one point, but many Jews left to seek out life in bigger cities. The 20th century was especially cruel to Mikulov. The Nazis Aryanized many of the industries and deported remaining Jews. After the war, many local industries—including the all-important wineries—were nationalized. Mikulov stagnated as a lonely outpost at the edge of the Iron Curtain.

Recent years have seen a slow revival. Much of the wine industry is back in private hands, and standards are rising. Day-trippers from Austria have spurred development of a nascent tourist industry. And after many decades of decline, the old Jewish Quarter is getting overdue attention. Although the Jewish community is still tiny—numbering just a handful of people—work is under way to try to preserve some of the remaining houses in the quarter. You can tour the quarter, where many of the houses are now marked with plaques explaining their significance. The Jewish cemetery is one of the largest in Central Europe, and a must-see if you're passing through.

Grape-harvesting time in October provides an ideal moment to visit and enjoy the local pastoral delights. Head for one of the many private *sklípeks* (wine cellars) built into the hills surrounding the town. If you visit in early September, try to hit Mikulov's renowned wine-harvest festival that kicks off the season with traditional music, folk dancing, and much guzzling of local Riesling.

GETTING HERE

Mikulov is easily reached by bus from Prague with a change at Brno's Zvonařka bus station. The trip takes a little more than four hours and costs about 255 Kč

Train service from Prague requires a change at Břeclav. It takes about four and a half hours and costs about 420 Kč. A high-speed train to Brno can be combined with a bus fro Brno to Mikulov, reducing the time substantially.

By car, the trip is south of Brno on Highway E65 to Břeclav and then east on Route 40. The trip takes a little more than 30 minutes from Brno.

Information Mikulov Tourist Information (⊠ *Nám. 1* ☎ *625–510–855* ⊕ *www. mikulov.cz*).

EXPLORING

Fodor's Choice **Jewish Cemetery.** Mikulov's massive and moving cemetery is not far from
★ Husova ulice, just off Brněnská. The cemetery dates to shortly after 1421 when Jews were forced to leave Vienna and Lower Austria. The oldest legible stone is from 1605 and the most recent are from the 19th century, giving a wide range of stylistic flourishes. Stones for Moravian rabbis are among the most interesting. Step into the ceremonial hall to view an exhibit of the cemetery's history. The cemetery is open in July and August, and during the rest of the year keys can be borrowed from the Tourist Information Center at Nám. 1. ⊠ *Off Brněnská ul.* ☜ *20 Kč*

Moravia is known for its verdant vineyards.

🕙 *July and Aug., Tues.–Sun. 10–noon and 1–6; at other times contact Mikulov Tourist Information Center.*

Jewish Quarter *(Upper Synagogue).* Little of Mikulov's once-thriving Jewish Quarter, Židovská čtvrt', still survives. The community once numbered several thousand people, and the town was the seat of the chief rabbi of Moravia from the 17th to the 19th century. Several respected Talmudic scholars, including Rabbis Jehuda Loew and David Oppenheimer, lived and taught here. What's left can be seen on a stroll down Husova ulice, which was once the center of the quarter. An information board near the corner with Brněnská ulice explains the significance of the community and what happened to it. The most important building still standing is the 16th-century **Altschul**. ✉ *Husova 11* 🎟 *20 Kč* 🕙 *May–Sept., Tues.–Sun. 10–5.*

Mikulov zámek *(Mikulov Château).* Looming over the tiny main square and surrounding area is this arresting château. Built as the Gothic-era residence of the noble Liechtenstein family in the 13th century, the château later served as the residence of the powerful Dietrichsteins. Napoléon Bonaparte also stayed here in 1805 while negotiating peace terms with the Austrians after winning the Battle of Austerlitz (Austerlitz is now known as Slavkov, near Brno). Sixty-one years later, Bismarck used the castle to sign a peace treaty with Austria. The castle's darkest days came at the end of World War II, when retreating Nazi SS units set fire to it. Much of what you see today—though it looks deceptively ancient—is relatively new, having been rebuilt after World War II. The château holds the **Regionální Muzeum** (Regional Museum), exhibiting period furniture and local wine-making items, including a remarkable wine cask, made in 1643, with a capacity of more than 22,000 gallons. ⊠ *Zámek 5* ☎ *519–309–019* 💳 *80 Kč* ⊙ *Apr. and Oct., Tues.–Sun. 9–4; May, June, and Sept., Tues.–Sun. 9–5; July and Aug., Tues.–Sun. 9–6.*

OFF THE BEATEN PATH

Just 12 km (7 mi) east of Mikulovis the **Château Lednice na Moravé**, a must-see if you happen to be in the area. The dining room alone, with resplendent blue-and-green silk wall coverings embossed with the Moravian eagle, makes the visit memorable. The grounds, not to be outdone by the sumptuous interior, have a 200-foot-tall minaret and a massive greenhouse filled with exotic flora. The absolute splendor of the palace and gardens contrasts sharply with the workaday reality of Lednice. ⊠ *Lednice* ☎ *519–340–128* ⊕ *www.zamek-lednice.com* 💳 *Tours 120 Kč each (2 circuits), foreign language guide 50 Kč extra; minaret 30 Kč* ⊙ *Apr. and Oct., Tues.–Sun. 9–noon and 1–4; May–Sept., Tues.–Sun. 9–noon and 1–6.*

WHERE TO STAY

¢–$
★

🏨 **Hotel Tanzberg.** Prim and nicely renovated, this hotel sits in the middle of the former Jewish quarter, on Husova ulice. The doubles are on the small side, but the suites, which cost just a little more, are quite roomy. Facilities are the best in Mikulov, particularly the ground-floor restaurant ($–$$), which serves a typical but delicately prepared selection of traditional Moravian dishes and some regional Jewish recipes from the 19th century. **Pros:** central location; historic building. **Cons:** few rooms; limited parking. ⊠ *Husova ul. 8* ☎ *519–510–692* ⊕ *www. hotel-tanzberg.cz* 🛏 *14 rooms* ⚴ *In-room: no a/c, Internet. In-hotel: restaurant, bar, bicycles, some pets allowed (fee)* ☰ *AE, MC, V* ❑ *BP.*

OLOMOUC

★ *77 km (48 mi) northeast of Brno; 275 km (165 mi) east of Prague.*

Olomouc (pronounced oh-loh-moats) is a handsome district capital, with some beautifully restored baroque houses along its broad central squares and the country's largest Trinity column—another UNESCO World Heritage Site. Its laid-back, small-town feel and the presence of a charming, inexpensive pension right in town make it an easy choice for an overnight stay.

Olomouc owes its relative prosperity to its loyalty to the Austro-Hungarian Empire. In the revolutionary days of the mid-19th century, when the rising middle classes throughout the empire were asserting their independence from the nobility, the residents of Olomouc remained true to the ruling Hapsburgs. During the revolutions of 1848 the royal family even fled here from Vienna for protection. Mozart, Mahler, and other famous composers stopped by on occasion, leaving behind a musical heritage that is still alive today with an active classical music scene.

The most prominent open space in Olomouc is the triangular Horní náměstí (Upper Square). Four of the city's half-dozen renowned **baroque fountains**, depicting Hercules (1687), Caesar (1724), Neptune (1695), and Jupiter (1707), dot the square and the adjacent other large square, Dolní náměstí (Lower Square) to the south.

A discount card called the **Olomouc Region Card** is valid for most tourist sights in and around the city, and is available for 180 Kč for 48 hours and 360 Kč for five days. Admission to the Town Hall tower, botanical gardens, zoo, Hrad Bouzov, Hrad Šternberk, and other sites is included. The card also provides discounts at some restaurants, pools, fitness centers, and hotels. You can buy the card—and get more information on discounts and deals—at the main tourist information center at Horní náměstí 1 and at many hotels, travel agencies, and tourist venues. The information center also can tell you about local tour operators that organize half-day outings to the area's castles.

GETTING HERE
Traveling from Prague, in addition to driving, you can take either a train or a bus. By car, follow the D1 motorway south to Brno and then follow the signs and turnoffs to Olomouc from Brno. The trip will take about three hours in moderate traffic.

Direct train travel from Prague takes at least 2¾ hours, and costs around 310 Kč for the 250-km (150-mi) trip. High-speed Pendolino trains also go there, usually from the Holešovice station, for 510 Kč.

Direct bus service from Prague's Florenc bus station takes at least three hours, and costs around 300 Kč for the 262-km (157-mi) trip.

Contacts Olomouc Tourist Information (✉ *Radnice, Horní nám.* ☎ *585–513– 385* ⊕ *www.tourism.olomouc.eu*).

EXPLORING
Arcidiecézní museum *(Archdiocesan Museum).* At this house in 1767 the young musical prodigy Wolfgang Amadeus Mozart, age 11, spent six weeks recovering from a mild attack of chicken pox and completed his Sixth Symphony. The 16-year-old King Wenceslas III suffered a much worse fate here in 1306, when he was murdered, putting an end to the Přemyslid dynasty. Now it houses treasures from the collections of the archdiocese, including golden monstrances, religious paintings, carved ivory objects, and a full-sized gilded coach. Modern art is also displayed in part of the building complex and included in the same admission, but is often a bit disappointing in comparison. ✉ *Václavské nám. 3* 🏛 *50 Kč (also includes Romanesque Bishop's Palace, when open)* ⏱ *Tues.–Sun. 10–6.*

Chrám svatého Mořice *(Church of St. Maurice).* Nothing is left of the original Church of St. Maurice that stood just north of the Horní náměstí in 1257. This is a new church started in 1412 on the same site and remodeled many times. Its current fierce, gray exterior dates from the middle of the 16th century. A sculpture of Christ on the Mount of Olives dates to the 15th century. The baroque organ inside, the largest in the Czech Republic, originally contained 2,311 pipes until it was expanded in the 1960s to more than 10,000 pipes. An international organ festival takes place in the church every September. ✉ *Jana Opletalova ul.* ⏱ *Hours are sporadic, but church is often open during day.*

Dóm svatého Václava *(Cathedral of St. Wenceslas).* Between the main square and this cathedral lies a peaceful neighborhood given over to huge buildings, mostly belonging either to the university or the archbishop. The church itself is impressive, but its Gothic appearance comes only from a 19th-century makeover. A plaque marks the fact that Pope John Paul II celebrated mass there in 1995. ⊠ *Václavské nám.* ⊘ *Mon., Tues, Fri., and Sat., 9–6, Wed. 9–4, Thurs., 9–5, Sun. 11–6.*

Kostel svatého Michala *(St. Michael's Church).* The interior of this triple-domed church casts a dramatic spell. The frescoes, the high and airy central dome, and the shades of rose, beige, and gray trompe-l'oeil marble on walls and arches work in concert to present a harmonious whole. The decoration followed a fire in 1709, only 30 years after the original construction. The architect and builder are not known, but it's surmised they are the same team that put up the Church of the Annunciation on Svatý Kopeček (Holy Hill), a popular Catholic pilgrimage site just outside Olomouc. ⊠ *Žerotínovo nám., 1 block uphill from Horní nám., along Školní ul.* ⊘ *Hours are sporadic, but church is often open during day.*

Fodor's Choice   **Morový sloup** *(Trinity Column).* In the northwest corner of Horní
★ náměstí this eccentric *Trinity column,* is one of the best surviving examples of the Olomouc baroque style, which was prevalent in this region of Moravia after the Thirty Years' War in the 17th century. At 35 meters (115 feet), it's the tallest column devoted to victims of the plague in the Czech Republic. The column alone (not the rest of the square) is a UNESCO World Heritage Site. Its construction began in 1717, but it was not completed until 1754, long after the death of its principal designer, Václav Render, who left all his wealth to the city of Olomouc so that the column could be finished. Inside is a small chapel that, unfortunately, is never open. ⊠ *Horní nám.*

Radnice *(Town Hall).* Olomouc's central square is marked by the bright, spire-bedecked Renaissance *town hall* with its 220-foot tower. The tower was constructed in the late 14th century. The astronomical clock on the outside was built in 1422, and once rivaled the one in Prague. It was mostly destroyed by an artillery shell on the last two days of World War II. The modern socialist-realist mosaic decorations of the current clock date from 1955. Be sure to look inside the town hall at the beautiful stairway. You can also visit a large Gothic banquet room in the main building, with scenes from the city's history, and a late-Gothic chapel. Tours of the tower and chapel are given several times daily; contact the tourist office in the town hall. ⊠ *Horní nám.* ☏ *585–513–385 tourist office* ⊠ *Tours up to 30 Kč* ⊘ *Daily 9–7, information center; 11–3, tower tours.*

QUICK
BITES

Wooden paneling and floral upholstery in the **Café Mahler** (⊠ *Horní nám.* 11) recall the taste of the 1880s, when Gustav Mahler briefly lived around the corner while working as a conductor at the theater on the other side of the Upper Square. It's a good spot for ice cream, cake, or coffee, or simply for sitting back and taking in the lovely view.

★ **Románský biskupský palace** *(Romanesque Bishop's Palace).* Next to the Cathedral of St. Wenceslas is a complex of buildings that for centuries were the center of the archdiocese. The oldest, commonly called Palác Přemyslovců *(Přemyslid Palace),* houses a museum where you can see

11

early-16th-century wall paintings decorating the Gothic cloisters and, upstairs, a wonderful series of Romanesque windows and displays of sculpted stonework fragments. This part of the building was used as a schoolroom some 700 years ago, and you can still make out drawings of animals engraved on the walls by young vandals. ⊠ *Václavské nám. 4* 🖆 *50 Kč (also includes Archdiocesan Museum)* ⊗ *May–Oct., Tues.–Sun. 10–6.*

OFF THE BEATEN PATH

Hrad Bouzov *(Bouzov Castle).* One of Moravia's most impressive castles—30 km (18 mi) west of Olomouc—has been featured in several fairy-tale films. Its present romanticized exterior comes from a remodeling at the turn of the 20th century, but the basic structure dates back to the 1300s. Owned by the Order of Teutonic Knights from the late 1600s up to the end of World War II, it was later confiscated by the state. Inside, the knights' hall has extensive carved-wood decorations and wall paintings that look old, even if many are reconstructions. Other rooms have collections of period furniture. The castle kitchen, which was used until 1945, is one of the best-preserved examples. Four tours are available, with the grand tour offering most of the highlights. The supplementary tour (doplňková trasa) includes a secret passage. You can easily arrange a tour from the tourist information office in Olomouc; the castle is included in the Olomouc Card. ⊠ *Bouzov 8, Bouzov* 🖀 *585–346–201* 🖆 *Classic tour 100 Kč (140 Kč with English commentary), grand tour 150 Kč (190 Kč with English commentary)* ⊗ *Apr. and Oct., weekends 9–4; May and Sept., Tues.–Sun. 9–5; June–Aug., daily 9–6.*

WHERE TO EAT AND STAY

$-$$
CAFÉ
✕ **Hanácká Hospoda.** Offering a lower-key, cheaper dining alternative to the Moravská, this popular local pub serves staples like pork, chicken, and duck, but nicely turned out. A quieter no-smoking room is available at the back. According to an inscription on the outside of the house, Mozart stayed here as a young boy on a trip with his parents. ⊠ *Dolní nám. 38* 🖀 *585–237–186* ⊟ *No credit cards.*

$$-$$$
CZECH
✕ **Moravská restaurace a vinárná.** Traditional Moravian dishes like roast duck with cabbage, chicken breast stuffed with almond butter, roast piglet, or fried Olomouc cheese are served in a rustic interior. The wine cellar, open weekdays, is a bit homier than the street-level restaurant. The staff sometimes wears folk costumes, and live musicians occasionally perform folk music of the region. International wines, including rare vintages, are available alongside a large selection of Moravian wine. ⊠ *Horní nám. 23* 🖀 *585–222–868* ⊟ *AE, MC, V.*

$$
🖼 **Arigone Hotel and Restaurant.** A renovated historic building blends a nice façade and a few salvageable details with modern rooms. Classic wooden furnishings help to add a little personality to the design. Split-level design opens up the space in the restaurant. **Pros:** a good blend of historic and modern architecture. **Cons:** parking is 300 yards away. ⊠ *Universitní 20* 🖀 *585–232–351* ⊕ *www.arigone.cz* ↰ *39 rooms* 🖧 *In-room: no a/c, Internet. In-hotel: restaurant, laundry service* ⊟ *DC, MC, V* ⥝❘ *BP.*

$ ⊡ **Flora**. The words "traditional communist-era hotel" don't evoke comfort, but this one was made much more inviting by a thorough makeover of the lobby and public areas. The rooms are small but clean, and the price is reasonable. It's a 15-minute walk from the main square. **Pros:** close to the main highways; lots of parking; several barrier-free rooms, spa and wellness services. **Cons:** unless you want to see a relic of Eastern bloc luxury, the hotel might not suit modern tastes. ⊠ *Krapkova 34* ☎ *585–422–200* ⊕ *www.hotelflora.cz* ⤳ *140 rooms, 4 suites* ⌂ *In-room: no a/c, Internet. In-hotel: restaurant, pool, spa, laundry services, Wi-Fi hotspot, some pets allowed (fee), parking (fee)* ⊟ *AE, DC, MC, V* ❡❍❘ *BP*.

$ ⊡ **U Dómu**. Each of the rooms in this quiet, family-run pension just off Vaclavské náměstí sleeps up to four and has a small kitchenette. Modern furnishings are somewhat dull, but the cleanliness of the rooms and the friendliness of the staff make up for it. It's an excellent value. **Pros:** quiet; near the center. **Cons:** limited number of rooms; on a steep street. ⊠ *Dómská 4* ☎ *585–220–502* ⊕ *udomu.3dpano.eu* ⤳ *6 rooms* ⌂ *In-room: no a/c, kitchen, Internet. In-hotel: bicycles, laundry service* ⊟ *AE, MC, V* ❡❍❘ *BP*.

Travel Smart Prague

GETTING HERE AND AROUND

Prague is divided into 10 major administrative districts (with numbers above 10 being used for administrative purposes for some of the larger public housing developments). Most visitors spend their time in "Prague 1," which encompasses the Old Town, Malá Strana, part of the New Town, and the Castle Area. Residents in conversation will often refer to the districts by number to orient themselves geographically ("x is in Prague 1" or "y is in Prague 7"). These district numbers correspond roughly to the city's traditional neighborhoods. The neighborhood of Vinohrady, which lies just to the east of Wenceslas Square, for example, is mostly in Prague 2. Other common neighborhoods and district numbers include Žižkov, Prague 3; Smíchov, Prague 5; and Holešovice, Prague 7. These names—along with the district numbers—appear on street signs.

▌AIR TRAVEL

Prague is served by a growing number of budget carriers, which connect the Czech capital to several cities in the United Kingdom and across the European continent. These airlines are a great and cheap way to travel within Europe—though since the flights are popular, be sure to book well in advance. Budget carriers, however, are usually not much help in cutting costs when traveling from North America. Most of these carriers operate out of secondary airports (for example, Stansted in London instead of Heathrow, where most trans-Atlantic flights land; Orly in Paris instead of the larger Charles de Gaulle airport). This means travelers must change not only airlines but also airports, which can add frustration and expense. Also, consider limits on both carry-on and checked baggage, which are often more stringent on budget carriers than on large international carriers. For flights within

> ### NAVIGATING PRAGUE
>
> Basic navigating vocabulary: *ulice* (street, abbreviated to ul.); *náměstí* (square, abbreviated to nám.); and *třída* (avenue). In Prague the blue signs mark the traditional street address, while the red signs are used to denote the number of the building for administrative purposes.

Europe, low-cost airlines are sometimes a viable alternative to bus and train travel.

The nonstop flight from New York to Prague takes about 8 hours, but the entire journey will take longer (12 to 15 hours) if you have to change planes at a European hub. The flight from London to Prague takes about 2 hours; the flight from Vienna to Prague takes less than an hour.

Airlines and Airports Airline and Airport Links.com (⊕ *www.airlineandairportlinks.com*) has links to many of the world's airlines and airports.

Airline Security Issues Transportation Security Administration (⊕ *www.tsa.gov*) has answers for almost every question that might come up.

AIRPORTS

Prague's Ruzyně Airport is the country's main international airport and lies about 15 km (10 mi) northwest of the city center. The airport has two terminals—*Sever 1* (North 1, or N1) and *Sever 2* (North 2, or N2)—so make sure to read your ticket carefully to see where you are arriving and departing from. The trip from the airport to the downtown area by car or taxi will take about 30 minutes—add another 20 minutes during rush hour (7 AM to 9 AM and 4 PM to 6 PM).

Airport Information Ruzyně Airport (☎ *220–113–314* ⊕ *www.prg.aero*).

GROUND TRANSPORTATION

There are several options for getting into town from the airport, depending on the amount of time you have, your budget, and the amount of luggage.

The cheapest option is Prague's municipal bus service, Bus 119, which leaves from just outside the arrivals area and makes the run to the Dejvická metro station (on the Green Line, A) every 15 minutes or so during weekdays and less frequently on weekends and evenings. The 20 Kč ticket—plus an extra 10 Kč ticket if you have a large bag—can be purchased at the yellow vending machine at the bus stop and includes a transfer to the metro. To reach Wenceslas Square, get off at Můstek station.

The Cedaz minibus shuttle links the airport with the central V Celnici street, adjacent to náměstí Republiky (Republic Square), which is not far from the Old Town Square. It runs regularly between 5:30 AM and 9:30 PM daily. The one-way fare to V Celnici is 120 Kč. You can also take a Cedaz minibus directly to your hotel for 480 Kč–960 Kč for up to four people, which is often less than the taxi fare.

A taxi ride to the center will set you back about 600 Kč–800 Kč; the fare will be higher for destinations outside the center and away from the airport. Be sure to agree on the fare with the driver before leaving the airport. AAA Radiotaxi has an exclusive concession to operate from the airport, but you can take any cab to the airport.

Prague Airport Shuttle offers transport to your hotel for a fixed price between 550 Kč and 800 Kč, depending on the number of passengers (one–eight). The company promises to wait up to an hour from your originally scheduled arrival if your flight is delayed or if customs and immigration are slow. Reservations must be made in advance via e-mail.

Contacts AAA Radiotaxi (☏ 222–333–222 ⊕ www.aaataxi.cz). **Cedaz** (☏ 220–111–111 ⊕ www.cedaz.cz). **Prague Airport Shuttle** (☏ 602–395–421 ⊕ www.prague-airport-shuttle.com).

FLIGHTS

ČSA (Czech Airlines), the Czech national carrier, offers nonstop flights from the United States (from New York's Newark airport) to Prague (daily flights during the busiest season); Delta offers nonstop flights from Atlanta. Most major U.S.-based airlines fly to Prague through codeshare arrangements with their European counterparts. However, nearly all the major European airlines fly there, so it's usually easy to connect through a major European airport (such as London–Heathrow, Paris, Amsterdam, or Vienna) and continue to Prague; indeed, flights between the United Kingdom and Prague are numerous and frequent, including some on cheap discount airlines, though in London most of these leave from Gatwick or Stansted airports rather than Heathrow, making them less attractive options for Americans. Fares from the United States tend to rise dramatically during the busy summer season, particularly from June through August or September. There are many discounts during the slow winter months.

Airline Contacts American Airlines (☏ 800/433–7300, 224–234–985 in Prague ⊕ www.aa.com). **Continental Airlines** (☏ 800/523–3273 for U.S. reservations, 800/231–0856 for international reservations, 221–665–133 in Prague ⊕ www.continental.com). **Czech Airlines** (ČSA ☏ 239–007–007 in Prague, 800/223–2365 in U.S. ⊕ www.csa.cz). **Delta Airlines** (☏ 800/221–1212 for U.S. reservations, 800/241–4141 for international reservations, 224–946–733 in Prague ⊕ www.delta.com). **United Airlines** (☏ 800/864–8331 for U.S. reservations, 800/538–2929 for international reservations ⊕ www.united.com).

Budget Airlines in Europe EasyJet (⊕ www.easyjet.com). **Germanwings** (⊕ www.germanwings.com). **Smart Wings** (☏ 900–166–565 in Prague, toll number, 255-700-827 outside Prague ⊕ www.smartwings.net).

▌BUS TRAVEL

The Czech complex of regional bus lines known collectively as ČSAD operates its dense network from the sprawling Florenc station. For information about routes and schedules, consult the confusingly displayed timetables posted at the station or visit the information window in the lower-level lobby, which is open daily from 6 AM to 9 PM. The company's Web site will give you bus and train information in English (click on the British flag).

Most, but not all, buses use the Florenc station. Some buses—primarily those heading to smaller destinations in the south of the country—depart from above Roztyly metro station (Red Line, C). You won't know beforehand which buses leave from Roztyly, so you will have to ask first at Florenc. There's no central information center at Roztyly; you simply have to sort out the timetables at the bus stops or ask someone.

Buses offer an easier and quicker alternative to trains for many destinations. The western Bohemian spa town of Karlovy Vary, for example, is an easy two-hour bus ride away. The same journey by train—because of the circuitous rail route—often takes six hours.

Bus Information ČSAD (*Florenc station* ✉ *Křižíkova 4, Karlín* ☎ *900-144-444* ⊕ *www. idos.cz* Ⓜ *Line B and C: Florenc*).

▌CAR TRAVEL

Traveling by car has some obvious advantages: it offers much more flexibility and is often quicker than a bus or train. But these advantages can be outweighed by the costs of the rental and gasoline, as well as the general hassles of driving in the Czech Republic. Most roads in the country are of the two-lane variety, and are often jammed with trucks. And then there's parking. It's impossible in Prague and often difficult in the larger cities and towns outside the capital. If you do decide to rent a car and drive, don't set

out without a large, up-to-date Český Autoatlas, available at gas stations and bookstores.

A special permit is required to drive on expressways and other four-lane highways. Rental cars should already have a permit affixed to the windshield. Temporary permits—for 15 days (200 Kč) or two months (300 Kč)—are available at border crossings, post offices, and some large service stations.

GASOLINE

Gas stations are plentiful on major thoroughfares and near large cities. Many are open around the clock. At least two grades of unleaded gasoline are sold, usually 91–93 octane (regular) and 94–98 octane (super), as well as diesel. Prices are per liter, and the average cost of gasoline is substantially higher than in the United States. The Czech word for gasoline is "benzin," and at the station you pump it yourself.

Finding a parking spot in Prague can be next to impossible. Most of the spaces in the city center, Prague 1, 2, and 3, are reserved for residents, so you'll have to look for public lots with machines that issue temporary permits (look for the big blue "P" on machines). To use the machines, insert the required amount of change—usually 10 Kč to 20 Kč an hour—then place the ticket in a visible spot on the dashboard. Violators will find their cars towed away or immobilized by a "boot" on the tire. Some hotels offer parking—and this is a real advantage—though you may have to pay extra. A few streets also have meter parking that sells tickets to put in your window, but finding a spot is a virtual impossibility. Changes in the parking policy are pending, due to complaints from local businesses.

Parking is generally unrestricted in the outer areas of the city, though vacant spots can still be hard to find. If you have a car and you need to get rid of it, try parking it on one of the streets in Prague 6 or Prague 7 across the river and north of the Old Town. There's an underground lot at Náměstí Jana Palacha, near Old Town Square. There are also park-and-ride (P+R) lots at distant suburban metro stations, including Skalka (Line A), Zličín and Černý Most (Line B), and Nádraží Holešovice and Opatov (Line C).

RULES OF THE ROAD

The Czech Republic follows the usual continental rules of the road. A right turn on red is permitted *only* when indicated by a green arrow. Signposts with yellow diamonds indicate a main road where drivers have the right of way. The speed limit is 130 kph (78 mph) on four-lane highways, 90 kph (56 mph) on open roads, and 50 kph (30 mph) in built-up areas and villages. Passengers under 12 years of age, or less than 150 cm (5 feet) in height, must ride in the back seat.

CAR RENTAL

Several major rental agencies have offices at the airport and also in the city. Prices can differ greatly, so be sure to shop around. Major firms like Avis and Hertz offer Western-style cars starting at around $45 per day or $300 per week, which includes insurance, damage waiver, and V.A.T. (value-added tax); cars equipped with automatic transmission and air-conditioning are available, but are generally more expensive. It's best to reserve your rental car before you leave home, and it may be less expensive as well. Smaller local companies, on the other hand, can rent Czech cars for significantly less, but the service and insurance coverage may be inferior.

Drivers from the United States need no international driving permit to rent a car in the Czech Republic, only a valid domestic license, along with the vehicle registration. If you intend to drive across a border, ask about restrictions on driving into other countries. The minimum age required for renting is usually 21 or older, and some companies also have maximum ages; be sure to inquire when making your arrangements. The Czech Republic requires that you have held your driver's license for at least a year before you can rent a car.

Major Rental Agencies Avis (☎ 235-362-420 ⊕ www.avis.com). **Budget** (☎ 220-113-253 ⊕ www.budget.com). **Hertz** (☎ 220-114-340 ⊕ www.hertz.com). **Europcar** (☎ 220-113-207 ⊕ www.europcar.com).

Wholesalers Auto Europe (☎ 888/223-5555 ⊕ www.autoeurope.com). **Europe by Car** (☎ 212/581-3040 in New York, 800/223-1516 ⊕ www.europebycar.com). **Eurovacations** (☎ 877/471-3876 ⊕ www.eurovacations.com). **Kemwel** (☎ 877/820-0668 ⊕ www.kemwel.com).

▌ PUBLIC TRANSIT TRAVEL

Prague has an excellent public transit system, which includes a clean and reliable underground subway system—called the metro—as well as an extensive tram and bus network. Metro stations are marked with an inconspicuous "M" sign. A refurbished old tram, No. 91, travels through the Old Town and Lesser Quarter on summer weekends. Beware of pickpockets, who often operate in large groups on crowded trams and metro cars and all other forms of transportation, including inter-city buses.

The basic, transferable metro and tram ticket costs 26 Kč. It permits 75 minutes of travel throughout the metro, tram, and bus network. Single-ride tickets cost 18 Kč and allow one 20-minute ride on a tram or bus, without transfer, or a metro journey of up to five stations lasting less than 30 minutes (transfer between lines is allowed). If you're carrying a big bag, you need to buy an additional 10 Kč ticket. A matter of politeness: Czechs keep to the right side of escalators, leaving the left side free to people who want to walk up or down. It just takes one person on the wrong side to block the entire escalator.

Tickets (*jízdenky*) can be bought at dispensing machines in the metro stations and at some newsstands. They can also be purchased via SMS over a mobile phone by calling 902–06–26 if you have an SIM card from a Czech service provider.

You can buy a one-day pass allowing unlimited use of the system for 100 Kč, a three-day pass for 330 Kč, or a five-day pass for 500 Kč. The latter two allow traveling with a child 6–15 years old for free. The passes can be purchased at the main metro stations, from ticket machines, and at some newsstands in the center. A pass is not valid until stamped in the orange machines in metro stations or aboard trams *and* the required information is entered on the back (there are instructions in English). Ticket inspectors look for tourists, and will fine you if a multiday pass isn't signed.

The trams and metros shut down around midnight, but special night trams, numbered 50 to 59, and some buses run all night. Night trams run at 30-minute intervals, and all routes intersect at the corner of Lazarská and Spálená streets in the New Town, near the Národní třída metro station. Schedules and regulations in English are on the transportation department's official Web site. Travel information centers provide all substantial information about public transport operation, routes, timetables, and so on. They are at major metro stations and at both terminals at the airport.

Validate your metro ticket at an orange stamping machine before descending the escalator. Trains are patrolled often; the fine for riding without a valid ticket is 950 Kč, but the fine is reduced if you pay on the spot. Tickets for buses are the same as those used for the metro, although you validate them at machines inside the bus or tram. Information about tickets, route changes, and fines is on the city transit company Web site.

Transit Information Web Sites Dopravní Podnik (⊕ www.dpp.cz).

Transit Information Centers Anděl (☎ 296–191–817). **Můstek** (☎ 296–191–817). **Muzeum** (☎ 296–191–817). **Nádraží** **Holešovice** (☎ 296–191–817). **Ruzyně Airport** (☎ 296–191–817).

Lost and Found Lost & Found (✉ Karoliny Světlé 5, Staré Město ☎ 224–235–085).

▌ TAXI TRAVEL

Taxis are a convenient way of getting around town, particularly in the evening, when the number of trams and metro trains starts to thin out. But be on the lookout for dishonest drivers, especially if you hail a taxi on the street or from one of the taxi stands at heavily touristed areas like Wenceslas Square. Typical scams include drivers doctoring the meter or failing to turn the meter on and then demanding an exorbitant sum at the end of the ride. In an honest cab, the meter starts at 40 Kč and increases by 28 Kč per km (½ mi) or 6 Kč per minute at rest. Most rides within town should cost no more than 150 Kč to 250 Kč. A loophole in the law allows drivers to set their own prices, even though the city has an official price. To counter this, the city has Fair Place stands with taxis that meet a minimum standard and agree to follow the set price list. Average prices are posted on a sign at each stand. The best way to avoid getting ripped off is to ask your hotel or restaurant to call a cab for you. If you have to hail a taxi on the street, agree with the driver on a fare before getting in. (If the driver says he can't tell you what the approximate fare will be, that's almost a sure sign he's giving you a line.) If you have access to a phone, a better bet is to call one of the many radio-operated companies, like AAA Taxi. The drivers are honest, and the dispatchers speak English.

Taxi Companies AAA Radiotaxi (☎ 222-333-222 ⊕ www.aaa-taxi.cz). **City Taxi** (☎ 257-257-257 ⊕ www.citytaxi.cz).

▌ TRAIN TRAVEL

Prague is serviced by two international train stations, so always make certain you know which station your train is using.

The main station, Hlavní Nádraží, is about 500 yards east of Wenceslas Square via Washingtonova ulice. The other international station is Nádraží Holešovice, in a suburban area about 2 km (1 mi) north of the city center along the metro Line C (Red Line). Nádraží Holešovice is frequently the point of departure for trains heading to Berlin, Vienna, and Budapest, as well as the high-speed train to Brno, Olomouc, and Ostrava in Moravia. Two other large stations in Prague service mostly local destinations. Smíchovské Nádraží—southwest of the city center across the Vltava (on metro Line B, Yellow Line)—services destinations to the west, including trains to Karlštejn. Masarykovo Nádraží, near Náměstí Republiky in the center of the city, services mostly suburban destinations.

For train times, consult the timetables posted at the stations. On timetables, departures (*odjezd*) appear on a yellow background; arrivals (*příjezd*) are on white. There are two information desks at the main station, Hlavní Nádraží. The main Čedok office downtown can advise on train times and schedules.

On arriving at Hlavní Nádraží, the best way to get to the center of town is by metro. The station lies on metro Line C (Red Line), and is just one stop from the top of Wenceslas Square (station: Muzeum)—travel in the direction of Haje station. You can also walk the 500 yards or so to the square, though the walk is not advisable late at night. A taxi ride from the main station to the center should cost about 100 Kč. To reach the city center from Nádraží Holešovice, take the metro Line C (Red Line) four stops to Muzeum; a taxi ride should cost roughly 200 Kč to 250 Kč.

The state-run rail system is called České dráhy (ČD). On longer runs, it's not really worth taking anything less than an express (*rychlík*) train, marked in red on the timetable. Tickets are inexpensive: a second-class ticket from Prague to Brno (a distance of 200 km) costs about 360 Kč.

A 40 Kč to 60 Kč supplement is charged for the excellent international expresses, EuroCity (EC) and InterCity (IC), and for domestic SuperCity (SC) schedules. An 86 Kč supplement applies to reserved seats on domestic journeys, or 200 Kč for the high-speed Pendolino train. If you haven't bought a ticket in advance, you can buy one aboard the train. It's possible to book sleepers (*lůžkový*) or the less-roomy couchettes (*lehátkový*) on most overnight trains. You do not need to validate your train ticket before boarding.

The Eurail Pass and the Eurail Youthpass are now valid for travel within the Czech Republic, and if you're traveling through to neighboring countries like Hungary, Austria, or Poland, it can be an economic way to bounce between the regions. (A three-country pass starts at 211 euros.) The European East Pass is also a good option for first-class travel on the national railroads of the Czech Republic, Austria, Hungary, Poland, and Slovakia. The pass allows five days of unlimited travel within a one-month period for $294 for first class and $205 for second class, and it must be purchased from Rail Europe before your departure. The many Czech rail passes available are useful chiefly to regular travelers. A discount applies to any group of 2 to 30 people traveling second class (*sleva pro skupiny*). It's always cheaper to buy a return ticket. Foreign visitors will find it easiest to inquire at the international booking offices of major stations for the latest discounts and passes that will apply to them. Rail schedules are available at ⊕ *www.idos.cz*.

Contacts Eurail (⊕ *www.eurail.com*). **Rail Europe** (✉ *44 S. Broadway, White Plains, NY* ☎ *800/622–8600* ⊕ *www.raileurope.com*).

Information Čedok (✉ *Na Příkopě 18, Nové Město* ☎ *224–197–111* ⊕ *www.cedok.cz*).

ESSENTIALS

■ ACCOMMODATIONS

APARTMENT AND HOUSE RENTALS

International Agencies Home Away (☎ 800/876–4319 ⊕ www.homeaway. com). **Interhome** (☎ 800/882–6864 ⊕ www.interhome.us). **Villas International** (☎ 415/499–9490 or 800/221–2260 ⊕ www. villasintl.com).

HOME EXCHANGES

With a direct home exchange you stay in someone else's home while they stay in yours. Some outfits also deal with vacation homes, so you're not actually staying in someone's full-time residence, just their vacant weekend place.

Exchange Clubs Home Exchange.com (☎ 800/877–8723 ⊕ www.homeexchange.com) $15.95 for a 3-month membership.

HOSTELS

Hostels offer bare-bones lodging at low, low prices—often in shared dorm rooms with shared baths—to people of all ages, though the primary market is young travelers, especially students. Prague has a reputation as a place for young people to party, and some independent hostels can be noisy and not very clean.

Many hostels are affiliated with Hostelling International (HI), an umbrella group of hostel associations with some 4,000 member properties in more than 80 countries. Other hostels are completely independent, and may be nothing more than a really cheap hotel.

Membership in any HI association, open to travelers of all ages, allows you to stay in HI-affiliated hostels at member rates. One-year membership is about $28 for adults; hostels charge about $10–$30 per night. Members have priority if the hostel is full; they're also eligible for discounts around the world, even on rail and bus travel in some countries.

Information Hostelling International—USA (☎ 301/495–1240 ⊕ www.hiusa.org).

■ COMMUNICATIONS

INTERNET

Internet is widely available at hotels, and many provide Wi-Fi. Cafés with Internet stations are also all over Prague, and you'll find you can check your e-mail everywhere from the local bookstore to the Laundromat. Many Internet cafés allow Skype calling internationally.

Contacts Cybercafes (⊕ www.cybercafes. com) lists more than 4,000 Internet cafés worldwide.

PHONES

The good news is that you can now make a direct-dial telephone call from virtually any point on earth. The bad news? You can't always do so cheaply. Calling from a hotel is almost always the most expensive option; hotels usually add huge surcharges to all calls, particularly international ones. In some countries you can phone from call centers or even the post office. Calling cards usually keep costs to a minimum, but only if you purchase them locally. And then there are mobile phones (⇨ *below*), which are sometimes more prevalent—particularly in the developing world—than land lines; as expensive as mobile phone calls can be, they are still usually a much cheaper option than calling from your hotel.

The country code for the Czech Republic is 420. To call the Czech Republic from outside the country, dial the international access prefix, then "420," and then the nine-digit Czech number. To call from the United States, for example, dial "011–420–xxx–xxx–xxx."

CALLING WITHIN THE CZECH REPUBLIC

Most people in Prague have mobile phones, but a reasonable phone booth network still exists. If you can't find a working booth on the street, the main post office is the best place to try. Once inside, follow signs for service provider O2. A concession room for the privately run main phone company has phones for international calls that can take coins or work with international calling cards.

Different pay phones accept Czech coins, euro coins, chip-based cards, or a combination of the three. Some phones allow for sending (but not receiving) SMSs and e-mail. The special chip-based phone cards called Trick are available for Kč 200 and up at O2 service stores, some post offices, and newsstands. In almost all phones, instructions are written in English. A five-minute domestic call is 10 Kč from a coin-operated phone, and international calls start at 10 Kč for 30 seconds. International calling cards, usable on any phone, are much cheaper. Calls from a pay phone to a mobile phone can be quite expensive. The dial tone is a series of alternating short and long buzzes.

You can reach an English-speaking operator from one of the major long-distance services on a toll-free number listed in the instructions on the public phone. The operator will connect your collect or credit-card call at the carrier's standard rates. In Prague many phone booths allow direct international dialing.

There are no regional or area codes in the Czech Republic. Numbers that start with the first three digits running from 601 to 777, however, are mobile phones and the charge may be correspondingly higher. When calling a Czech number from within the Czech Republic, do not use the country code or any prefixes; simply dial the nine-digit number.

CALLING OUTSIDE THE CZECH REPUBLIC

When dialing out of the country, the country code is 1 for the United States and Canada. To dial overseas directly, first dial 00 and then the country code of the country you are calling. A call to the United States or Canada, for example, would begin 00-1, followed by the U.S. or Canadian area code and number.

The post office telephone operator can place your international call, or simply ask the receptionist at your hotel to put the call through for you. In the latter instance, the surcharges and rates will probably be very high.

Access Codes AT&T (☎ *0/042–000–101*). **BT Direct** (☎ *0/042–004–401*). **CanadaDirect** (☎ *0/042–000–151*). **MCI** (☎ *0/042–000–112*). **Sprint** (☎ *0/042–087–187*).

Other Contacts International Directory Assistance (☎ *1181*).

CALLING CARDS

With the prepaid O2 Karta X (300 Kč to 1,000 Kč), rates to the United States or United Kingdom are roughly 9 Kč per minute; a call to Hong Kong costs about 12 Kč per minute. The cards are available at many money-changing stands, newsstands, and O2 service outlets and can work with any phone once you enter a 14-digit code. You do not need to find a booth with a card slot to use the cards. Newsstands also carry other brands of cards with low rates, such as SmartCall.

MOBILE PHONES

If you have a multiband phone (some countries use different frequencies than what's used in the United States) and your service provider uses the world-standard GSM network (as do T-Mobile, Cingular, and Verizon), you can probably use your phone abroad. Roaming fees can be steep, however: 99¢ a minute is considered reasonable. And overseas you normally pay the toll charges for incoming calls. It's almost always cheaper to send a text message than to make a call, since text messages have a very low set fee (often less than 5¢).

If you just want to make local calls, consider buying a new SIM card (note that your provider may have to unlock your phone for you to use a different SIM card) and a prepaid service plan in the destination. You'll then have a local number and can make local calls at local rates. If your trip is extensive, you could also simply buy a new cell phone in your destination, as the initial cost will be offset over time.

■ TIP➔ If you travel internationally frequently, save one of your old mobile phones or buy a cheap one on the Internet; ask your cell-phone company to unlock it for you, and take it with you as a travel phone, buying a new SIM card with pay-as-you-go service in each destination.

Contacts **Cellular Abroad** (☎ 800/287–5072 ⊕ www.cellularabroad.com) rents and sells GSM phones and sells SIM cards that work in many countries. **Mobal** (☎ 888/888–9162 ⊕ www.mobalrental.com) rents mobiles and sells GSM phones (starting at $49) that will operate in 140 countries. Per-call rates vary throughout the world. **Planet Fone** (☎ 888/988–4777 ⊕ www.planetfone.com) rents cell phones, but the per-minute rates are expensive. AAA members often receive discounts.

■ CUSTOMS AND DUTIES

There are few restrictions on what you can take out of the Czech Republic. The main exception is items with special historical or cultural value. To be exported, an antique or work of art must have an export certificate. Reputable shops should be willing to advise customers on how to comply with the regulations. If a shop can't provide proof of the item's suitability for export, be wary. Now that the Czech Republic is in the Schengen zone, there should be no restrictions on bringing cigarettes and alcohol to neighboring countries. Austria, however, has cracked down on people with more than a carton of cigarettes due to the lack of required German-language health warnings. Large knives and martial-arts items, common in Czech tourist shops, are also illegal in much of Europe, even though border checks have been dropped.

Under certain circumstances you can receive a refund of usually around 22% value-added tax payable on purchases over 1,000 Kč, provided the goods are taken out of the country soon after purchase. Ask about "Tax Free Shopping" at the store when you purchase the goods, and make sure to collect all of the necessary stamps and receipts. You can get a cash refund at the airport. Many downtown stores specializing in fashion, glass, or other popular items have a tax-free sticker on the door, meaning they have the proper forms for reclaiming tax.

U.S. Information **U.S. Customs and Border Protection** (⊕ www.cbp.gov).

■ ELECTRICITY

The electrical current in Eastern and Central Europe is 220 volts, 50 cycles alternating current (AC); wall outlets generally take plugs with two round prongs.

Consider making a small investment in a universal adapter, which has several types of plugs in one lightweight, compact unit. Most laptops and mobile phone chargers are dual voltage (i.e., they operate equally well on 110 and 220 volts), so require only an adapter. These days the same is true of small appliances such as hair dryers. Always check labels and manufacturer instructions to be sure. Don't use 110-volt outlets marked FOR SHAVERS ONLY for high-wattage appliances such as hair dryers.

Contacts **Steve Kropla's Help for World Traveler's** (⊕ www.kropla.com) has information on electrical and telephone plugs around the world. **Walkabout Travel Gear** (⊕ www.walkabouttravelgear.com) has good coverage about electricity under "adapters."

■ EMERGENCIES

Doctors and Dentists **American Dental Associates** (✉ V Celnici 4, Nové Město ☎ 221–181–121).

Foreign Embassy **U.S. Embassy** (✉ Tržiště 15, Malá Strana ☎ 257–022–000 ⊕ www.usembassy.cz).

General Emergency Contacts **Ambulance** (☎ 155). **Autoklub Bohemia Assistance**

(☎ *1240*). **State Police** (☎ *158*). **Prague City Police** (☎ *156*). **ÚAMK Emergency Roadside Assistance** (☎ *1230* ⊕ *www.uamk.cz*).

Hospitals and Clinics Na Homolce Hospital (✉ *Roentgenova 2* ☎ *257–271–111* ⊕ *www. homolka.cz*).

Pharmacies Lékárna U Anděla (✉ *Štefánikova 6, Smíchov* ☎ *257–320–918*). **Lékárna** (✉ *Belgická 37, Nové Město* ☎ *222–513–396*).

■ HEALTH

Make sure food has been thoroughly cooked and is served to you fresh and hot. If you have problems, mild cases of traveler's diarrhea may respond to Imodium (known generically as loperamide) or Pepto-Bismol. Be sure to drink plenty of fluids; if you can't keep fluids down, seek medical help immediately.

Infectious diseases can be airborne or passed via mosquitoes and ticks and through direct or indirect physical contact with animals or people. Some, including Norwalk-like viruses that affect your digestive tract, can be passed along through contaminated food. Condoms can help prevent most sexually transmitted diseases, but they aren't absolutely reliable, and their quality varies from country to country. Speak with your physician and/or check the CDC or World Health Organization Web sites for health alerts, particularly if you're pregnant, traveling with children, or have a chronic illness.

OVER-THE-COUNTER REMEDIES

Pharmacies in Prague are well stocked with prescription and nonprescription drugs, though you may have trouble persuading a pharmacist to fill a foreign prescription. It's best to bring from home all of the prescribed medications you are likely to need. Pharmacies are generally open during regular business hours from 9 AM to 6 PM, with some offering night and weekend service. A new law requires a standard 30 Kč fee per prescription.

During off-hours, pharmacies will often post the name and address of the nearest open pharmacy on their doors. Pharmacies not only sell prescription medicines but are the only licensed dealers of typical over-the-counter products like pain relievers and cough medicines. Most standard U.S. over-the-counter products have Czech equivalents. Aspirin is widely available. However items such as aspirin cannot be found outside pharmacies. The most common non-aspirin pain reliever is Ibalgin (ibuprofen), sold in 200 mg and 400 mg doses.

■ **TIP**→ Pharmacists may not speak English or know a drug's non-Czech brand name, but will certainly know the drug's generic name ("acetaminophen" for "Tylenol," for example). Be sure to call a drug by its generic name when asking for it.

SHOTS AND MEDICATIONS

If you plan on doing a lot of hiking or camping, note that tick-borne Lyme disease is a serious risk in the woodlands of the Czech Republic. Schedule vaccinations well in advance of departure, because some require several doses, and others may cause uncomfortable side effects.

To avoid problems clearing customs, diabetic travelers carrying needles and syringes should have on hand a letter from their physician confirming their need for insulin injections.

■ HOURS OF OPERATION

Though hours vary, most banks are open weekdays from 8 AM to 5 PM. Private currency exchange offices usually have longer hours, and some are open all night.

Gas stations on the main roads are open 24 hours a day.

In season (from May through September), most museums, castles, and other major sights are open daily—except Monday—from about 9 AM to 4 PM. Hours vary at other times during the year, and some attractions in smaller, off-the-beaten-track places shut down altogether from November to March.

Most pharmacies are open weekdays from about 9 AM to 6 PM, and are closed weekends. For emergencies, some pharmacies maintain weekend hours, though these can change from week to week. Ask someone locally for advice.

Most stores are open weekdays from 9 AM to 6 PM, but a growing number now are open to 9 PM. Some larger grocery stores open as early as 6 AM, and a few of the hypermarkets in Prague (usually well outside of town along the metro lines) are open 24 hours. Department stores often stay open until 9 or even 10 PM. Outside Prague, most stores close for the weekend at noon on Saturday, although you may find a grocery store open at night or on the weekend.

HOLIDAYS

January 1; Easter Monday; May 1 (Labor Day); May 8 (Liberation Day); July 5 (Sts. Cyril and Methodius Day); July 6 (Jan Hus Day); September 28 (Day of Czech Statehood); October 28 (Czech National Day); November 17 (Day of a Struggle for Liberty and Democracy, aka "Velvet Revolution" Day); and December 24, 25, and 26 (Christmas Eve, Christmas Day, Boxing Day).

▌MAIL

It takes about a week for letters and postcards to reach the United States. Remember to pay a little extra for airmail; otherwise your letters will be sent by ship. The opening hours of post offices vary—the smaller the place, the shorter the hours. Most large post offices are open from 8 AM to 7 PM on weekdays. The main post office in Prague is open 22 hours, with a two-hour break after midnight. Orange post-office boxes can be found around the city, usually attached to the side of a building.

At this writing, postcards and letters up to 20 grams in weight cost 18 Kč to send.

You can buy stamps at post offices, hotels, newsstands, and shops that sell postcards.

If you don't know where you'll be staying, American Express mail service is a great convenience, available at no charge to anyone holding an American Express credit card or carrying American Express traveler's checks. There are several offices in Prague. You can also have mail held *poste restante* (general delivery) at post offices in major towns, but the letters should be marked *Pošta 1,* to designate the city's main post office; in Prague the poste restante window is at the main post office. You'll be asked for identification when you collect your mail.

Information American Express (✉ Na Příkopě, Nové Město ☎ 222–800–111 ⊕ www.americanexpress.com).

Main Branch Prague Main Post Office (✉ *Jindřišská ul. 14* ⊕ www.cpost.cz).

SHIPPING PACKAGES

The Czech postal service, Česká pošta, runs an Express Mail Service (EMS). You can post your EMS parcel at any post office, and Česká pošta can supply forms for customs clearance. Delivery times vary between one and five days, though material is often delayed by American customs. You may not send currency, travel checks, precious metals, or stones through Express Mail. Not every post office offers a pickup service.

Many other private international express carriers also serve the Czech Republic.

Some major stores can make their own arrangements to ship purchases home on behalf of their customers. A number of freight and cargo services operate international delivery services, and these can generally be relied upon. An average shipping time to the United States is 21 days (4 days for air cargo). There's no reason not to use the reliable Česká pošta, which delivers anything up to 30 kg.

Express Services DHL (☎ 800–103–000 ⊕ www.dhl.cz). **EMS** (☎ 800–104–410 ⊕ www.cpost.cz). **FedEx** (☎ 800–133–339 ⊕ www.

fedex.com/cz_english). **UPS** (☎ *800–181–111* ⊕ *www.ups.com*).

Information Art Trans (✉ *Mlynska 60/2, Bubeneč* ☎ *235–362–202* ⊕ *www.shipping.cz*).

∎ MONEY

The Czech crown has been quite strong, and many of the bargains people expect might no longer exist. Prices are approaching those of Western Europe quite rapidly. Hotel prices in particular are often higher than the facilities would warrant, but prices at tourist resorts outside the capital are lower and, in the outlying areas and off the beaten track, very low. The story is similar for restaurants, with Prague being comparable to the United States and Western Europe, whereas outlying towns are much more reasonable. The prices for castles, museums, and other sights are rising, but still low by outside standards.

ATMs are common in Prague and most towns in the Czech Republic, and more often than not are part of the Cirrus and Plus networks, meaning you can get cash easily. Outside of urban areas, machines can be scarce, and you should plan to carry enough cash to meet your needs.

In Czech an ATM is called a *bankomat*, and a PIN is also a PIN, just as in English.

Prices throughout this guide are given for adults. Substantially reduced fees are almost always available for children, students, and senior citizens.

Banks in the United States never have every foreign currency on hand, and it may take as long as a week to order. If you're planning to exchange funds before leaving home, don't wait until the last minute.

ATMS AND BANKS

Your own bank will probably charge a fee for using ATMs abroad; the foreign bank you use may also charge a fee. Nevertheless, you'll usually get a better rate of exchange at an ATM than you will at a currency-exchange office or even when changing money in a bank. And extracting funds as you need them is a safer option than carrying around a large amount of cash.

∎ TIP➔ PIN numbers with more than four digits are not recognized at ATMs in many countries. If yours has five or more, remember to change it before you leave.

ATMs are safe and reliable. Instructions are in English. If in doubt, use machines attached to established banks like Česká Spořitelna, Komerčni Banka, and ČSOB.

CREDIT CARDS

Throughout this guide, the following abbreviations are used: **AE,** American Express; **DC,** Diners Club; **MC,** Master-Card; and **V,** Visa.

It's a good idea to inform your credit-card company before you travel, especially if you're going abroad and don't travel internationally very often. Otherwise, the credit-card company might put a hold on your card owing to unusual activity—not a good thing halfway through your trip. Record all your credit-card numbers—as well as the phone numbers to call if your cards are lost or stolen—in a safe place, so you're prepared should something go wrong. Both MasterCard and Visa have general numbers you can call (collect if you're abroad) if your card is lost, but you're better off calling the number of your issuing bank, since Master-Card and Visa usually just transfer you to your bank; your bank's number is usually printed on your card.

If you plan to use your credit card for cash advances, you'll need to apply for a PIN at least two weeks before your trip. Although it's usually cheaper (and safer) to use a credit card abroad for large purchases (so you can cancel payments or be reimbursed if there's a problem), note that some credit-card companies *and* the banks that issue them add substantial percentages to all foreign transactions, whether they're in a foreign currency or not. Check on these fees before leaving home, so there won't be any surprises when you get the bill.

■TIP➜ Before you charge something, ask the merchant whether he or she plans to do a dynamic currency conversion (DCC). In such a transaction the credit-card *processor* (shop, restaurant, or hotel, not Visa or MasterCard) converts the currency and charges you in dollars. In most cases you'll pay the merchant a 3% fee for this service in addition to any credit-card company and issuing-bank foreign-transaction surcharges.

Dynamic currency conversion programs are becoming increasingly widespread. Merchants who participate in them are supposed to ask whether you want to be charged in dollars or the local currency, but they don't always do so. And even if they do offer you a choice, they may well avoid mentioning the additional surcharges. The good news is that you *do* have a choice. And if this practice really gets your goat, you can avoid it entirely thanks to American Express; with its cards, DCC simply isn't an option.

Visa, MasterCard, and American Express are widely accepted by major hotels, restaurants, and stores, Diners Club less so. Smaller establishments and those off the beaten track, unsurprisingly, are less likely to accept credit cards.

Reporting Lost Cards American Express (✆ 888/937–2639 ⊕ www.americanexpress. com). **Diners Club** (✆ 0/267–197–450 ⊕ www.dinersclub.com). **MasterCard** (✆ 800/627–8372 in U.S., 636/722–7111 collect from abroad ⊕ www.mastercard.com). **Visa** (✆ 800/847–2911 ⊕ www.visa.com).

CURRENCY AND EXCHANGE

Though discussions continue regarding a currency change to the euro in 2015, for now the unit of currency in the Czech Republic is the *koruna* (plural: koruny) or crown (Kč), which is divided into 100 *haléřů*, or hellers. The 50-heller coin, the last of the small denominations, was phased out in 2008, but prices are still marked in hellers. There are coins of 1, 2, 5, 10, 20, and 50 Kč; and notes of 100,

200, 500, 1,000, 2,000, and 5,000 Kč. Notes of 1,000 Kč and up may not always be accepted for small purchases. Notes for 50 Kč have been phased out as of April 2011 and are no longer being accepted.

Try to avoid exchanging money at hotels or private exchange booths, including the ubiquitous Chequepoint and Exact Change booths. They routinely take commissions of 8% to 10%, in addition to giving poor rates. The best places to exchange money are at bank counters, where the commissions average 1% to 3%, or at ATMs. The koruna is fully convertible, which means it can be purchased outside the country and exchanged into other currencies. Of course, never change money with people on the street. Not only is it illegal, but you will almost definitely be ripped off.

On arrival at the airport, the best bets for exchanging money are the ATM machines lined up in the terminal just as you leave the arrivals area. The currency-exchange windows at the airport, happily, offer rates that are no worse than you will find anywhere in town, if not quite as good as those at banks.

At this writing the exchange rate was around 20 Kč to the U.S. dollar.

■TIP➜ Even if a currency-exchange booth has a sign promising no commission, rest assured that there's some kind of huge, hidden fee. (Oh . . . that's right. The sign didn't say no *fee*.) And as for rates, you're almost always better off getting foreign currency at an ATM or exchanging money at a bank.

Exchange Services **Exchange** (✉ *nám. Franze Kafka 2*).

TIPPING

Service is not usually included in restaurant bills. In pubs or ordinary places, simply round up the bill to the next multiple of 10 (if the bill comes to 83 Kč, for example, give the waiter 90 Kč); in nicer places, 10% is considered appropriate for good food and service. Tip porters who bring bags to your rooms 40 Kč–50 Kč total. For room service, a 20 Kč tip is enough. In taxis, round the bill up by 10%. Give tour guides and helpful concierges between 50 Kč and 100 Kč for services rendered.

PACKING

Prague's climate is continental, so in summer plan on relatively warm days and cool nights. Spring tends to be wet and cool; fall is drier but also on the chilly side. In winter, pack plenty of warm clothes and plan to use them. An umbrella is a good idea any time of year. Note that areas in higher elevations tend to stay very cool even in midsummer.

In general, pack for comfort rather than for style. Casual dress is the norm for everyday wear, including at most restaurants. Men will need a sport coat for an evening out at a concert or the opera. Shorts for men are not as common in Prague as they are in North America. In the evening, long pants are the norm, even in summer.

Many areas are best seen on foot, so take a pair of sturdy walking shoes and be prepared to use them. High heels can present considerable problems on the cobblestone streets of Prague.

Some items that you take for granted at home are occasionally unavailable or of questionable quality in Eastern and Central Europe, though the situation has been steadily improving. Toiletries and personal-hygiene products are relatively easy to find, but it's always a good idea to bring necessities when traveling in outlying areas, especially on weekends.

PASSPORTS

Citizens of the United States need only a valid passport to enter the Czech Republic, and can stay for as long as 90 days without a visa. It's a good idea to make sure your passport is valid for at least six months on entry. If you plan on living or working in the Czech Republic, be advised that long-term and work visas must be obtained outside the country. Contact the Czech embassy or consulate in your home country well in advance of your trip. The Czech Republic is now part of the Schengen area, meaning that once a visitor enters one of countries in the zone, which covers most of Europe, he or she will not have to show a passport at each border; a visitor's three-month stay begins upon the first point of entry into the Schengen area. Travelers are still required to have a valid passport, and spot checks still occur.

RESTROOMS

Public restrooms are more common, and cleaner, than they used to be in the Czech Republic. You nearly always have to pay 5 Kč to 10 Kč to the attendant. Restaurant and bar toilets are generally for customers only, but if you're discreet no one will care if you just drop by to use the facilities.

SAFETY

Crime rates are relatively low in Prague, but travelers should be wary of pickpockets in crowded areas, especially on metros and trams, and at railway stations. Trams popular with tourists, such as the Number 22 tram, which circumnavigates most of the major sites, are also popular with pickpockets. In general, always keep your valuables on your person—purses, backpacks, or cameras are easy targets if they are hung on or placed next to chairs.

Violent crime is extremely rare, and you shouldn't experience any problems of this sort. That said, you should certainly take the typical precautions you would take in any large city.

Although nothing is likely to happen, it is not wise for a woman to go alone to a bar or nightclub or to wander the streets late at night. When traveling by train at night, seek out compartments that are well populated.

As with any city popular with tourists, Prague has its share of scams. The most common rip-offs are dishonest taxi drivers, pickpockets in the trams and metros, and the ubiquitous offers to "change money" on the street. All these are easily avoided if you take precautions. If you have to hail a cab on the street, ask the driver what the approximate fare will be before you get in (if he can't tell you, that's a bad sign), and ask for a receipt (*paragon*) at the end of the ride. In trams and metros watch your valuables carefully. And never exchange money on the street unless you want to end up with a handful of fake and worthless bills.

■ TIP→ Distribute your cash, credit cards, IDs, and other valuables between a deep front pocket, an inside jacket or vest pocket, and a hidden money pouch. Don't reach for the money pouch once you're in public.

■ SPORTS AND THE OUTDOORS

Czechs are avid sportsmen and sportswomen. In the summertime, Prague empties out as residents head to their country cottages to hike or bike in clean air. In winter the action shifts to the mountains, a few hours to the north and east of the city, for decent downhill and cross-country skiing. If the ponds freeze over in Prague's Stromovka Park, kids nab their skates for pickup ice-hockey games—a national mania.

The most popular spectator sport, bar none, is ice hockey. Czechs are world hockey champions, and the Czech gold medal at the Nagano Winter Olympics in 1998 is held up as a national achievement practically on par with the 1989 Velvet Revolution. If you're here in wintertime, witness the fervor by seeking out tickets to an Extraliga game. The main Prague teams are Sparta and Slavia.

Soccer plays a perennial second fiddle to hockey, although the Czech national soccer team ranks among the best in the world. Prague's main professional team, Sparta, hosts its home games at Toyota Arena near Letná. If you're interested in seeing a hockey or soccer game during your stay, the best place to find out

what's going on (and where) is the weekly sports page of the *Prague Post*, or inquire at your hotel.

BICYCLING
Much of the Czech Republic is a cyclist's dream of gently sloping tracks for pedalers. The capital, however, can be unkind to bicyclers. Prague's ubiquitous tram tracks and cobblestones make for hazardous conditions—as do the legions of tourist groups clogging the streets. Nevertheless, cycling is increasingly popular, and there are now several adequate yellow-marked cycling trails that crisscross the city. From April to October two bike-rental companies provide decent bikes—as well as locks, helmets, and maps.

City Bike (✉ *Králodvorská 5, Staré Město* ☎ *776–180–284* ⊕ *www.citybike-prague. com prague online.cz/citybike* Ⓜ *Line B: Nám. Republiky*) runs guided tours leaving at 10:30, 1:30, and 4:30. Your English-speaking guides offer fun tidbits of history and point out architecture, but do not offer a full tour. The ride's pace is comfortable for those who haven't taken a spin in a while.

One of the multicultural teams from **Praha Bike** (✉ *Dlouhá 24, Staré Město* ☎ *732– 388–880* ⊕ *www.prahabike.cz* Ⓜ *Line B: Nám. Republiky*) can casually guide you around one of two routes; tours are at 11:30 and 2:30, which are considered the "classic city" tours, and 5:30, which is the "panoramic" tour that hits all of the best vantage points in the city (so don't forget your camera).

HOCKEY
A feverish national fixation, ice hockey becomes a full-blown obsession during the World Championships (held every year in late spring) and the Winter Olympics.

The Czech national hockey league, Extraliga, is one of the most competitive in the world, and the best players regularly move on to the North American National Hockey League. Slavia Praha and Sparta are the two best teams, both in Prague. Hockey season runs from September to

March. Tickets cost between 130 Kč and 550 Kč and are reasonably easy to get.

Although a relative giant in the Czech Republic, **HC Slavia Praha** (⊠ *O2 Arena, Očálařská, Vysočany* ☎ *266–771–000* ⊕ *www.hc-slavia.cz* Ⓜ *Line B: Českomoravská*) usually finds itself chasing the leaders of the pack in international matches.

HC Sparta Praha (⊠ *Arena HC Sparta, Za Elektrárnou 419, Holešovice* ☎ *266–727–443* ⊕ *www.hcsparta.cz* Ⓜ *Line C: Nádraží Holešovice*) was the national champion at this writing, and is routinely regarded as the premier team in an excellent local league—until players are lured across the Atlantic. Come to spot the next Jágr or Hašek.

PARKS AND PLAYGROUNDS

Praguers are gluttons for a sunny day in the park. A pleasant weekend afternoon brings out plenty of sun-worshippers and Frisbee-tossers, with their blankets, books, and dogs. Two of the city's best beer gardens can be found at Letná and Riegrovy Sady.

Kampa. Under the noses of the throng on Charles Bridge: take the steps off the bridge onto Na Kampě and follow the wide cobbled street to the end; Kampa is a diminutive gem hidden in the heart of Malá Strana. It's a location for lazing in the sunshine and resting your eyes from all the busy baroque architecture, with a playground for when the kids grow restless from the endless palaces and churches. ⊠ *Malá Strana* Ⓜ *Tram to Malostranské nám.*

Letná. With killer views of the city across the river, this park is eternally busy. It has a huge restaurant and beer garden, to chill out in like a local, located around Letenský zámeček, near the intersection of Kostelní and Muzejní. The large grassy northern plateau sometimes holds concerts or political rallies, but is also a great place to throw a Frisbee or kick a soccer ball. An excellent playground sits in the center near the tennis courts, just to the west of Letenský zámeček. ⊠ *Holešovice* Ⓜ *Tram to Sparta.*

Riegrovy Sady. This lush park climbs sharply up the slopes of Vinohrady. On the east side of the park, lovely landscaping surrounds one of the best beer gardens in Prague and a large playground. It offers lavish views of Prague Castle on the distant horizon. ⊠ *Vinohrady* Ⓜ *Line A: Jiřího z Poděbrad.*

Stromovka. King of all Prague parks, these lands were formerly royal hunting grounds. Today the deer have been usurped by horse riders and dog lovers. Remarkably rustic for a city-based park, it's primarily a place for walking rather than loafing about. The racket from the ramshackle amusements at Výstaviště exhibition grounds (found at the park's eastern entrance where Dukelských hrdinů meets U Výstaviště) stresses the fact that you remain city-bound. ⊠ *Holešovice* Ⓜ *Tram to Výstaviště.*

SKIING

Czechs are enthusiastic and gifted skiers, and the country's northern border regions with Germany and Poland hold many small ski resorts. Czechs generally acknowledge the Krkonoše Mountains, which straddle a border with Poland, to be the best. Experienced skiers may find the hills here a little small and the facilities not quite up to international standards. (Hard-core Czech skiers usually head to Austria or France.) Nevertheless, if you're here in midwinter and you get a good snowfall, the Czech resorts can make for a fun overnight trip from the capital. All the area ski resorts are regularly served by buses leaving from Florenc.

Černá Hora (⊠ *Cernohorská 265, Janské Lázně* ☎ *499–875–186* ⊕ *www.cernahora.cz*) is 180 km (112 mi, about a four-hour drive) east of Prague. The resort has a cable car, one chairlift, and a couple of drag lifts. The "Black Mountain" is not the biggest of ski resorts, but is often fairly quiet, meaning less waiting and a nice unofficial run, with plenty of forest to explore, directly under the cable car.

On weekends, when you want to take in some crisp mountain air and clap on a pair of skis, head for **Harrachov** (⊠ *Harrachov* ☏ *432–529–600* ⊕ *www.harrachov. cz*). In the west of the Krkonoše, around 120 km (74 mi, a three-hour drive) from the capital, the resort offers red and blue runs served by two chairlifts and 11 rope tows. This small and friendly resort is ideal for beginners and intermediates.

The biggest and most popular ski resort in the Czech Republic is **Skiareal Špindlerův Mlýn** (⊠ *Špindlerův Mlýn* ☏ *499–467– 102* ⊕ *www.skiarealspindl.cz*), which is 160 km (99 mi, about a 3½-hour drive) from Prague. The twin slopes, Svatý Petr and Medvedín, gaze at each other over the small village and offer blue, red, and black runs served by four chairlifts and numerous rope tows. Weekends here are mobbed to a point well past frustration.

SOCCER

Games for the domestic Czech league, the Gambrinus liga, run from August to May with a break in December and January. The games and the fans tend to be somewhat lackluster. Tickets are plentiful enough on match days (except for tournaments). International matches are hosted at Sparta's stadium.

AC Sparta Praha (⊠ *Toyota Arena Milady Horákové 98, Letná* ☏ *296–111–400* ⊕ *www.sparta.cz* Ⓜ *Line A: Sparta*) has an enthusiastic fan base, with the stadium roar to match. Although Sparta has seen its fortunes dip a little recently, the team remains a domestic Goliath and a stone-slinging David in European competition.

Reduced in the early 21st century to bringing up the rear in the capital are second-division **FC Bohemians Praha** (⊠ *Doliček stadion, Vršovická 31, Vršovice* ☏ *271– 721–459* ⊕ *www.fc-bohemians.cz* Ⓜ *Tram to Vršovice Nám.*).

Sparta's success is much to the chagrin of its bitter rivals **SK Slavia Praha** (⊠ *Eden Stadium 1460/10 Vladivostocká, Vršovice*

☏ *234–710–380* ⊕ *www.slavia.cz* Ⓜ *Tram lines 6, 7, 22 or 24 to Slavia*), which now plays in the new Eden Stadium.

TENNIS

Tennis is one of the favorite local sports, but the national passion remains at a simmer instead of a rolling boil. The best-known Czech players have been Ivan Lendl and, by ethnicity at least, Martina Navratilova. But there are a crop of younger players out there trying to crowd into the top 10. Prague is blessed with several public tennis courts. Most are cinder or clay surface.

At **Bendvík** (⊠ *Diskařská 1, Hradčany* ☏ *251–611–129* Ⓜ *Tram 15, 22, or 23 to Malovanka*) indoor courts cost 250 Kč to 430 Kč per hour, outdoor courts 100 Kč to 200 Kč per hour.

Some of the city's best tennis courts are found right next door to the tennis stadium, **Česky Lawn Tennis Klub** (⊠ *Ostrov Štvanice 38, Holešovice* ☏ *222–316–317* Ⓜ *Line C: Vltavská*), which in its time has hosted ATP events. Open to the public for 300 Kč–600 Kč per hour are 10 outdoor courts and 6 indoor courts, all hard surface or clay, despite the name.

▌ TAXES

Taxes are usually included in the prices of hotel rooms, restaurant meals, and items purchased in shops. The price on the tag is what you'll pay at the register. The airport departure tax, about 600 Kč, is usually included in the price of airline tickets.

The Czech V.A.T. is called DPH (daň z přidané hodnoty), and there are two rates. The higher one (19%) covers nearly everything—gifts, souvenirs, clothing, and food in restaurants. Food in grocery stores and books are taxed by 9%. Exported goods are exempt from the tax, which can be refunded. All tourists outside the EU are entitled to claim the tax back if they spend more than 1,000 Kč in one shop on the same day. Global Refund processes V.A.T. refunds in the Czech Republic and will give you your refund in cash (U.S. dollars or euros) from a booth at the airport; be aware that the Czech Republic does *not* provide a postage-paid mailer for V.A.T. refund forms, unlike most other European countries.

When making a purchase, ask for a V.A.T. refund form and find out whether the merchant gives refunds—not all stores do, nor are they required to. Have the form stamped like any customs form by customs officials when you leave the country or, if you're visiting several European Union countries, when you leave the EU. After you're through passport control, take the form to a refund-service counter for an on-the-spot refund (which is usually the quickest and easiest option), or mail it to the address on the form (or the envelope with it) after you arrive home. You receive the total refund stated on the form, but the processing time can be long, especially if you request a credit-card adjustment.

Global Refund is a Europe-wide service with 240,000 affiliated stores and more than 700 refund counters at major airports and border crossings. Its refund form, called a Tax Free Check, is the most common across the European continent. The service issues refunds in the form of cash, check, or credit-card adjustment.

V.A.T. Refunds Global Refund (☎ 800/566–9828 ⊕ www.globalrefund.com).

▌ TIME

The Czech Republic is on Central European Time (CET), one hour ahead of Greenwich Mean Time and six hours ahead of the Eastern time zone of the United States.

▌ TOURS

Major U.S. agencies often plan trips covering Prague and the Czech Republic. Abercrombie & Kent, Inc. is one agency that offers package tours to the area. The largest Czech agency, Čedok, also offers package tours.

GUIDED TOURS

Tours of Prague come under the supervision of Prague Information Service, which is reliable and always informative. The partly city-funded company organizes walking tours in Prague's city center and in the outskirts, including excursions from Prague. Arrangements can be made with them for many tailor-made tours. Non-registered guides can also be found, but unless they come with a personal recommendation from someone you trust, their services cannot be guaranteed. The Information Service rents GPS sets programmed with monument sites, restaurants, and cultural events for people who want to tour on their own; the price is 450 Kč for four hours (a deposit is required).

One small private company that does an excellent tour of the city is Custom Travel Services, operated by Jaroslav Pesta. The service offers a wide range of touring options. A full-day private walking tour of Prague with a boat ride for two or three people is 3,300 Kč, or 3,900 Kč for five to six people. The firm offers 100 different tours across the country, and also will customize a tour according to your interests.

Information Custom Travel Services (☎ 608–866–454 ⊕ www.privatepragueguide. com.com). **Prague Information Service** (☎ 236–002–569 ⊕ www.pis.cz).

WALKING TOURS

Theme walking tours are popular in Prague. You can choose from tours on medieval architecture, "Velvet Revolution" walks, visits to communist monuments, and any number of pub crawls. Each year, four or five small operators do these tours, which generally last a couple of hours and cost 150 Kč to more than 1,000 Kč. Inquire at Prague Information Service or a major ticket agency for the current season's offerings. Most walks start at the clock tower on Old Town Square.

A special guide service is available in the Czech Republic, designed to examine and explain the country's Jewish history. The company, Wittmann Tours, offers several different tours within Prague and also outside, including the Terezín concentration camp.

Information Wittmann Tours (☎ 222–252–472 ⊕ www.wittmann-tours.com).

DAY TOURS AND GUIDES
BOAT TOURS

You can take a 30- to 60-minute boat trip along the Vltava year-round with several boat companies that are based on the quays near the Malá Strana side of the Charles Bridge. It's not really necessary to buy tickets in advance, though you can; boats leave as they fill up. One of the cruise companies stands out, and it's on the Old Town side of the bridge. Prague-Venice Cruises operates restored, classic canal boats from the late 19th century; the company operates one larger boat that holds 35 passengers and eight smaller boats that hold 12 passengers.

■**TIP→ Take one of the smaller boats— particularly one of the uncovered ones—if you can, for a more intimate narrated cruise of about 45 minutes along the Vltava and nearby canals.**

Refreshments are included in all cruises. You actually set sail from beneath the last remaining span of Judith's Bridge (the Roman-built precursor to the Charles Bridge). Look for the touts in sailor suits right before the bridge; they will direct you to the ticket office. Cruises are offered daily from 10:30 to 6 from November through February, until 8 from March through June and September through October, and until 11 in July and August. Cruises cost 290 Kč.

Information Prague-Venice Cruises (☎ 776–776–779 ⊕ www.prague-venice.cz).

BUS TOURS

Čedok offers a 3½-hour "Prague Castle Tour," a combination bus and walking venture that covers the castle and major sights around town in English. The price is about 850 Kč. Stop by the main office for information on other tours and for information on tour departure points. You can also arrange a personalized walking tour. Times and itineraries are negotiable; prices start at around 400 Kč per hour.

Very similar tours by other operators also depart daily from Náměstí Republicy, Národní třída near Jungmannovo náměstí, and Wenceslas Square. Prices are generally a couple of hundred crowns less than for Čedok's tours.

Information Čedok (☎ 224–197–242 ⊕ www.cedok.cz). **Martin Tour** (☎ 224–212–473 ⊕ www.martintour.cz). **Precious Legacy Tours** (☎ 222–321–954 ⊕ www.legacytours.cz). **Premiant City Tour** (☎ 224–946–922 ⊕ www.premiant.cz). **Travel Plus** (☎ 224–990–990 ⊕ www.travel.cz). **Wittmann Tours** (☎ 222–252–472 ⊕ www.wittmann-tours.com).

SPECIAL-INTEREST TOURS

One reason visitors come to the Czech Republic is to connect with their Jewish heritage. Wittmann Tours provides not only coverage of the main sights in Prague, but excursions to smaller Czech towns and to Trebíč.

Recommended Companies Abercrombie & Kent (☎ 800/554–7016 in U.S. ⊕ www.abercrombiekent.com). **Čedok** (☎ 221–447–242 ⊕ www.cedok.com). **Wittmann Tours** (☎ 222–252–472 ⊕ www.wittmann-tours.com).

■ VISITOR INFORMATION

ONLINE TRAVEL TOOLS

All About Prague Czech Tourist Authority (⊕ www.czechtourism.com).

Currency Conversion Google (⊕ www.google.com) does currency conversion. Just type in the amount you want to convert and an explanation of how you want it converted (e.g., "14 Swiss francs in dollars"), and then voilà. **Oanda.com** (⊕ www.oanda.com) also allows you to print out a handy table with the current day's conversion rates. **XE.com**

(⊕ www.xe.com) is a good currency conversion Web site.

Safety Transportation Security Administration (*TSA* ⊕ www.tsa.gov).

Time Zones Timeanddate.com (⊕ www.timeanddate.com/worldclock) can help you figure out the correct time anywhere in the world.

Weather Accuweather.com (⊕ www.accuweather.com) is an independent weather-forecasting service. **Weather.com** (⊕ www.weather.com) is the Web site for the Weather Channel.

Other Resources CIA World Factbook (⊕ https://www.cia.gov/library/publications/the-world-factbook/index.html) has profiles of every country in the world. It's a good source if you need some quick facts and figures.

VISITOR INFORMATION

The Prague Information Service maintains three helpful information offices—the most useful, and most overcrowded, is in the former Town Hall building (just to the left of the clock tower) on Old Town Square. The office can advise on walking tours, as well as answer basic questions and arrange accommodation.

Before You Leave Czech Tourist Authority (⊕ www.czechtourism.com).

In Prague Prague Information Service (*PIS* ✉ Staroměstská radnice [Old Town Hall], Staré Město 🕾 No phone ⊕ www.pis.cz ✉ Hlavní nádraží, lower hall, Staré Město 🕾 No phone ✉ Malostranská mostecká věž, Malá Strana 🕾 No phone).

INDEX

PHOTO CREDITS

1, wrangel/iStockphoto. 2-3, lillisphotography/iStockphoto. Chapter 1: Experience Prague 8-9, Matthew Dixon/iStockphoto. 10, vladislav.bezrukov/Flickr. 11 (left), Bartlomiej K. Kwieciszewski/iStockphoto. 11 (right), nadi555/Shutterstock. 14, gracious_tiger/Shutterstock. 15 (left), S.Borisov/Shutterstock. 15 (right), jmilles/Flickr. 16 (left), GrLb71/Shutterstock. 16 (top right), Ivo Brezina/Shutterstock. 16 (bottom right), Eugeny Shevchenko/iStockphoto. 17 (top left), atelier22/Shutterstock. 17 (bottom left), Anastazzo/Shutterstock. 17 (right), PHB.cz (Richard Semik)/Shutterstock. 18 (left), Brian K./Shutterstock. 18 (right), illisphotography/iStockphoto. 20, Boudikka/Shutterstock. 21 (left), Stanislav Bokach/Shutterstock. 21 (right), Ray_from_LA /Flickr. 22, knottyboy/Flickr. 23 (left), Elena Solodovnikova/iStockphoto. 23 (right), Michal Boubin, www.siloto.cz/iStockphoto. 26, haridas/Wikimedia Commons. Chapter 2: Exploring Prague 27, Fribus Ekaterina/Shutterstock. 28, courtyardpix/iStockphoto. 29, WH CHOW/Shutterstock. 30-31, Ekaterina Fribus/iStockphoto. 32, Matthew Dixon/iStockphoto. 40-41, Dmitry Agafontsev/Shutterstock. 43, Roberto Gennaro/iStockphoto. 48, Kajano/Shutterstock. 51, simonechoule/Flickr. 54-55, courtyardpix/Shutterstock. 59, Nataliya Hora/Shutterstock. 60, Tupungato/Shutterstock. 63, Jozef Sedmak/Shutterstock. 64, hammondovi/iStockphoto. 68 and 72, Javier Larrea/age fotostock. 74-75, René Mattes/age fotostock. 76, Peter Zurek/Shutterstock. 80, Igumnova Irina/Shutterstock. 83, Vadim Balantsev/Shutterstock. 85, Razvan Chirnoaga/Shutterstock. 86, Martin Spurny/Shutterstock. 90, Ionia/Shutterstock. Chapter 3: Where to Eat 93, magicinfoto/Shutterstock. 94, CÉLESTE Restaurant & Bar. 96, Ian Bull. 97, Peter Vitale/Four Seasons Hotel Prague. 98, Jon Bennett/Flickr. 99 (bottom), Dezidor/Wikimedia Commons. 99 (top), Juan de Vojníkov/Wikimedia Commons. 100, jmilles/Flickr. 101 (bottom), CÉLESTE Restaurant & Bar. 101 (top), La Degustation. 105, Peter Vitale/Four Seasons Hotel Prague. 110, CÉLESTE Restaurant & Bar. 116, Frank Chmura / age fotostock. 123, Ian Bull. Chapter 4: Where to Stay 125, Mandarin Oriental Prague. 126, HOTEL LE PALAIS PRAGUE. 129, Mandarin Oriental Prague. 137 (top), Mamaison Hotels & Residences. 137 (bottom), garybembridge/Flickr. 144 (top), Golden Well Hotel. 144 (bottom), Mandarin Oriental Prague. 151 (top and bottom), HOTEL LE PALAIS PRAGUE. Chapter 5: The Performing Arts 155, Massimiliano Pieraccini/iStockphoto. 157, greynforty/Flickr. 163, David V./Shutterstock. 169, RENAULT Philippe / age fotostock. 170-71, WOW Projects. 172, Sergi Marin Casas/Flickr. Chapter 6: Nightlife 175, John Sigler/iStockphoto. 177, robertpaulyoung/Flickr. 178, Dino/Shutterstock. 179 (bottom), jerrroen/Flickr. 179 (top), Company Pivovary Staropramen. 180, loopiss/iStockphoto. 187, Cloud 9/Hilton Prague & Hilton Prague Old Town. 189, Peter Zurek - Big Original/iStockphoto. 192, Jim Milles/Flickr. Chapter 7: Shopping 195, Peter Erik Forsberg / age fotostock. 197, ahisgett/Flickr. 198, Peter Zurek - Big Original/iStockphoto. 200, Annavee/Shutterstock. 208-09, Javier Larrea / age fotostock. 214, HermÈs/Flickr. 216, Guillén Pérez/Flickr. 219, jean schweitzer/Shutterstock. Chapter 8: Day Trips from Prague 221, DEA / M BORCHI / age fotostock. 222 (top), Pecold/Shutterstock. 222 (bottom), Canoneer/Shutterstock. 223 (top), Filip Fuxa/Shutterstock. 223 (bottom), Jozef Sedmak/Shutterstock. 225, LWY/Flickr. 229, hornyak/Shutterstock. 230, Matt Ragen/Shutterstock. 237, Vaclav Ostadal / age fotostock. 243, Emmanuel Dyan/Flickr. Chapter 9: Southern Bohemia 245, Elena Terletskaya/Shutterstock. 246 (bottom), kohy/Shutterstock. 246 (top), Roman Pavlik/Shutterstock. 247, BESTWEB/Shutterstock. 249, Ionia/Shutterstock. 254, Peter Zurek/Shutterstock. 259, julius fekete/Shutterstock. 264, Eleonoracerna/Shutterstock. 267, spfotocz/Shutterstock. Chapter 10: Western Bohemia 271, Pavel Kosek/Shutterstock. 272 (bottom), Jita/Shutterstock. 272 (top), Pavel Kosek/Shutterstock. 273 and 275, Andrea Seemann/Shutterstock. 278, marchello_/Shutterstock. 283, Ionia/Shutterstock. 288, Alexander Cherednichenko/Shutterstock. 292, Pavel Kosek/Shutterstock. 296, Palis Michalis/Shutterstock. 298, Norbert Aepli/Wikimedia Commons. 299, Stefan Kiefer / age fotostock. Chapter 11: Excursion to Moravia 303, 1potter1/Shutterstock. 304 (bottom), Pavel Kosek/Shutterstock. 304 (top), Beentree/Wikimedia Commons. 305, Karel Gallas/iStockphoto. 307, Sedlacek/Shutterstock. 310, Ales Liska/Shutterstock. 313, Vera Kailova/Shutterstock.

NOTES